OXFORD SHAKESPEARE CONCORDANCES

OXFORD SHAKESPEARE CONCORDANCES

AS YOU LIKE IT

A CONCORDANCE TO THE TEXT
OF THE FIRST FOLIO

OXFORD
AT THE CLARENDON PRESS
1969

Oxford University Press, Ely House, London W. 1

GLASGOW NEW YORK TORONTO MELBOURNE WELLINGTON
CAPE TOWN SALISBURY IBADAN NAIROBI LUSAKA ADDIS ABABA
BOMBAY CALCUTTA MADRAS KARACHI LAHORE DACCA
KUALA LUMPUR SINGAPORE HONG KONG TOKYO JOHANNESBURG

FILMSET BY COMPUTAPRINT LIMITED
AND PRINTED IN GREAT BRITAIN
AT THE UNIVERSITY PRESS, OXFORD
BY VIVIAN RIDLER
PRINTER TO THE UNIVERSITY

GENERAL INTRODUCTION

IN this series of Oxford Shakespeare Concordances, a separate volume is devoted to each of the plays. The text for each concordance is the one chosen as copy-text by Dr. Alice Walker for the Oxford Old Spelling Shakespeare now in preparation.

Each concordance takes account of every word in the text, and represents their occurrence by frequency counts, line numbers, and reference lines, or a selection of these according to the interest of the particular word. The number of words which have frequency counts only has been kept as low as possible. The introduction to each volume records the facsimile copy of the text from which the concordance was prepared, a table of Folio through line numbers and Globe edition act and scene numbers, a list of the misprints corrected in the text, and an account of the order of printing, and the proof-reading, abstracted from Professor Charlton Hinman's *The Printing and Proof-Reading of the First Folio of Shakespeare* (Oxford, 1963).

The following notes on the main features of the concordances may be helpful.[1]

A. *The Text*

The most obvious misprints have been corrected, on conservative principles, and have been listed for each play in the introduction to the corresponding concordance. Wrong-fount letters have been silently corrected.

Obvious irregularities on the part of the original compositor—for example the anomalous absence of full stops after speech prefixes—have been normalized and noted. Colons, semicolons, exclamation and interrogation marks after italicized words have been modernized to roman fount after current practice, since this aspect of

---

[1] An account of the principles and methods by which the concordances were edited appears in *Studies in Bibliography*, vol. 22, 1969.

compositorial practice would not normally be studied from a concordance. The spacing of words in the original printed texts, particu-
larly in 'justified' lines, is extremely variable; spacing has been
normalized on the basis of the compositor's practice as revealed in
the particular column or page.

For ease of reference, the contractions *S.*, *L.*, *M.*, and forms such
as *Mist.* and tildes, have been expanded when the compositor's own
preferred practice is clear, and the expansion has been noted in the
text. For M^r, the superior character has been lowered silently.
Superior characters like the circumflex in *baâ* and those in y̒, y̐, y̑, and
w̑, have been ignored. The reader should find little difficulty in dis-
tinguishing the original form of the pronominal contractions when
they are encountered in the text. They are listed under Y and W
respectively.

B. *Arrangement of entries*

The words in the text are arranged alphabetically, with numerals
and & and &c listed at the end. Words starting with I and J, and U
and V, will be found together under I and V respectively. The reader
should note that the use of U for the medial V (and I for J) leads in
some cases to an unfamiliar order of entry. For example, ADUISED is
listed before ADULTERY. The reader will usually find the word he
wants if he starts his inquiry at the modern spelling, for when the old
spelling differs considerably from the modern spelling, a reference
such as 'ENFORCE *see* inforce' will direct the reader to the entry in the
concordance.

In hyphenated compounds where the hyphen is the second or third
character of the heading-word (as in A-BOORD), the hyphenated form
may be listed some distance from other occurrences of the same word
in un-hyphenated form. In significant cases, references are given to
alert the user.

Under the heading-word, the line numbers or lines of context are
in the order of the text. The heading-word is followed by a frequency
count of the words in short and long (that is, marked with an
asterisk) lines, and the reference lines. When a word has been treated
as one to have a frequency count only, or a list of the line numbers

and count, any further count which follows will refer to the reference lines listed under the same heading. Where there are two counts but no reference lines (as with AN), the first count refers to the speech prefix.

C. *Special Forms*

(*a*) The following words have not been given context lines and line references but are dealt with only by the counting of their frequency:

A AM AND ARE AT BE BY HE I IN IS IT OF ON SHE THE THEY TO WAS WE WITH YOU

These forms occur so often in most texts that the reader can locate them more easily by examining the text of the play than he could by referring to an extensive listing in the concordance.

Homographs of these words (for example I = *ay*) have been listed in full and are given separate counts under the same heading-word.

(*b*) A larger number of words, consisting mainly of variant spellings, have been given line references as well as frequency counts.

These words are: ACTUS AN AR ART ATT AU BEE BEEING BEEN BEENE BEING BENE BIN BUT CAN CANST CE COULD COULDST DE DECIMA DES DID DIDD DIDDEST DIDDST DO DOE DOES DOEST DOETH DONE DOO DOOE DOOES DOOEST DOOING DOON DOONE DOOS DOOST DOOTH DOS DOST DOTH DU E EN EST ET ETC FINIS FOR FROM HA HAD HADST HAH HAS HAST HATH HAUE HEE HEEL HEELE HEL HELL HER HIM HIR HIS IE IF IL ILL ILLE INTO LA LE LES MA MAIE MAIEST MAIST MAY ME MEE MIGHT MIGHTEST MIGHTST MINE MOI MOY MY NE NO NOE NON NONA NOR NOT O OCTAUA OFF OH OR OU OUR OUT PRIMA PRIMUS QUARTA QUARTUS QUE QUINTA QUINTUS SCAENA SCENA SCOENA SECUNDA SECUNDUS SEPTIMA SEPTIMUS SEXTA SHAL SHALL SHALT SHEE SHOLD SHOLDE SHOLDST SHOULD SHOULDE SHOULDST SIR SO SOE TE TERTIA TERTIUS THAT THEE THEIR THEIRE THEM THEN THER THERE THESE THEYR THIS THOSE THOU THY TIS TU VN VNE VOS VOSTRE VOUS VS WAST WEE WER WERE WERT WHAT WHEN WHER WHERE WHICH WHO WHOM WHOME WHY WIL WILL WILT WILTE WOLD WOLDE WOLDST WOULD WOULDE WOULDEST WOULDST YE YEE YF YOUE YOUR YT & &C 1 2 3 4.

Homographs of words on this list (e.g. *bee* = n.) have been listed in full, and also have separate counts.

(*c*) All speech prefixes, other than *All.*, *Both.*, and those which represent the names of actors, have been treated as count-only words. In some cases, however, where a speech prefix corresponds to a form already on the count-only list (e.g. *Is.*), a full entry has been given. In some other cases, when two counts are given for the same heading-word for no apparent reason, the count which does not correspond to the following full references or to the list of line references is that of the speech prefix form (for example AN in *The Tempest*).

(*d*) Hyphenated compounds such as *all-building-law* have been listed under the full form, and also under each main constituent after the first. In this example there are entries under ALL-BUILDING-LAW, BUILDING, and LAW. When, however, one of the constituents of the compound is a word on the count- or location-only list ((*a*) or (*b*) above), it is dealt with in whichever of these two lists applies. References such as 'AT *see also* bemock't-at-stabs' are given to assist the reader in such cases.

Simple or non-hyphenated compounds such as *o'th'King* have been listed only under the constituent parts—in this example under OTH and KING.

(*e*) 'Justified' lines where the spellings *may* have been affected by the compositor's need to fit the text to his measure are distinguished by an asterisk at the beginning of the reference line. If only location is being given, the asterisk occurs before the line reference. If only frequency counts are being given, the number *after* the asterisk records the frequency of forms occurring in 'justified' lines. Lines which do not extend to the full width of the compositor's measure have not been distinguished as 'justified' lines, even though in many cases the shorter line may have affected the spelling.

D. *Line Numbers*

The lines in each text have been numbered from the first *Actus Primus* or stage direction and thereafter in normal reading order, including all stage directions and act and scene divisions. Each typographical line has been counted as a unit when it contains matter for inclusion in the concordance. Catchwords are not included in the count. The only general exception is that turn-overs are regarded as belonging to their base-lines; where a turn-over occurs on a line by itself, it has been reckoned as part of the base-line, and the line containing only the turn-over has not been counted as a separate line. Turn-overs may readily be distinguished by vertical stroke and single bracket after the last word of the base-line; for example *brought with* | (*child,*.

When two or more lines have been joined in order to provide a fuller context, the line-endings are indicated by a vertical stroke |, and the line reference applies to that part of the line before the vertical stroke. For the true line-numbers of words in the following part of the context line, the stated line-number should be increased by one each time a vertical stroke occurs, save when the next word is a turn-over.

The numbering of the quarto texts has been fitted to that of the corresponding Folio texts; lines in the Quarto which do not occur in the Folio are prefixed by +. The line references are similarly specified. The line references of these concordances therefore provide a consistent permanent numbering of each typographical line of text, based on the First Folio.

PROGRAM CHANGES

Preparation of concordances to the first few texts, and the especial complexity of *Wiv.*, have enabled some improvements to be made to the main concordance program. For texts other than *Tmp.*, *TGV*, *MM*, and *Err.*, the concordances have been prepared with the improved program.

Speech-prefixes now have separate entries under the appropriate heading-word and follow any other entry under the same heading-word. Entries under AN in *Wiv.*, AND and TO in *TN*, and AD in *AYL* offer examples. This alteration provides a clearer record of the total number of occurrences of words which occur both as speech-prefixes and also as forms on the 'count only' or 'locations only' lists.

Another modification supplies a more precise reference to the location of words such as BEENE for which line numbers but no full lines are given. When a 'location only' word is encountered to the right of the 'end-of-line' bar (which shows that lines of text have been joined together in order to provide a sufficient context), the line number is now adjusted to supply the exact reference. In the concordances to the texts listed above, users will find that in some instances the particular occurrence of a 'location only' word which they wish to consult in the text is to be found in the line after the one specified in the concordance; this depends on whether lines have been joined in the computer-readable version of the text from which the concordance was made. It is not expected that readers will be seriously inconvenienced by this. Should a concordance to the First Folio be published, it will, of course, incorporate all improvements.

AS YOU LIKE IT

The concordance to *AYL* was prepared from the Lee facsimile of the First Folio (Oxford, 1902). Professor Charlton Hinman (*Printing and Proof-Reading*, Oxford, 1963) records that the Lee facsimile contains the corrected formes R1:6ᵛ and S2:5ᵛ (v. 1, p. 261–2), and observes that one or two other pages in this quire might also have been proof-corrected. Such a page may be R3ᵛ in the Yale facsimile where, for the manifestly incorrect speech-prefix *Ol.* in Lee at 1. 1701, may be seen the correct *Clo.* His order of printing for this portion of the Folio (v. 2, p. 514–15) reads:

Cx By	Cx Dz	Cx Dz	By Cx/Dz	Cx Dz	Cx By	By Cx	By Cx
Q3ᵛ:4	Q3:4ᵛ	Q2ᵛ:5	Q2:5ᵛ	Q1ᵛ:6	Q1:6ᵛ	R3ᵛ:4	R3:4ᵛ

By Cx	By Cx	By Cx	By By	By By	By By	By By	By By ‖
R2ᵛ:5	R2:5ᵛ	R1ᵛ:6	R1:6ᵛ	S3ᵛ:4	S3:4ᵛ	S2ᵛ:5	S2:5ᵛ ‖

By By	By By
S1ᵛ:6	S1:6ᵛ

TABLE OF LINE AND ACT/SCENE NUMBERS

Page	Col.	Comp.	F line nos.	Globe act/scene nos.
Q3	a	C	1–51	1.1.1–1.1.52
	b	C	52–102	1.1.106
Q3ᵛ	a	C	103–68	1.1.179
	b	C	169–228	1.2.64
Q4	a	B	229–93	1.2.139
	b	B	294–357	1.2.207
Q4ᵛ	a	D	358–423	1.2.267
	b	D	424–82	1.3.25
Q5	a	D	483–547	1.3.88
	b	D	548–608	2.1.2
Q5ᵛ	a	C	609–74	2.1.66
	b	D	675–728	2.3.24
Q6	a	D	729–88	2.4.6
	b	D	789–852	2.4.68
Q6ᵛ	a	B	853–912	2.5.25
	b	B	913–70	2.6.19
R1	a	B	971–1031	2.6.57
	b	B	1032–96	2.7.119
R1ᵛ	a	B	1097–159	2.7.179
	b	B	1160–212	3.2.12
R2	a	B	1213–78	3.2.86
	b	B	1279–342	3.2.152

Page	Col.	Comp.	F line nos.	Globe act/scene nos.
R2ᵛ	a	B	1343–407	3.2.225
	b	B	1408–72	3.2.298
R3	a	B	1473–538	3.2.370
	b	B	1539–604	3.2.449
R3ᵛ	a	B	1605–64	3.3.56
	b	B	1665–724	3.4.15
R4	a	C	1725–82	3.5.11
	b	C	1783–848	3.5.76
R4ᵛ	a	C	1849–914	3.5.159
	b	C	1915–75	4.1.62
R5	a	C	1976–2041	4.1.131
	b	C	2042–107	4.1.206
R5ᵛ	a	C	2108–61	4.3.13
	b	C	2162–226	4.3.77
R6	a	C	2227–92	4.3.139
	b	C	2293–351	5.1.12
R6ᵛ	a	B	2352–410	5.2.2
	b	B	2411–74	5.2.73
S1	a	B	2475–535	5.3.5
	b	B	2536–93	5.4.17
S1ᵛ	a	B	2594–659	5.4.89
	b	B	2660–723	5.4.154
S2	a	B	2724–59	5.4.188
	b	B	2760–97 (Finis)	5.4.229

These errors, etc. have been corrected in the text:

Q3ᵛ	223	whetstone. (indistinct colon)		R3	1473	mofl
	226	farher.			1487	Lacky.
Q4ᵛ	430	Te			1580	*Ros:*
Q5	497	*Duk*ʌ		R4	1802	wouuds
	539	per			1810	hau
	591	by		R4ᵛ	1862	extermin'd·
Q5ᵛ	657	must:			1973	youare
	690	Centlewoman		R5ᵛ	2116	in,in
	701	*Exunt.*		R6	2296	I
R1	1011	braiue,		R6ᵛ	2358	eouer'd.
	1022	Wiithall,			2379	sit.
	1060	why			2397	police:
	1061	any. manBut			2455	heauinesse.
R1ᵛ	1111	out.		S1	2520	wlll
	1114	*Du*ʌ*Sen.*			2532	[*Clo.*]
	1147	*Du*ʌ*Sen.*		S1ᵛ	2605	daughrer:
R2	1226	pood			2656	ro
R2ᵛ	1373	berimʌd		S2	2748	wete
	1448	*Iaq*ʌ			2751	sharc

December, 1968   T. H. H.

AS YOU LIKE IT

A = 217*224, 7*2
Oliuer. Marry sir be better employed, and be naught | a while.   38
Saw her a bed, and in the morning early,   686
*comming a night to *Iane Smile*, and I remember the kis- | sing   830
For my sake be comfortable, hold death a while   959
Sayes, very wisely, it is ten a clocke: 995
Ros. I pray you, what i'st a clocke?   1490
Orl. I must attend the Duke at dinner, by two a clock | I will be with
thee againe.   2086
Ros. How say you now, is it not past two a clock? | And heere much
Orlando.   2148
Ros. Read. *Why, thy godhead laid a part*,   2193
ABANDON = *2
*you Clowne, abandon: which is in the vulgar, leaue the   2389
*is, abandon the society of this Female, or Clowne   2392
ABANDOND = 1
Ile stay to know, at your abandon'd caue. *Exit*.   2773
ABANDONED = 1
Left and abandoned of his veluet friend;   658
ABED *see* bed
ABHOMINABLE = *1
Ros. Those that are in extremity of either, are abho- | minable   1921
ABHORRE = 1
Abhorre it, feare it, doe not enter it.   732
ABLE = 1
My fortunes were more able to releeue her.   862
ABOUE = 1
With thy chaste eye, from thy pale spheare aboue   1203
ABOUT = 5*2
*cleare all: nothing remaines, but that I kindle the boy | thither, which
now Ile goe about. *Exit*.   167
Of him I was about to call his Father,   725
As yet to question you about your fortunes: 1153
Cel. And a chaine that you once wore about his neck: 1377
*about you, demonstrating a carelesse desolation: but you   1565
A sheep-coat, fenc'd about with Oliue-trees.   2227
Lay sleeping on his back; about his necke   2258
ABRUPTLY = 1
Abruptly as my passion now makes me, | Thou hast not lou'd.   823

1

ABSENCE = 1
By reason of his absence there is nothing — 870
ABSENT = 2
If he be absent, bring his Brother to me, — 698
I should not seeke an absent argument — 1183
ABUSD = 1
None could be so abus'd in sight as hee. — 1851
ABUSES = *2
*that are sicke. There is a man haunts the Forrest, that a-|buses — 1545
*madnesse, that blinde rascally boy, that abuses euery — 2119
ACCENT = *1
*Orl. Your accent is something finer, then you could | purchase in so
remoued a dwelling. — 1529
ACCESSE = 1
*Den. So please you, he is heere at the doore, and im-|portunes accesse
to you. — 92
ACCORD = 2
*Adam. Sweet Masters bee patient, for your Fathers | remembrance, be
at accord. — 63
You, to his loue must accord, — 2707
ACCORDING = 1*2
*to sweare, and to forsweare, according as mariage binds — 2633
*Clo. According to the fooles bolt sir, and such dulcet | diseases. — 2640
According to the measure of their states. — 2752
ACCOUSTREMENTS = *1
*are no such man; you are rather point deuice in your
ac-|coustrements, — 1566
ACCUSTOMD = 1
Whose heart th'accustom'd sight of death makes hard — 1774
ACORNE = 1
vnder a tree like a drop'd Acorne. — 1429
ACQUAINT = *2
*Cha. Marry doe I sir: and I came to acquaint you — 122
*to acquaint you withall, that either you might stay him — 131
ACQUAINTANCE = 1*2
Or haue acquaintance with mine owne desires, — 508
*Orl. Is't possible, that on so little acquaintance you — 2409
*pouertie of her, the small acquaintance, my sodaine wo-|ing, — 2414
ACQUAINTED = *2
*Iaq. You are ful of prety answers: haue you not bin ac-|quainted — 1464
*Iaq. I prethee, pretty youth, let me better acquainted | with thee. — 1917
ACQUIT = *1
*some broken limbe, shall acquit him well: your brother — 127
ACRES = 1
Betweene the acres of the Rie, — 2557
ACTION = 1
By the sterne brow, and waspish action — 2157
ACTIONS = 2
How many actions most ridiculous, — 812
*girle goes before the Priest, and certainely a Womans | thought runs
before her actions. — 2049
ACTOR = 1
Ile proue a busie actor in their play. Exeunt. — 1768
ACTS = 1
His Acts being seuen ages. At first the Infant, — 1122
ACTUS l.1 604 1179 1915 2339 = 5

AD = *1
   *he would not haue spoke such a word. *Ex. Orl. Ad.*   84
AD = 6*1
ADAM see also Ad. = 6*5
   Enter Orlando and Adam.   2
   Orlando. | *As I remember *Adam*, it was vpon this fashion   3
   *gentility with my education. This is it *Adam* that   23
   Orlan. Goe a-part *Adam*, and thou shalt heare how | he will shake me
   vp.   30
   Heere feele we not the penaltie of *Adam*,   611
   Enter Orlando and Adam.   703
   Ad. Why whether *Adam* would'st thou haue me go?   733
   Enter Orlando, & Adam.   950
   Orl. Why how now *Adam*? No greater heart in thee: 954
   Cheerely good *Adam. Exeunt*   970
   Enter Orlando with Adam.   1146
ADAM = 2*2
ADDREST = 1
   Addrest a mightie power, which were on foote   2732
ADIEU = 2*2
   Orl. I am glad of your departure: Adieu good Mon-|sieur
   Melancholly.   1485
   Orl. With no lesse religion, then if thou wert indeed | my *Rosalind*: so
   adieu.   2103
   such offenders, and let time try: adieu. *Exit.*   2106
   Phe. If sight & shape be true, why then my loue adieu   2695
ADMIRED = 1
   Trees, wherein *Rosalind* is so admired?   1575
ADOPTED = 1
   His yongest sonne, and would not change that calling | To be adopted
   heire to *Fredricke.*   396
ADORATION = 1
   All adoration, dutie, and obseruance,   2503
ADUENTURE = 1*1
   *your selfe with your iudgment, the feare of your aduen-|ture   339
   I haue by hard aduenture found mine owne.   827
ADUERSITIE = 1
   Sweet are the vses of aduersitie   618
AFFAIRES = 1
   He dies that touches any of this fruite, | Till I, and my affaires are
   answered.   1074
AFFAIRS = *1
   *but a part of the thousand part of a minute in the affairs   1961
AFFECTION = 1*2
   *perforce, I will render thee againe in affection: by   189
   *it cannot bee sounded: my affection hath an vnknowne | bottome, like
   the Bay of Portugall.   2113
   Cel. Or rather bottomlesse, that as fast as you poure | affection in, it
   runs out.   2115
AFFECTIONS = 1
   Cel. Come, come, wrastle with thy affections.   479
AFFLICT = 1
   Afflict me with thy mockes, pitty me not,   1806
AFTER = 12*3
   Orl. You meane to mocke me after: you should not   369
   After my flight: now goe in we content   602
   And after one houre more, 'twill be eleuen,   998

AFTER *cont*.

After a voyage: He hath strange places cram'd	1013
Who after me, hath many a weary steppe	1107
If the Cat will after kinde, | *so be sure will Rosalinde:*	1301
*wonderfull, and yet againe wonderful, and after that out | of all hooping.	1388
After the Shepheard that complain'd of loue,	1755
No faith proud Mistresse, hope not after it,	1818
To gleane the broken eares after the man	1876
Ros. Now tell me how long you would haue her, af-|ter you haue possest her?	2052
And after some small space, being strong at heart,	2305
Phe. That will I, should I die the houre after.	2587
After some question with him, was conuerted	2737
And after, euery of this happie number	2749

AGAINE = 7*9

*goe alone againe, Ile neuer wrastle for prize more: and	157
*perforce, I will render thee againe in affection: by	189
*then with safety of a pure blush, thou maist in ho-|nor come off againe.	197
To bring againe these foolish runawaies. *Exeunt*.	701
*cods, and giuing her them againe, said with weeping	834
Turning againe toward childish trebble pipes,	1141
*wonderfull, and yet againe wonderful, and after that out | of all hooping.	1388
*parted he with thee? And when shalt thou see him a-|gaine? Answer me in one word.	1417
I maruell why I answer'd not againe,	1906
Orl. I must attend the Duke at dinner, by two a clock | I will be with thee againe.	2086
He left a promise to returne againe	2250
*word againe, it was not well cut, he wold send me word	2649
*If againe, it was not well cut, he disabled my iudgment:	2651
*this is called, the reply churlish. If againe it was not well	2652
*reproofe valiant. If againe, it was not well cut, he wold	2654
And all their Lands restor'd to him againe	2740

AGAINST *see also* 'gainst = 4*10

*is within mee, begins to mutinie against this seruitude.	25
*in disguis'd against mee to try a fall: to morrow sir I	125
*shall runne into, in that it is a thing of his owne search, | and altogether against my will.	133
*contriuer against mee his naturall brother: therefore vse	142
*grace himselfe on thee, hee will practise against thee by	146
I breake my shins against it.	840
*Ile go sleepe if I can: if I cannot, Ile raile against all | the first borne of Egypt.	945
Of what we thinke against thee.	1192
*more plentie in it, it goes much against my stomacke.	1220
*wee two, will raile against our Mistris the world, and all | our miserie.	1470
against whom I know most faults.	1473
*Lectors against it, and I thanke God, I am not a Wo-|man	1535
*clamorous then a Parrat against raine, more new-fang-|led	2060
*of Irish Wolues against the Moone: I will helpe you	2517

AGE = 7*2

And vnregarded age in corners throwne,	746
Be comfort to my age: here is the gold,	749
Therefore my age is as a lustie winter,	756

AGE *cont*.
Opprest with two weake euils, age, and hunger,	1109
And so he playes his part. The sixt age shifts	1136
That the stretching of a span, | *buckles in his summe of age.*	1329
*and the foolish Chronoclers of that age, found it was	2016
*Vnder an old Oake, whose bows were moss'd with age	2255
Will. Fiue and twentie Sir. | *Clo*. A ripe age: Is thy name *William*?	2360

AGEN = *1
Clo. Your lips wil feele them the sooner. Shallow a- |gen: a more sounder instance, come.	1257

AGES = 1 *1
His Acts being seuen ages. At first the Infant,	1122
*'tis a Word too great for any mouth of this Ages size, to	1420

AGOE = 1
'Tis but an houre agoe, since it was nine,	997

AH = *1
*Ah, sirra, a body would thinke this was well counterfei- |ted,	2321

AIME = 1
That from the Hunters aime had tane a hurt,	641

AIRE = 1
In the bleake aire. Come, I wil beare thee	966

ALACKE = 1
Alacke, in me, what strange effect	2201

ALAS = 3 *4
take his part with weeping. | *Ros*. Alas.	294
Cel. Alas, he is too yong: yet he looks successfully	317
Ros. Alas, what danger will it be to vs,	572
Ros. Alas poore Shepheard searching of they would,	826
Ros. Alas the day, what shall I do with my doublet &	1413
Ros. Alas, deere loue, I cannot lacke thee two houres.	2085
Sil. Call you this chiding? | *Cel*. Alas poore Shepheard.	2213

ALBEIT = 1 *1
*of my father in mee, as you, albeit I confesse your com- |ming	52
To leaue this place; Albeit you haue deseru'd	430

ALIAS = 1
Enter Rosaline for Ganimed, Celia for Aliena, and | *Clowne*, alias *Touchstone*.	782

ALIENA = 4 *3
Cel. Something that hath a reference to my state: | No longer *Celia*, but *Aliena*.	592
Enter Rosaline for Ganimed, Celia for Aliena, and | *Clowne*, alias *Touchstone*.	782
*selfe coragious to petty-coate; therefore courage, good | *Aliena*.	790
*how deepe I am in loue: ile tell thee *Aliena*, I cannot be	2121
Aliena: say with her, that she loues mee; consent with	2416
Go you, and prepare *Aliena*; for looke you,	2425
*brother marries *Aliena*, shall you marrie her. I know in- |to	2472

ALL = 63 *27
*hiding from me all gentleman-like qualities: the spirit	69
*deuise, of all sorts enchantingly beloued, and indeed	163
*cleare all: nothing remaines, but that I kindle the boy | thither, which now Ile goe about. *Exit*.	167
Cel. All the better: we shalbe the more Marketable.	262
Ros. With bils on their neckes: Be it knowne vnto | all men by these presents.	286
*making such pittiful dole ouer them, that all the behol- |ders	293
Orl. I attend them with all respect and dutie.	330

AS YOU LIKE IT

ALL *cont*.
    And all the world was of my Fathers minde,   399
    But iustly as you haue exceeded all promise, | Your Mistris shall be
    happie.   408
    Are all throwne downe, and that which here stands vp   416
    That he misconsters all that you haue done: 433
    Cel. But is all this for your Father?   469
    Duk. Thus doe all Traitors,   513
    That I did suite me all points like a man,   581
    The enemie of all your graces liues   722
    All this I giue you, let me be your seruant,   750
    In all your businesse and necessities.   759
    In lieu of all thy paines and husbandrie,   769
    *runne into strange capers; but as all is mortall in   836
    nature, so is all nature in loue, mortall in folly.   837
    Cor. And to you gentle Sir, and to you all.   854
    *the Duke wil drinke vnder this tree; he hath bin all this | day to looke
    you.   919
    Iaq. And I haue bin all this day to auoid him: 921
    *Ile go sleepe if I can: if I cannot, Ile raile against all | the first borne
    of Egypt.   945
    Of all opinion that growes ranke in them,   1020
    And all th'imbossed sores, and headed euils,   1041
    I thought that all things had bin sauage heere,   1084
    Du Sen. Thou seest, we are not all alone vnhappie: 1114
    Ia. All the world's a stage, | And all the men and women, meerely
    Players;   1118
    And whistles in his sound. Last Scene of all,   1142
    And let me all your fortunes vnderstand. *Exeunt*.   1178
    Thy Lands and all things that thou dost call thine,   1189
    Clo. Truly thou art damn'd, like an ill roasted Egge, | all on one side.   1235
    *to a crooked-pated olde Cuckoldly Ramme, out of all   1279
    *Hir worth being mounted on the winde, | through all the world beares
    Rosalinde*.   1288
    All the pictures fairest Linde, | are but blacke to Rosalinde: 1290
    Will I Rosalinda write, | teaching all that reade, to know   1335
    With all Graces wide enlarg'd, | nature presently distill'd   1341
    Ros. O yes, I heard them all, and more too, for some   1362
    *wonderfull, and yet againe wonderful, and after that out | of all
    hooping.   1388
    *much at once, or none at all. I pre'thee take the Corke   1397
    *wee two, will raile against our Mistris the world, and all | our miserie.   1470
    Ros. There were none principal, they were all like   1540
    *brambles; all (forsooth) defying the name of *Rosalinde*.   1548
    Wil you go? | *Orl*. With all my heart, good youth.   1609
    all shal flout me out of my calling. *Exeunt*   1707
    Now I doe frowne on thee with all my heart,   1786
    That you insult, exult, and all at once   1809
    Sell when you can, you are not for all markets: 1833
    And be not proud, though all the world could see,   1850
    But that's all one: omittance is no quittance: 1907
    Sil. Phebe, with all my heart.   1910
    *is all these: but it is a melancholy of mine owne, com-|pounded   1931
    *lispe, and weare strange suites; disable all the benefits   1949
    *haue you bin all this while? you a louer? and you   1954
    *almost six thousand yeeres old, and in all this time there   2007
    Hero of Cestos. But these are all lies, men haue died   2017

6

ALL *cont*.

Ros. Yes faith will I, fridaies and saterdaies, and all.	2026
Orl. So do all thoughts, they are wing'd.	2051
*mend mee, and by all pretty oathes that are not dange-|rous,	2095
Ros. Well, Time is the olde Iustice that examines all	2105
And play the swaggerer, beare this, beare all:	2162
Of me, and all that I can make,	2210
A Lyonnesse, with vdders all drawne drie,	2265
Which all this while had bled: and now he fainted,	2302
Awd. Faith the Priest was good enough, for all the | olde gentlemans saying.	2343
*other. For all your Writers do consent, that *ipse* is hee:	2385
*good: for my fathers house, and all the reuennew, that	2418
Sil. It is to be all made of sighes and teares, | And so am I for *Phebe*.	2491
Sil. It is to be all made of faith and seruice, | And so am I for *Phebe*.	2496
Sil. It is to be all made of fantasie,	2501
All made of passion, and all made of wishes, .	2502
All adoration, dutie, and obseruance,	2503
All humblenesse, all patience, and impatience,	2504
All puritie, all triall, all obseruance: | And so am I for *Phebe*.	2505
Aud. I do desire it with all my heart: and I hope it is	2534
Can do all this that he hath promised?	2576
Orl. That would I, were I of all kingdomes King.	2585
Ros. I haue promis'd to make all this matter euen:	2594
To make these doubts all euen. *Exit Ros. and Celia*.	2601
*of verie strange beasts, which in all tongues, are call'd | Fooles.	2614
Clo. Salutation and greeting to you all.	2616
*the Lye direct: all these you may auoyd, but the	2670
And all their Lands restor'd to him againe	2740
Play Musicke, and you Brides and Bride-groomes all,	2755

ALLIES = 1

you to your land, and loue, and great allies:	2766

ALLOTTERY = *1

*a gentleman, or giue mee the poore allottery my	72

ALLOW = *1

*endure it: therefore allow me such exercises as may be-|come	71

ALLOWES = *1

*nations allowes you my better, in that you are the first	49

ALLS = 1*1

*breakes his staffe like a noble goose; but all's braue that	1751
Inuite the Duke, and all's contented followers:	2424

ALMOST = 4*3

*meanes or other: for I assure thee, (and almost with	149
Almost to bursting, and the big round teares	645
From seauentie yeeres, till now almost fourescore	775
I faint almost to death.	847
Orl. I almost die for food, and let me haue it.	1081
*natiuitie, and almost chide God for making you that	1951
*almost six thousand yeeres old, and in all this time there	2007

ALONE = 4*2

*goe alone againe, Ile neuer wrastle for prize more: and	157
Leaue me alone to woe him; Let's away	598
To that which had too much: then being there alone,	657
Du Sen. Thou seest, we are not all alone vnhappie:	1114
I had as liefe haue beene my selfe alone.	1449
*of his owne getting; hornes, euen so poore men alone:	1664

ALONG = 8*1
Else had she with her Father rang'd along.	529
Say what thou canst, Ile goe along with thee.	569
The like doe you, so shall we passe along, | And neuer stir assailants.	577
Cel. Heele goe along ore the wide world with me,	597
Did steale behinde him as he lay along	637
Vpon the brooke that brawles along this wood,	639
Full of the pasture, iumps along by him	661
But come thy waies, weele goe along together,	770
Cel. There lay hee stretch'd along like a Wounded | knight.	1434

ALREADY = *1
Oli. Where will the old Duke liue? | *Cha*. They say hee is already in the Forrest of *Arden*,	114

ALSO = 1
Your Grace was wont to laugh is also missing,	689

ALTHOUGH = 2
Doth very foolishly, although he smart	1028
although thy breath be rude.	1159

ALTOGETHER = 2*2
*shall runne into, in that it is a thing of his owne search, | and altogether against my will.	133
*owne people, who best know him, that I am altogether	165
Come, warble, come. | *Song. Altogether heere*.	925
*me altogether: I wil marrie you, if euer I marrie Wo-|man,	2519

ALWAIES = *1
*our whetstone: for alwaies the dulnesse of the foole, is	223

AM = 43*31

AMAZE = 1
Le Beu. You amaze me Ladies: I would haue told	274

AMBITION = 1*1
*yong fellow of France, full of ambition, an enuious	140
Who doth ambition shunne,	927

AMBITIOUS = 1*1
I am ambitious for a motley coat. | *Du Sen*. Thou shalt haue one.	1016
*which is ambitious: nor the Lawiers, which is politick:	1929

AMBLES = 1*2
*with diuers persons: Ile tel you who Time ambles with-|all,	1499
Orl. Who ambles Time withal?	1507
*of heauie tedious penurie. These Time ambles | withal.	1513

AMEN = *1
Clo. Amen. A man may if he were of a fearful heart,	1657

AMIEN = 1

AMIENS see also Amy. = 1
To day my Lord of *Amiens*, and my selfe,	636

AMONG = 1
capricious Poet honest *Ouid* was among the Gothes.	1620

AMONGST = 1*1
And he did render him the most vnnaturall | That liu'd amongst men.	2273
*in heere sir, amongst the rest of the Country copulatiues	2632

AMY = 6*3

AMYENS = 3
Enter Duke Senior: Amyens, and two or three Lords | like Forresters.	605
Enter, Amyens, Iaques, & others.	889
Enter Duke Senior, Amyens, Iaques, Orlan-|do, Oliuer, Celia.	2573

AN *l*.*13 *140 *160 *282 283 535 638 803 997 1006 1106 1183 1197 *1235 *1358 1374 1407 *1531 *1533 *1559 1646 1721 *1957 *1959 *2061 *2113 2159 *2216 2233 2251 *2255 *2634 *2671 *2674 2736 = 17*18

ANATHOMIZD = 1
    The Wise-mans folly is anathomiz'd   1030
ANATHOMIZE = *1
    *but should I anathomize him to thee, as hee is, I must   152
AND = 402*250, 2*4
    And if he will come to me.   942
    Iaq. And you will not be answer'd with reason, | I must dye.   1076
    Iaq. Nay then God buy you, and you talke in blanke | verse.   1946
    *haue you bin all this while? you a louer? and you   1954
    Ros. Nay, and you be so tardie, come no more in my   1965
    *would you say to me now, and I were your verie, verie | *Rosalind*?   1983
ANGER = 2
    Cel. With his eies full of anger.   497
    Fall in loue with my anger. If it be so, as fast   1840
ANGRY = 1
    It beares an angry tenure; pardon me,   2159
ANIE = *3
    *had anie; or if he had, he had sworne it away, before   244
    *so faire and excellent Ladies anie thing. But let your   348
    *was not anie man died in his owne person (*videlicet*) in   2008
ANIMALS = *1
    *him but growth, for the which his Animals on his   17
ANNIMALL = 1
    The wretched annimall heau'd forth such groanes   643
ANNIMALS = 1
    To fright the Annimals, and to kill them vp   670
ANON = 1
    The Fluxe of companie: anon a carelesse Heard   660
ANOTHER = 6*8
    *Musicke in his sides? Is there yet another doates vpon   304
    Hadst thou descended from another house: 390
    I would thou had'st told me of another Father. | *Exit Duke*.   392
    No, let my Father seeke another heire: 563
    Cours'd one another downe his innocent nose   646
    But I am shepheard to another man,   863
    Come, more, another stanzo: Cal you'em stanzo's?   907
    Clo. That is another simple sinne in you, to bring the   1275
    *one another, as halfepence are, euerie one fault seeming   1541
    *married of him then of another, for he is not like to mar-|rie   1696
    *serue me such another tricke, neuer come in my sight | more.   1955
    *but they ask'd one another the reason: no sooner knew   2444
    *it is, to looke into happines through another mans eies: 2453
    Iaq. There is sure another flood toward, and these   2612
ANSWER = 2*5
    *parted he with thee? And when shalt thou see him a-|gaine? Answer
    me in one word.   1417
    *say I and no, to these particulars, is more then to answer | in a
    Catechisme.   1421
    Orl. Not so: but I answer you right painted cloath,   1466
    *shall neuer take her without her answer, vnlesse you take   2080
    *my troth, we that haue good wits, haue much to answer   2352
    Will. I sir, I thanke God. | *Clo*. Thanke God: A good answer.   2364
    *cut, he would answer I spake not true: this is call'd the   2653
ANSWERD = 2
    Iaq. And you will not be answer'd with reason, | I must dye.   1076
    I maruell why I answer'd not againe,   1906

ANSWERE = 1
Oli. That will I: for I must beare answere backe   2334
ANSWERED = 1
He dies that touches any of this fruite, | Till I, and my affaires are
answered.   1074
ANSWERES = 1
As she answeres thee with frowning lookes, ile sauce   1841
ANSWERS = *1
Iaq. You are ful of prety answers: haue you not bin ac-|quainted   1464
ANTICKE = 1
Vnder an oake, whose anticke roote peepes out   638
ANTIQUE = 1
The constant seruice of the antique world,   761
ANTIQUITIE = 1
And high top, bald with drie antiquitie: 2256
ANY = 19*9
Oli. Now Sir, what make you heere? | *Orl*. Nothing: I am not taught to
make any thing.   32
*dost him any slight disgrace, or if hee doe not mightilie   145
*learne mee how to remember any extraordinary plea-|sure.   175
Ros. But is there any else longs to see this broken   303
*one should be lam'd with reasons, and the other mad | without any.   467
1 *Lo*. I cannot heare of any that did see her,   684
If he for gold will giue vs any foode,   846
That little cares for buying any thing.   876
Iaq. Well then, if euer I thanke any man, Ile thanke   912
If it do come to passe, that any man turne Asse: 937
If this vncouth Forrest yeeld any thing sauage,   956
If there liue any thing in this Desert.   969
That can therein taxe any priuate party: 1045
Vnclaim'd of any man. But who come here?   1061
He dies that touches any of this fruite, | Till I, and my affaires are
answered.   1074
If euer sate at any good mans feast: 1092
Has't any Philosophie in thee shepheard?   1221
*'tis a Word too great for any mouth of this Ages size, to   1420
Orl. Can you remember any of the principall euils,   1538
*as louing your selfe, then seeming the Lo-|uer of any other.   1567
Orl. Did you euer cure any so?   1585
*for no passion truly any thing; as boyes and women are   1592
Clo. I wil not take her on guift of any man.   1677
Then any of her lineaments can show her.   1829
*was neuer any thing so sodaine, but the sight of two   2439
*to set her before your eyes to morrow, humane as she is, | and without
any danger.   2475
Clo. If any man doubt that, let him put mee to my   2620
at any thing, and yet a foole.   2678
ANYTHING *see* thing
APACE = *2
*speake apace: I would thou couldst stammer, that thou   1394
Clo. Come apace good *Audrey*, I wil fetch vp your   1615
APART *see* a-part
APE = *1
*then an ape, more giddy in my desires, then a mon-|key: 2061
APES = *1
*of two dog-Apes. And when a man thankes me hartily,   914

APISH = *1
  *liking, proud, fantastical, apish, shallow, inconstant, ful   1590
APPARELL = *1
  *apparell, and to cry like a woman: but I must comfort   788
APPARRELL = *2
  *in mans apparrell? Looks he as freshly, as he did the day | he
  Wrastled?   1424
  *Ros. Not out of your apparrell, and yet out of your | suite: 1999
APPEARE = *1
  *impossible to me, if it appeare not inconuenient to you,   2474
APPEARES = 1
  Orl. Oh good old man, how well in thee appeares   760
APPLAUSE = 1
  High commendation, true applause, and loue;   431
APPLY = 1
  For in my youth I neuer did apply | Hot, and rebellious liquors in my
  bloud,   752
APPOINTED = *1
  *place appointed for the wrastling, and they are ready to | performe it.   307
APPROACH = 2
  1.Lord. He saues my labor by his owne approach.   981
  This seene, Orlando did approach the man,   2270
APPROACHD = 1
  Who with her head, nimble in threats approach'd | The opening of his
  mouth: but sodainly   2260
APRILL = *1
  *are Aprill when they woe, December when they wed: 2056
APTER = *1
  *you Loue beleeue it, which I warrant she is apter to do,   1571
ARAY = 1*1
  Who gaue me fresh aray, and entertainment,   2297
  *I say I am a Magitian: Therefore put you in your best a- |ray,   2479
ARDEN = 2*2
  Oli. Where will the old Duke liue? | *Cha. They say hee is already in
  the Forrest of Arden,   114
  Ros. Why, whether shall we goe? | Cel. To seeke my Vncle in the
  Forrest of Arden.   570
  Ros. Well, this is the Forrest of Arden.   797
  *Clo. I, now am I in Arden, the more foole I, when I   798
ARE = 46*64
ARGUMENT = 3
  sent in this foole to cut off the argument?   216
  Grounded vpon no other argument,   447
  I should not seeke an absent argument   1183
ARKE = *1
  *couples are comming to the Arke. Here comes a payre   2613
ARME = 4
  Support him by the arme: giue me your hand,   1177
  There stript himselfe, and heere vpon his arme   2300
  I pray you will you take him by the arme.   2317
  thee weare thy heart in a scarfe. | Orl. It is my arme.   2430
ARMED = *1
  *to your wiues for: but he comes armed in his   1974
ARMES = 2
  At the armes end: I wil heere be with thee presently,   960
  Mewling, and puking in the Nurses armes: 1123

ARROWES = 1
He hath t'ane his bow and arrowes, and is gone forth   2152
ARROWS = 1
Then shall you know the wounds inuisible | That Loues keene arrows make.   1802
ART *l*.240 391 427 *519 541 588 763 838 963 *1067 1157 1158 1176 1233 *1235 *1241 1269 1556 *1635 1872 *2064 2189 2366 2370 2380 *2722 2724 = 20*7, *2
*no wit by Nature, nor Art, may complaine of good | breeding, or comes of a very dull kindred.   1228
*his Art, and yet not damnable. If you do loue *Rosalinde*   2470
AS = 84*78
Orlando. | *As I remember *Adam*, it was vpon this fashion   3
*Crownes, and as thou saist, charged my bro- | ther   6
*dunghils are as much bound to him as I: besides this no- | thing   18
*place of a brother, and as much as in him lies, mines my   22
*were there twenty brothers betwixt vs: I haue as much   51
*of my father in mee, as you, albeit I confesse your com- | ming   52
*endure it: therefore allow me such exercises as may be- | come   71
*of her Vncle, then his owne daughter, and neuer two La- | dies loued as they doe.   112
carelesly as they did in the golden world.   119
*loth to foyle him, as I must for my owne honour if hee   129
*from his intendment, or brooke such disgrace well as he   132
*thy discretion, I had as liefe thou didst breake his necke   143
*as his finger. And thou wert best looke to't; for if thou   144
*but should I anathomize him to thee, as hee is, I must   152
*of thy loue to me were so righteously temper'd, as mine | is to thee.   182
Cel. Which he will put on vs, as Pigeons feed their | young.   259
Ros. As wit and fortune will. | *Clo*. Or as the destinies decrees.   269
*I come but in as others do, to try with him the strength | of my youth.   334
Ros. My Father lou'd Sir *Roland* as his soule,   398
But iustly as you haue exceeded all promise, | Your Mistris shall be happie.   408
So neere our publike Court as twentie miles, | Thou diest for it.   503
(As I doe trust I am not) then deere Vncle,   510
Neuer so much as in a thought vnborne,   511
They are as innocent as grace it selfe;   515
(Maides as we are) to trauell forth so farre?   573
As manie other mannish cowards haue,   586
The seasons difference, as the Icie phange   612
Did steale behinde him as he lay along   637
As worldlings doe, giuing thy sum of more   656
Their graces serue them but as enemies,   714
Therefore my age is as a lustie winter,   756
That cannot so much as a blossome yeelde,   768
*the weaker vessell, as doublet and hose ought to show it   789
Though in thy youth thou wast as true a louer   808
As euer sigh'd vpon a midnight pillow: 809
As sure I thinke did neuer man loue so: 811
Or if thou hast not sat as I doe now,   819
Abruptly as my passion now makes me, | Thou hast not lou'd.   823
*runne into strange capers; but as all is mortall in   836
As a Weazel suckes egges: More, I pre'thee more.   902
I thinke of as many matters as he, but I giue   923
Heere shall he see, grosse fooles as he,   941
As I do liue by foode, I met a foole,   987

AS *cont*.

Which is as drie as the remainder bisket	1012
Withall, as large a Charter as the winde,	1022
The why is plaine, as way to Parish Church:	1026
As sensuall as the brutish sting it selfe,	1040
Doth it not flow as hugely as the Sea,	1046
When such a one as shee, such is her neighbor?	1052
As yet to question you about your fortunes:	1153
Thou art not so vnkinde, as mans ingratitude	1157
Freize, freize, thou bitter skie that dost not bight so nigh | *as benefitts*	
forgot:	1164
as freind remembred not. | *Heigh ho, sing, &c.*	1167
As you haue whisper'd faithfully you were,	1170
And as mine eye doth his effigies witnesse,	1171
Thou art right welcome, as thy masters is:	1176
*respect it is not in the Court, it is tedious. As it is a spare	1218
*life (looke you) it fits my humor well: but as there is no	1219
*at the Court, are as ridiculous in the Countrey, as	1244
*is not the grease of a Mutton, as wholesome as the sweat	1253
*might'st powre this conceal'd man out of thy mouth, as	1395
*in mans apparrell? Looks he as freshly, as he did the day | he	
Wrastled?	1424
Cel. It is as easie to count Atomies as to resolue the	1426
I had as liefe haue beene my selfe alone.	1449
Iaq. God buy you, let's meet as little as we can.	1452
Iaq. What stature is she of? | *Orl*. Iust as high as my heart.	1462
detect the lazie foot of time, as wel as a clocke.	1495
Orl. And why not the swift foote of time? Had not | that bin as	
proper?	1496
*go as softly as foot can fall, he thinkes himselfe too soon | there.	1517
Ros. As the Conie that you see dwell where shee is | kindled.	1527
*to be touch'd with so many giddie offences as hee	1536
*one another, as halfepence are, euerie one fault seeming	1541
*as louing your selfe, then seeming the Lo-|uer of any other.	1567
Ros. But are you so much in loue, as your rimes speak?	1578
*as wel a darke house, and a whip, as madmen do:	1581
*for no passion truly any thing; as boyes and women are	1592
*as cleane as a sound sheepes heart, that there shal not | be one spot of	
Loue in't.	1600
Clo. I am heere with thee, and thy Goats, as the most	1619
*sweare in Poetrie, may be said as Louers, they do feigne.	1632
*may come heereafter. But be it, as it may bee,	1650
*though? Courage. As hornes are odious, they are neces-|sarie.	1660
*No, no, the noblest Deere hath them as huge as the Ras-|call:	1665
*Is the single man therefore blessed? No, as a wall'd	1666
Clo. As the Oxe hath his bow sir, the horse his curb,	1686
*and the Falcon her bels, so man hath his desires, and as	1687
*this fellow wil but ioyne you together, as they ioyne	1692
Cel. As good cause as one would desire, | Therefore weepe.	1714
Ros. And his kissing is as ful of sanctitie, | As the touch of holy bread.	1723
*but for his verity in loue, I doe thinke him as	1733
concaue as a couered goblet, or a Worme-eaten nut.	1734
*told him of as good as he, so he laugh'd and let mee goe.	1744
*But what talke wee of Fathers, when there is such a man | as *Orlando*?	1745
*as a puisny Tilter, y spurs his horse but on one side,	1750
Sil. O deere *Phebe*, | If euer (as that euer may be neere)	1799
As till that time I shall not pitty thee.	1807

13

AS *cont*.

As by my faith, I see no more in you	1811
Then she a woman. 'Tis such fooles as you	1825
Fall in loue with my anger. If it be so, as fast	1840
As she answeres thee with frowning lookes, ile sauce	1841
None could be so abus'd in sight as hee.	1851
In parcells as I did, would haue gone neere	1899
sight, I had as liefe be woo'd of a Snaile.	1966
Orl. What's that? | *Ros*. Why hornes: w such as you are faine to be be-|holding	1972
Ros. I, but when? | *Orl*. Why now, as fast as she can marrie vs.	2042
Ros. By my life, she will doe as I doe. | *Orl*. O but she is wise.	2067
*you would proue, my friends told mee as much, and I	2089
Cel. Or rather bottomlesse, that as fast as you poure | affection in, it runs out.	2115
I know not the contents, but as I guesse	2156
Which she did vse, as she was writing of it,	2158
I am but as a guiltlesse messenger.	2160
Were man as rare as Phenix: 'od's my will,	2165
The royall disposition of that beast | To prey on nothing, that doth seeme as dead:	2268
As how I came into that Desert place.	2295
He sent me hither, stranger as I am	2306
*so neere the hart, as your gesture cries it out: when your	2471
*to set her before your eyes to morrow, humane as she is, | and without any danger.	2475
*you, and you shal be married to morrow: As you loue	2523
*Rosalind meet, as you loue Phebe meet, and as I loue no	2524
As those that feare they hope, and know they feare.	2578
*to sweare, and to forsweare, according as mariage binds	2633
*sir, in a poore house, as your Pearle in your foule oy-|ster.	2637
*bodie more seeming *Audry*) as thus sir: I did dislike the	2645
*Clo. O sir, we quarrel in print, by the booke: as you	2664
*thought but of an If; as if you saide so, then I saide so:	2674
*Iaq. Is not this a rare fellow my Lord? He's as good	2677
As the Winter to fowle Weather:	2710
As we do trust, they'l end in true delights. *Exit*	2775
*women) for the loue you beare to men, to like as much	2787
*of this Play, as please you: And I charge you (O men)	2788
*for the loue you beare to women (as I perceiue by your	2789
*I would kisse as many of you as had beards that	2792
*I defi'de not: And I am sure, as many as haue good	2794
As you Like it.	2798

ASIDE = 2

Ros. Peace, here comes my sister reading, stand aside.	1322
Loe what befell: he threw his eye aside,	2253

ASK = 1

Phe. Thinke not I loue him, though I ask for him,	1883

ASKD = 1*1

Cel. It is no boast, being ask'd, to say we are.	2240
*but they ask'd one another the reason: no sooner knew	2444

ASKE = 3*2

Ile aske him what he would: Did you call Sir?	419
*heere? Did he aske for me? Where remaines he? How	1416
*Orl. You should aske me what time o'day: there's no | clocke in the Forrest.	1491
and aske me what you will, I will grant it.	2024

14

ASKE *cont*.
Ros. I might aske you for your Commission, 2047
ASKT = *1
*with him: he askt me of what parentage I was; I 1743
ASPECT = 1
Would they worke in milde aspect? 2202
ASSAID = 1
Ros. But Cosen, what if we assaid to steale 594
ASSAILANTS = 1
The like doe you, so shall we passe along, | And neuer stir assailants. 577
ASSE = 1
If it do come to passe, that any man turne Asse: 937
ASSEMBLY = 1 *1
*but the wood, no assembly but horne-beasts. But what 1659
That bring these tidings to this faire assembly. 2729
ASSIGND = 1
In their assign'd and natiue dwelling place. 671
ASSOONE = *1
*Ros. Me beleeue it? You may assoone make her that 1570
ASSURE = 1 *1
*meanes or other: for I assure thee, (and almost with 149
Ros. Counterfeit, I assure you. 2327
ASSUREDLY = 1
Cor. Assuredly the thing is to be sold: 883
AT = 34*23
ATHWART = *1
*them brauely, quite trauers athwart the heart of his lo-|uer, 1749
ATOMIES = *1
*Cel. It is as easie to count Atomies as to resolue the 1426
ATOMYES = 1
Who shut their coward gates on atomyes, 1784
ATTALANTAS = 1 *1
Attalanta's *better part*, | *sad* Lucrecia's *Modestie*. 1345
Attalanta's heeles. Will you sitte downe with me, and 1469
ATTEMPT = 1 *1
and giue ouer this attempt. 342
*stagger in this attempt: for heere wee haue no Temple 1658
ATTEND = 3 *1
Orl. I attend them with all respect and dutie. 330
*Orl. I must attend the Duke at dinner, by two a clock | I will be with
thee againe. 2086
Clo. Trip *Audry*, trip *Audry*, I attend, | I attend. *Exeunt* 2405
ATTENDANTS = 2
Flourish. Enter Duke, Lords, Orlando, Charles, | *and Attendants.* 311
The Ladies her attendants of her chamber 685
ATTENDS = *1
*confirmer of false reckonings, he attends here in the for-|rest on the
Duke your father. 1740
ATTIRE = 1
Cel. Ile put my selfe in poore and meane attire, 575
ATTONE = 1
When earthly things made eauen | *attone together.* 2684
ATTORNEY = *1
*Ros. No faith, die by Attorney: the poore world is 2006
AUD = 4*6
AUDIENCE = 2
Cel. Giue me audience, good Madam. | Ros. Proceed. 1432

AUDIENCE *cont.*
    2.Bro. Let me haue audience for a word or two: 2727.
AUDREY *see also Aud., Awd.* = 5*4
    Enter Clowne, Audrey, & Iaques.   1614
    *Clo. Come apace good *Audrey*, I wil fetch vp your   1615
    *Goates, Audrey: and how *Audrey* am I the man yet?   1616
    Ol. Come sweete *Audrey*, | We must be married, or we must liue in
    baudrey: 1701
    Will. Good eu'n *Audrey*.   2354
    Enter Clowne and Audrey.   2531
    *Clo. To morrow is the ioyfull day *Audrey*, to morow | will we be
    married.   2532
    Enter Clowne and Audrey.   2610
AUDRIE = 1
    **such a foolish song. God buy you, and God mend your | voices. Come
    Audrie. Exeunt.*   2570
AUDRY = 2*1
    Clo. Trip *Audry*, trip *Audry*, I attend, | I attend. *Exeunt*   2405
    *bodie more seeming Audry) as thus sir: I did dislike the   2645
AUGMENTING = 1
    Stood on th'extremest verge of the swift brooke, | Augmenting it with
    teares.   649
AUNSWER = *1
    *Le Beu. What colour Madame? How shall I aun-|swer you?   267
AUOID = 2
    **I will no longer endure it, though yet I know no wise | remedy how to
    auoid it.   26
    Iaq. And I haue bin all this day to auoid him: 921
AUOIDE = *1
    **Lye direct: and you may auoide that too, with an If. I   2671
AUOYD = *1
    **the Lye direct: all these you may auoyd, but the   2670
AWAIE = 1
    Duk. Beare him awaie: | What is thy name yong man?   382
AWAKED = 1
    From miserable slumber I awaked.   2284
AWARE *see* ware
AWAY = 5*11
    **borne, but the same tradition takes not away my bloud,   50
    **be his heire; for what hee hath taken away from thy fa-|ther   188
    *Clow. Mistresse, you must come away to your father.   226
    **had anie; or if he had, he had sworne it away, before   244
    *Cel. No, thy words are too precious to be cast away   463
    Cel. Hem them away.   477
    Leaue me alone to woe him; Let's away   598
    *Ros. No: I wil not cast away my physick, but on those   1544
    *Clo. Truly, and to cast away honestie vppon a foule   1645
    *Oliuer leaue me not behind thee: But winde away, bee   1704
    **me: 'tis but one cast away, and so come death: two o' | clocke is your
    howre.   2091
    And with indented glides, did slip away   2263
    The Lyonnesse had torne some flesh away,   2301
    **(to wit) I kill thee, make thee away, translate thy life in-|to   2394
    *Cor. Our Master and Mistresse seekes you: come a-|way, away.   2403
AWD = *2
AWDRIE = 2*3
    Enter Clowne and Awdrie.   2340

AWDRIE *cont*.

*Clow. We shall finde a time *Awdrie*, patience gen- |tle *Awdrie*.	2341
*Clow. A most wicked Sir *Oliuer*, *Awdrie*, a most vile	2345
*Mar-text. But *Awdrie*, there is a youth heere in the | Forrest layes	
claime to you.	2346

AXE = 1

Falls not the axe vpon the humbled neck,	1775

AY *see* I

A-PART = *1

*Orlan. Goe a-part *Adam*, and thou shalt heare how | he will shake me	
vp.	30

BACK = 1*1

*Ros. He cals vs back: my pride fell with my fortunes,	418
Lay sleeping on his back; about his necke	2258

BACKE = 2*1

*Cel. How now backe friends: Shepheard, go off a lit- |tle:	1356
Oli. Twice did he turne his backe, and purpos'd so:	2279
Oli. That will I: for I must beare answere backe	2334

BAD = 2

Clo. Truely the tree yeelds bad fruite.	1314
*or spitting, or saying we are hoarse, which are the onely | prologues to	
a bad voice.	2542

BAGGAGE = *1

*though not with bagge and baggage, yet with | scrip and scrippage.	
Exit.	1359

BAGGE = *1

*though not with bagge and baggage, yet with | scrip and scrippage.	
Exit.	1359

BALD = 1

And high top, bald with drie antiquitie:	2256

BALLAD = 1

Sighing like Furnace, with a wofull ballad	1127

BALLS = 1

Your bugle eye-balls, nor your cheeke of creame	1820

BAND = *1

*may bee chosen out of the grosse band of the vnfaith- |full:	2100

BANDS = 1

To ioyne in *Hymens* bands,	2703

BANDY = *1

*with thee, or in bastinado, or in steele: I will bandy	2396

BANISHD = 6

The other is daughter to the banish'd Duke,	441
Which I haue past vpon her, she is banish'd.	545
Hath banish'd me his daughter? | *Ros*. That he hath not.	558
Then doth your brother that hath banish'd you:	635
Heere come two of the banish'd Dukes Pages.	2536
His crowne bequeathing to his banish'd Brother,	2739

BANISHED = 1*4

*olde newes: that is, the old Duke is banished by his yon- |ger	101
*Oli. Can you tell if *Rosalind* the Dukes daughter bee | banished with	
her Father?	106
*could teach me to forget a banished father, you must not	174
*waight that I loue thee; if my Vncle thy banished father	178
*had banished thy Vncle the Duke my Father, so thou	179

BANISHMENT = 1

To libertie, and not to banishment. *Exeunt*.	603

BANISHT = 1
So was I when your highnesse banisht him;   521
BANKET = 1
His banket is prepar'd. *Exeunt*   948
BANKRUPT = 1
Vpon that poore and broken bankrupt there?   665
BARBARY = *1
*thee, then a Barbary cocke-pidgeon ouer his hen, more   2059
BARE = 1*1
Of bare distresse, hath tane from me the shew   1071
*of a married man, more honourable then the bare   1668
BARGAINE = 1
Phe. So is the bargaine.   2590
BARKES = 2*1
And in their barkes my thoughts Ile charracter,   1206
Iaq. I pray you marre no more trees with Writing | Loue-songs in their
barkes.   1454
*barkes; hangs Oades vpon Hauthornes, and Elegies on   1547
BARRE = 1
Hy. Peace hoa: I barre confusion,   2699
BARRES = *1
*me: hee lets mee feede with his Hindes, barres mee the   21
BASE = 1
Or with a base and boistrous Sword enforce   736
BASER = *1
*and perpend: Ciuet is of a baser birth then Tarre, the   1264
BASEST = 1
Or what is he of basest function,   1053
BASKD = 1
Who laid him downe, and bask'd him in the Sun,   988
BASTARD = *1
Ros. No, that same wicked Bastard of *Venus*, that was   2117
BASTINADO = *1
*with thee, or in bastinado, or in steele: I will bandy   2396
BATCHELLER = *1
*brow of a Batcheller: and by how much defence is bet-|ter   1669
BATHD = 1
Teares our recountments had most kindely bath'd,   2294
BATLER = *1
*of her batler, and the Cowes dugs that her prettie   831
BATTELL = 1
Made him giue battell to the Lyonnesse: 2282
BAUDREY = 1
Ol. Come sweete *Audrey*, | We must be married, or we must liue in
baudrey: 1701
BAWD = *1
*liuing, by the copulation of Cattle, to be bawd to a Bel-|weather,   1277
BAY = 1
*it cannot bee sounded: my affection hath an vnknowne | bottome, like
the Bay of Portugall.   2113
BE *see also* shalbe = 101*59
BEARD = 3*6
With eyes seuere, and beard of formall cut,   1134
Is his head worth a hat? Or his chin worth a beard?   1401
Cel. Nay, he hath but a little beard.   1402
*thankful: let me stay the growth of his beard, if thou   1404
*which you haue not: a beard neglected, which you   1560

BEARD *cont*.

*in beard, is a yonger brothers reuennew) then your	1562
*cut of a certaine Courtiers beard: he sent me word, if I	2646
*said his beard was not cut well, hee was in the minde it	2647
*Iaq. And how oft did you say his beard was not well | cut?	2657

BEARDED = 1

Full of strange oaths, and bearded like the Pard,	1129

BEARDS = 2*2

and sweare by your beards that I am a knaue.	239
Cel. By our beards (if we had them) thou art.	240
*I would kisse as many of you as had beards that	2792
*beards, or good faces, or sweet breaths, will for my kind	2795

BEARE = 13*11

Duk. Beare him awaie: | What is thy name yong man?	382
Ros. I doe beseech your Grace | Let me the knowledge of my fault	
beare with me:	505
Whether to goe, and what to beare with vs,	565
To beare your griefes your selfe, and leaue me out:	567
*Cel. I pray you beare with me, I cannot goe no fur-|ther.	792
*Clo. For my part, I had rather beare with you, then	794
*beare you: yet I should beare no crosse if I did beare	795
In the bleake aire. Come, I wil beare thee	966
*of them had in them more feete then the Verses would | beare.	1363
*Cel. That's no matter: the feet might beare y verses.	1365
*Ros. I, but the feet were lame, and could not beare	1366
Phe. For no ill will I beare you.	1843
And yet it is not, that I beare thee loue,	1867
And thou shalt beare it, wilt thou Siluius?	1909
Then sing him home, the rest shall beare this burthen;	2139
And play the swaggerer, beare this, beare all:	2162
Oli. That will I: for I must beare answere backe	2334
*I speake not this, that you should beare a good opinion	2463
*Clo. Vpon a lye, seuen times remoued: (beare your	2644
*women) for the loue you beare to men, to like as much	2787
*for the loue you beare to women (as I perceiue by your	2789

BEARES = 4

Oh what a world is this, when what is comely | Enuenoms him that	
beares it?	717
When that I say the City woman beares	1049
Hir worth being mounted on the winde, | through all the world beares	
Rosalinde.	1288
It beares an angry tenure; pardon me,	2159

BEAST = 3

Du Sen. I thinke he be transform'd into a beast,	973
Meaning me a beast.	2198
The royall disposition of that beast | To prey on nothing, that doth	
seeme as dead:	2268

BEASTS = *2

*but the wood, no assembly but horne-beasts. But what	1659
*of verie strange beasts, which in all tongues, are call'd | Fooles.	2614

BEAU see also Beu. = 1

Enter le Beau. | Ros. With his mouth full of newes.	257

BEAUTIE = 1*1

Beautie prouoketh theeues sooner then gold.	574
*honestie coupled to beautie, is to haue Honie a sawce to | Sugar.	1640

BEAUTY = 1

Ouer the wretched? what though you haue no beauty	1810

19

BECAUSE = 3*4
Because I doe. Looke, here comes the Duke.	496
Ros. Were it not better,	Because that I am more then common tall,	579
Thy tooth is not so keene, because thou art not seene,	1158
*that hath not the Gowt: for the one sleepes easily be-|cause	1509
*he cannot study, and the other liues merrily, be-|cause	1510
Orl. I take some ioy to say you are, because I would	be talking of	
her.	2002
*ones eyes, because his owne are out, let him bee iudge,	2120

BECOME = 1*2
*endure it: therefore allow me such exercises as may be-	come	71
that teares do not become a man.	1712
*to begge will not become mee. My way is to coniure	2785

BECOMES = 2*1
Orl. I will no further offend you, then becomes mee	for my good.	79
Ros. Though it be pittie to see such a sight, it well	becomes the	
ground.	1436
But sure hee's proud, and yet his pride becomes him;	1888

BED = 6
Saw her a bed, and in the morning early,	686
They found the bed vntreasur'd of their Mistris.	687
Then without Candle may goe darke to bed:	1812
met your wiues wit going to your neighbours bed.	2077
O blessed bond of boord and bed:	2717
you to a long, and well-deserued bed:	2767

BEE *l*.*63 *106 *128 *201 *324 *350 *354 1292 *1317 1323 *1381 *1403
*1650 *1695 *1704 *2058 *2100 *2113 *2120 *2134 *2221 *2358 *2447
*2521 = 2*22

BEENE *see also* bene, bin *l*.*180 *386 813 1091 1449 *2330 *2432 = 3*4

BEEST = 1*1
| Within these ten daies if that thou beest found | 502 |
| *reasonable match. If thou bee'st not damn'd for this, the | 1280 |

BEFELL = 1
| Loe what befell: he threw his eye aside, | 2253 |

BEFORE = 9*9
Oli. Know you before whom sir?	*Orl*. I, better then him I am before	
knowes mee: I	45
before me is neerer to his reuerence.	*Oli*. What Boy.	53
Oli. What, you wrastle to morrow before the new	Duke,	120
*had anie; or if he had, he had sworne it away, before	244
haue mockt me before: but come your waies.	370
Had I before knowne this yong man his sonne,	400
Your praise is come too swiftly home before you.	712
Before I come, thou art a mocker of my labor.	963
*before you came: for looke heere what I found on a	1372
Orl. I would kisse before I spoke.	1985
Orl. Who could be out, being before his beloued	Mistris?	1994
*Grecian club, yet he did what hee could to die before,	2010
*girle goes before the Priest, and certainely a Womans	thought runs	
before her actions.	2049
Who quickly fell before him, in which hurtling	2283
*before marriage; they are in the verie wrath of	2448
*to set her before your eyes to morrow, humane as she is,	and without	
any danger.	2475

BEG = *2
| *Oli*. And what wilt thou do? beg when that is spent? | 75 |
| *Orl*. What, would'st thou haue me go & beg my food, | 735 |

BEGAN = 2
My Lungs began to crow like Chanticleere,   1003
This Carroll they began that houre,   2561
BEGGE = *1
*to begge will not become mee. My way is to coniure   2785
BEGGER = *2
*married vnder a bush like a begger? Get you to church,   1690
*good play? I am not furnish'd like a Begger, therefore   2784
BEGGERLY = *1
*the beggerly thankes. Come sing; and you that wil not | hold your
tongues.   916
BEGIN = 1*3
*Oli. Is it euen so, begin you to grow vpon me? I will   85
Ros. You must begin, will you *Orlando*.   2038
Du Se. Proceed, proceed: wee'l begin these rights,   2774
*you, and Ile begin with the Women. I charge you (O   2786
BEGINNING = 2*1
Le Beu. I wil tell you the beginning: and if it please   277
Cel. Well, the beginning that is dead and buried.   281
Cel. I could match this beginning with an old tale.   283
BEGINS = *3
*there begins my sadnesse: My brother *Iaques* he keepes   8
*is within mee, begins to mutinie against this seruitude.   25
Ros. Then she puts you to entreatie, and there begins | new matter.   1992
BEGOT = 1*2
*that saies such a father begot villaines: wert thou   59
*begot of thought, conceiu'd of spleene, and borne of   2118
That heere were well begun, and wel begot: 2748
BEGS = 1
But first begs pardon: will you sterner be   1776
BEGUN = 1
That heere were well begun, and wel begot: 2748
BEHALFE = *1
*nor cannot insinuate with you in the behalfe of a   2783
BEHAUIOUR = *1
*the behauiour of the Countrie is most mockeable at the   1245
BEHIND = *2
*stay behind her; she is at the Court, and no lesse beloued   111
Oliuer leaue me not behind thee: But winde away, bee   1704
BEHINDE = 1*1
Did steale behinde him as he lay along   637
*minute behinde your houre, I will thinke you the most   2097
BEHOLDERS = *1
*making such pittiful dole ouer them, that all the behol- | ders   293
BEHOLDING = *1
Orl. What's that? | *Ros*. Why hornes: w such as you are faine to be
be- | holding   1972
BEING l.*109 629 657 807 1122 1237 1288 *1588 *1689 *1697 1835 *1994
*2015 2240 2290 2305 *2383 = 10*7
BELEEFE = *1
*little measure draw a beleefe from you, to do your selfe   2466
BELEEUE = 1*5
Orl. Faire youth, I would I could make thee beleeue | (I Loue.   1569
Ros. Me beleeue it? You may assoone make her that   1570
*you Loue beleeue it, which I warrant she is apter to do,   1571
*good, and not to grace me. Beleeue then, if you please,   2467
Du Sen. Dost thou beleeue *Orlando*, that the boy   2575

BELEEUE *cont*.
    Orl. I sometimes do beleeue, and somtimes do not,   2577
BELEEUES = 1
    And she beleeues where euer they are gone   695
BELL = 1
    And haue with holy bell bin knowld to Church,   1098
BELLY = 2
    In faire round belly, with good Capon lin'd,   1133
    Cel. So you may put a man in your belly.   1399
BELOUED = *3
    *stay behind her; she is at the Court, and no lesse beloued   111
    *deuise, of all sorts enchantingly beloued, and indeed   163
    Orl. Who could be out, being before his beloued | Mistris?   1994
BELS = 1*1
    If euer beene where bels haue knoll'd to Church: 1091
    *and the Falcon her bels, so man hath his desires, and as   1687
BELWEATHER = *1
    *liuing, by the copulation of Cattle, to be bawd to a Bel-|weather,   1277
BENE *l*.1039 = 1
BENEFITS = *2
    Ros. I would wee could doe so: for her benefits are   203
    *lispe, and weare strange suites; disable all the benefits   1949
BENEFITTS = 1
    Freize, freize, thou bitter skie that dost not bight so nigh | as benefitts
    forgot: 1164
BEQUEATH = 1
    you to your former Honor, I bequeath   2763
BEQUEATHED = *1
    *bequeathed me by will, but poore a thousand   5
BEQUEATHING = 1
    His crowne bequeathing to his banish'd Brother,   2739
BERIMD = *1
    *Palme tree; I was neuer so berim'd since *Pythagoras* time   1373
BESEECH = 1*2
    Orl. I beseech you, punish mee not with your harde   346
    Orl. Yes I beseech your Grace, I am not yet well | breath'd.   378
    Ros. I doe beseech your Grace | Let me the knowledge of my fault
    beare with me: 505
BESIDES = 3*4
    *better, for besides that they are faire with their feeding,   14
    *dunghils are as much bound to him as I: besides this no-|thing   18
    Besides his Coate, his Flockes, and bounds of feede   868
    Cor. Besides, our hands are hard.   1256
    Cel. Was, is not is: besides, the oath of Louer is no   1738
    Besides, I like you not: if you will know my house,   1846
    *then you make a woman: besides, he brings his destinie | with him.   1970
BEST = 2*4
    *as his finger. And thou wert best looke to't; for if thou   144
    *owne people, who best know him, that I am altogether   165
    *your Ladiships, you may see the end, for the best is yet   278
    Orl. 'Tis a fault I will not change, for your best ver-|tue: I am wearie of
    you.   1475
    Hee'll make a proper man: the best thing in him   1889
    *I say I am a Magitian: Therefore put you in your best a-|ray,   2479
BESTOW = 1
    You wil bestow her on *Orlando* heere?   2582

BEU = 4
*wise men haue makes a great shew; Heere comes Mon-|sieur the *Beu*.   255
Boon-iour Monsieur le Beu, what's the newes?   263
Cel. Call him hether good Monsieuer *Le Beu*. | *Duke*. Do so: Ile not be
by.   326
Enter Le Beu.   426
BEU = 6*8
BEWARE = *1
*therefore beware my censure, and keep your pro-|mise.   2101
BID = 2*5
Clo. No by mine honor, but I was bid to come for you   228
*broke my sword vpon a stone, and bid him take that for   829
My gentle *Phebe*, did bid me giue you this: 2155
*bid the Duke to the Nuptiall. But O, how bitter a thing   2452
*bid your friends: for if you will be married to mor-|row, you shall: and
to *Rosalind* if you will.   2480
Iaq. Good my Lord, bid him welcome: This is the   2617
offer, when I make curt'sie, bid me farewell. *Exit*.   2796
BIG = 1
Almost to bursting, and the big round teares   645
BIGGE = 1
For his shrunke shanke, and his bigge manly voice,   1140
BIGHT = 1
Freize, freize, thou bitter skie that dost not bight so nigh | *as benefitts*
forgot: 1164
BILL = 1
Pigeons bill, so wedlocke would be nibling.   1688
BILS = *1
Ros. With bils on their neckes: Be it knowne vnto | all men by these
presents.   286
BIN *l*.*919 921 *1009 1084 1098 *1464 1497 *1531 *1651 *1954 *2013
2607 2619 *2622 = 6*8
BINDE = 1
They that reap must sheafe and binde, | *then to cart with Rosalinde*.   1305
BINDS = *1
*to sweare, and to forsweare, according as mariage binds   2633
BIRD = *1
*your head, and shew the world what the bird hath done | to her owne
neast.   2109
BIRDS = 2
vnto the sweet Birds throte: 894
When Birds do sing, hey ding a ding, ding.   2551
BIRTH = *2
*you that keeping for a gentleman of my birth, that dif-|fers   12
*and perpend: Ciuet is of a baser birth then Tarre, the   1264
BISKET = 1
Which is as drie as the remainder bisket   1012
BIT = 1
I will not touch a bit.   1110
BITE *see* bight
BITES = 1
Which when it bites and blowes vpon my body   614
BITTER = 4*1
Freize, freize, thou bitter skie that dost not bight so nigh | *as benefitts*
forgot: 1164
Her with bitter words: why looke you so vpon me?   1842
I will be bitter with him, and passing short;   1913

BITTER *cont*.
 Chewing the food of sweet and bitter fancie,   2252
 *bid the Duke to the Nuptiall. But O, how bitter a thing   2452
BITTERNESSE = 1
 In bitternesse; the common executioner   1773
BLACK = 1
 He said mine eyes were black, and my haire blacke,   1904
BLACKE = 3
 All the pictures fairest Linde, | *are but blacke to Rosalinde:*   1290
 'Tis not your inkie browes, your blacke silke haire,   1819
 He said mine eyes were black, and my haire blacke,   1904
BLACKER = 1
 Such Ethiop words, blacker in their effect   2184
BLAME = 3*1
 Phe. If this be so, why blame you me to loue you?   2510
 Sil. If this be so, why blame you me to loue you?   2511
 Orl. If this be so, why blame you me to loue you?   2512
 Ros. Why do you speake too, Why blame you mee | to loue you. 2513
BLANKE = *1
 Iaq. Nay then God buy you, and you talke in blanke | verse.   1946
BLEAKE = 1
 In the bleake aire. Come, I wil beare thee   966
BLED = 1
 Which all this while had bled: and now he fainted,   2302
BLESSED = 1*1
 *Is the single man therefore blessed? No, as a wall'd   1666
 O blessed bond of boord and bed: 2717
BLESSING = *1
 *on his blessing to breed mee well: and   7
BLEST = *1
 Orl. I thanke ye, and be blest for your good comfort.   1113
BLEW = *1
 Ros. A leane cheeke, which you haue not: a blew eie   1558
BLINDE = *2
 *mightily misplaced, and the bountifull blinde woman | doth most
 mistake in her gifts to women.   204
 *madnesse, that blinde rascally boy, that abuses euery   2119
BLOCKE = 1
 Is but a quintine, a meere liuelesse blocke.   417
BLOOD = 1*1
 Of a diuerted blood, and bloudie brother.   741
 *and blood breakes: a poore virgin sir, an il-fauor'd thing   2634
BLOODY = 2
 Then he that dies and liues by bloody drops?   1777
 Ros. But for the bloody napkin? | *Oli*. By and by: 2291
BLOSSOME = 1
 That cannot so much as a blossome yeelde,   768
BLOUD = 2*3
 *of bloud you should so know me: the courtesie of   48
 *borne, but the same tradition takes not away my bloud,   50
 For in my youth I neuer did apply | Hot, and rebellious liquors in my
 bloud,   752
 Died in this bloud, vnto the Shepheard youth,   2309
 Oli. Many will swoon when they do look on bloud.   2312
BLOUDIE = 1
 Of a diuerted blood, and bloudie brother.   741

25

BLOUDY = 1
He sends this bloudy napkin; are you he? 2243
BLOW = 3
To blow on whom I please, for so fooles haue: 1023
Song. | *Blow, blow, thou winter winde,* 1155
BLOWES = 1
Which when it bites and blowes vpon my body 614
BLUSH = 1*2
*blush, and weepe, and thou must looke pale and | wonder. 153
*then with safety of a pure blush, thou maist in ho-|nor come off
againe. 197
In the which hope, I blush, and hide my Sword. 1096
BOAST = 2
Heauen thankes, and make no boast of them. 924
Cel. It is no boast, being ask'd, to say we are. 2240
BOB = 1
Seeme senselesse of the bob. If not, 1029
BODIE = 2*1
Cleanse the foule bodie of th'infected world, 1034
Therefore heauen Nature charg'd, | that one bodie should be fill'd 1339
*bodie more seeming *Audry*) as thus sir: I did dislike the 2645
BODY = 2*1
Which when it bites and blowes vpon my body 614
Thus most inuectiuely he pierceth through | The body of Countrie,
Citie, Court, 666
*Ah, sirra, a body would thinke this was well counterfei-|ted, 2321
BOISTROUS = 1
Or with a base and boistrous Sword enforce 736
BOLD = *1
Cel. Yong Gentleman, your spirits are too bold for 336
BOLDEND = *1
Du Sen. Art thou thus bolden'd man by thy distres? 1067
BOLT = *1
Clo. According to the fooles bolt sir, and such dulcet | diseases. 2640
BOND = 2
Are deerer then the naturall bond of Sisters: 444
O blessed bond of boord and bed: 2717
BONDAGE = *1
*death, thy libertie into bondage: I will deale in poy-|son 2395
BONNET = *1
*hose should be vngarter'd, your bonnet vnbanded, your 1563
BONNIE = 1
The bonnie priser of the humorous Duke? 711
BOOKE = *1
Clo. O sir, we quarrel in print, by the booke: as you 2664
BOOKES = 1*2
*Findes tongues in trees, bookes in the running brookes, 622
O *Rosalind,* these Trees shall be my Bookes, 1205
*haue bookes for good manners: I will name you the de-|grees. 2665
BOON-IOUR = 1
Boon-iour Monsieur le Beu, what's the newes? 263
BOORD = 1
O blessed bond of boord and bed: 2717
BOORISH = *1
*societie: which in the boorish, is companie, of this fe-|male: 2390
BORE = 1
And thy father bore it, 2143

26

BORE-SPEARE = 1
A bore-speare in my hand, and in my heart   583
BORNE = 4*2
*borne, but the same tradition takes not away my bloud,   50
*Ile go sleepe if I can: if I cannot, Ile raile against all | the first borne
of Egypt.   945
*begot of thought, conceiu'd of spleene, and borne of   2118
It was a crest ere thou wast borne,   2141
Will. William, sir. | Clo. A faire name. Was't borne i'th Forrest heere? 2362
But my good Lord, this Boy is Forrest borne,   2606
BORROW = *1
*Cel. You must borrow me Gargantuas mouth first: 1419
BOSOME = 1
Whose heart within his bosome is.   2690
BOTH = 5*4
*Clo. Stand you both forth now: stroke your chinnes,   238
*Cel. It is yong Orlando, that tript vp the Wrastlers | heeles, and your
heart, both in an instant.   1406
*stronger then the word of a Tapster, they are both the   1739
By giuing loue your sorrow, and my griefe | Were both extermin'd. 1861
Oli. Orlando doth commend him to you both,   2241
*both, that we may enioy each other: it shall be to your   2417
2.Pa. I faith, y'faith, and both in a tune like two | gipsies on a horse. 2544
*Sil. Though to haue her and death, were both one | thing.   2592
Both from his enterprize, and from the world: 2738
BOTTLE = *1
*Wine comes out of a narrow-mouth'd bottle: either too   1396
BOTTOM = *1
*Cel. West of this place, down in the neighbor bottom   2228
BOTTOME = 1
*it cannot bee sounded: my affection hath an vnknowne | bottome, like
the Bay of Portugall.   2113
BOTTOMLESSE = *1
*Cel. Or rather bottomlesse, that as fast as you poure | affection in, it
runs out.   2115
BOUGHES = 1
Vnder the shade of melancholly boughes,   1088
BOUGHT = 1*1
*Cel. Hee hath bought a paire of cast lips of Diana: a   1725
And he hath bought the Cottage and the bounds   1881
BOUND = 1*1
*dunghils are as much bound to him as I: besides this no- | thing 18
Briefe, I recouer'd him, bound vp his wound,   2304
BOUNDEN = 1
Orl. I rest much bounden to you: fare you well.   454
BOUNDS = 2
Besides his Coate, his Flockes, and bounds of feede   868
And he hath bought the Cottage and the bounds   1881
BOUNTIFULL = *1
*mightily misplaced, and the bountifull blinde woman | doth most
mistake in her gifts to women.   204
BOW = 1*1
*Clo. As the Oxe hath his bow sir, the horse his curb,   1686
He hath t'ane his bow and arrowes, and is gone forth   2152
BOWES = 1
But vpon the fairest bowes, | or at euerie sentence end;   1333

BOWS = *1
*Vnder an old Oake, whose bows were moss'd with age   2255
BOY = 7*2
before me is neerer to his reuerence. | *Oli*. What Boy.   53
*cleare all: nothing remaines, but that I kindle the boy | thither, which
now Ile goe about. *Exit*.   167
Then, the whining Schoole-boy with his Satchell   1124
'Tis but a peeuish boy, yet he talkes well,   1884
*madnesse, that blinde rascally boy, that abuses euery   2119
Such garments, and such yeeres: the boy is faire,   2235
Du Sen. Dost thou beleeue *Orlando*, that the boy   2575
Du Sen. I do remember in this shepheard boy,   2602
But my good Lord, this Boy is Forrest borne,   2606
BOYES = *1
*for no passion truly any thing; as boyes and women are   1592
BOYS = 1*1
Rowland de Boys, he was my father, and he is thrice a vil-|laine   58
Orl. *Orlando* my Liege, the yongest sonne of Sir Ro-|*land de Boys*.   384
BOYSTEROUS = 1
Ros. Why, tis a boysterous and a cruell stile,   2180
BRAGGE = *1
*Rammes, and *Cesars* Thrasonicall bragge of I came, saw,   2440
BRAIN = *1
Cel. I warrant you, with pure loue, & troubled brain,   2150
BRAINE = 2
They haue the gift to know it: and in his braine,   1011
Like Turke to Christian: womens gentle braine   2182
BRAINES = *1
*a loue cause: *Troilous* had his braines dash'd out with a   2009
BRAMBLES = *1
*brambles; all (forsooth) defying the name of *Rosalinde*.   1548
BRANCH = *1
*horns vpon his head, for a branch of victory; haue you   2131
BRAUE = *6
*Farewel good Mr *Oliuer*: Not O sweet *Oliuer*, O braue   1703
Cel. O that's a braue man, hee writes braue verses,   1747
*speakes braue words, sweares braue oathes, and breakes   1748
*breakes his staffe like a noble goose; but all's braue that   1751
BRAUELY = *1
*them brauely, quite trauers athwart the heart of his lo-|uer,   1749
BRAUERIE = 1
That sayes his brauerie is not on my cost,   1054
BRAWLES = 1
Vpon the brooke that brawles along this wood,   639
BREAD = 1
Ros. And his kissing is as ful of sanctitie, | As the touch of holy bread. 1723
BREAKE = 2*5
*thy discretion, I had as liefe thou didst breake his necke   143
*mine honor I will, and when I breake that oath, let mee   190
Will sodainly breake forth: Sir, fare you well,   451
I breake my shins against it.   840
Ros. Breake an houres promise in loue? hee that   1959
*will diuide a minute into a thousand parts, and breake   1960
*if you breake one iot of your promise, or come one   2096
BREAKES = *3
*speakes braue words, sweares braue oathes, and breakes   1748
*breakes his staffe like a noble goose; but all's braue that   1751

BREAKES *cont.*
*and blood breakes: a poore virgin sir, an il-fauor'd thing   2634
BREAKE-PROMISE = *1
*patheticall breake-promise, and the most hollow louer,   2098
BREAKING = 1*1
*first time that euer I heard breaking of ribbes was sport | for Ladies.   300
rib-breaking? Shall we see this wrastling Cosin?   305
BREATH = 1
although thy breath be rude.   1159
BREATHD = 1
Orl. Yes I beseech your Grace, I am not yet well | breath'd.   378
BREATHER = *1
Orl. I wil chide no breather in the world but my selfe   1472
BREATHS = *2
*pleas'd me, complexions that lik'd me, and breaths that   2793
*beards, or good faces, or sweet breaths, will for my kind   2795
BRED = 1*2
*not from the stalling of an Oxe? his horses are bred   13
*loues her, being euer from their Cradles bred together,   109
Of smooth ciuility: yet am I in-land bred,   1072
BREED = 1*1
*on his blessing to breed mee well: and   7
her childe her selfe, for she will breed it like a foole.   2083
BREEDING = 1*1
*no wit by Nature, nor Art, may complaine of good | breeding, or
comes of a very dull kindred.   1228
Iaq. And wil you (being a man of your breeding) be   1689
BRIDES = 1
Play Musicke, and you Brides and Bride-groomes all,   2755
BRIDE-GROOMES = 1
Play Musicke, and you Brides and Bride-groomes all,   2755
BRIEFE = 3
Some, how briefe the Life of man | runs his erring pilgrimage,   1327
In briefe, he led me to the gentle Duke,   2296
Briefe, I recouer'd him, bound vp his wound,   2304
BRIEFLY = 1
Clo. Instance, briefly: come, instance.   1249
BRIERS = 1
how full of briers is this working day world.   471
BRIGHT = 1*1
*And thou wilt show more bright, & seem more vertuous   542
If the scorne of your bright eine   2199
BRING = 11*2
1 *Lor.* Ile bring you to him strait. *Exeunt.*   678
If he be absent, bring his Brother to me,   698
To bring againe these foolish runawaies. *Exeunt.*   701
Bring vs where we may rest our selues, and feed: 857
I wil either be food for it, or bring it for foode to thee: 957
And if I bring thee not something to eate,   961
Seeke him with Candle: bring him dead, or liuing   1186
Clo. That is another simple sinne in you, to bring the   1275
Cel. You bring me out. Soft, comes he not heere?   1446
Bring vs to this sight, and you shall say   1767
You say, if I bring in your *Rosalinde,*   2581
Ros. And you say you wil haue her, when I bring hir?   2584
That bring these tidings to this faire assembly.   2729

BRINGS = 2*1

*then you make a woman: besides, he brings his destinie | with him.	1970
He that brings this loue to thee,	2205
Left on your right hand, brings you to the place:	2230

BRINGST = 1

Cel. I would sing my song without a burthen, thou | bring'st me out of tune.	1441

BROKE = 1*2

*him, and broke three of his ribbes, that there is little	290
Or if thou hast not broke from companie,	822
*broke my sword vpon a stone, and bid him take that for	829

BROKEN = 3*2

*some broken limbe, shall acquit him well: your brother	127
Ros. But is there any else longs to see this broken	303
Vpon that poore and broken bankrupt there?	665
To gleane the broken eares after the man	1876
His broken promise, and to giue this napkin	2308

BROOKE = 2*2

*from his intendment, or brooke such disgrace well as he	132
Vpon the brooke that brawles along this wood,	639
Stood on th'extremest verge of the swift brooke, | Augmenting it with teares.	649
Orl. He is drown'd in the brooke, looke but in, and | you shall see him.	1479

BROOKES = *1

*Findes tongues in trees, bookes in the running brookes,	622

BROTHER *see also* 2.*Bro.* = 20*19

*Crownes, and as thou saist, charged my bro- | ther	6
*there begins my sadnesse: My brother *Iaques* he keepes	8
*deerely hir'd: but I (his brother) gaine nothing vnder	16
*place of a brother, and as much as in him lies, mines my	22
Adam. Yonder comes my Master, your brother.	29
*God made, a poore vnworthy brother of yours with | idlenesse.	36
*know you are my eldest brother, and in the gentle con- | dition	47
Orl. Come, come elder brother, you are too yong in | (this.	55
*not my brother, I would not take this hand from thy	60
*brother the new Duke, and three or foure louing	102
*your yonger brother *Orlando* hath a disposition to come	124
*some broken limbe, shall acquit him well: your brother	127
*contriuer against mee his naturall brother: therefore vse	142
From tyrant Duke, vnto a tyrant Brother.	456
Then doth your brother that hath banish'd you:	635
Duk. Send to his brother, fetch that gallant hither,	697
If he be absent, bring his Brother to me,	698
Your brother, no, no brother, yet the sonne	723
Of a diuerted blood, and bloudie brother.	741
Finde out thy brother wheresoere he is,	1185
I neuer lou'd my brother in my life.	1194
Cor. Heere comes yong Mr *Ganimed,* my new Mistris- | ses Brother.	1283
And browner then her brother: are not you	2238
And found it was his brother, his elder brother.	2271
Cel. O I haue heard him speake of that same brother,	2272
Cel. Are you his brother?	2285
*I pray you tell your brother how well I counterfei- | ted: heigh-ho.	2322
How you excuse my brother, *Rosalind.*	2335
Ros. God saue you brother. | *Ol.* And you faire sister.	2427
Ros. Did your brother tell you how I counterfeyted	2435

BROTHER *cont.*

*and ouercome. For your brother, and my sister, no soo-|ner	2441
*of heart heauinesse, by how much I shal thinke my bro-|ther	2455
*brother marries *Aliena*, shall you marrie her. I know in-|to	2472
Me thought he was a brother to your daughter:	2605
Enter Second Brother.	2726
His brother heere, and put him to the sword:	2734
His crowne bequeathing to his banish'd Brother,	2739

BROTHERLY = *1

*this day liuing. I speake but brotherly of him,	151

BROTHERS = 3*5

*were there twenty brothers betwixt vs: I haue as much	51
*selfe notice of my Brothers purpose heerein, and haue by	137
Duk Sen. Now my Coe-mates, and brothers in exile:	607
Till thou canst quit thee by thy brothers mouth,	1191
*in beard, is a yonger brothers reuennew) then your	1562
Committing me vnto my brothers loue,	2298
*and they shooke hands, and swore brothers. Your If, is	2675
Thou offer'st fairely to thy brothers wedding:	2744

BROUGHT = 2

Hymen from Heauen brought her,	2687
Yea brought her hether.	2688

BROW = 3*1

Made to his Mistresse eye-brow. Then, a Soldier,	1128
Ros. Nay, but the diuell take mocking: speake sadde | brow, and true	
maid.	1408
*brow of a Batcheller: and by how much defence is bet-|ter	1669
By the sterne brow, and waspish action	2157

BROWES = 1

'Tis not your inkie browes, your blacke silke haire,	1819

BROWNER = 2

Cel. Something browner then Iudasses:	1718
And browner then her brother: are not you	2238

BRUTISH = 1

As sensuall as the brutish sting it selfe,	1040

BUBBLE = 1

Seeking the bubble Reputation | Euen in the Canons mouth: And then,	
the Iustice	1131

BUCKLES = 1

That the stretching of a span, | *buckles in his summe of age.*	1329

BUGLE = 1

Your bugle eye-balls, nor your cheeke of creame	1820

BURGERS = 1

Being natiue Burgers of this desert City,	629

BURIED = 1

Cel. Well, the beginning that is dead and buried.	281

BURND = 1

That a maidens heart hath burn'd.	2190

BURNE = 1*1

To burne the lodging where you vse to lye,	727
*the propertie of raine is to wet, and fire to burne: That	1225

BURS = *2

Cel. They are but burs, Cosen, throwne vpon thee	472
Ros. I could shake them off my coate, these burs are | in my heart.	475

BURSTING = 1

Almost to bursting, and the big round teares	645

BURTHEN = 1*4
*Du Sen. Welcome: set downe your venerable bur-|then, and let him
feede.   1147
*Cel. I would sing my song without a burthen, thou | bring'st me out of
tune.   1441
*he feeles no paine: the one lacking the burthen of   1511
*leane and wasteful Learning; the other knowing no bur-|then   1512
Then sing him home, the rest shall beare this burthen;   2139
BUSH = 1*2
*married vnder a bush like a begger? Get you to church,   1690
Into a bush, vnder which bushes shade   2264
*no bush, 'tis true, that a good play needes no Epilogue.   2779
BUSHES = 1*1
Into a bush, vnder which bushes shade   2264
*Yet to good wine they do vse good bushes: and good   2780
BUSIE = 1
Ile proue a busie actor in their play. Exeunt.   1768
BUSINESSE = 1
In all your businesse and necessities.   759
BUT 1.*5 *16 *17 *50 *100 *128 *139 *151 *152 *166 *167 *186 *195
*221 *228 *241 *296 *303 *323 *334 *348 *350 *351 *363 365 370 388
391 408 412 417 440 445 448 457 469 *472 *483 533 591 593 594 651
694 714 731 742 757 764 767 770 776 778 *788 *799 810 *836 *843 863
871 *874 897 *913 923 962 975 997 1010 1037 1055 1061 1073 1086 1104
1182 1184 *1214 *1216 *1217 *1219 *1222 *1246 1291 1293 *1319 1333
1343 *1366 *1369 *1381 1383 1402 *1408 *1423 *1427 *1448 1450 *1466
*1472 *1479 *1505 *1531 *1544 *1561 *1565 *1573 *1578 *1588 *1603
*1650 *1659 *1692 *1695 *1704 *1711 1713 *1728 *1733 1736 *1745
*1750 *1751 1772 1776 1792 1795 1804 1827 1830 1868 1871 1880 1884
1885 1888 1893 1900 1907 *1931 *1961 1963 *1974 *1979 *2014 *2017
*2018 *2022 2042 *2048 *2057 2066 2068 *2091 *2112 2156 2160 2175
2176 2231 2261 2277 2280 2288 2291 *2330 *2336 *2346 2369 *2373
*2410 *2415 2434 *2439 *2442 *2443 *2444 *2445 *2452 2563 *2569
2588 2606 *2635 *2642 *2670 *2673 *2674 *2769 *2777 = 88*104
BUTCHERIE = 1
This is no place, this house is but a butcherie;   731
BUTCHERS = 1
Should be called tyrants, butchers, murtherers.   1785
BUTTER-WOMENS = 1
*and suppers, and sleeping hours excepted: it is the right | Butter-
womens ranke to Market.   1295
BUY = 4*4
*father left me by testament, with that I will goe buy my | fortunes.   73
Can in this desert place buy entertainment,   856
*Ros. What is he that shall buy his flocke and pasture?   873
Buy thou the Cottage, pasture, and the flocke,   878
And buy it with your Gold right sodainly. Exeunt.   887
Iaq. God buy you, let's meet as little as we can.   1452
*Iaq. Nay then God buy you, and you talke in blanke | verse.   1946
*such a foolish song. God buy you, and God mend your | voices. Come
Audrie. Exeunt.   2570
BUYING = 1
That little cares for buying any thing.   876
BY see also a = 40*47, 1
Ros. But for the bloody napkin? | Oli. By and by: 2291

CAGE = *1
*he taught me how to know a man in loue: in which cage | of rushes, I
am sure you art not prisoner.   1555
CAKES = *1
*they were good Pan-cakes, and swore by his Honor the   231
CAL = 1*1
Come, more, another stanzo: Cal you'em stanzo's?   907
*you: but that they cal complement is like th'encounter   913
CALD = *1
*Ros. It may wel be cal'd Ioues tree, when it droppes | forth fruite.   1430
CALL = 12*7
*more properly) staies me heere at home vnkept: for call   11
Oli. Call him in: 'twill be a good way: and to mor-|row the wrastling is. 94
Cel. Call him hether good Monsieuer Le Beu. | Duke. Do so: Ile not be
by.   326
Ile aske him what he would: Did you call Sir?   419
Cel. What shall I call thee when thou art a man?   588
And therefore looke you call me Ganimed.   590
(Yet not the son, I will not call him son)   724
Of him I was about to call his Father,   725
*Iaq. 'Tis a Greeke inuocation, to call fools into a cir-|cle.   944
Call me not foole, till heauen hath sent me fortune,   992
Thy Lands and all things that thou dost call thine,   1189
*Ros. I would cure you, if you would but call me Rosa-|lind,   1603
*Ros. Nay, you must call mee Rosalind: Come sister, | will you go?
Exeunt.   1611
*Cel. It pleases him to call you so: but he hath a Rosa-|lind of a better
leere then you.   1979
*and the most vnworthy of her you call Rosalinde, that   2099
Sil. Call you this railing?   2192
Sil. Call you this chiding? | Cel. Alas poore Shepheard.   2213
That he in sport doth call his Rosalind.   2310
*Ol. Neither call the giddinesse of it in question; the   2413
CALLD = 1*5
But what will you be call'd?   591
*of verie strange beasts, which in all tongues, are call'd | Fooles.   2614
*was: this is call'd the retort courteous. If I sent him   2648
*he cut it to please himselfe: this is call'd the quip modest.   2650
*cut, he would answer I spake not true: this is call'd the   2653
*say, I lie: this is call'd the counter-checke quarrelsome: 2655
CALLED = 1*1
Should be called tyrants, butchers, murtherers.   1785
*this is called, the reply churlish. If againe it was not well   2652
CALLING = 2
His yongest sonne, and would not change that calling | To be adopted
heire to Fredricke.   396
all shal flout me out of my calling. Exeunt   1707
CALLS = 3
Enter Dennis. | Den. Calls your worship?   88
She calls me proud, and that she could not loue me   2164
And to that youth hee calls his Rosalind,   2242
CALS = 1*2
*Le Beu. Monsieur the Challenger, the Princesse cals | for you.   328
*Ros. He cals vs back: my pride fell with my fortunes,   418
Cor. Who cals? | Clo. Your betters Sir.   850
CALT = *1
*Clo. Good euen good Mr what ye cal't: how do you   1681

CAME = 3*6
```
*Cha. Marry doe I sir: and I came to acquaint you                        122
*come in: therefore out of my loue to you, I came hither                 130
*Cha. I am heartily glad I came hither to you: if hee                    155
*before you came: for looke heere what I found on a                      1372
monstrous, til his fellow-fault came to match it.                        1542
*Rosa. Marry to say, she came to seeke you there: you                    2079
As how I came into that Desert place.                                    2295
*Rammes, and Cesars Thrasonicall bragge of I came, saw,                  2440
And to the skirts of this wilde Wood he came;                            2735
```
CAN l.*106 *321 *324 *375 415 445 625 681 739 856 901 *945 951 974
    *1036 1045 1051 1151 1374 1452 *1517 *1538 *1579 *1691 1787 1798
    1821 1829 1833 *2032 2043 2191 2210 *2459 *2468 *2518 2576
    *2662 = 23*15
CANDLE = 2
```
Seeke him with Candle: bring him dead, or liuing                         1186
Then without Candle may goe darke to bed:                                1812
```
CANNOT = 11*13
```
Le Beu. He cannot speake my Lord.                                        381
I cannot speake to her, yet she vrg'd conference.                        425
Ros. Yet your mistrust cannot make me a Traitor;                        517
I cannot liue out of her companie.                                       547
It cannot be, some villaines of my Court | Are of consent and sufferance
in this.                                                                 682
1 Lo. I cannot heare of any that did see her,                           684
That cannot so much as a blossome yeelde,                                768
Yet fortune cannot recompence me better                                 779
*Cel. I pray you beare with me, I cannot goe no fur-|ther.             792
*Amy. My voice is ragged, I know I cannot please | you.                903
*Ile go sleepe if I can: if I cannot, Ile raile against all | the first borne
of Egypt.                                                               945
Du. Not see him since? Sir, sir, that cannot be:                        1181
*diuell himselfe will haue no shepherds, I cannot see else | how thou
shouldst scape.                                                         1281
*he cannot study, and the other liues merrily, be-|cause              1510
*Clo. When a mans verses cannot be vnderstood, nor                     1623
Orl. Pray thee marrie vs. | Cel. I cannot say the words.               2036
*her without her tongue: o that woman that cannot                      2081
*Ros. Alas, deere loue, I cannot lacke thee two houres.                2085
*it cannot bee sounded: my affection hath an vnknowne | bottome, like
the Bay of Portugall.                                                   2113
*how deepe I am in loue: ile tell thee Aliena, I cannot be             2121
for: we shall be flouting: we cannot hold.                             2353
*loue, and they will together. Clubbes cannot part | them.            2449
*Ros. Why then to morrow, I cannot serue your turne | for Rosalind?    2457
*nor cannot insinuate with you in the behalfe of a                     2783
```
CANONS = 1
```
Seeking the bubble Reputation | Euen in the Canons mouth: And then,
the Iustice                                                            1131
```
CANST l.569 807 1191 1789 1868 = 5
CAPABLE = 1
```
The Cicatrice and capable impressure | Thy palme some moment
keepes: but now mine eyes                                              1794
```
CAPARISOND = *1
```
*I am caparison'd like a man, I haue a doublet and hose in             1391
```
CAPERS = *1
```
*runne into strange capers; but as all is mortall in                   836
```

CAPON = 1
In faire round belly, with good Capon lin'd,   1133
CAPRICIOUS = 1
capricious Poet honest *Ouid* was among the Gothes.   1620
CARE = 3*1
Clo. I care not for my spirits, if my legges were not | wearie.   785
Iaq. Nay, I care not for their names, they owe mee | nothing. Wil you
sing?   909
But what care I for words? yet words do well   1885
Ros. I care not if I haue: it is my studie   2486
CARELESLY = 1
carelesly as they did in the golden world.   119
CARELESSE = 1*1
The Fluxe of companie: anon a carelesse Heard   660
*about you, demonstrating a carelesse desolation: but you   1565
CARES = 1
That little cares for buying any thing.   876
CARLOT = 1
That the old *Carlot* once was Master of.   1882
CARRIES = *1
*carries his house on his head; a better ioyncture I thinke   1969
CARROLL = 1
This Carroll they began that houre,   2561
CART = 1
They that reap must sheafe and binde, | then to cart with Rosalinde.   1305
CARUE = 1
Run, run *Orlando*, carue on euery Tree,   1209
CARUED = *1
*thy name should be hang'd and carued vpon these trees?   1370
CARUING = *1
*our yong plants with caruing *Rosalinde* on their   1546
CASE = *1
*What a case am I in then, that am neither a good Epi-|logue,   2782
CASEMENT = *1
*wit, and it will out at the casement: shut that, and   2071
CAST = *5
Cel. No, thy words are too precious to be cast away   463
Ros. No: I wil not cast away my physick, but on those   1544
Clo. Truly, and to cast away honestie vppon a foule   1645
Cel. Hee hath bought a paire of cast lips of *Diana*: a   1725
*me: 'tis but one cast away, and so come death: two o' | clocke is your
howre.   2091
CAT = 1*1
*verie vncleanly fluxe of a Cat. Mend the instance Shep-|heard.   1265
If the Cat will after kinde, | so be sure will Rosalinde: 1301
CATCH = 1*1
Cel. I would I were inuisible, to catch the strong fel-|low by the legge.
Wrastle.   372
our very petty-coates will catch them.   474
CATECHISME = 1
*say I and no, to these particulars, is more then to answer | in a
Catechisme.   1421
CATERS = 1
Yea prouidently caters for the Sparrow,   748
CATLIKE = 1
Lay cowching head on ground, with catlike watch   2266

CATTLE = *2
  *liuing, by the copulation of Cattle, to be bawd to a Bel-|weather,   1277
  *for the most part, cattle of this colour: would now like   1593
CAUE = 3
  Go to my Caue, and tell mee. Good old man,   1175
  Who led me instantly vnto his Caue,   2299
  Ile stay to know, at your abandon'd caue. *Exit.*   2773
CAUGHT = 1
  That thou with license of free foot hast caught,   1042
CAUSE = 6*4
  Ros. I haue more cause. | *Cel.* Thou hast not Cosen,   555
  *good pasture makes fat sheepe: and that a great cause of   1226
  Ros. But haue I not cause to weepe?   1713
  Cel. As good cause as one would desire, | Therefore weepe.   1714
  Haue more cause to hate him then to loue him,   1902
  *a loue cause: *Troilous* had his braines dash'd out with a   2009
  Clo. 'Faith we met, and found the quarrel was vpon | the seuenth
  cause.   2626
  Iaq. How seuenth cause? Good my Lord, like this | fellow.   2628
  Iaq. But for the seuenth cause. How did you finde   2642
  the quarrell on the seuenth cause?   2643
CEL = 58*49
CELIA see also Cel. = 12
  Enter Celia and Rosaline.   459
  Duk. I *Celia*, we staid her for your sake,   528
  Cel. Something that hath a reference to my state: | No longer *Celia*, but
  Aliena.   592
  *Enter Rosaline for Ganimed, Celia for Aliena, and | Clowne, alias
  Touchstone.*   782
  Enter Celia with a writing.   1321
  Enter Rosalind & Celia.   1709
  Enter Rosalind, Celia, and Corin.   1778
  Enter Rosalind, and Celia, and Iaques.   1916
  Enter Rosalind and Celia.   2147
  Enter Duke Senior, Amyens, Iaques, Orlan-|do, Oliuer, Celia.   2573
  To make these doubts all euen. *Exit Ros. and Celia.*   2601
  Enter Hymen, Rosalind, and Celia. | Still Musicke.   2681
CELLIA = 1*1
  Enter Rosalind, and Cellia.   170
  Ros. Deere *Cellia*; I show more mirth then I am mi-|stresse   172
CENSURE = 1*1
  *fellowes, and betray themselues to euery mo-|derne censure, worse
  then drunkards.   1922
  *therefore beware my censure, and keep your pro-|mise.   2101
CERTAINE = *2
  Clo. Of a certaine Knight, that swore by his Honour   230
  *cut of a certaine Courtiers beard: he sent me word, if I   2646
CERTAINELY = *1
  *girle goes before the Priest, and certainely a Womans | thought runs
  before her actions.   2049
CERTAINLY = 1
  Cel. Nay certainly there is no truth in him. | *Ros.* Doe you thinke so?   1730
CESARS = *1
  *Rammes, and *Cesars* Thrasonicall bragge of I came, saw,   2440
CESTOS = *1
  Hero of Cestos. But these are all lies, men haue died   2017

36

CHA = 1*5
CHAINE = *1
  Cel. And a chaine that you once wore about his neck: 1377
CHALLENGD = *1
  Ros. Young man, haue you challeng'd *Charles* the | Wrastler?   331
CHALLENGER = *2
  Le Beu. Monsieur the Challenger, the Princesse cals | for you.   328
  Orl. No faire Princesse: he is the generall challenger,   333
CHALLENGERS = 1*1
  *there is such oddes in the man: In pitie of the challen-|gers   322
  A stile for challengers: why, she defies me,   2181
CHAMBER = 1
  The Ladies her attendants of her chamber   685
CHANGE = 6
  His yongest sonne, and would not change that calling | To be adopted
  heire to *Fredricke*.   396
  Wilt thou change Fathers? I will giue thee mine: 553
  And doe not seeke to take your change vpon you,   566
  Amien. I would not change it, happy is your Grace   624
  change you colour? | *Ros*. I pre'thee who?   1378
  Orl. 'Tis a fault I will not change, for your best ver-|tue: I am wearie of
  you.   1475
CHANGEABLE = *1
  *youth, greeue, be effeminate, changeable, longing, and   1589
CHANGES = *1
  *Maides are May when they are maides, but the sky chan-|ges   2057
CHANTICLEERE = 1
  My Lungs began to crow like Chanticleere,   1003
CHAPPELL = 1
  shal we go with you to your Chappell?   1675
CHAR = *1
CHARGD = 1*1
  *father charg'd you in his will to giue me good educati-|on: 67
  Therefore heauen Nature charg'd, | *that one bodie should be fill'd*   1339
CHARGE = 2*3
  I charge thee be not thou more grieu'd then I am.   554
  that he laid to the charge of women?   1539
  *loue me, I charge her to loue thee: if she will not, I will   2220
  *you, and Ile begin with the Women. I charge you (O   2786
  *of this Play, as please you: And I charge you (O men)   2788
CHARGED = *1
  *Crownes, and as thou saist, charged my bro-|ther   6
CHARLES see also Cha., Char. = 5*8
  Oli. Was not *Charles* the Dukes Wrastler heere to | speake with me?   90
  Enter Charles.   96
  Oli. Good Mounsier *Charles*: what's the new newes | at the new Court?   98
  Oli. Charles, I thanke thee for thy loue to me, which   135
  *but he is resolute. Ile tell thee *Charles*, it is the stubbor-|nest   139
  *Farewell good *Charles*. Now will I stirre this Game-|ster: 159
  Le Beu. The eldest of the three, wrastled with *Charles*   288
  *the Dukes Wrastler, which *Charles* in a moment threw   289
  Flourish. Enter Duke, Lords, Orlando, Charles, | *and Attendants*.   311
  Ros. Young man, haue you challeng'd *Charles* the | Wrastler?   331
  Duk. How do'st thou *Charles*?   380
  Or Charles, or something weaker masters thee.   428
  That did but lately foile the synowie *Charles*,   694

CHARLES = *1
CHARRACTER = 1
And in their barkes my thoughts Ile charracter,   1206
CHARTER = 1
Withall, as large a Charter as the winde,   1022
CHASE = 1*1
*Sonne deerelie? By this kinde of chase, I should hate   489
In pitteous chase: and thus the hairie foole,   647
CHASTE = 2
With thy chaste eye, from thy pale spheare aboue   1203
The faire, the chaste, and vnexpressiue shee. *Exit*   1210
CHASTITY = 1
the very yce of chastity is in them.   1727
CHECKE = *2
Ros. Nay, you might keepe that checke for it, till you   2076
*say, I lie: this is call'd the counter-checke quarrelsome: 2655
CHEEKE = 4*1
Helens cheeke, but not his heart, | Cleopatra's *Maiestie:*   1343
Ros. A leane cheeke, which you haue not: a blew eie   1558
You meet in some fresh cheeke the power of fancie,   1801
Your bugle eye-balls, nor your cheeke of creame   1820
Then that mixt in his cheeke: 'twas iust the difference   1896
CHEERE = 2
Liue a little, comfort a little, cheere thy selfe a little.   955
Oli. Be of good cheere youth: you a man?   2318
CHEEREFULL = 1
Prethee be cheerefull; know'st thou not the Duke   557
CHEERELY = 2
Wel said, thou look'st cheerely,   964
Cheerely good *Adam. Exeunt*   970
CHESSENUT = 1
Your Chessenut was euer the onely colour.   1722
CHEWING = 1
Chewing the food of sweet and bitter fancie,   2252
CHID = 1
Whiles you chid me, I did loue,   2203
CHIDE = 2*3
Orl. I wil chide no breather in the world but my selfe   1472
Phe. Sweet youth, I pray you chide a yere together,   1837
I had rather here you chide, then this man wooe.   1838
For what had he to doe to chide at me?   1903
*natiuitie, and almost chide God for making you that   1951
CHIDING = 3
And churlish chiding of the winters winde,   613
Du Sen. Most mischeeuous foule sin, in chiding sin: 1038
Sil. Call you this chiding? | *Cel*. Alas poore Shepheard.   2213
CHILDE = 1*2
Cel. You know my Father hath no childe, but I, nor   186
*a mans good wit seconded with the forward childe, vn- | derstanding: 1624
her childe her selfe, for she will breed it like a foole.   2083
CHILDES = *1
Ros. No, some of it is for my childes Father: Oh   470
CHILDISH = 1
Turning againe toward childish trebble pipes,   1141
CHILDISHNESSE = 1
Is second childishnesse, and meere obliuion,   1144

CHILDREN = 2
  Marrie his kisses are Iudasses owne children. 1719
  That makes the world full of ill-fauourd children: 1826
CHIMNEY = 1
  *'twill out at the key-hole: stop that, 'twill flie with the | smoake out at
  the chimney. 2072
CHIN = 2
  Is his head worth a hat? Or his chin worth a beard? 1401
  delay me not the knowledge of his chin. 1405
CHINNES = *1
  *Clo. Stand you both forth now: stroke your chinnes, 238
CHOAKE = 1
  And hauing that do choake their seruice vp, 765
CHOPT = *1
  *chopt hands had milk'd; and I remember the wooing 832
CHOSEN = *1
  *may bee chosen out of the grosse band of the vnfaith- | full: 2100
CHRISTEND = 1
  *Orl. There was no thought of pleasing you when she | was christen'd. 1460
CHRISTIAN = 1
  Like Turke to Christian: womens gentle braine 2182
CHRONOCLERS = *1
  *and the foolish Chronoclers of that age, found it was 2016
CHURCH = 3*1
  The why is plaine, as way to Parish Church: 1026
  If euer beene where bels haue knoll'd to Church: 1091
  And haue with holy bell bin knowld to Church, 1098
  *married vnder a bush like a begger? Get you to church, 1690
CHURLISH = 2*2
  And churlish chiding of the winters winde, 613
  My master is of churlish disposition, 865
  *this is called, the reply churlish. If againe it was not well 2652
  *Quip-modest: the third, the reply Churlish: the fourth, 2667
CICATRICE = 1
  The Cicatrice and capable impressure | Thy palme some moment
  keepes: but now mine eyes 1794
CIPHER = 1
  Orl. Which I take to be either a foole, or a Cipher. 1482
CIRCLE = 1*1
  *Iaq. 'Tis a Greeke inuocation, to call fools into a cir- | cle. 944
  Obscured in the circle of this Forrest. 2611
CIRCUMSTANCE = *1
  *the sixt, the Lye with circumstance: the sea- | uenth, 2669
CIRCUMSTANTIAL = *1
  *Clo. I durst go no further then the lye circumstantial: 2659
CIRCUMSTANTIALL = 1
  and so to lye circumstantiall, and the lye direct. 2656
CITIE = 2
  Thus most inuectiuely he pierceth through | The body of Countrie,
  Citie, Court, 666
  What woman in the Citie do I name, 1048
CITIZENS = 1
  Sweepe on you fat and greazie Citizens, 663
CITY = 2
  Being natiue Burgers of this desert City, 629
  When that I say the City woman beares 1049

CIUET = 1*1
  Courtiers hands are perfum'd with Ciuet.   1261
  *and perpend: Ciuet is of a baser birth then Tarre, the   1264
CIUILITY = 2
  That in ciuility thou seem'st so emptie?   1069
  Of smooth ciuility: yet am I in-land bred,   1072
CIUILL = 1
  Tonges Ile hang on euerie tree, | that shall ciuill sayings shoe.   1325
CLAIME = 1
  Mar-text. But *Awdrie*, there is a youth heere in the | Forrest layes
  claime to you.   2346
CLAMOROUS = *1
  *clamorous then a Parrat against raine, more new-fang- | led   2060
CLAP = *1
  *1.*Pa*. Shal we clap into't roundly, without hauking,   2541
CLAPT = *1
  *of loue, it may be said of him that *Cupid* hath clapt   1962
CLAWES = 1
  Ros. I thought thy heart had beene wounded with | the clawes of a
  Lion.   2432
CLE = *1
  Cle. So, so, is good, very good, very excellent good: 2368
CLEANE = *1
  *as cleane as a sound sheepes heart, that there shal not | be one spot of
  Loue in't.   1600
CLEANLIEST = 1
  matter, the cleanliest shift is to kisse.   1990
CLEANSE = 1
  Cleanse the foule bodie of th'infected world,   1034
CLEARE = *1
  *cleare all: nothing remaines, but that I kindle the boy | thither, which
  now Ile goe about. *Exit*.   167
CLEOPATRAS = 1
  Helens cheeke, but not his heart, | Cleopatra's *Maiestie:*   1343
CLIMBE = *1
  *which they will climbe incontinent, or else bee inconti- | nent   2447
CLO = 17*50
CLOATH = *1
  Orl. Not so: but I answer you right painted cloath,   1466
CLOCK = 1*1
  Orl. I must attend the Duke at dinner, by two a clock | I will be with
  thee againe.   2086
  Ros. How say you now, is it not past two a clock? | And heere much
  Orlando.   2148
CLOCKE = 5
  Sayes, very wisely, it is ten a clocke: 995
  Ros. I pray you, what i'st a clocke?   1490
  Orl. You should aske me what time o'day: there's no | clocke in the
  Forrest.   1491
  detect the lazie foot of time, as wel as a clocke.   1495
  *me: 'tis but one cast away, and so come death: two o' | clocke is your
  howre.   2091
CLOW = *5
CLOWN = *1
  *2.*Lor*. My Lord, the roynish Clown, at whom so oft,   688
CLOWNE see also Clo., Clow. = 8*3
  Enter Clowne.   212

CLOWNE cont.
Enter Rosaline for Ganimed, Celia for Aliena, and | Clowne, alias
Touchstone.   782
Clo. Holla; you Clowne. | *Ros.* Peace foole, he's not thy kinsman.   848
Enter Corin & Clowne.   1211
Enter Clowne, Audrey, & Iaques.   1614
Enter Clowne and Awdrie.   2340
Clo. It is meat and drinke to me to see a Clowne, by   2351
*you Clowne, abandon: which is in the vulgar, leaue the   2389
*is, abandon the society of this Female, or Clowne   2392
Enter Clowne and Audrey.   2531
Enter Clowne and Audrey.   2610
CLOWNISH = 1
The clownish Foole out of your Fathers Court: 595
CLUB = *1
*Grecian club, yet he did what hee could to die before,   2010
CLUBBES = *1
*loue, and they will together. Clubbes cannot part | them.   2449
CO = *1
COAT = 5
That their discharge did stretch his leatherne coat   644
Are now on sale, and at our sheep-coat now   869
I am ambitious for a motley coat. | *Du Sen.* Thou shalt haue one.   1016
and come euerie day to my Coat, and woe me.   1604
A sheep-coat, fenc'd about with Oliue-trees.   2227
COATE = 1*2
Ros. I could shake them off my coate, these burs are | in my heart.   475
*selfe coragious to petty-coate; therefore courage, good | *Aliena*.   790
Besides his Coate, his Flockes, and bounds of feede   868
COATES = 1
our very petty-coates will catch them.   474
COCKE = 1
Iaq. Of what kinde should this Cocke come of?   1066
COCKE-PIDGEON = *1
*thee, then a Barbary cocke-pidgeon ouer his hen, more   2059
CODS = *1
*cods, and giuing her them againe, said with weeping   834
COE-MATES = *1
Duk Sen. Now my Coe-mates, and brothers in exile: 607
COLD = 1
Euen till I shrinke with cold, I smile, and say   615
COLOUR = 6*2
Cel. Sport: of what colour?   266
Le Beu. What colour Madame? How shall I aun-|swer you?   267
change you colour? | *Ros.* I pre'thee who?   1378
*for the most part, cattle of this colour: would now like   1593
Ros. His very haire | Is of the dissembling colour.   1716
Ros. I'faith his haire is of a good colour.   1720
Cel. An excellent colour: 1721
Your Chessenut was euer the onely colour: 1722
COLOURED = 1
A freestone coloured hand: I verily did thinke   2174
COMBINE = 1
Thy faith, my fancie to thee doth combine.   2725
COME = 42*28
*them? what prodigall portion haue I spent, that I should | come to such
penury?   41

41

COME *cont.*

Orl. Come, come elder brother, you are too yong in | (this.	55
*your yonger brother *Orlando* hath a disposition to come	124
*come in: therefore out of my loue to you, I came hither	130
*come to morrow, Ile giue him his payment: if euer hee	156
*then with safety of a pure blush, thou maist in ho-|nor come off again.	197
Clow. Mistresse, you must come away to your father.	226
Clo. No by mine honor, but I was bid to come for you	228
Duke. Come on, since the youth will not be intreated	313
*I come but in as others do, to try with him the strength | of my youth.	334
Char. Come, where is this yong gallant, that is so	361
haue mockt me before: but come your waies.	370
*vpon curs, throw some of them at me; come lame mee | with reasons.	464
Cel. Come, come, wrastle with thy affections.	479
Du Sen. Come, shall we goe and kill vs venison?	627
Did come to languish; and indeed my Lord	642
Your praise is come too swiftly home before you.	712
Come not within these doores: within this roofe	721
Ad. No matter whether, so you come not here.	734
But come thy waies, weele goe along together,	770
That you will feed on: but what is, come see,	871
Come hither, come hither, come hither:	895
Come, more, another stanzo: Cal you 'em stanzo 's?	907
*the beggerly thankes. Come sing; and you that wil not | hold your tongues.	916
Come, warble, come. | *Song. Altogether heere.*	925
Come hither, come hither, come hither,	931
If it do come to passe, that any man turne Asse:	937
And if he will come to me.	942
Before I come, thou art a mocker of my labor.	963
In the bleake aire. Come, I wil beare thee	966
Who can come in, and say that I meane her,	1051
Vnclaim'd of any man. But who come here?	1061
Iaq. Of what kinde should this Cocke come of?	1066
Clo. Instance, briefly: come, instance.	1249
*of a man? Shallow, shallow: A better instance I say: | Come.	1254
Clo. Your lips wil feele them the sooner. Shallow a-|gen: a more sounder instance, come.	1257
Clo. Come Shepheard, let vs make an honorable re-|treit,	1358
and come euerie day to my Coat, and woe me.	1604
Ros. Nay, you must call mee *Rosalind:* Come sister, | will you go? *Exeunt.*	1611
Clo. Come apace good *Audrey,* I wil fetch vp your	1615
*may come heereafter. But be it, as it may bee,	1650
Ol. Come sweete *Audrey,* | We must be married, or we must liue in baudrey:	1701
Rosa. But why did hee sweare hee would come this | morning, and comes not?	1728
Ros. O come, let vs remoue,	1765
Phe. But till that time | Come not thou neere me: and when that time comes,	1804
Come Sister: Shepheardesse, looke on him better	1849
Come, to our flocke, *Exit.*	1852
*serue me such another tricke, neuer come in my sight | more.	1955
Orl. My faire *Rosalind,* I come within an houre of my | promise.	1957
Ros. Nay, and you be so tardie, come no more in my	1965

COME *cont*.

Ros. Come, wooe me, wooe mee: for now I am in a	1981
Ros. By this hand, it will not kill a flie: but come,	2022
*good thing: Come sister, you shall be the Priest, and	2033
*me: 'tis but one cast away, and so come death: two o'│ clocke is your	
howre.	2091
*if you breake one iot of your promise, or come one	2096
*out of the sight of *Orlando*: Ile goe finde a shadow, and │ sigh till he	
come.	2122
Ros. Come, come, you are a foole,	2171
Cel. Come, you looke paler and paler: pray you draw │ homewards:	
good sir, goe with vs.	2332
Cor. Our Master and Mistresse seekes you: come a-│way, away.	2403
Heere come two of the banish'd Dukes Pages.	2536
Clo. By my troth well met: come, sit, sit, and a song.	2539
*such a foolish song. God buy you, and God mend your │ voices. Come	
Audrie. *Exeunt*.	2570

COMELY = 1

Oh what a world is this, when what is comely │ Enuenoms him that	
beares it?	717

COMES = 12*11

Adam. Yonder comes my Master, your brother.	29
*wise men haue makes a great shew; Heere comes Mon-│sieur the *Beu*.	255
Le Beu. There comes an old man, and his three sons.	282
Because I doe. Looke, here comes the Duke.	496
Ros. I, be so good *Touchstone*: Look you, who comes	802
*no wit by Nature, nor Art, may complaine of good │ breeding, or	
comes of a very dull kindred.	1228
Cor. Heere comes yong Mr *Ganimed*, my new Mistris-│ses Brother.	1283
Ros. Peace, here comes my sister reading, stand aside.	1322
*Wine comes out of a narrow-mouth'd bottle: either too	1396
Ros. O ominous, he comes to kill my Hart.	1440
Cel. You bring me out. Soft, comes he not heere?	1446
*Heere comes Sir *Oliuer*: Sir *Oliuer Mar-text* you are │	1673
Rosa. But why did hee sweare hee would come this │ morning, and	
comes not?	1728
youth mounts, and folly guides: who comes heere?	1752
Phe. But till that time │ Come not thou neere me: and when that time	
comes,	1804
Ros. I, of a Snaile: for though he comes slowly, hee	1968
*to your wiues for: but he comes armed in his	1974
To sleepe: looke who comes heere.	2153
*true louer hence, and not a word; for here comes more │ company.	
Exit. *Sil*.	2222
in the world: here comes the man you meane.	2349
Heere comes my *Rosalinde*.	2426
*Looke, here comes a Louer of mine, and a louer of hers.	2483
*couples are comming to the Arke. Here comes a payre	2613

COMFORT = 3*2

Would he not be a comfort to our trauaile?	596
Be comfort to my age: here is the gold,	749
*apparell, and to cry like a woman: but I must comfort	788
Liue a little, comfort a little, cheere thy selfe a little.	955
Orl. I thanke ye, and be blest for your good comfort.	1113

COMFORTABLE = 1

For my sake be comfortable, hold death a while	959

COMMAND = 1
And take vpon command, what helpe we haue | 1102
COMMANDMENT = 1
Of sterne command'ment. But what ere you are | 1086
COMMANDS = *1
*woman, Ile meet: so fare you wel: I haue left you com- | mands. | 2525
COMMEND = 2*1
Your daughter and her Cosen much commend | 692
Oli. *Orlando* doth commend him to you both, | 2241
Ros. I shall deuise something: but I pray you com- | mend | 2336
COMMENDATION = 1
High commendation, true applause, and loue; | 431
COMMENTING = 1
2.*Lord*. We did my Lord, weeping and commenting | Vpon the sobbing
Deere. | 673
COMMING = *5
*of my father in mee, as you, albeit I confesse your com- | ming | 52
*to doe, and heere where you are, they are comming to | performe it. | 279
Cel. Yonder sure they are comming. Let vs now stay | and see it. | 309
*comming a night to *Iane Smile*, and I remember the kis- | sing | 830
*couples are comming to the Arke. Here comes a payre | 2613
COMMING-ON = *1
*now I will be your *Rosalind* in a more comming-on dis- | position: | 2023
COMMISSION = 1
Ros. I might aske you for your Commission, | 2047
COMMITTING = 1
Committing me vnto my brothers loue, | 2298
COMMON = 3*1
Ros. Were it not better, | Because that I am more then common tall, | 579
A theeuish liuing on the common rode? | 737
In bitternesse; the common executioner | 1773
*which in the common, is woman: which toge- | ther, | 2391
COMPACT = 1*1
Du Sen. If he compact of iarres, grow Musicall, | 977
Ros. Patience once more, whiles our co(m)pact is vrg'd: | 2580
COMPANIE = 7*2
To keepe his daughter companie, whose loues | 443
I cannot liue out of her companie. | 547
The Fluxe of companie: anon a carelesse Heard | 660
That youth is surely in their companie. | 696
Or if thou hast not broke from companie, | 822
He is too disputeable for my companie: | 922
That your poore friends must woe your companie, | 983
*companie, I am verie glad to see you, euen a toy in hand | 1683
*societie: which in the boorish, is companie, of this fe- | male: | 2390
COMPANY = 2*1
Iaq. I thanke you for your company, but good faith | 1448
Thy company, which erst was irkesome to me | 1869
*true louer hence, and not a word; for here comes more | company.
Exit. Sil. | 2222
COMPLAIND = 1
After the Shepheard that complain'd of loue, | 1755
COMPLAINE = *1
*no wit by Nature, nor Art, may complaine of good | breeding, or
comes of a very dull kindred. | 1228
COMPLECTION = *1
Ros. Good my complection, dost thou think though | 1390

COMPLEMENT = *1
*you: but that they cal complement is like th'encounter   913
COMPLEXION = 2*1
  Betweene the pale complexion of true Loue,   1761
  Is his complexion: and faster then his tongue   1890
  *in your complexion, that it was a passion of ear-|nest.   2325
COMPLEXIONS = *1
  *pleas'd me, complexions that lik'd me, and breaths that   2793
COMPOUNDED = *1
  *is all these: but it is a melancholy of mine owne, com-|pounded   1931
CONCAUE = 1
  concaue as a couered goblet, or a Worme-eaten nut.   1734
CONCEALD = *1
  *might'st powre this conceal'd man out of thy mouth, as   1395
CONCEIT = *1
  *that I know you are a Gentleman of good conceit: 2462
CONCEITE = 1
  Thy conceite is neerer death, then thy powers.   958
CONCEIUD = *1
  *begot of thought, conceiu'd of spleene, and borne of   2118
CONCEIUE = 1
  More suites you to conceiue, then I to speake of.   435
CONCLUSION = 1
  'Tis I must make conclusion | Of these most strange euents: 2700
COND = *1
  *with goldsmiths wiues, & cond the(m) out of rings   1465
CONDITION = 1*2
  *know you are my eldest brother, and in the gentle con-|dition   47
  *Ros. Well, I will forget the condition of my estate, | to reioyce in
  yours.   184
  Yet such is now the Dukes condition,   432
CONDUCT = 2
  Goe hence a little, and I shall conduct you | If you will marke it.   1763
  In his owne conduct, purposely to take   2733
CONFERENCE = 1
  I cannot speake to her, yet she vrg'd conference.   425
CONFESSE = 1*3
  *of my father in mee, as you, albeit I confesse your com-|ming   52
  *thoughts, wherein I confesse me much guiltie to denie   347
  *then to confesse she do's: that is one of the points, in the   1572
  You lacke a mans heart. | Ros. I doe so, I confesse it: 2319
CONFESSES = 1
  Hisperia the Princesse Gentlewoman | Confesses that she secretly
  ore-heard   690
CONFINES = 1
  Should in their owne confines with forked heads   630
CONFIRMER = *1
  *confirmer of false reckonings, he attends here in the for-|rest on the
  Duke your father.   1740
CONFUSION = 1
  Hy. Peace hoa: I barre confusion,   2699
CONIE = *1
  Ros. As the Conie that you see dwell where shee is | kindled.   1527
CONIURE = *1
  *to begge will not become mee. My way is to coniure   2785
CONQUEROUR = *1
  *Conquerour, and it would doe well to set the Deares   2130

CONSCIENCES = *1
*which women stil giue the lie to their consciences. But 1573
CONSENT = 2*3
It cannot be, some villaines of my Court | Are of consent and sufferance
in this. 682
*holy-day humor, and like enough to consent: What 1982
*other. For all your Writers do consent, that *ipse* is hee: 2385
Aliena: say with her, that she loues mee; consent with 2416
Orl. You haue my consent. 2422
CONSENTING = *1
*nor sodaine consenting: but say with mee, I loue 2415
CONSIDER = *1
Cel. Do I prethee, but yet haue the grace to consider, 1711
CONSIST = 1
If their purgation did consist in words, 514
CONSTANT = 2
The constant seruice of the antique world, 761
Betwixt the constant red, and mingled Damaske. 1897
CONTEMPLATION = *2
D Sen. And did you leaue him in this contemplation? 672
*and indeed the sundrie contemplation of my trauells, in 1933
CONTEMPLATIUE = 1
That Fooles should be so deepe contemplatiue: 1004
CONTENT = 4*3
After my flight: now goe in we content 602
Weele light vpon some setled low content. 772
*was at home I was in a better place, but Trauellers must | be content. 799
*meanes, and content, is without three good frends. That 1224
*glad of other mens good content with my harme: 1272
Doth my simple feature content you? 1617
*I wil content you, if what pleases you contents 2522
CONTENTED = 1
Inuite the Duke, and all's contented followers: 2424
CONTENTS = 3*1
I know not the contents, but as I guesse 2156
Sil. No, I protest, I know not the contents, | *Phebe* did write it. 2169
*I wil content you, if what pleases you contents 2522
If truth holds true contents. 2704
CONTRACT = *1
*the contract of her marriage, and the day it is solemnizd: 1504
CONTRIUE = *1
Cel. Was't you that did so oft contriue to kill him? 2287
CONTRIUER = *1
*contriuer against mee his naturall brother: therefore vse 142
CONUERSION = 1
To tell you what I was, since my conuersion 2289
CONUERST = *1
*yeare old conuerst with a Magitian, most profound in 2469
CONUERTED = 1
After some question with him, was conuerted 2737
CONUERTITES = 1
Iaq. To him will I: out of these conuertites, 2761
COPE = 1
Du Sen. Show me the place, | I loue to cope him in these sullen fits, 675
COPULATION = *1
*liuing, by the copulation of Cattle, to be bawd to a Bel-|weather, 1277

COPULATIUES = *1
*in heere sir, amongst the rest of the Country copulatiues   2632
COR = 14*8
CORAGIOUS = *1
*selfe coragious to petty-coate; therefore courage, good | *Aliena*.   790
CORIN see also *Co., Cor.* = 7*1
  Enter Corin and Siluius.   801
  Sil. Oh *Corin*, that thou knew'st how I do loue her.   805
  Sil. No *Corin*, being old, thou canst not guesse,   807
  Enter Corin & Clowne.   1211
  Enter Corin.   1753
  **Corin*. Mistresse and Master, you haue oft enquired   1754
  Enter Rosalind, Celia, and Corin.   1778
  Enter Corin.   2402
CORKE = *1
*much at once, or none at all. I pre'thee take the Corke   1397
CORNE = 1
  That o're the greene corne feild did passe,   2549
CORNERS = 1
And vnregarded age in corners throwne,   746
COSEN = 6*3
  **Cha*. O no; for the Dukes daughter her Cosen so   108
  Cel. Gentle Cosen, | Let vs goe thanke him, and encourage him: 403
  **Cel*. Why Cosen, why *Rosaline*: *Cupid* haue mercie,   460
  **Cel*. They are but burs, Cosen, throwne vpon thee   472
  Ros. Me Vncle. | *Duk.* You Cosen,   500
  Ros. I haue more cause. | *Cel.* Thou hast not Cosen,   555
  Ros. But Cosen, what if we assaid to steale   594
Your daughter and her Cosen much commend   692
  Cel. There is more in it; Cosen *Ganimed*.   2313
COSENS = *1
  **Ros*. Then there were two Cosens laid vp, when the   466
COSIN = 1
rib-breaking? Shall we see this wrastling Cosin?   305
COST = 2
The cost of Princes on vnworthy shoulders?   1050
That sayes his brauerie is not on my cost,   1054
COTE *see* coat
COTTAGE = 2
Buy thou the Cottage, pasture, and the flocke,   878
And he hath bought the Cottage and the bounds   1881
COUER = *3
  **Amy*. Wel, Ile end the song. Sirs, couer the while,   918
  **Clo*. Good eu'n gentle friend. Couer thy head, couer   2357
COUERD = 1*1
heere Sir: Nay, pray be couer'd.   1684
*thy head: Nay prethee bee couer'd. How olde are you | Friend?   2358
COUERED = 1
concaue as a couered goblet, or a Worme-eaten nut.   1734
COUETOUSNESSE = 1
  Phe. Why that were couetousnesse: 1865
COULD *l.*174 *180 *203 283 412 *475 478 *787 881 *1366 *1529 *1549
  *1569 1850 1851 *1994 *2010 *2069 2078 2164 2183 2197 *2518
  *2672 = 10*14
COULDST *l.*1394 = *1
COUNSAILE = 1
  Le Beu. Good Sir, I do in friendship counsaile you   429

COUNSEL = 2*2
  *would counsel you to a more equall enterprise. We   340
  *some good counsel, for he seemes to haue the Quotidian | of Loue
  vpon him.   1550
  loue too: yet I professe curing it by counsel.   1584
  Iaq. Goe thou with mee, | And let me counsel thee.   1699
COUNSELLORS = 1
  This is no flattery: these are counsellors   616
COUNT = *2
  Cel. It is as easie to count Atomies as to resolue the   1426
  Clo. By my troth yes: I count it but time lost to heare   2569
COUNTENANCE = 2*2
  *nature gaue mee, his countenance seemes to take from   20
  And therefore put I on the countenance   1085
  *countenance you are; or I will scarce thinke you haue   1952
  Then in their countenance: will you heare the letter?   2185
COUNTER = 1
  Iaq. What, for a Counter, would I do, but good?   1037
COUNTERCHECKE = *1
  *the Reproofe valiant: the fift, the Counterchecke quar- | relsome: 2668
COUNTERFEIT = 3*1
  Now counterfeit to swound, why now fall downe,   1788
  Oli. This was not counterfeit, there is too great te- | stimony   2324
  Ros. Counterfeit, I assure you.   2327
  Oli. Well then, take a good heart, and counterfeit to | be a man.   2328
COUNTERFEITED = *2
  *Ah, sirra, a body would thinke this was well counterfei- | ted,   2321
  *I pray you tell your brother how well I counterfei- | ted: heigh-ho.   2322
COUNTERFEITING = 1
  my counterfeiting to him: will you goe? | *Exeunt*.   2337
COUNTERFEYTED = *1
  Ros. Did your brother tell you how I counterfeyted   2435
COUNTER-CHECKE = *1
  *say, I lie: this is call'd the counter-checke quarrelsome: 2655
COUNTREY = *1
  *at the Court, are as ridiculous in the Countrey, as   1244
COUNTRIE = 1*2
  Thus most inuectiuely he pierceth through | The body of Countrie,
  Citie, Court,   666
  *the behauiour of the Countrie is most mockeable at the   1245
  *of your owne Countrie: be out of loue with your   1950
COUNTRY = 1*2
  *with a Medler: then it will be the earliest fruit i'th coun- | try: 1316
  These prettie Country folks would lie. | *In spring time*, &c.   2559
  *in heere sir, amongst the rest of the Country copulatiues   2632
COUPLE = 1
  *promis'd to meete me in this place of the Forrest, and to | couple vs.   1653
COUPLED = 1*1
  Still we went coupled and inseperable.   537
  *honestie coupled to beautie, is to haue Honie a sawce to | Sugar.   1640
COUPLES = *1
  *couples are comming to the Arke. Here comes a payre   2613
COURAGE = *2
  *selfe coragious to petty-coate; therefore courage, good | *Aliena*.   790
  *though? Courage. As hornes are odious, they are neces- | sarie.   1660
COURSD = 1
  Cours'd one another downe his innocent nose   646

COURT = 10*7
*Oli. Good Mounsier *Charles*: what's the new newes | at the new Court? 98
Charles. There's no newes at the Court Sir, but the 100
*stay behind her; she is at the Court, and no lesse beloued 111
And get you from our Court. 499
So neere our publike Court as twentie miles, | Thou diest for it. 503
The clownish Foole out of your Fathers Court: 595
More free from perill then the enuious Court? 610
Thus most inuectiuely he pierceth through | The body of Countrie,
Citie, Court, 666
It cannot be, some villaines of my Court | Are of consent and sufferance
in this. 682
*respect it is not in the Court, it is tedious. As it is a spare 1218
Was't euer in Court, Shepheard? | *Cor*. No truly. 1231
Cor. For not being at Court? your reason. 1237
Clo. Why, if thou neuer was't at Court, thou neuer 1238
*at the Court, are as ridiculous in the Countrey, as 1244
*Court. You told me, you salute not at the Court, but 1246
And throwne into neglect the pompous Court. | 2.*Bro*. He hath. 2759
COURTEOUS = *2
*was: this is call'd the retort courteous. If I sent him 2648
*The first, the Retort courteous: the second, the 2666
COURTESIE = *2
*of bloud you should so know me: the courtesie of 48
*you kisse your hands; that courtesie would be vncleanlie | if Courtiers
were shepheards. 1247
COURTIER = 1*1
Iaq. O worthie Foole: One that hath bin a Courtier 1009
the Forrest: he hath bin a Courtier he sweares. 2619
COURTIERS = 2*3
*you kisse your hands, that courtesie would be vncleanlie | if Courtiers
were shepheards. 1247
Clo. Why do not your Courtiers hands sweate? and 1252
Courtiers hands are perfum'd with Ciuet. 1261
*nor the Courtiers, which is proud: nor the Souldiers, 1928
*cut of a certaine Courtiers beard: he sent me word, if I 2646
COURTLY = 1
Cor. You haue too Courtly a wit, for me, Ile rest. 1267
COURTSHIP = *1
*in his youth an inland man, one that knew Courtship too 1533
COUSIN = 1
Du. How now daughter, and Cousin: | Are you crept hither to see the
wrastling? 318
COWARD = 1
Who shut their coward gates on atomyes, 1784
COWARDS = 1
As manie other mannish cowards haue, 586
COWCHING = 1
Lay cowching head on ground, with catlike watch 2266
COWES = *1
*of her batler, and the Cowes dugs that her prettie 831
COZ = 2*5
Cel. I pray thee *Rosalind*, sweet my Coz, be merry. 171
Ros. From henceforth I will Coz, and deuise sports: 193
Cel. I'faith (Coz) tis he. 1410
Ros. O coz, coz, coz: my pretty little coz, that thou 2111

COZE = 3
Cel. Were I my Father (Coze) would I do this? 394
Shall we goe Coze? | *Cel*. I: fare you well faire Gentleman. 413
Cel. Will you goe Coze? | *Ros*. Haue with you: fare you well. *Exit*. 422
COZEN = 1
Giue vs some Musicke, and good Cozen, sing. 1154
CRADLES = *1
*loues her, being euer from their Cradles bred together, 109
CRAMD = 2
Ros. Then shal we be newes-cram'd. 261
After a voyage: He hath strange places cram'd 1013
CRAMPE = *1
*and being taken with the crampe, was droun'd, 2015
CREAME = 1
Your bugle eye-balls, nor your cheeke of creame 1820
CREATURE = *1
Cel. No; when Nature hath made a faire creature, 213
CREDIT = *1
*wrastle for my credit, and hee that escapes me without 126
CREEPING = 2
Loose, and neglect the creeping houres of time: 1089
And shining morning face, creeping like snaile 1125
CREPT = 1
Du. How now daughter, and Cousin: | Are you crept hither to see the
wrastling? 318
CREST = 1
It was a crest ere thou wast borne, 2141
CRIDE = 2
neuer cri'de, haue patience good people. 1355
And cride in fainting vpon *Rosalinde*. 2303
CRIES = 1*1
Iaq. Why who cries out on pride, 1044
*so neere the hart, as your gesture cries it out: when your 2471
CROOKED-PATED = *1
*to a crooked-pated olde Cuckoldly Ramme, out of all 1279
CROP = 1
That I shall thinke it a most plenteous crop . 1875
CROSSE = 1*1
*beare you: yet I should beare no crosse if I did beare 795
You and you, no crosse shall part; 2705
CROW = 1
My Lungs began to crow like Chanticleere, 1003
CROWNE = 2
Song. | *Wedding is great Iunos crowne*, 2715
His crowne bequeathing to his banish'd Brother, 2739
CROWNED = 2
And thou thrice crowned Queene of night suruey 1202
For loue is crowned with the prime. | *In spring time*, *&c*. 2555
CROWNES = 2*1
*Crownes, and as thou saist, charged my bro-|ther 6
*physicke your ranckenesse, and yet giue no thousand| crownes
neyther: holla *Dennis*. 86
Ad. But do not so: I haue fiue hundred Crownes, 742
CRUELL = 1*1
*your yeares: you haue seene cruell proofe of this mans 337
Ros. Why, tis a boysterous and a cruell stile, 2180

CRUELTIE = 1
Yet heard too much of *Phebes* crueltie.   2187
CRY = 2*2
  Ros. I would try if I could cry hem, and haue him.   478
  *apparell, and to cry like a woman: but I must comfort   788
  Cel. Cry holla, to the tongue, I prethee: it curuettes   1438
  Cry the man mercy, loue him, take his offer,   1834
CUCKOLDLY = *1
  *to a crooked-pated olde Cuckoldly Ramme, out of all   1279
CUP = *1
  *of a cup into a glasse, by filling the one, doth empty the   2384
CUPID = *2
  Cel. Why Cosen, why *Rosaline: Cupid* haue mercie,   460
  *of loue, it may be said of him that *Cupid* hath clapt   1962
CURB = *1
  Clo. As the Oxe hath his bow sir, the horse his curb,   1686
CURD = *1
  *and to liue in a nooke meerly Monastick: and thus I cur'd   1598
CURE = 1*1
  Orl. Did you euer cure any so?   1585
  Ros. I would cure you, if you would but call me *Rosa-|lind*,   1603
CURED = 1*1
  *and the reason why they are not so punish'd and cured, is   1582
  Orl. I would not be cured, youth.   1602
CURING = 1
  loue too: yet I professe curing it by counsel.   1584
CURS = *1
  *vpon curs, throw some of them at me; come lame mee | with reasons.   464
CURTELAX = 1
  A gallant curtelax vpon my thigh,   582
CURTSIE = 1
  offer, when I make curt'sie, bid me farewell. *Exit.*   2796
CURUETTES = *1
  Cel. Cry holla, to the tongue, I prethee: it curuettes   1438
CUSTOME = 1
  Hath not old custome made this life more sweete   608
CUT = 4*7
  sent in this foole to cut off the argument?   216
  He will haue other meanes to cut you off;   729
  With eyes seuere, and beard of formall cut,   1134
  *cut of a certaine Courtiers beard: he sent me word, if I   2646
  *said his beard was not cut well, hee was in the minde it   2647
  *word againe, it was not well cut, he wold send me word   2649
  *he cut it to please himselfe: this is call'd the quip modest.   2650
  *If againe, it was not well cut, he disabled my iudgment: 2651
  *cut, he would answer I spake not true: this is call'd the   2653
  *reproofe valiant. If againe, it was not well cut, he wold   2654
  Iaq. And how oft did you say his beard was not well | cut?   2657
CUTTER = *1
  *fortune makes natures naturall, the cutter off of natures | witte.   218
DAIES = 3*1
  *speake no more of him, you'l be whipt for taxation one | of these
  daies.   249
  Within these ten daies if that thou beest found   502
  Ros. I was seuen of the nine daies out of the wonder,   1371
  That haue endur'd shrew'd daies, and nights with vs,   2750

DAMASKE = 1
Betwixt the constant red, and mingled Damaske. 1897
DAMNABLE = *1
*his Art, and yet not damnable. If you do loue *Rosalinde* 2470
DAMNATION = *1
*and sinne is damnation: Thou art in a parlous state shep-|heard. 1241
DAMND = 1*3
    Clo. Then thou art damn'd. | *Cor*. Nay, I hope. 1233
    *Clo. Truly thou art damn'd, like an ill roasted Egge, | all on one side. 1235
    *Clo. Wilt thou rest damn'd? God helpe thee shallow 1268
    *reasonable match. If thou bee'st not damn'd for this, the 1280
DANCING = 1
I am for other, then for dancing meazures. | *Du Se*. Stay, *Iaques*, stay. 2770
DANGER = 2
    Ros. Alas, what danger will it be to vs, 572
    *to set her before your eyes to morrow, humane as she is, | and without
any danger. 2475
DANGEROUS = *1
*mend mee, and by all pretty oathes that are not dange-|rous, 2095
DAPLED = 1
And yet it irkes me the poore dapled fooles 628
DARKE = 1*1
*as wel a darke house, and a whip, as madmen do: 1581
Then without Candle may goe darke to bed: 1812
DARTED = 1
Which I haue darted at thee, hurt thee not, 1796
DASHD = *1
*a loue cause: *Troilous* had his braines dash'd out with a 2009
DAUGHTER = 11*7
    Oli. Can you tell if *Rosalind* the Dukes daughter bee | banished with
her Father? 106
    Cha. O no; for the Dukes daughter her Cosen so 108
    *of her Vncle, then his owne daughter, and neuer two La-|dies loued as
they doe. 112
    Du. How now daughter, and Cousin: | Are you crept hither to see the
wrastling? 318
Which of the two was daughter of the Duke, 437
    Le Beu. Neither his daughter, if we iudge by manners, 439
But yet indeede the taller is his daughter, 440
The other is daughter to the banish'd Duke, 441
To keepe his daughter companie, whose loues 443
    Duk. Thou art thy Fathers daughter, there's enough. 519
Hath banish'd me his daughter? | *Ros*. That he hath not. 558
Your daughter and her Cosen much commend 692
*Keepe you your word, O Duke, to giue your daughter, 2595
You yours *Orlando*, to receiue his daughter: 2596
Me thought he was a brother to your daughter: 2605
Good Duke receiue thy daughter, 2686
    Du Se. If there be truth in sight, you are my daughter. 2693
Euen daughter welcome, in no lesse degree. 2723
DAUGHTERS = 1
Some liuely touches of my daughters fauour. 2603
DAY = 8*11
*Gentlemen flocke to him euery day, and fleet the time 118
*this day liuing. I speake but brotherly of him, 151
    Clo. Thus men may grow wiser euery day. It is the 299
how full of briers is this working day world. 471

DAY *cont*.

To day my Lord of *Amiens*, and my selfe,	636
*the Duke wil drinke vnder this tree; he hath bin all this | day to looke	
you.	919
Iaq. And I haue bin all this day to auoid him:	921
**Ros*. Alas the day, what shall I do with my doublet z	1413
*in mans apparrell? Looks he as freshly, as he did the day | he	
Wrastled?	1424
**Orl*. You should aske me what time o'day: there's no | clocke in the	
Forrest.	1491
*the contract of her marriage, and the day it is solemnizd:	1504
*me his Loue, his Mistris: and I set him euerie day	1587
and come euerie day to my Coat, and woe me.	1604
Orl. Good day, and happinesse, deere *Rosalind*.	1945
*holy-day humor, and like enough to consent: What	1982
Orl. For euer, and a day.	2054
**Ros*. Say a day, without the euer: no, no *Orlando*, men	2055
**Clo*. To morrow is the ioyfull day *Audrey*, to morow | will we be	
married.	2532
Duke Frederick hearing how that euerie day	2730

DAYES = 1 *1

If euer you haue look'd on better dayes:	1090
**Du Sen*. True is it, that we haue seene better dayes,	1097

DE *l*.*58 386 = 1 *1

DEAD = 3 *3

Cel. Well, the beginning that is dead and buried.	281
*neuer gracious: if kil'd, but one dead that is willing to	351
Seeke him with Candle: bring him dead, or liuing	1186
*it strikes a man more dead then a great rec-|koning	1625
**Phe*. Dead Shepheard, now I find thy saw of might,	1853
The royall disposition of that beast | To prey on nothing, that doth	
seeme as dead:	2268

DEALE = *1

*death, thy libertie into bondage: I will deale in poy-|son	2395

DEARE – 2 *1

*turne monster: therefore my sweet *Rose*, my deare *Rose*, | be merry.	191
Iaq. Which is he that killed the Deare? | *Lord*. Sir, it was I.	2127
Musicke, Song. | *What shall he haue that kild the Deare?*	2136

DEARES = *1

*Conquerour, and it would doe well to set the Deares	2130

DEATH = 4 *3

I faint almost to death.	847
Thy conceite is neerer death, then thy powers.	958
For my sake be comfortable, hold death a while	959
Whose heart th'accustom'd sight of death makes hard	1774
*me: 'tis but one cast away, and so come death: two o' | clocke is your	
howre.	2091
*death, thy libertie into bondage: I will deale in poy-|son	2395
**Sil*. Though to haue her and death, were both one | thing.	2592

DEBILITIE = 1

The meanes of weaknesse and debilitie,	755

DEBTER = 1

Then to die well, and not my Masters debter. *Exeunt*.	780

DECEIUD = *2

**Ros*. Fare you well: praie heauen I be deceiu'd in you.	359
*1.*Pa*. you are deceiu'd Sir, we kept time, we lost not | our time.	2567

DECEMBER = *1
*are Aprill when they woe, December when they wed: 2056
DECREES = 1
Ros. As wit and fortune will. | *Clo*. Or as the destinies decrees. 269
DEED = 1
Aud. I do not know what Poetical is: is it honest in | deed and word: is
it a true thing? 1628
DEEDE = 1
Thou should'st haue better pleas'd me with this deede, 389
DEEDS = 1
And little wreakes to finde the way to heauen | By doing deeds of
hospitalitie. 866
DEEPE = 1*2
That Fooles should be so deepe contemplatiue: 1004
*didst know how many fathome deepe I am in loue: but 2112
*how deepe I am in loue: ile tell thee *Aliena*, I cannot be 2121
DEERE = 8*5
Ros. Deere *Cellia*; I show more mirth then I am mi- | stresse 172
(As I doe trust I am not) then deere Vncle, 510
Cel. Deere Soueraigne heare me speake. 527
Poore Deere quoth he, thou mak'st a testament 655
2.*Lord*. We did my Lord, weeping and commenting | Vpon the sobbing
Deere. 673
Adam. Deere Master, I can go no further: 951
*No, no, the noblest Deere hath them as huge as the Ras- | call: 1665
Sil. O deere *Phebe*, | If euer (as that euer may be neere) 1799
Orl. Good day, and happinesse, deere *Rosalind*. 1945
Orl. Pardon me deere *Rosalind*. 1964
Ros. Alas, deere loue, I cannot lacke thee two houres. 2085
Ros. Oh my deere *Orlando*, how it greeues me to see 2429
Du Se. O my deere Neece, welcome thou art to me, 2722
DEERELIE = *2
Ros. The Duke my Father lou'd his Father deerelie. 487
*Sonne deerelie? By this kinde of chase, I should hate 489
DEERELY = *2
*deerely hir'd: but I (his brother) gaine nothing vnder 16
*him, for my father hated his father deerely; yet I hate | not *Orlando*. 490
DEERER = 1
Are deerer then the naturall bond of Sisters: 444
DEEREST = 1
Of manie faces, eyes, and hearts, | *to haue the touches deerest pris'd*. 1349
DEERLY = *1
Ros. By my life I do, which I tender deerly, though 2478
DEFENCE = *1
*brow of a Batcheller: and by how much defence is bet- | ter 1669
DEFIDE = *1
*I defi'de not: And I am sure, as many as haue good 2794
DEFIES = 1
A stile for challengers: why, she defies me, 2181
DEFYING = *1
*brambles; all (forsooth) defying the name of *Rosalinde*. 1548
DEGREE = 1
Euen daughter welcome, in no lesse degree. 2723
DEGREES = *3
*degrees, haue they made a paire of staires to marriage, 2446
Iaq. Can you nominate in order now, the degrees of | the lye. 2662
*haue bookes for good manners: I will name you the de- | grees. 2665

54

DELAY = 1 *1
  *my disposition? One inch of delay more, is a South-sea   1392
  delay me not the knowledge of his chin.   1405
DELIGHT = *1
  *Du. You wil take little delight in it, I can tell you   321
DELIGHTS = 1
  As we do trust, they'l end in true delights. *Exit*   2775
DEMONSTRATING = *1
  *about you, demonstrating a carelesse desolation: but you   1565
DEN = 1 *1
DENIDE = 1
  Orl. How if the kisse be denide?   1991
DENIE = 1 *1
  *thoughts, wherein I confesse me much guiltie to denie   347
  Or else by him my loue denie,   2211
DENNIS see also Den. = 2
  *physicke your ranckenesse, and yet giue no thousand | crownes
  neyther: holla *Dennis*.   86
  Enter Dennis. | *Den.* Calls your worship?   88
DEPART = 1
  *will kill thee a hundred and fifty wayes, therefore trem- | ble and
  depart.   2398
DEPARTURE = *1
  Orl. I am glad of your departure: Adieu good Mon- | sieur
  Melancholly.   1485
DEPENDS = 1
  Tell me whereon the likelihoods depends?   518
DERIUE = 1
  Or if we did deriue it from our friends,   523
DESCENDED = 1
  Hadst thou descended from another house: 390
DESCRIPTION = 1
  Then should I know you by description,   2234
DESERT = 6
  Being natiue Burgers of this desert City,   629
  Can in this desert place buy entertainment,   856
  If there liue any thing in this Desert.   969
  That in this desert inaccessible,   1087
  Cel. Why should this Desert bee, | *for it is vnpeopled? Noe:*   1323
  As how I came into that Desert place.   2295
DESERUD = 2
  Sticks me at heart: Sir, you haue well deseru'd,   406
  To leaue this place; Albeit you haue deseru'd   430
DESERUE = 1
  Cel. Why should I not? doth he not deserue well?   493
DESERUED = 1
  you to a long, and well-deserued bed: 2767
DESERUES = 1 *2
  Ros. Loue is meerely a madnesse, and I tel you, de- | serues   1580
  Ros. Doe you pitty him? No, he deserues no pitty: 2215
  your patience, and your vertue, well deserues it.   2764
DESIRE = 5 *6
  I shall desire more loue and knowledge of you.   453
  Iaq. I do not desire you to please me,   905
  I do desire you to sing: 906
  Orl. I do desire we may be better strangers.   1453
  Cel. As good cause as one would desire, | Therefore weepe.   1714

DESIRE *cont*.

Rosalind. Why then, can one desire too much of a	2032
*when he had a desire to eate a Grape, would open	2375
Aud. I do desire it with all my heart: and I hope it is	2534
*no dishonest desire, to desire to be a woman of y world?	2535
Clo. God'ild you sir, I desire you of the like: I presse	2631

DESIRES = 2*2

Cel. Your hearts desires be with you.	360
Or haue acquaintance with mine owne desires,	508
*and the Falcon her bels, so man hath his desires, and as	1687
*then an ape, more giddy in my desires, then a mon- | key:	2061

DESIROUS = 1

desirous to lie with his mother earth?	362

DESOLATION = *1

*about you, demonstrating a carelesse desolation: but you	1565

DESPERATE = 1

Of many desperate studies, by his vnckle,	2608

DESPIGHT *see also* dispight = 1

That I made yesterday in despight of my Inuention.	934

DESPIGHTFULL = 1

To seeme despightfull and vngentle to you:	2487

DESPISER = 1

Or else a rude despiser of good manners,	1068

DESTINIE = *1

*then you make a woman: besides, he brings his destinie | with him.	1970

DESTINIES = 1

Ros. As wit and fortune will. | *Clo*. Or as the destinies decrees.	269

DETAIND = 1

And here detain'd by her vsurping Vncle	442

DETECT = 1

detect the lazie foot of time, as wel as a clocke.	1495

DEUICE = 1*1

*are no such man; you are rather point deuice in your ac- | coustrements,	1566
This is a Letter of your owne deuice.	2168

DEUILL *see* diuell

DEUISD = 1

Thus Rosalinde *of manie parts*, | *by Heauenly Synode was deuis'd*,	1347

DEUISE = 2*4

*poyson, entrap thee by some treacherous deuise, and ne- | uer	147
*deuise, of all sorts enchantingly beloued, and indeed	163
Ros. From henceforth I will Coz, and deuise sports:	193
Therefore deuise with me how we may flie	564
Deuise the fittest time, and safest way	600
Ros. I shall deuise something: but I pray you com- | mend	2336

DIALL = 2

And then he drew a diall from his poake,	993
And I did laugh, sans intermission | An houre by his diall. Oh noble foole,	1005

DIANA = *2

Cel. Hee hath bought a paire of cast lips of *Diana*: a	1725
*I will weepe for nothing, like *Diana* in the Foun- | taine,	2062

DID *l*.119 388 419 512 514 523 530 581 637 642 644 652 *672 673 684 694 744 752 754 *795 811 817 1001 1005 *1414 *1416 *1424 1585 *1728 1891 1899 *2010 2155 2158 2170 2174 2177 2195 2196 2203 2239 2254 2263 2270 2273 2277 2279 *2287 *2435 2549 *2642 *2645 *2657 = 42*12

DIDST = 3*3
*thy discretion, I had as liefe thou didst breake his necke 143
Sil. Oh thou didst then neuer loue so hartily, 815
Cel. Didst thou heare these verses? 1361
Cel. But didst thou heare without wondering, how 1369
*Now if thou wert a Poet, I might haue some hope | thou didst feigne. 1636
*didst know how many fathome deepe I am in loue: but 2112
DIE *see also* dye = 11*2
And in the greatnesse of my word you die. | *Exit Duke, &c*. 550
Then to die well, and not my Masters debter. *Exeunt*. 780
O I die for food. Heere lie I downe, 952
I wil giue thee leaue to die: but if thou diest 962
To some shelter, and thou shalt not die | For lacke of a dinner, 967
Orl. I almost die for food, and let me haue it. 1081
Heauen would that shee these gifts should haue, | *and I to liue and die her*
slaue. 1351
Orl. Then in mine owne person, I die. 2005
Ros. No faith, die by Attorney: the poore world is 2006
*Grecian club, yet he did what hee could to die before, 2010
And then Ile studie how to die. 2212
*was old Sir *Rowlands* will I estate vpon you, and heere | liue and die a
Shepherd. 2419
Phe. That will I, should I die the houre after. 2587
DIED = 1*3
*that hee would haue followed her exile, or haue died to 110
*was not anie man died in his owne person (*videlicet*) in 2008
Hero of Cestos. But these are all lies, men haue died 2017
Died in this bloud, vnto the Shepheard youth, 2309
DIES = 2*1
*none is like to haue; and truely when he dies, thou shalt 187
He dies that touches any of this fruite, | Till I, and my affaires are
answered. 1074
Then he that dies and liues by bloody drops? 1777
DIEST = 2
So neere our publike Court as twentie miles, | Thou diest for it. 503
I wil giue thee leaue to die: but if thou diest 962
DIFFERENCE = 2
The seasons difference, as the Icie phange 612
Then that mixt in his cheeke: 'twas iust the difference 1896
DIFFERS = *1
*you that keeping for a gentleman of my birth, that dif-|fers 12
DIGNITIE = 1
Meane time, forget this new-falne dignitie, 2753
DIMINISH = 1
That reason, wonder may diminish 2713
DING = 3
When Birds do sing, hey ding a ding, ding. 2551
DINNER = 1*1
To some shelter, and thou shalt not die | For lacke of a dinner, 967
Orl. I must attend the Duke at dinner, by two a clock | I will be with
thee againe. 2086
DINNERS = *1
Clo. Ile rime you so, eight yeares together; dinners, 1294
DIRECT = 1*3
and so to lye circumstantiall, and the lye direct. 2656
*nor he durst not giue me the lye direct: and so wee mea-|sur'd swords,
and parted. 2660

DIRECT *cont*.

*the Lye direct: all these you may auoyd, but the	2670
*Lye direct: and you may auoide that too, with an If. I	2671

DISABLE = *1

*lispe, and weare strange suites; disable all the benefits	1949

DISABLED = *1

*If againe, it was not well cut, he disabled my iudgment:	2651

DISCHARGE = 1

That their discharge did stretch his leatherne coat	644

DISCORD = 1

We shall haue shortly discord in the Spheares:	978

DISCOUERIE = *1

*of discouerie. I pre'thee tell me, who is it quickely, and	1393

DISCRETION = *1

*thy discretion, I had as liefe thou didst breake his necke	143

DISDAINE = 1

And the red glowe of scorne and prowd disdaine,	1762

DISDAINFULL = 1

Praising the proud disdainfull Shepherdesse | That was his Mistresse.	1757

DISEASES = 1

*Clo. According to the fooles bolt sir, and such dulcet | diseases.	2640

DISGORGE = 1

Would'st thou disgorge into the generall world.	1043

DISGRACE = *3

*from his intendment, or brooke such disgrace well as he	132
*dost him any slight disgrace, or if hee doe not mightilie	145
*Ros. I could finde in my heart to disgrace my mans	787

DISGUISD = *1

*in disguis'd against mee to try a fall: to morrow sir I	125

DISH = 1

slut, were to put good meate into an vncleane dish.	1646

DISHONEST = *1

*no dishonest desire, to desire to be a woman of y world?	2535

DISLIKE = *1

*bodie more seeming Audry) as thus sir: I did dislike the	2645

DISPATCH = 1*1

Duk. Mistris, dispatch you with your safest haste,	498
*wel met. Will you dispatch vs heere vnder this tree, or	1674

DISPIGHT = *1

*in dispight of a fall: but turning these iests out of seruice,	483

DISPLEASURE = 1

Hath tane displeasure 'gainst his gentle Neece,	446

DISPOSD = *1

*z I wil do that when you are dispos'd to be merry:	2063

DISPOSITION = 3*3

*your yonger brother Orlando hath a disposition to come	124
My Fathers rough and enuious disposition	405
My master is of churlish disposition,	865
*my disposition? One inch of delay more, is a South-sea	1392
*now I will be your Rosalind in a more comming-on dis-|position:	2023
The royall disposition of that beast | To prey on nothing, that doth seeme as dead:	2268

DISPUTEABLE = 1

He is too disputeable for my companie:	922

DISSEMBLING = 1

Ros. His very haire | Is of the dissembling colour.	1716

DISSWADE = *2
  *vnder-hand meanes laboured to disswade him from it;   138
  *youth, I would faine disswade him, but he will not   323
DISTILLD = 1
  With all Graces wide enlarg'd, | nature presently distill'd   1341
DISTRES = *1
  *Du Sen. Art thou thus bolden'd man by thy distres?   1067
DISTRESSE = 1
  Of bare distresse, hath tane from me the shew   1071
DITTIE = *1
  *great matter in the dittie, yet y note was very vntunable   2566
DIUELL = *2
  *diuell himselfe will haue no shepherds, I cannot see else | how thou
  shouldst scape.   1281
  *Ros. Nay, but the diuell take mocking: speake sadde | brow, and true
  maid.   1408
DIUERS = *2
  *Ros. By no meanes sir; Time trauels in diuers paces,   1498
  *with diuers persons: Ile tel you who Time ambles with- | all,   1499
DIUERTED = 1
  Of a diuerted blood, and bloudie brother.   741
DIUIDE = *1
  *will diuide a minute into a thousand parts, and breake   1960
DO l.*75 253 327 *334 *343 *352 394 429 495 699 708 738 739 742 765
  805 864 905 906 937 987 *1036 1037 1047 1048 1058 1190 1198 *1252
  *1413 *1443 1453 1459 *1488 *1571 *1581 *1628 *1632 *1633 *1635
  *1681 *1711 1712 1771 1814 1822 1844 1885 2051 *2063 2197 *2312
  *2372 2378 2379 *2385 2400 *2465 *2466 *2468 *2470 *2478 *2513
  *2534 2551 2576 *2577 2588 2602 2742 2747 2775 *2780 = 45*31
DOATES = *1
  *Musicke in his sides? Is there yet another doates vpon   304
DOE l.114 *122 *145 *195 *203 *279 407 496 505 509 510 513 566 577
  587 634 656 664 715 732 758 819 1299 *1311 1731 *1733 1771 1786 1798
  1860 1871 1903 1920 *2034 *2048 2066 2067 *2069 *2130 2166 *2215
  2275 2288 2320 *2330 = 33*13, 1
  Whiles (like a Doe) I go to finde my Fawne,   1105
DOG = 1
  Not a word? | Ros. Not one to throw at a dog.   461
DOGGE = 1*1
  Oli. Get you with him, you olde dogge.   81
  *Adam. Is old dogge my reward: most true, I haue   82
DOG-APES = *1
  *of two dog-Apes. And when a man thankes me hartily,   914
DOING = 1
  And little wreakes to finde the way to heauen | By doing deeds of
  hospitalitie.   866
DOLE = *1
  *making such pittiful dole ouer them, that all the behol- | ders   293
DONE l.433 1375 *2109 *2484 = 2*2
DOOMBE = 1
  Firme, and irreuocable is my doombe,   544
DOORE = *1
  *Den. So please you, he is heere at the doore, and im- | portunes accesse
  to you.   92
DOORES = 1*1
  Come not within these doores: within this roofe   721
  *the wiser, the waywarder: make the doores vpon a wo- | mans   2070

DORES = *1
*Duke. More villaine thou. Well push him out of dores   1195
DOS l.*1572 = *1
DOST l.*145 380 1164 1189 *1390 2575 = 4*2
DOTH l.205 *488 493 635 659 747 927 1027 1028 1046 1171 1204 *1423
  1502 1515 1617 2231 2241 2269 2310 *2373 *2384 2515 2725
  2765 = 21*4
DOUBLET = *4
  *the weaker vessell, as doublet and hose ought to show it   789
  *I am caparison'd like a man, I haue a doublet and hose in   1391
  *Ros. Alas the day, what shall I do with my doublet &   1413
  *we must haue your doublet and hose pluckt ouer   2108
DOUBT = *1
  *Clo. If any man doubt that, let him put mee to my   2620
DOUBTS = 1
  To make these doubts all euen. Exit Ros. and Celia.   2601
DOWN = *1
  *Cel. West of this place, down in the neighbor bottom   2228
DOWNE = 8*3
  *Cel. If I had a thunderbolt in mine eie, I can tell who | should downe.
  Shout.   375
  Are all throwne downe, and that which here stands vp   416
  Cours'd one another downe his innocent nose   646
  O I die for food. Heere lie I downe,   952
  Who laid him downe, and bask'd him in the Sun,   988
  *Du Sen. Sit downe and feed, & welcom to our table   1082
  And therefore sit you downe in gentlenesse,   1101
  *Du Sen. Welcome: set downe your venerable bur- | then, and let him
  feede.   1147
  *Attalanta's heeles. Will you sitte downe with me, and   1469
  Now counterfeit to swound, why now fall downe,   1788
  But Mistris, know your selfe, downe on your knees   1830
DOWNRIGHT = *1
  *Ros. You haue heard him sweare downright he was.   1737
DOWRIE = *1
  *of them. Well, that is the dowrie of his wife, 'tis none   1663
DRAUE = *1
  *him: now weepe for him, then spit at him; that I draue   1595
DRAW = *2
  *Cel. Come, you looke paler and paler: pray you draw | homewards:
  good sir, goe with vs.   2332
  *little measure draw a beleefe from you, to do your selfe   2466
DRAWNE = 2
  Hast thou beene drawne to by thy fantasie?   813
  A Lyonnesse, with vdders all drawne drie,   2265
DREAME = 1
  If that I doe not dreame, or be not franticke,   509
DREW = 1
  And then he drew a diall from his poake,   993
DRIE = 3
  Which is as drie as the remainder bisket   1012
  And high top, bald with drie antiquitie: 2256
  A Lyonnesse, with vdders all drawne drie,   2265
DRINK = *1
  *it is a figure in Rhetoricke, that drink being powr'd out   2383

DRINKE = 1*2
   *the Duke wil drinke vnder this tree; he hath bin all this | day to looke
   you.   919
   out of thy mouth, that I may drinke thy tydings.   1398
   *Clo. It is meat and drinke to me to see a Clowne, by   2351
DRIUEN = *1
   *what straights of Fortune she is driuen, and it is not   2473
DROP = 1
   Could not drop forth such giant rude inuention,   2183
DROPD = 1
   vnder a tree like a drop'd Acorne.   1429
DROPPES = *1
   *Ros. It may wel be cal'd Ioues tree, when it droppes | forth fruite.   1430
DROPS = 2
   Of drops, that sacred pity hath engendred: 1100
   Then he that dies and liues by bloody drops?   1777
DROUND = *1
   *and being taken with the crampe, was droun'd,   2015
DROWND = *1
   *Orl. He is drown'd in the brooke, looke but in, and | you shall see
   him.   1479
DRUNKARDS = 1
   *fellowes, and betray themselues to euery mo- | derne censure, worse
   then drunkards.   1922
DSEN = *1
DU = 2*1
DUCDAME = 4
   Ducdame, ducdame, ducdame: 940
   Amy. What's that Ducdame?   943
DUGS = *1
   *of her batler, and the Cowes dugs that her prettie   831
DUK = 9*5
   Duk. You shall trie but one fall.   365
   Duk. No more, no more.   377
   Duk. How do'st thou *Charles?*   380
   Duk. Beare him awaie: | What is thy name yong man?   382
   Duk. I would thou hadst beene son to some man else,   386
   Duk. Mistris, dispatch you with your safest haste,   498
   Ros. Me Vncle. | *Duk.* You Cosen,   500
   Duk. Thus doe all Traitors,   513
   Duk. Thou art thy Fathers daughter, there's enough.   519
   Duk. I *Celia,* we staid her for your sake,   528
   Duk. She is too subtile for thee, and her smoothnes;   538
   Duk. You are a foole: you Neice prouide your selfe,   548
   Duk. Can it be possible that no man saw them?   681
   Duk. Send to his brother, fetch that gallant hither,   697
DUKDOME = *1
   Ros. So was I when your highnes took his Dukdome,   520
*DUKE see also D Sen., Du., Du Se., Du Sen., Duk Sen. = 27*12*
   *olde newes: that is, the old Duke is banished by his yon- | ger   101
   *brother the new Duke, and three or foure louing   102
   *him, whose lands and reuenues enrich the new Duke,   104
   Oli. Where will the old Duke liue? | *Cha.* They say hee is already in
   the Forrest of *Arden,*   114
   Oli. What, you wrastle to morrow before the new | Duke.   120
   *had banished thy Vncle the Duke my Father, so thou   179
   Flourish. Enter Duke, Lords, Orlando, Charles, | and Attendants.   311

DUKE cont.
*be misprised: we wil make it our suite to the Duke, that	344
I would thou had'st told me of another Father. | *Exit Duke*.	392
The Duke is humorous, what he is indeede	434
Which of the two was daughter of the Duke,	437
The other is daughter to the banish'd Duke,	441
But I can tell you, that of late this Duke	445
From tyrant Duke, vnto a tyrant Brother.	456
Ros. The Duke my Father lou'd his Father deerelie.	487
Enter Duke with Lords.	494
Because I doe. Looke, here comes the Duke.	496
And in the greatnesse of my word you die. | *Exit Duke, &c*.	550
Prethee be cheerefull; know'st thou not the Duke	557
Enter Duke Senior: Amyens, and two or three Lords | *like Forresters*.	605
Enter Duke, with Lords.	680
The bonnie priser of the humorous Duke?	711
*the Duke wil drinke vnder this tree; he hath bin all this | day to looke you.	919
Amy. And Ile go seeke the Duke,	947
Enter Duke Sen. & Lord, like Out-lawes.	972
Be truly welcome hither: I am the Duke	1173
Enter Duke, Lords, & Oliuer.	1180
*confirmer of false reckonings, he attends here in the for-|rest on the Duke your father.	1740
Ros. I met the Duke yesterday, and had much que-|stion	1742
Orl. I must attend the Duke at dinner, by two a clock | I will be with thee againe.	2086
Iaq. Let's present him to the Duke like a Romane	2129
In briefe, he led me to the gentle Duke,	2296
Inuite the Duke, and all's contented followers:	2424
*bid the Duke to the Nuptiall. But O, how bitter a thing	2452
Enter Duke Senior, Amyens, Iaques, Orlan-|do, Oliuer, Celia.	2573
*Keepe you your word, O Duke, to giue your daughter,	2595
Good Duke receiue thy daughter,	2686
Duke Frederick hearing how that euerie day	2730
The Duke hath put on a Religious life,	2758

DUKE = 2*3
DUKEDOME = 1
A land it selfe at large, a potent Dukedome.	2746

DUKES = 2*4
Oli. Was not *Charles* the Dukes Wrastler heere to | speake with me?	90
Oli. Can you tell if *Rosalind* the Dukes daughter bee | banished with her Father?	106
Cha. O no; for the Dukes daughter her Cosen so	108
*the Dukes Wrastler, which *Charles* in a moment threw	289
Yet such is now the Dukes condition,	432
Heere come two of the banish'd Dukes Pages.	2536

DUKSEN = *1
DULCET = *1
Clo. According to the fooles bolt sir, and such dulcet | diseases.	2640

DULL = 2*1
*but Natures, who perceiueth our naturall wits too dull	221
*no wit by Nature, nor Art, may complaine of good | breeding, or comes of a very dull kindred.	1228
Ros. Peace you dull foole, I found them on a tree.	1313

DULNESSE = *1
*our whetstone: for alwaies the dulnesse of the foole, is	223

DUNGHILS = *1
*dunghils are as much bound to him as I: besides this no-|thing   18
DURST = *2
   *Clo. I durst go no further then the lye circumstantial: 2659
   *nor he durst not giue me the lye direct: and so wee mea-|sur'd swords,
   and parted.   2660
DUSE = 3*6
DUSEN = 12*7
DUTIE = 3
   Orl. I attend them with all respect and dutie.   330
   When seruice sweate for dutie, not for meede: 762
   All adoration, dutie, and obseruance,   2503
DWEL = 1
   Orl. Where dwel you prettie youth?   1523
DWELL = *1
   *Ros. As the Conie that you see dwell where shee is | kindled.   1527
DWELLING = 2
   In their assign'd and natiue dwelling place.   671
   *Orl. Your accent is something finer, then you could | purchase in so
   remoued a dwelling.   1529
DWELS = *1
   *that that no man else will: rich honestie dwels like a mi-|ser   2636
DYE = 1
   Iaq. And you will not be answer'd with reason, | I must dye.   1076
DYED see died
DYEST = *1
   *thou perishest: or to thy better vnderstanding, dyest; or   2393
EACH = *1
   *both, that we may enioy each other: it shall be to your   2417
EARE = 1
   For I must tell you friendly in your eare,   1832
EARES = 1
   To gleane the broken eares after the man   1876
EARLIEST = *1
   *with a Medler: then it will be the earliest fruit i'th coun-|try: 1316
EARLY = 1
   Saw her a bed, and in the morning early,   686
EARNE = *1
   *Cor. Sir, I am a true Labourer, I earne that I eate: get   1270
EARNEST = *4
   *loue no man in good earnest, nor no further in sport ney-|ther,   196
   *let vs talke in good earnest: Is it possible in such a so-|daine,   484
   *Ros. By my troth, and in good earnest, and so God   2094
   *in your complexion, that it was a passion of ear-|nest.   2325
EARTH = 1
   desirous to lie with his mother earth?   362
EARTHLY = 1
   When earthly things made eauen | attone together.   2684
EARTHQUAKES = *1
   *meete; but Mountaines may bee remoou'd with Earth-|quakes, and so
   encounter.   1381
EASE = 1*1
   Leauing his wealth and ease,   938
   *the worse at ease he is: and that hee that wants money,   1223
EASIE = *1
   *Cel. It is as easie to count Atomies as to resolue the   1426

EASILY = *1
    *that hath not the Gowt: for the one sleepes easily be-|cause   1509
EAST = 1
    *Ros. From the east to westerne Inde, | no iewel is like Rosalinde,   1286
EAT = *1
    *Orlan. Shall I keepe your hogs, and eat huskes with   40
EATE = 5*3
    Rose at an instant, learn'd, plaid, eate together,   535
    And if I bring thee not something to eate,   961
    Orl. Forbeare, and eate no more.   1063
    Iaq. Why I haue eate none yet.   1064
    *Cor. Sir, I am a true Labourer, I earne that I eate: get   1270
    *when he had a desire to eate a Grape, would open   2375
    *that Grapes were made to eate, and lippes to open.   2377
    Phe. I wil not eate my word, now thou art mine,   2724
EATEN = 1*1
    concaue as a couered goblet, or a Worme-eaten nut.   1734
    *from time to time, and wormes haue eaten them, but not | for loue.   2018
EATES = 1
    Seeking the food he eates,   929
EAUEN = 1
    When earthly things made eauen | attone together.   2684
EBBE = 1
    Till that the wearie verie meanes do ebbe.   1047
EDUCATION = *2
    *gentility with my education. This is it Adam that   23
    *father charg'd you in his will to giue me good educati-|on: 67
EEKE = 1
    Cel. And mine to eeke out hers.   358
EFFECT = 2
    Such Ethiop words, blacker in their effect   2184
    Alacke, in me, what strange effect   2201
EFFEMINATE = *1
    *youth, greeue, be effeminate, changeable, longing, and   1589
EFFIGIES = 1
    And as mine eye doth his effigies witnesse,   1171
EGGE = *1
    *Clo. Truly thou art damn'd, like an ill roasted Egge, | all on one side.   1235
EGGES = 1
    As a Weazel suckes egges: More, I pre'thee more.   902
EGYPT = 1
    *Ile go sleepe if I can: if I cannot, Ile raile against all | the first borne
    of Egypt.   945
EIE = *2
    *Cel. If I had a thunderbolt in mine eie, I can tell who | should downe.
    Shout.   375
    *Ros. A leane cheeke, which you haue not: a blew eie   1558
EIES = 3*3
    *strength, if you saw your selfe with your eies, or knew   338
    *faire eies, and gentle wishes go with mee to my triall;   349
    Cel. With his eies full of anger.   497
    And sat at good mens feasts, and wip'd our eies   1099
    I thinke she meanes to tangle my eies too: 1817
    *it is, to looke into happines through another mans eies: 2453
EIGHT = 1*1
    *Clo. Ile rime you so, eight yeares together; dinners,   1294
    Here's eight that must take hands,   2702

EINE = 1
If the scorne of your bright eine   2199
EITHER = 2*3
   *to acquaint you withall, that either you might stay him   131
   I wil either be food for it, or bring it for foode to thee: 957
   *Wine comes out of a narrow-mouth'd bottle: either too   1396
   Orl. Which I take to be either a foole, or a Cipher.   1482
   Ros. Those that are in extremity of either, are abho- | minable   1921
EKE *see* eeke
ELDER = 1*1
   Orl. Come, come elder brother, you are too yong in | (this.   55
   And found it was his brother, his elder brother.   2271
ELDEST = *2
   *know you are my eldest brother, and in the gentle con- | dition   47
   Le Beu. The eldest of the three, wrastled with *Charles*   288
ELEGIES = *1
   *barkes; hangs Oades vpon Hauthornes, and Elegies on   1547
ELEUEN = 1
   And after one houre more, 'twill be eleuen,   998
ELSE = 5*7
   Ros. But is there any else longs to see this broken   303
   Duk. I would thou hadst beene son to some man else,   386
   Else had she with her Father rang'd along.   529
   Cor. Else are they very wretched.   852
   Or else a rude despiser of good manners,   1068
   *diuell himselfe will haue no shepherds, I cannot see else | how thou
   shouldst scape.   1281
   Ros. Then there is no true Louer in the Forrest, else   1493
   Ros. Or else shee could not haue the wit to doe this: 2069
   Or else by him my loue denie,   2211
   *which they will climbe incontinent, or else bee inconti- | nent   2447
   Or else refusing me to wed this shepheard: 2598
   *that that no man else will: rich honestie dwels like a mi- | ser   2636
EM = 1
   Come, more, another stanzo: Cal you 'em stanzo's?   907
EMBRACE = *1
   *pray you for your owne sake to embrace your own safe- | tie,   341
EMPLOY = 1
   I will endure; and Ile employ thee too: 1870
EMPLOYD = 1
   Then thine owne gladnesse, that thou art employd.   1872
EMPLOYED = *1
   Oliuer. Marry sir be better employed, and be naught | a while.   38
EMPTIE = 2
   *onely in the world I fil vp a place, which may bee better | supplied,
   when I haue made it emptie.   354
   That in ciuility thou seem'st so emptie?   1069
EMPTY = *1
   *of a cup into a glasse, by filling the one, doth empty the   2384
EMULATION = *1
   *is emulation: nor the Musitians, which is fantasticall;   1927
EMULATOR = *1
   *emulator of euery mans good parts, a secret & villanous   141
ENCHANTINGLY = *1
   *deuise, of all sorts enchantingly beloued, and indeed   163
ENCOUNTER = 1*1
   *you: but that they cal complement is like th'encounter   913

ENCOUNTER *cont*.
*meete; but Mountaines may bee remoou'd with Earth- |quakes, and so
encounter.   1381
ENCOURAGE = 1
Cel. Gentle Cosen, | Let vs goe thanke him, and encourage him: 403
END = 3*7
*they are taught their mannage, and to that end Riders   15
*I hope I shall see an end of him; for my soule (yet   160
*your Ladiships, you may see the end, for the best is yet   278
Amy. Wel, Ile end the song. Sirs, couer the while,   918
At the armes end: I wil heere be with thee presently,   960
But vpon the fairest bowes, | or at euerie sentence end;   1333
*I wil marrie thee: and to that end, I haue bin with Sir   1651
*It is said, many a man knowes no end of his goods;   1661
*right: Many a man has good Hornes, and knows no end   1662
As we do trust, they'l end in true delights. *Exit*   2775
ENDS = 2
That ends this strange euentfull historie,   1143
First, in this Forrest, let vs do those ends   2747
ENDURD = 1*1
*and play false straines vpon thee? not to be en- |dur'd.   2217
That haue endur'd shrew'd daies, and nights with vs,   2750
ENDURE = 1*2
*I will no longer endure it, though yet I know no wise | remedy how to
auoid it.   26
*endure it: therefore allow me such exercises as may be- |come   71
I will endure; and Ile employ thee too: 1870
ENEMIE = 3*1
But I did finde him still mine enemie: 388
The enemie of all your graces liues   722
Heere shall he see no enemie,   896
*enemie, I haue vndone three Tailors, I haue had foure   2623
ENEMIES = 2
Sir, you haue wrastled well, and ouerthrowne | More then your enemies.   420
Their graces serue them but as enemies,   714
ENFORCE = 1
Or with a base and boistrous Sword enforce   736
ENFORCEMENT = 1
Let gentlenesse my strong enforcement be,   1095
ENGAGE = 1
That were with him exil'd. This to be true, | I do engage my life.   2741
ENGENDRED = 1
Of drops, that sacred pity hath engendred: 1100
ENGLAND = *1
*like the old *Robin Hood* of *England*: they say many yong   117
ENIOY = 1*1
*And louing woo? and wooing, she should graunt? And | will you
perseuer to enioy her?   2411
*both, that we may enioy each other: it shall be to your   2417
ENLARGD = 1
With all Graces wide enlarg'd, | nature presently distill'd   1341
ENOUGH = 1*5
Ros. My Fathers loue is enough to honor him enough;   248
Duk. Thou art thy Fathers daughter, there's enough.   519
*holy-day humor, and like enough to consent: What   1982
Iaq. Sing it: 'tis no matter how it bee in tune, so it | make noyse
enough.   2134

ENOUGH *cont*.
Awd. Faith the Priest was good enough, for all the | olde gentlemans
   saying.   2343
ENQUIRE = 1
   The owner of the house I did enquire for?   2239
ENQUIRED = *1
Corin. Mistresse and Master, you haue oft enquired   1754
ENRICH = *1
*him, whose lands and reuenues enrich the new Duke,   104
ENSUE = *1
Cel. Doth it therefore ensue that you should loue his   488
ENTAME = 1
   That can entame my spirits to your worship: 1821
ENTER = 54
   Enter Orlando and Adam.   2
   Enter Oliuer.   28
   Enter Dennis. | *Den*. Calls your worship?   88
   Enter Charles.   96
   Enter Rosalind, and Cellia.   170
   Enter Clowne.   212
   Enter le Beau. | *Ros*. With his mouth full of newes.   257
   Flourish. Enter Duke, Lords, Orlando, Charles, | *and Attendants*.   311
   Enter Le Beu.   426
   Enter Celia and Rosaline.   459
   Enter Duke with Lords.   494
   Enter Duke Senior: Amyens, and two or three Lords | *like Forresters*.   605
   Enter Duke, with Lords.   680
   Enter Orlando and Adam.   703
   Abhorre it, feare it, doe not enter it.   732
   Enter Rosaline for Ganimed, Celia for Aliena, and | *Clowne*, alias
   Touchstone.   782
   Enter Corin and Siluius.   801
   Enter, Amyens, Iaques, & others.   889
   Enter Orlando, & Adam.   950
   Enter Duke Sen. & Lord, like Out-lawes.   972
   Enter Iaques.   980
   Enter Orlando.   1062
   Enter Orlando with Adam.   1146
   Enter Duke, Lords, & Oliuer.   1180
   Enter Orlando.   1200
   Enter Corin & Clowne.   1211
   Enter Rosalind.   1285
   Enter Celia with a writing.   1321
   Enter Orlando & Iaques.   1445
   Enter Clowne, Audrey, & Iaques.   1614
   Enter Sir Oliuer Mar-text.   1672
   Enter Rosalind & Celia.   1709
   Enter Corin.   1753
   Enter Siluius and Phebe.   1770
   Enter Rosalind, Celia, and Corin.   1778
   Enter Rosalind, and Celia, and Iaques.   •   1916
   Enter Orlando.   1941
   Enter Iaques and Lords, Forresters.   2126
   Enter Rosalind and Celia.   2147
   Enter Siluius.   2151
   Enter Oliuer.   2224
   Enter Clowne and Awdrie.   2340

ENTER *cont.*
ENTERPRISE = *1
*would counsel you to a more equall enterprise. We   340
ENTERPRIZE = 1
Both from his enterprize, and from the world: 2738
ENTERTAINE = *1
*him, now loath him: then entertaine him, then forswear   1594
ENTERTAINMENT = 2
Can in this desert place buy entertainment,   856
Who gaue me fresh aray, and entertainment,   2297
ENTRANCES = 1
They haue their *Exits* and their Entrances,   1120
ENTRAP = *1
*poyson, entrap thee by some treacherous deuise, and ne-|uer   147
ENTREAT *see also* intreat = *1
Cha. No, I warrant your Grace you shall not entreat   366
ENTREATED = *1
*bee entreated. Speake to him Ladies, see if you can | mooue him.   324
ENTREATIE = *1
Ros. Then she puts you to entreatie, and there begins | new matter.   1992
ENTREATIES = 1
I should haue giuen him teares vnto entreaties,   401
ENUENOMS = 1
Oh what a world is this, when what is comely | Enuenoms him that
beares it?   717
ENUIE = *1
*that I weare; owe no man hate, enuie no mans happi-|nesse: 1271
ENUIOUS = 2*1
*yong fellow of France, full of ambition, an enuious   140
My Fathers rough and enuious disposition   405
More free from perill then the enuious Court?   610
EPILOGUE = *3
Ros. It is not the fashion to see the Ladie the Epi-|logue: 2776
*no bush, 'tis true, that a good play needes no Epilogue.   2779
*What a case am I in then, that am neither a good Epi-|logue,   2782
EPILOGUES = *1
*playes proue the better by the helpe of good Epilogues: 2781
EQUALL = *1
*would counsel you to a more equall enterprise. We   340
EQUALLY = 1
*from her wheele, that her gifts may henceforth bee | bestowed equally.   201
ERE = 5*1
Ere he should thus haue ventur'd.   402
And ere we haue thy youthfull wages spent,   771
Cor. I partly guesse: for I haue lou'd ere now.   806

ERE *cont*.
Of sterne command'ment. But what ere you are   1086
*for you'l be rotten ere you bee halfe ripe, and that's | the right vertue
of the Medler.   1317
It was a crest ere thou wast borne,   2141
EREWHILE = *1
Cor. That yong Swaine that you saw heere but ere-|while,   874
ERRAND = 1
Sil. My errand is to you, faire youth,   2154
ERRING = 1
Some, how briefe the Life of man | runs his erring pilgrimage,   1327
ERST = 1
Thy company, which erst was irkesome to me   1869
ESCAPES = *1
*wrastle for my credit, and hee that escapes me without   126
ESPECIALLY = *1
*so much in the heart of the world, and especially of my   164
ESTATE = *2
Ros. Well, I will forget the condition of my estate, | to reioyce in
yours.   184
*was old Sir *Rowlands* will I estate vpon you, and heere | liue and die a
Shepherd.   2419
ESTEEMD = 1
The world esteem'd thy father honourable,   387
ESTEEME = *1
*do I labor for a greater esteeme then may in some   2465
ETHIOP = 1
Such Ethiop words, blacker in their effect   2184
EUEN *see also* eauen = 10*4
Oli. Is it euen so, begin you to grow vpon me? I will   85
Ros. Is yonder the man? | *Le Beu*. Euen he, Madam.   315
Euen till I shrinke with cold, I smile, and say   615
Euen with the hauing, it is not so with thee: 766
Ros. Peace I say; good euen to your friend.   853
1.*Lord*. My Lord, he is but euen now gone hence,   975
Euen by the squandring glances of the foole.   1031
Seeking the bubble Reputation | Euen in the Canons mouth: And then,
the Iustice   1131
*of his owne getting; hornes, euen so poore men alone: 1664
Clo. Good euen good Mr what ye cal't: how do you   1681
*companie, I am verie glad to see you, euen a toy in hand   1683
Ros. I haue promis'd to make all this matter euen: 2594
To make these doubts all euen. *Exit Ros. and Celia*.   2601
Euen daughter welcome, in no lesse degree.   2723
EUENING *see* euen, eu'n
EUENTFULL = 1
That ends this strange euentfull historie,   1143
EUENTS = 1
'Tis I must make conclusion | Of these most strange euents: 2700
EUER *see also* ere = 20*7
*loues her, being euer from their Cradles bred together,   109
*come to morrow, Ile giue him his payment: if euer hee   156
euer he saw those Pancakes, or that Mustard.   245
*first time that euer I heard breaking of ribbes was sport | for Ladies.   300
And she beleeues where euer they are gone   695
As euer sigh'd vpon a midnight pillow: 809
But if thy loue were euer like to mine,   810

EUER *cont*.

That euer loue did make thee run into, | Thou hast not lou'd.	817
Iaq. Well then, if euer I thanke any man, Ile thanke	912
If euer you haue look'd on better dayes:	1090
If euer beene where bels haue knoll'd to Church:	1091
If euer sate at any good mans feast:	1092
If euer from your eye-lids wip'd a teare,	1093
Was't euer in Court, Shepheard? | *Cor*. No truly.	1231
Orl. Did you euer cure any so?	1585
Your Chessenut was euer the onely colour:	1722
Sil. O deere *Phebe*, | If euer (as that euer may be neere)	1799
Who euer lov'd, that lou'd not at first sight?	1854
Sil. Where euer sorrow is, reliefe would be:	1859
Orl. For euer, and a day.	2054
Ros. Say a day, without the euer: no, no *Orlando*, men	2055
Did you euer heare such railing?	2195
But kindnesse, nobler euer then reuenge,	2280
*me altogether: I wil marrie you, if euer I marrie Wo-|man,	2519
*if euer I satisfi'd man, and you shall bee married to mor-|row.	2521
Orl. My Lord, the first time that I euer saw him,	2604

EUERIE = 8*6

That euerie eye, which in this Forrest lookes,	1207
Tonges Ile hang on euerie tree, | that shall ciuill sayings shoe.	1325
But vpon the fairest bowes, | or at euerie sentence end;	1333
The quintessence of euerie sprite, | heauen would in little show.	1337
*sighing euerie minute, and groaning euerie houre wold	1494
*one another, as halfepence are, euerie one fault seeming	1541
*sleeue vnbutton'd, your shoo vnti'de, and euerie thing	1564
*me his Loue, his Mistris: and I set him euerie day	1587
*of teares, full of smiles; for euerie passion something, and	1591
and come euerie day to my Coat, and woe me.	1604
'Tis Hymen peoples euerie towne,	2718
To Hymen, God of euerie Towne.	2721
Duke Frederick hearing how that euerie day	2730

EUERY = 5*5

*Gentlemen flocke to him euery day, and fleet the time	118
*emulator of euery mans good parts, a secret & villanous	141
Clo. Thus men may grow wiser euery day. It is the	299
Sermons in stones, and good in euery thing.	623
Sans teeth, sans eyes, sans taste, sans euery thing.	1145
Shall see thy vertue witnest euery where.	1208
Run, run *Orlando*, carue on euery Tree,	1209
*fellowes, and betray themselues to euery mo-|derne censure, worse	
then drunkards.	1922
*madnesse, that blinde rascally boy, that abuses euery	2119
And after, euery of this happie number	2749

EUERYTHING *see* euery

EUILS = 2*1

And all th'imbossed sores, and headed euils,	1041
Opprest with two weake euils, age, and hunger,	1109
Orl. Can you remember any of the principall euils,	1538

EUN = 3*1

Will. Good eu'n *Audrey*.	2354
Aud. God ye good eu'n *William*.	2355
Will. And good eu'n to you Sir.	2356
Clo. Good eu'n gentle friend. Couer thy head, couer	2357

EWES = *3
*Cor. Why we are still handling our Ewes, and their | Fels you know
are greasie.   1250
*and the greatest of my pride, is to see my Ewes graze, & | my Lambes
sucke.   1273
*Ewes and the Rammes together, and to offer to get your   1276
EX = *1
*he would not haue spoke such a word. Ex. Orl. Ad.   84
EXAMINES = *1
*Ros. Well, Time is the olde Iustice that examines all   2105
EXCEEDED = 1
But iustly as you haue exceeded all promise, | Your Mistris shall be
happie.   408.
EXCELLENT = 2*3
*Le Beu. Three proper yong men, of excellent growth | and presence. 284
*so faire and excellent Ladies anie thing. But let your   348
Ros. Oh excellent yong man.   374
Cel. An excellent colour.   1721
*Cle. So, so, is good, very good, very excellent good: 2368
EXCEPTED = *1
*and suppers, and sleeping hours excepted: it is the right | Butter-
womens ranke to Market.   1295
EXCUSE = 4
excuse for me heereafter, to leaue my wife.   1698
Orl. And what wit could wit haue, to excuse that?   2078
To tell this story, that you might excuse   2307
How you excuse my brother, Rosalind.   2335
EXECUTIONER = 2
In bitternesse; the common executioner   1773
Phe. I would not be thy executioner,   1779
EXEMPT = 1
And this our life exempt from publike haunt,   621
EXERCISES = *1
*endure it: therefore allow me such exercises as may be- | come   71
EXEUNT = 19
To libertie, and not to banishment. Exeunt.   603
1.Lor. Ile bring you to him strait. Exeunt.   678
To bring againe these foolish runawaies. Exeunt.   701
Then to die well, and not my Masters debter. Exeunt.   780
And buy it with your Gold right sodainly. Exeunt.   887
His banket is prepar'd. Exeunt   948
Cheerely good Adam. Exeunt   970
And let me all your fortunes vnderstand. Exeunt.   1178
Do this expediently, and turne him going. Exeunt   1198
*Ros. Nay, you must call mee Rosalind: Come sister, | will you go?
Exeunt.   1611
all shal flout me out of my calling. Exeunt   1707
Ile proue a busie actor in their play. Exeunt.   1768
Goe with me Siluius. Exeunt.   1914
Cel. And Ile sleepe. Exeunt.   2124
Is not a thing to laugh to scorne. Exeunt.   2145
my counterfeiting to him: will you goe? | Exeunt.   2337
Clo. Trip Audry, trip Audry, I attend, | I attend. Exeunt   2405
Sil. Ile not faile, if I liue. | Phe. Nor I. | Orl. Nor I. Exeunt. 2527
*such a foolish song. God buy you, and God mend your | voices. Come
Audrie. Exeunt.   2570

EXILD = 1
That were with him exil'd. This to be true, | I do engage my life.   2741
EXILE = *3
*Lords haue put themselues into voluntary exile with   103
*that hee would haue followed her exile, or haue died to   110
*Duk .Sen. Now my Coe-mates, and brothers in exile: 607
EXIT see also Ex. = 17
so God keepe your worship. Exit.   158
*cleare all: nothing remaines, but that I kindle the boy | thither, which
now Ile goe about. Exit.   167
I would thou had'st told me of another Father. | Exit Duke.   392
Cel. Will you goe Coze? | Ros. Haue with you: fare you well. Exit.   422
But heauenly Rosaline. Exit   457
And in the greatnesse of my word you die. | Exit Duke, &c.   550
O Phebe, Phebe, Phebe. Exit.   825
The faire, the chaste, and vnexpressiue shee. Exit   1210
*though not with bagge and baggage, yet with | scrip and scrippage.
Exit.   1359
Come, to our flocke, Exit.   1852
such offenders, and let time try: adieu. Exit.   2106
*true louer hence, and not a word; for here comes more | company.
Exit. Sil.   2222
Aud. Do good William. | Will. God rest you merry sir. Exit   2400
To make these doubts all euen. Exit Ros. and Celia.   2601
Ile stay to know, at your abandon'd caue. Exit.   2773
As we do trust, they'l end in true delights. Exit   2775
offer, when I make curt'sie, bid me farewell. Exit.   2796
EXITS = 1
They haue their Exits and their Entrances,   1120
EXPEDIENTLY = 1
Do this expediently, and turne him going. Exeunt   1198
EXPERIENCE = 1*2
Iaq. Yes, I haue gain'd my experience.   1940
*Ros. And your experience makes you sad: I had ra-|ther   1942
*haue a foole to make me merrie, then experience to   1943
EXPRESSE = *1
*Orl. Neither rime nor reason can expresse how much.   1579
EXTENT = 1
And let my officers of such a nature | Make an extent vpon his house
and Lands: 1196
EXTERMIND = 1
By giuing loue your sorrow, and my griefe | Were both extermin'd.   1861
EXTRACTED = *1
*of many simples, extracted from many obiects,   1932
EXTRAORDINARY = *1
*learne mee how to remember any extraordinary plea-|sure.   175
EXTREMEST = 1
Stood on th'extremest verge of the swift brooke, | Augmenting it with
teares.   649
EXTREMITY = 1*1
*Ros. Those that are in extremity of either, are abho-|minable   1921
And turn'd into the extremity of loue.   2172
EXULT = 1
That you insult, exult, and all at once   1809
EYE see also eie = 10
And looking on it, with lacke-lustre eye,   994
And as mine eye doth his effigies witnesse,   1171

EYE *cont*.

With thy chaste eye, from thy pale spheare aboue	1203
That euerie eye, which in this Forrest lookes,	1207
Thou tellst me there is murder in mine eye,	1781
Now shew the wound mine eye hath made in thee,	1791
Did make offence, his eye did heale it vp:	1891
Whiles the eye of man did wooe me,	2196
Oli. If that an eye may profit by a tongue,	2233
Loe what befell: he threw his eye aside,	2253

EYES *see also* eies = 11*2

With eyes seuere, and beard of formall cut,	1134
Sans teeth, sans eyes, sans taste, sans euery thing.	1145
Of manie faces, eyes, and hearts, | to haue the touches deerest pris'd.	1349
That eyes that are the frailst, and softest things,	1783
And if mine eyes can wound, now let them kill thee:	1787
Lye not, to say mine eyes are murtherers:	1790
The Cicatrice and capable impressure | Thy palme some moment keepes: but now mine eyes	1794
Nor I am sure there is no force in eyes | That can doe hurt.	1797
He said mine eyes were black, and my haire blacke,	1904
nothing, is to haue rich eyes and poore hands.	1939
*ones eyes, because his owne are out, let him bee iudge,	2120
Orl. Wounded it is, but with the eyes of a Lady.	2434
*to set her before your eyes to morrow, humane as she is, | and without any danger.	2475

EYE-BALLS = 1

Your bugle eye-balls, nor your cheeke of creame	1820

EYE-BROW = 1

Made to his Mistresse eye-brow. Then, a Soldier,	1128

EYE-LIDS = 1

If euer from your eye-lids wip'd a teare,	1093

FACE = 4

And with a kinde of vmber smirch my face,	576
And shining morning face, creeping like snaile	1125
Most truly limn'd, and liuing in your face,	1172
Let no face bee kept in mind, | but the faire of Rosalinde.	1292

FACES = 1*1

Of manie faces, eyes, and hearts, | to haue the touches deerest pris'd.	1349
*beards, or good faces, or sweet breaths, will for my kind	2795

FACTION = *1

*with thee in faction, I will ore-run thee with policie: I	2397

FAILE = 2

And you within it: if he faile of that	728
Sil. Ile not faile, if I liue. | *Phe*. Nor I. | *Orl*. Nor I. *Exeunt*.	2527

FAINE = 1*2

*youth, I would faine disswade him, but he will not	323
Iaq. I would faine see this meeting.	1655
Orl. What's that? | *Ros*. Why hornes: w such as you are faine to be be-|holding	1972

FAINING = *1

Clo. No trulie: for the truest poetrie is the most fai-|ning,	1630

FAINT = 1

I faint almost to death.	847

FAINTED = 1

Which all this while had bled: and now he fainted,	2302

FAINTING = 1

And cride in fainting vpon *Rosalinde*.	2303

FAINTS = 1
Here's a yong maid with trauaile much oppressed, | And faints for
succour.   858
FAIRE = 13*11
*better, for besides that they are faire with their feeding,   14
*Cel. 'Tis true, for those that she makes faire, she scarce   206
*Cel. No; when Nature hath made a faire creature,   213
Le Beu. Faire Princesse, | you haue lost much good sport.   264
*Orl. No faire Princesse: he is the generall challenger,   333
*so faire and excellent Ladies anie thing. But let your   348
*faire eies, and gentle wishes go with mee to my triall;   349
Shall we goe Coze? | Cel. I: fare you well faire Gentleman.   413
Cor. Faire Sir, I pittie her,   860
And sayes, if Ladies be but yong, and faire,   1010
In faire round belly, with good Capon lin'd,   1133
The faire, the chaste, and vnexpressiue shee. Exit   1210
Let no face bee kept in mind, | but the faire of Rosalinde.   1292
*Orl. Faire youth, I would I could make thee beleeue | (I Loue.   1569
*Aud. Well, I am not faire, and therefore I pray the | Gods make me
honest.   1643
*Orl. My faire Rosalind, I come within an houre of my | promise.   1957
*haue liu'd manie a faire yeere though Hero had turn'd   2012
Sil. My errand is to you, faire youth,   2154
Shee saies I am not faire, that I lacke manners,   2163
*Oliu. Good morrow, faire ones: pray you, (if you | know)   2225
Such garments, and such yeeres: the boy is faire,   2235
Will. William, sir. | Clo. A faire name. Was't borne i'th Forrest heere? 2362
Ros. God saue you brother. | Ol. And you faire sister.   2427
That bring these tidings to this faire assembly.   2729
FAIRELY = 1
Thou offer'st fairely to thy brothers wedding: 2744
FAIREST = 2
All the pictures fairest Linde, | are but blacke to Rosalinde: 1290
But vpon the fairest bowes, | or at euerie sentence end;   1333
FAITH see also i'faith = 9*7
Ros. No faith, hate him not for my sake.   492
*Iaq. I thanke you for your company, but good faith   1448
*Orlan. Now by the faith of my loue, I will; Tel me | where it is.   1605
As by my faith, I see no more in you   1811
No faith proud Mistresse, hope not after it,   1818
*Ros. A Traueller: by my faith you haue great rea-|son   1936
*Ros. No faith, die by Attorney: the poore world is   2006
Ros. Yes faith will I, fridaies and saterdaies, and all.   2026
*Awd. Faith the Priest was good enough, for all the | olde gentlemans
saying.   2343
Art rich? | Will. 'Faith sir, so, so.   2366
Sil. It is to be all made of faith and seruice, | And so am I for Phebe.   2496
2.Pa. I faith, y'faith, and both in a tune like two | gipsies on a horse. 2544
*Clo. 'Faith we met, and found the quarrel was vpon | the seuenth
cause.   2626
*Du Se. By my faith, he is very swift, and sententious   2639
Thy faith, my fancie to thee doth combine.   2725
you to a loue, that your true faith doth merit: 2765
FAITHFUL = 1
you are there followed by a faithful shepheard,   2488
FAITHFULL = 3
I will your very faithfull Feeder be,   886

74

FAITHFULL *cont.*
Will the faithfull offer take   2209
You'l giue your selfe to this most faithfull Shepheard.   2589
FAITHFULLY = 1
As you haue whisper'd faithfully you were,   1170
FALCON = *1
*and the Falcon her bels, so man hath his desires, and as   1687
FALL = 7*6
*in disguis'd against mee to try a fall: to morrow sir I   125
*may she not by Fortune fall into the fire? though nature   214
Duk. You shall trie but one fall.   365
*in dispight of a fall: but turning these iests out of seruice,   483
*you should fall into so strong a liking with old Sir | *Roulands* yongest
sonne?   485
Du Sen. Welcome, fall too: I wil not trouble you,   1152
*go as softly as foot can fall, he thinkes himselfe too soon | there.   1517
Now counterfeit to swound, why now fall downe,   1788
Fall in loue with my anger. If it be so, as fast   1840
Ros. I pray you do not fall in loue with mee,   1844
To fall in loue with him: but for my part   1900
And fall into our Rusticke Reuelrie: 2754
With measure heap'd in ioy, to'th Measures fall.   2756
FALLING = 1
let me see, what thinke you of falling in Loue?   194
FALLS = 1
Falls not the axe vpon the humbled neck,   1775
FALNE = 1*1
Ros. Hees falne in loue with your foulnesse, & shee'll   1839
Meane time, forget this new-falne dignitie,   2753
FALSE = *3
*This is the verie false gallop of Verses, why doe you in- | fect your selfe
with them?   1311
*confirmer of false reckonings, he attends here in the for- | rest on the
Duke your father.   1740
*and play false straines vpon thee? not to be en- | dur'd.   2217
FALSER = 1
For I am falser then vowes made in wine: 1845
FANCIE = 3
You meet in some fresh cheeke the power of fancie,   1801
Chewing the food of sweet and bitter fancie,   2252
Thy faith, my fancie to thee doth combine.   2725
FANCIE-MONGER = *1
*If I could meet that Fancie-monger, I would giue him   1549
FANGE *see* phange
FANGLED = 1
*clamorous then a Parrat against raine, more new-fang- | led   2060
FANTASIE = 2
Hast thou beene drawne to by thy fantasie?   813
Sil. It is to be all made of fantasie,   2501
FANTASTICAL = *2
*liking, proud, fantastical, apish, shallow, inconstant, ful   1590
Ol. Tis no matter; Ne're a fantastical knaue of them   1706
FANTASTICALL – *1
*is emulation: nor the Musitians, which is fantasticall;   1927
FARE = 5*2
Ros. Fare you well: praie heauen I be deceiu'd in you.   359
But fare thee well, thou art a gallant youth,   391

75

FARE *cont*.
Shall we goe Coze? | *Cel*. I: fare you well faire Gentleman.   413
Cel. Will you goe Coze? | *Ros*. Haue with you: fare you well. *Exit*.   422
Will sodainly breake forth: Sir, fare you well,   451
Orl. I rest much bounden to you: fare you well.   454
*woman, Ile meet: so fare you wel: I haue left you com-|mands.   2525
FAREWEL = *1
*Farewel good Mr *Oliuer*: Not O sweet *Oliuer*, O braue   1703
FAREWELL *see also* fare = 1*3
*Farewell good *Charles*. Now will I stirre this Game-|ster: 159
Iaq. Ile tarrie no longer with you, farewell good sig-|nior Loue.   1483
Ros. Farewell Mounsieur Trauellor: looke you   1948
offer, when I make curt'sie, bid me farewell. *Exit*.   2796
FAREYOUWELL = 1
So take her to thee Shepheard, fareyouwell.   1836
FARRE = 1
(Maides as we are) to trauell forth so farre?   573
FARWEL = 1
And measure out my graue. Farwel kinde master.   953
FASHION = 4*2
Orlando. | *As I remember *Adam*, it was vpon this fashion   3
'Tis iust the fashion; wherefore doe you looke   664
Thou art not for the fashion of these times,   763
Ros. *Ioue*, *Ioue*, this Shepherds passion, | Is much vpon my fashion.   841
Orl. And so had I: but yet for fashion sake   1450
Ros. It is not the fashion to see the Ladie the Epi-|logue: 2776
FAST = 2*1
Fall in loue with my anger. If it be so, as fast   1840
Ros. I, but when? | *Orl*. Why now, as fast as she can marrie vs.   2042
Cel. Or rather bottomlesse, that as fast as you poure | affection in, it
runs out.   2115
FASTER = 1
Is his complexion: and faster then his tongue   1890
FASTING = 1
And thanke heauen, fasting, for a good mans loue;   1831
FAT = 1*1
Sweepe on you fat and greazie Citizens,   663
*good pasture makes fat sheepe: and that a great cause of   1226
FATHER = 17*20
*grieues me, and the spirit of my Father, which I thinke   24
*of my father in mee, as you, albeit I confesse your com-|ming   52
Rowland de Boys, he was my father, and he is thrice a vil-|laine   58
*that saies such a father begot villaines: wert thou   59
*father charg'd you in his will to giue me good educati-|on: 67
*of my father growes strong in mee, and I will no longer   70
*father left me by testament, with that I will goe buy my | fortunes.   73
Oli. Can you tell if *Rosalind* the Dukes daughter bee | banished with
her Father?   106
*could teach me to forget a banished father, you must not   174
*waight that I loue thee; if my Vncle thy banished father   178
*had banished thy Vncle the Duke my Father, so thou   179
*to take thy father for mine; so wouldst thou, if the truth   181
Cel. You know my Father hath no childe, but I, nor   186
*be his heire; for what hee hath taken away from thy fa-|ther   188
Clow. Mistresse, you must come away to your father.   226
Clo. One that old *Fredericke* your Father loues.   247
*third: yonder they lie, the poore old man their Father,   292

FATHER *cont*.

The world esteem'd thy father honourable,	387
I would thou had'st told me of another Father. | *Exit Duke*.	392
Cel. Were I my Father (Coze) would I do this?	394
Ros. My Father lou'd Sir *Roland* as his soule,	398
Cel. But is all this for your Father?	469
Ros. No, some of it is for my childes Father: Oh	470
Ros. The Duke my Father lou'd his Father deerelie.	487
*him, for my father hated his father deerely; yet I hate | not *Orlando*.	490
What's that to me, my Father was no Traitor,	524
Else had she with her Father rang'd along.	529
No, let my Father seeke another heire:	563
Of him I was about to call his Father:	725
The thriftie hire I saued vnder your Father,	743
That lou'd your Father, the residue of your fortune,	1174
*confirmer of false reckonings, he attends here in the for- | rest on the Duke your father.	1740
Thy fathers father wore it,	2142
And thy father bore it,	2143
Ros. Ile haue no Father, if you be not he:	2696

FATHERS = 6*5

Adam. Sweet Masters bee patient, for your Fathers | remembrance, be at accord.	63
Ros. My Fathers loue is enough to honor him enough;	248
And all the world was of my Fathers minde,	399
My Fathers rough and enuious disposition	405
And pittie her, for her good Fathers sake;	449
Duk. Thou art thy Fathers daughter, there's enough.	519
Wilt thou change Fathers? I will giue thee mine:	553
The clownish Foole out of your Fathers Court:	595
*But what talke wee of Fathers, when there is such a man | as *Orlando*?	1745
Thy fathers father wore it,	2142
*good: for my fathers house, and all the reuennew, that	2418

FATHOME = *1

*didst know how many fathome deepe I am in loue: but	2112

FAULT = 4*2

Ros. I doe beseech your Grace | Let me the knowledge of my fault beare with me:	505
Iaq. The worst fault you haue, is to be in loue.	1474
Orl. 'Tis a fault I will not change, for your best ver- | tue: I am wearie of you.	1475
*one another, as halfepence are, euerie one fault seeming	1541
monstrous, til his fellow-fault came to match it.	1542
*make her fault her husbands occasion, let her neuer nurse	2082

FAULTS = 1

against whom I know most faults.	1473

FAUORD = *1

*and blood breakes: a poore virgin sir, an il-fauor'd thing	2634

FAUOUR = 2

Of femall fauour, and bestowes himselfe | Like a ripe sister: the woman low	2236
Some liuely touches of my daughters fauour.	2603

FAUOURD = 1*1

Clo. No truly, vnlesse thou wert hard fauour'd: for	1639
That makes the world full of ill-fauourd children:	1826

FAUOUREDLY = 1
*Orl. I pray you marre no moe of my verses with rea-|ding them
ill-fauouredly.   1456
FAWNE = 1
Whiles (like a Doe) I go to finde my Fawne,   1105
FAYNING = 1
Most frendship, is fayning; most Louing, meere folly: 1161
FEARE = 4*2
*your selfe with your iudgment, the feare of your aduen-|ture   339
Lye there what hidden womans feare there will,   584
Abhorre it, feare it, doe not enter it.   732
*to be sad: I feare you haue sold your owne Lands,   1937
As those that feare they hope, and know they feare.   2578
FEARFUL = *1
*Clo. Amen. A man may if he were of a fearful heart,   1657
FEAST = 1
If euer sate at any good mans feast: 1092
FEASTS = 1
And sat at good mens feasts, and wip'd our eies   1099
FEATURE = 1
Doth my simple feature content you?   1617
FEATURES = *2
*Aud. Your features, Lord warrant vs: what features?   1618
FEED = 2*2
*Cel. Which he will put on vs, as Pigeons feed their | young.   259
Bring vs where we may rest our selues, and feed: 857
That you will feed on: but what is, come see,   871
*Du Sen. Sit downe and feed, & welcom to our table   1082
FEEDE = 4*1
*me: hee lets mee feede with his Hindes, barres mee the   21
Take that, and he that doth the Rauens feede,   747
Besides his Coate, his Flockes, and bounds of feede   868
*Du Sen. Welcome: set downe your venerable bur-|then, and let him
feede.   1147
Feede your selues with questioning: 2712
FEEDER = 1
I will your very faithfull Feeder be,   886
FEEDETH = 1
The sight of Louers feedeth those in loue: 1766
FEEDING = *1
*better, for besides that they are faire with their feeding,   14
FEELE = 1*1
Heere feele we not the penaltie of *Adam*,   611
*Clo. Your lips wil feele them the sooner. Shallow a-|gen: a more
sounder instance, come.   1257
FEELES = *1
*he feeles no paine: the one lacking the burthen of   1511
FEELINGLY = 1
That feelingly perswade me what I am: 617
FEET = *2
*Cel. That's no matter: the feet might beare y verses.   1365
*Ros. I, but the feet were lame, and could not beare   1366
FEETE = *1
*of them had in them more feete then the Verses would | beare.   1363
FEIGNE = 1*1
*sweare in Poetrie, may be said as Louers, they do feigne.   1632
*Now if thou wert a Poet, I might haue some hope | thou didst feigne.   1636

FEILD = 1
That o're the greene corne feild did passe,   2549
FEL = *1
'*well: for there he fel in loue. I haue heard him read ma-|ny   1534
FELL = 1*1
Ros. He cals vs back: my pride fell with my fortunes,   418
Who quickly fell before him, in which hurtling   2283
FELLOW = 2*4
*yong fellow of France, full of ambition, an enuious   140
Cel. I would I were inuisible, to catch the strong fel-|low by the legge.
Wrastle.   372
*this fellow wil but ioyne you together, as they ioyne   1692
Ros They say you are a melancholly fellow.   1919
Iaq. How seuenth cause? Good my Lord, like this | fellow.   2628
Iaq. Is not this a rare fellow my Lord? He's as good   2677
FELLOWES = *1
*fellowes, and betray themselues to euery mo-|derne censure, worse
then drunkards.   1922
FELLOW-FAULT = 1
monstrous, til his fellow-fault came to match it.   1542
FELS = 1
Cor. Why we are still handling our Ewes, and their | Fels you know
are greasie.   1250
FEMALE = *2
*societie: which in the boorish, is companie, of this fe-|male: 2390
*is, abandon the society of this Female, or Clowne   2392
FEMALL = 1
Of femall fauour, and bestowes himselfe | Like a ripe sister: the woman
low   2236
FENCD = 1
A sheep-coat, fenc'd about with Oliue-trees.   2227
FETCH = *2
Duk. Send to his brother, fetch that gallant hither,   697
Clo. Come apace good *Audrey*, I wil fetch vp your   1615
FIE = *1
Du Sen. Fie on thee. I can tell what thou wouldst do.   1036
FIELDS = *1
*in respect it is in the fields, it pleaseth mee well: but in   1217
FIFT = *1
*the Reproofe valiant: the fift, the Counterchecke quar-|relsome: 2668
FIFTY = *1
*will kill thee a hundred and fifty wayes, therefore trem-|ble and
depart.   2398
FIGURE = 1*1
Iaq. There I shal see mine owne figure.   1481
*it is a figure in Rhetoricke, that drink being powr'd out   2383
FIL = *1
*onely in the world I fil vp a place, which may bee better | supplied,
when I haue made it emptie.   354
FILLD = 1
Therefore heauen Nature charg'd, | that one bodie should be fill'd   1339
FILLING = *1
*of a cup into a glasse, by filling the one, doth empty the   2384
FIND = *1
Phe. Dead Shepheard, now I find thy saw of might,   1853
FINDE = 9*5
*thou shalt finde I will most kindly requite: I had my   136

FINDE *cont*.

But I did finde him still mine enemie:	388
Ile make him finde him: do this sodainly;	699
Ros. I could finde in my heart to disgrace my mans	787
And little wreakes to finde the way to heauen | By doing deeds of hospitalitie.	866
For I can no where finde him, like a man.	974
Whiles (like a Doe) I go to finde my Fawne,	1105
Duke Sen. Go finde him out,	1111
Finde out thy brother wheresoere he is,	1185
He that sweetest rose will finde, | *must finde Loues pricke, & Rosalinde*.	1309
*out of the sight of *Orlando*: Ile goe finde a shadow, and | sigh till he come.	2122
Clow. We shall finde a time *Awdrie*, patience gen- |tle *Awdrie*.	2341
Iaq. But for the seuenth cause. How did you finde	2642

FINDES = *1

*Findes tongues in trees, bookes in the running brookes,	622

FINDING = *1

*propositions of a Louer: but take a taste of my finding	1427

FINER = *1

Orl. Your accent is something finer, then you could | purchase in so remoued a dwelling.	1529

FINGER = *1

*as his finger. And thou wert best looke to't; for if thou	144

FINIS *l*.2797 = 1

FINISH = 1

How thus we met, and these things finish.	2714

FIRE = *2

*may she not by Fortune fall into the fire? though nature	214
*the propertie of raine is to wet, and fire to burne: That	1225

FIRME = 1

Firme, and irreuocable is my doombe,	544

FIRST = 11*5

*nations allowes you my better, in that you are the first	49
*first time that euer I heard breaking of ribbes was sport | for Ladies.	300
*him to a second, that haue so mightilie perswaded him | from a first.	367
First, for his weeping into the needlesse streame;	654
*Ile go sleepe if I can: if I cannot, Ile raile against all | the first borne of Egypt.	945
Orl. You touch'd my veine at first, the thorny point	1070
Limpt in pure loue: till he be first suffic'd,	1108
His Acts being seuen ages. At first the Infant,	1122
Cel. You must borrow me Gargantuas mouth first:	1419
But first begs pardon: will you sterner be	1776
Who euer lov'd, that lou'd not at first sight?	1854
Ros. Nay, you were better speake first, and when you	1986
When from the first to last betwixt vs two,	2293
Orl. My Lord, the first time that I euer saw him,	2604
*The first, the Retort courteous: the second, the	2666
First, in this Forrest, let vs do those ends	2747

FITS = 1*1

Du Sen. Show me the place, | I loue to cope him in these sullen fits,	675
*life (looke you) it fits my humor well: but as there is no	1219

FITTEST = 1

Deuise the fittest time, and safest way	600

FIUE = 2

Ad. But do not so: I haue fiue hundred Crownes,	742

FIUE *cont*.

Will. Fiue and twentie Sir. | *Clo*. A ripe age: Is thy name *William*? 2360
FLATTERING = *1
   *thought no lesse: that flattering tongue of yours wonne 2090
FLATTERS = 1
   'Tis not her glasse, but you that flatters her, 1827
FLATTERY = 1
   This is no flattery: these are counsellors 616
FLATTRED = *1
   *purgation, I haue trod a measure, I haue flattred a Lady, 2621
FLEECES = 1
   And do not sheere the Fleeces that I graze: 864
FLEET = *1
   *Gentlemen flocke to him euery day, and fleet the time 118
FLESH = 1*1
   *of a good peece of flesh indeed: learne of the wise 1263
   The Lyonnesse had torne some flesh away, 2301
FLIE = 1*2
   Therefore deuise with me how we may flie 564
   Ros. By this hand, it will not kill a flie: but come, 2022
   *'twill out at the key-hole: stop that, 'twill flie with the | smoake out at
the chimney. 2072
FLIES = 1
   Why then my taxing like a wild-goose flies 1060
FLIGHT = 1
   After my flight: now goe in we content 602
FLOCKE = 2*2
   *Gentlemen flocke to him euery day, and fleet the time 118
   Ros. What is he that shall buy his flocke and pasture? 873
   Buy thou the Cottage, pasture, and the flocke, 878
   Come, to our flocke, *Exit*. 1852
FLOCKES – 1
   Besides his Coate, his Flockes, and bounds of feede 868
FLOOD = *1
   Iaq. There is sure another flood toward, and these 2612
FLOURISH = 1
   Flourish. Enter Duke, Lords, Orlando, Charles, | and Attendants. 311
FLOUT = 1*1
   *hath giuen vs wit to flout at Fortune, hath not Fortune 215
   all shal flout me out of my calling. *Exeunt* 1707
FLOUTING = 1
   for: we shall be flouting: we cannot hold. 2353
FLOW = 1
   Doth it not flow as hugely as the Sea, 1046
FLOWER = 1
   How that a life was but a Flower, | In spring time, &c. 2563
FLUXE = 1*1
   The Fluxe of companie: anon a carelesse Heard 660
   *verie vncleanly fluxe of a Cat. Mend the instance Shep-|heard. 1265
FLYE = 1
   I flye thee, for I would not iniure thee: 1780
FOGGY = 1
   Like foggy South, puffing with winde and raine, 1823
FOILD = *1
   *wherein if I bee foil'd, there is but one sham'd that was 350
FOILE = 1
   That did but lately foile the synowie *Charles*, 694

FOLKS = 1
These prettie Country folks would lie. | In spring time, &c. 2559
FOLLOW = 2
Ad. Master goe on, and I will follow thee 773
You foolish Shepheard, wherefore do you follow her 1822
FOLLOWED = 1*1
*that hee would haue followed her exile, or haue died to 110
you are there followed by a faithful shepheard, 2488
FOLLOWERS = 1
Inuite the Duke, and all's contented followers: 2424
FOLLY = 7*1
If thou remembrest not the slightest folly, 816
nature, so is all nature in loue, mortall in folly. 837
And they that are most gauled with my folly, 1024
The Wise-mans folly is anathomiz'd 1030
His folly to the mettle of my speech, 1056
Most frendship, is fayning: most Louing, meere folly: 1161
youth mounts, and folly guides: who comes heere? 1752
**Du Se*. He vses his folly like a stalking-horse, and vn-|der 2679
FOND = 1
Why would you be so fond to ouercome 710
FOOD = 8*1
**Orl*. What, would'st thou haue me go & beg my food, 735
Seeking the food he eates, 929
O I die for food. Heere lie I downe, 952
I wil either be food for it, or bring it for foode to thee: 957
Orl. I almost die for food, and let me haue it. 1081
Orl. Then but forbeare your food a little while: 1104
And giue it food. There is an old poore man, 1106
Chewing the food of sweet and bitter fancie, 2252
Food to the suck'd and hungry Lyonnesse? 2278
FOODE = 3
If he for gold will giue vs any foode, 846
I wil either be food for it, or bring it for foode to thee: 957
As I do liue by foode, I met a foole, 987
FOOLE = 28*8
sent in this foole to cut off the argument? 216
*our whetstone: for alwaies the dulnesse of the foole, is 223
Ros. Where learned you that oath foole? 229
Thou art a foole, she robs thee of thy name, 541
**Duk*. You are a foole: you Neice prouide your selfe, 548
The clownish Foole out of your Fathers Court: 595
In pitteous chase: and thus the hairie foole, 647
**Clo.* I, now am I in *Arden*, the more foole I, when I 798
Clo. Holla; you Clowne. | *Ros.* Peace foole, he's not thy kinsman. 848
Iaq. A Foole, a foole: I met a foole i'th Forrest, 985
A motley Foole (a miserable world:) 986
As I do liue by foode, I met a foole, 987
In good set termes, and yet a motley foole. 990
Good morrow foole (quoth I:) no Sir, quoth he, 991
Call me not foole, till heauen hath sent me fortune, 992
The motley Foole, thus morall on the time, 1002
And I did laugh, sans intermission | An houre by his diall. Oh noble
foole, 1005
A worthy foole: Motley's the onely weare. 1007
Du Sen. What foole is this? 1008
**Iaq.* O worthie Foole: One that hath bin a Courtier 1009

FOOLE *cont*.

With obseruation, the which he vents | In mangled formes. O that I were a foole,	1014
Hee, that a Foole doth very wisely hit,	1027
Euen by the squandring glances of the foole.	1031
Ros. Out Foole. | *Clo*. For a taste.	1297
Ros. Peace you dull foole, I found them on a tree.	1313
*Iaq. By my troth, I was seeking for a Foole, when I | found you.	1477
Orl. Which I take to be either a foole, or a Cipher.	1482
Iaq. A materiall foole.	1642
*haue a foole to make me merrie, then experience to	1943
her childe her selfe, for she will breed it like a foole.	2083
Ros. Come, come, you are a foole,	2171
*The Foole doth thinke he is wise, but the wiseman	2373
*knowes himselfe to be a Foole. The Heathen Philoso- |pher,	2374
at any thing, and yet a foole.	2678

FOOLERIE = *2

*wit that fooles haue was silenced, the little foolerie that	254
*in holiday foolerie, if we walke not in the trodden paths	473

FOOLES = 6*3

Clo. The more pittie that fooles may not speak wise-|ly, what Wisemen do foolishly.	251
*wit that fooles haue was silenced, the little foolerie that	254
And yet it irkes me the poore dapled fooles	628
Heere shall he see, grosse fooles as he,	941
That Fooles should be so deepe contemplatiue:	1004
To blow on whom I please, for so fooles haue:	1023
Then she a woman. 'Tis such fooles as you	1825
*of verie strange beasts, which in all tongues, are call'd | Fooles.	2614
Clo. According to the fooles bolt sir, and such dulcet | diseases.	2640

FOOLISH = 2*2

To bring againe these foolish runawaies. *Exeunt*.	701
You foolish Shepheard, wherefore do you follow her	1822
*and the foolish Chronoclers of that age, found it was	2016
*such a foolish song. God buy you, and God mend your | voices. Come *Audrie. Exeunt*.	2570

FOOLISHLY = 2

Clo. The more pittie that fooles may not speak wise-|ly, what Wisemen do foolishly.	251
Doth very foolishly, although he smart	1028

FOOLS = *1

Iaq. 'Tis a Greeke inuocation, to call fools into a cir-|cle.	944

FOOT = 2*1

That thou with license of free foot hast caught,	1042
detect the lazie foot of time, as wel as a clocke.	1495
*go as softly as foot can fall, he thinkes himselfe too soon | there.	1517

FOOTE = 1*1

Orl. And why not the swift foote of time? Had not | that bin as proper?	1496
Addrest a mightie power, which were on foote	2732

FOR *l*.*10 *11 *12 *14 *17 *61 *63 80 *108 *126 *128 *129 *135 *144 *149 *157 *160 *181 *188 *203 *206 *217 *222 *223 *228 *243 *249 *253 *278 301 *306 *307 329 *336 *341 *352 *353 411 448 449 469 *470 *490 492 495 504 528 *538 568 654 677 748 752 762 763 764 782 *785 *794 796 806 *829 *835 846 859 861 876 879 909 922 952 957 959 968 974 1016 1023 1037 1039 1081 *1113 1140 1149 1151 1237 1267 *1280 1298 *1317 1324 *1362 *1372 *1380 *1416 *1420 *1448 1450 1451 1475

FOR *cont*.
  *1477 *1509 *1516 *1520 *1534 *1550 *1561 *1591 *1592 *1593 *1595
*1630 *1635 *1639 *1649 *1658 *1682 *1696 1698 *1733 1780 1789 1831
1832 1833 1843 1845 1858 1871 1883 1885 1892 1900 1903 1944 *1951
*1968 *1974 *1981 *1987 *1989 *2013 2019 2021 *2044 2046 2047 *2048
2054 *2062 *2076 2083 *2084 *2131 2132 2181 2186 *2218 *2221 *2222
2239 2267 2276 2291 2334 *2343 2353 *2382 *2385 2386 *2418 2425
*2441 2456 2458 *2461 *2465 *2480 2492 2493 2494 2495 2497 2498
2499 2500 2506 2507 2508 2509 2540 2555 *2642 *2665 2691 2692 2727
2768 *2769 2770 *2787 *2789 *2795 = 109*101

FORBEARE = 3
Orl. Forbeare, and eate no more.   1063
And know some nourture: But forbeare, I say,   1073
Orl. Then but forbeare your food a little while: 1104

FORCE = 3
Du Sen. What would you haue? | Your gentlenesse shall force, more
then your force   1078
Nor I am sure there is no force in eyes | That can doe hurt.   1797

FOREHEAD = 1*1
Nor did not with vnbashfull forehead woe,   754
*Towne is more worthier then a village, so is the fore- | head   1667

FORGET = 1*2
*could teach me to forget a banished father, you must not   174
Ros. Well, I will forget the condition of my estate, | to reioyce in
yours.   184
Meane time, forget this new-falne dignitie,   2753

FORGOT = 1
*Freize, freize, thou bitter skie that dost not bight so nigh | as benefitts
forgot:*   1164

FORGOTTEN = 1
Cor. Into a thousand that I haue forgotten.   814

FORKED = 1
Should in their owne confines with forked heads   630

FORMALL = 1
With eyes seuere, and beard of formall cut,   1134

FORMER = 1
you to your former Honor, I bequeath   2763

FORMES = 1
With obseruation, the which he vents | In mangled formes. O that I
were a foole,   1014

FORREST = 17*7
Oli. Where will the old Duke liue? | *Cha*. They say hee is already in
the Forrest of *Arden*,   114
Ros. Why, whether shall we goe? | *Cel*. To seeke my Vncle in the
Forrest of *Arden*.   570
Ros. Well, this is the Forrest of *Arden*.   797
If this vncouth Forrest yeeld any thing sauage,   956
Iaq. A Foole, a foole: I met a foole i'th Forrest,   985
That euerie eye, which in this Forrest lookes,   1207
Clo. You haue said: but whether wisely or no, let the | Forrest iudge.   1319
Ros. But doth he know that I am in this Forrest, and   1423
Orl. You should aske me what time o'day: there's no | clocke in the
Forrest.   1491
Ros. Then there is no true Louer in the Forrest, else   1493
skirts of the Forrest, like fringe vpon a petticoat.   1525
*that are sicke. There is a man haunts the Forrest, that a- | buses   1545
*the way, you shal tell me, where in the Forrest you liue: 1608

FORREST *cont.*

*promis'd to meete me in this place of the Forrest, and to | couple vs.	1653
*confirmer of false reckonings, he attends here in the for-|rest on the	
Duke your father.	1740
Where in the Purlews of this Forrest, stands	2226
Within an houre, and pacing through the Forrest,	2251
Mar-text. But *Awdrie*, there is a youth heere in the | Forrest layes	
claime to you.	2346
Will. *William*, sir. | *Clo*. A faire name. Was't borne i'th Forrest heere?	2362
But my good Lord, this Boy is Forrest borne,	2606
Obscured in the circle of this Forrest.	2611
the Forrest: he hath bin a Courtier he sweares.	2619
Men of great worth resorted to this forrest,	2731
First, in this Forrest, let vs do those ends	2747

FORRESTER = 1*1

*that habit play the knaue with him, do you hear For-|(rester.	1488
no song Forrester for this purpose? | *Lord*. Yes Sir.	2132

FORRESTERS = 2

Enter Duke Senior: Amyens, and two or three Lords | like Forresters.	605
Enter Iaques and Lords, Forresters.	2126

FORSOOTH = *1

*brambles; all (forsooth) defying the name of *Rosalinde*.	1548

FORSWEAR = *1

*him, now loath him: then entertaine him, then forswear	1594

FORSWEARE = *2

*of madnes, w was to forsweare the ful stream of y world,	1597
*to sweare, and to forsweare, according as mariage binds	2633

FORSWORN = *1

*you sweare by that that is not, you are not forsworn: no	242

FORSWORNE = 1

not the Knight forsworne.	234

FORTH = 6*2

Clo. Stand you both forth now: stroke your chinnes,	238
Will sodainly breake forth: Sir, fare you well,	451
(Maides as we are) to trauell forth so farre?	573
The wretched annimall heau'd forth such groanes	643
Ros. It may wel be cal'd Ioues tree, when it droppes | forth fruite.	1430
*(good youth) he went but forth to wash him in the Hel-|lespont,	2014
He hath t'ane his bow and arrowes, and is gone forth	2152
Could not drop forth such giant rude inuention,	2183

FORTUNE = 9*8

Cel. Let vs sit and mocke the good hous+wife For-|*tune*	200
*Fortune reignes in gifts of the world, not in the | lineaments of Nature.	210
*may she not by Fortune fall into the fire? though nature	214
*hath giuen vs wit to flout at Fortune, hath not Fortune	215
Ros. Indeed there is fortune too hard for nature, when	217
*fortune makes natures naturall, the cutter off of natures | witte.	218
Ros. As wit and fortune will. | *Clo*. Or as the destinies decrees.	269
Ros. Gentleman, | Weare this for me: one out of suites with fortune	410
That can translate the stubbornnesse of fortune | Into so quiet and so	
sweet a stile.	625
Yet fortune cannot recompence me better	779
And rail'd on Lady Fortune in good termes,	989
Call me not foole, till heauen hath sent me fortune,	992
That lou'd your Father, the residue of your fortune,	1174
fortune, and preuents the slander of his wife.	1975
*what straights of Fortune she is driuen, and it is not	2473

FORTUNE *cont*.
Shal share the good of our returned fortune,   2751
FORTUNES = 5*3
   *father left me by testament, with that I will goe buy my | fortunes.   73
   Ros. Nay now thou goest from Fortunes office to Na- | tures: 209
   Cel. Peraduenture this is not Fortunes work neither,   220
   Ros. He cals vs back: my pride fell with my fortunes,   418
   At seauenteene yeeres, many their fortunes seeke   777
   My fortunes were more able to releeue her.   862
   As yet to question you about your fortunes: 1153
   And let me all your fortunes vnderstand. *Exeunt*.   1178
FORWARD = 1*1
   the wrastling might not go forward.   345
   *a mans good wit seconded with the forward childe, vn- | derstanding: 1624
FORWARDNESSE = 1
   His owne perill on his forwardnesse.   314
FOSTER = 1
   Which I did store to be my foster Nurse,   744
FOUGHT = 1
   quarrels, and like to haue fought one.   2624
FOULE = 6*2
   Cleanse the foule bodie of th'infected world,   1034
   Du Sen. Most mischeeuous foule sin, in chiding sin: 1038
   Clo. Truly, and to cast away honestie vppon a foule   1645
   Aud. I am not a slut, though I thanke the Goddes I | am foule.   1647
   Foule is most foule, being foule to be a scoffer.   1835
   *sir, in a poore house, as your Pearle in your foule oy- | ster.   2637
FOULNESSE = *2
   Clo. Well, praised be the Gods, for thy foulnesse; slut- | tishnesse   1649
   Ros. Hees falne in loue with your foulnesse, & shee'll   1839
FOUND = 6*4
   Within these ten daies if that thou beest found   502
   They found the bed vntreasur'd of their Mistris.   687
   I haue by hard aduenture found mine owne.   827
   Ros. Peace you dull foole, I found them on a tree.   1313
   *before you came: for looke heere what I found on a   1372
   *him, and rellish it with good obseruance. I found him   1428
   Iaq. By my troth, I was seeking for a Foole, when I | found you.   1477
   *and the foolish Chronoclers of that age, found it was   2016
   And found it was his brother, his elder brother.   2271
   Clo. 'Faith we met, and found the quarrel was vpon | the seuenth
   cause.   2626
FOUNTAINE = *1
   *I will weepe for nothing, like *Diana* in the Foun- | taine,   2062
FOURE = *2
   *brother the new Duke, and three or foure louing   102
   *enemie, I haue vndone three Tailors, I haue had foure   2623
FOURESCORE = 2
   From seauentie yeeres, till now almost fourescore   775
   But at fourescore, it is too late a weeke,   778
FOURTH = *1
   *Quip-modest: the third, the reply Churlish: the fourth,   2667
FOWLE = 1
   As the Winter to fowle Weather.   2710
FOYLE = *1
   *loth to foyle him, as I must for my owne honour if hee   129

FRAILST = 1
That eyes that are the frailst, and softest things,   1783
FRANCE = *1
*yong fellow of France, full of ambition, an enuious   140
FRANTICKE = 1
If that I doe not dreame, or be not franticke,   509
FREDERICK = 1
Duke Frederick hearing how that euerie day   2730
FREDERICKE = 1
Clo. One that old *Fredericke* your Father loues.   247
FREDRICKE = 1
His yongest sonne, and would not change that calling | To be adopted
heire to *Fredricke*.   396
FREE = 3
More free from perill then the enuious Court?   610
That thou with license of free foot hast caught,   1042
Then he hath wrong'd himselfe: if he be free,   1059
FREESTONE = 1
A freestone coloured hand: I verily did thinke   2174
FREIND = 1
as *freind* remembred not. | *Heigh ho, sing, &c.*   1167
FREIZE = 2
*Freize, freize, thou bitter skie that dost not bight so nigh | as benefitts
forgot:*   1164
FRENDS = *1
*meanes, and content, is without three good frends. That   1224
FRENDSHIP = 1
Most frendship, is fayning; most Louing, meere folly: 1161
FRESH = 2
You meet in some fresh cheeke the power of fancie,   1801
Who gaue me fresh aray, and entertainment,   2297
FRESHLY = *1
*in mans apparrell? Looks he as freshly, as he did the day | he
Wrastled?   1424
FRIDAIES = 1
Ros. Yes faith will I, fridaies and saterdaies, and all.   2026
FRIEND = 5*2
Left and abandoned of his veluet friend;   658
Ros. Peace I say; good euen to your friend.   853
Some of violated vowes, | twixt the soules of friend, and friend: 1331
Clo. Good eu'n gentle friend. Couer thy head, couer   2357
*thy head: Nay prethee bee couer'd. How olde are you | Friend?   2358
*I haue bin politicke with my friend, smooth with mine   2622
FRIENDLY = 1
For I must tell you friendly in your eare,   1832
FRIENDS = 2*5
*be so: I shall do my friends no wrong, for I haue none to   352
Or if we did deriue it from our friends,   523
That your poore friends must woe your companie,   983
Cel. How now backe friends: Shepheard, go off a lit- | tle: 1356
Cel. O Lord, Lord, it is a hard matter for friends to   1380
*you would proue, my friends told mee as much, and I   2089
*bid your friends: for if you will be married to mor- | row, you shall: and
to *Rosalind* if you will.   2480
FRIENDSHIP = 1
Le Beu. Good Sir, I do in friendship counsaile you   429

87

FRIGHT = 1
To fright the Annimals, and to kill them vp   670
FRINGE = 1
skirts of the Forrest, like fringe vpon a petticoat.   1525
FROM *l.*13 *20 *60 *69 *109 *132 *138 *188 *193 *201 *209 368 390
455 456 499 523 601 610 621 641 775 822 *833 993 999 1000 1071 1093
1203 1286 1467 *1596 *1932 *2018 2249 2284 2293 *2466 2600 2687
2738 = 27*16
FROSTIE = 1
Frostie, but kindely; let me goe with you,   757
FROWNE = 2
Now I doe frowne on thee with all my heart,   1786
for I protest her frowne might kill me.   2021
FROWNING = 1
As she answeres thee with frowning lookes, ile sauce   1841
FRUIT = *1
*with a Medler: then it will be the earliest fruit i'th coun- | try: 1316
FRUITE = 3
He dies that touches any of this fruite, | Till I, and my affaires are
answered.   1074
Clo. Truely the tree yeelds bad fruite.   1314
*Ros. It may wel be cal'd Ioues tree, when it droppes | forth fruite.   1430
FUL = 1*3
*Iaq. You are ful of prety answers: haue you not bin ac- | quainted   1464
*liking, proud, fantastical, apish, shallow, inconstant, ful   1590
*of madnes, w was to forsweare the ful stream of y world,   1597
Ros. And his kissing is as ful of sanctitie, | As the touch of holy bread.   1723
FULL = 9*4
*yong fellow of France, full of ambition, an enuious   140
*gentle, neuer school'd, and yet learned, full of noble   162
*Cel. Heerein I see thou lou'st mee not with the full   177
Enter le Beau. | Ros. With his mouth full of newes.   257
how full of briers is this working day world.   471
Cel. With his eies full of anger.   497
Full of the pasture, iumps along by him   661
For then he's full of matter.   677
Full of strange oaths, and bearded like the Pard,   1129
Full of wise sawes, and moderne instances,   1135
Thy Huntresse name, that my full life doth sway.   1204
*of teares, full of smiles; for euerie passion something, and   1591
That makes the world full of ill-fauourd children: 1826
FUNCTION = 1
Or what is he of basest function,   1053
FURNACE = 1
Sighing like Furnace, with a wofull ballad   1127
FURNISHD = 1*1
vnseasonably. He was furnish'd like a Hunter.   1439
*good play? I am not furnish'd like a Begger, therefore   2784
FURTHER = 2*4
*Orl. I will no further offend you, then becomes mee | for my good.   79
*loue no man in good earnest, nor no further in sport ney- | ther,   196
*Cel. I pray you beare with me, I cannot goe no fur- | ther.   792
Adam. Deere Master, I can go no further: 951
But doe not looke for further recompence   1871
*Clo. I durst go no further then the lye circumstantial: 2659
GAIND = 1
Iaq. Yes, I haue gain'd my experience.   1940

GAINE = *1
*deerely hir'd: but I (his brother) gaine nothing vnder   16
GAINST = 2
Hath tane displeasure 'gainst his gentle Neece,   446
And on my life his malice 'gainst the Lady   450
GALLANT = 2*2
*Char. Come, where is this yong gallant, that is so   361
But fare thee well, thou art a gallant youth,   391
A gallant curtelax vpon my thigh,   582
*Duk. Send to his brother, fetch that gallant hither,   697
GALLOP = 1*1
*This is the verie false gallop of Verses, why doe you in-|fect your selfe
with them?   1311
Orl. Who doth he gallop withal?   1515
GALLOPS = *1
*who Time trots withal, who Time gallops withal,   1500
GALLOWES = *1
*Ros. With a theefe to the gallowes: for though hee   1516
GAMESTER = *1
*Farewell good Charles. Now will I stirre this Game-|ster: 159
GANIMED = 8*1
And therefore looke you call me Ganimed.   590
Enter Rosaline for Ganimed, Celia for Aliena, and | Clowne, alias
Touchstone.   782
*Cor. Heere comes yong Mr Ganimed, my new Mistris-|ses Brother.   1283
Cel. Why how now Ganimed, sweet Ganimed.   2311
Cel. There is more in it; Cosen Ganimed.   2313
Phe. And I for Ganimed.   2493
Phe. And I for Ganimed.   2498
Phe. And so am I for Ganimed.   2507
GARGANTUAS = *1
*Cel. You must borrow me Gargantuas mouth first: 1419
GARMENTS = 2
Wintred garments must be linde, | so must slender Rosalinde: 1303
Such garments, and such yeeres: the boy is faire,   2235
GASPE = 1
To the last gaspe with truth and loyaltie,   774
GATES = 1
Who shut their coward gates on atomyes,   1784
GAUE = 1*1
*nature gaue mee, his countenance seemes to take from   20
Who gaue me fresh aray, and entertainment,   2297
GAULED = 1
And they that are most gauled with my folly,   1024
GENERALL = 1*1
*Orl. No faire Princesse: he is the generall challenger,   333
Would'st thou disgorge into the generall world.   1043
GENERALLY = 1
hath generally tax'd their whole sex withal.   1537
GENTILITY = *1
*gentility with my education. This is it Adam that   23
GENTLE = 10*6
*know you are my eldest brother, and in the gentle con-|dition   47
*gentle, neuer school'd, and yet learned, full of noble   162
*faire eies, and gentle wishes go with mee to my triall;   349
Cel. Gentle Cosen, | Let vs goe thanke him, and encourage him: 403
Hath tane displeasure 'gainst his gentle Neece,   446

GENTLE *cont*.

Orl. Who's there? | *Ad*. What my yong Master, oh my gentle master,	704
And wherefore are you gentle, strong, and valiant?	709
No more doe yours: your vertues gentle Master	715
Cor. And to you gentle Sir, and to you all.	854
*Ros. O most gentle Iupiter, what tedious homilie of	1353
Phe. Why I am sorry for thee gentle *Siluius*.	1858
My gentle *Phebe*, did bid me giue you this:	2155
Like Turke to Christian: womens gentle braine	2182
In briefe, he led me to the gentle Duke,	2296
*Clow. We shall finde a time *Awdrie*, patience gen-|tle *Awdrie*.	2341
*Clo. Good eu'n gentle friend. Couer thy head, couer	2357

GENTLEMAN = 3*5

*you that keeping for a gentleman of my birth, that dif-|fers	12
*a gentleman, or giue mee the poore allottery my	72
*Cel. Yong Gentleman, your spirits are too bold for	336
Ros. Gentleman, | Weare this for me: one out of suites with fortune	410
Shall we goe Coze? | *Cel*. I: fare you well faire Gentleman.	413
*that I know you are a Gentleman of good conceit:	2462
1.*Pa*. Wel met honest Gentleman.	2538
*Motley-minded Gentleman, that I haue so often met in	2618

GENTLEMANS = 1

*Awd. Faith the Priest was good enough, for all the | olde gentlemans	
saying.	2343

GENTLEMAN-LIKE = *1

*hiding from me all gentleman-like qualities: the spirit	69

GENTLEMEN = *2

*Gentlemen flocke to him euery day, and fleet the time	118
*Clo. Truly yong Gentlemen, though there was no	2565

GENTLENESSE = 4

Du Sen. What would you haue? | Your gentlenesse shall force, more	
then your force	1078
Moue vs to gentlenesse.	1080
Let gentlenesse my strong enforcement be,	1095
And therefore sit you downe in gentlenesse,	1101

GENTLEWOMAN = 1

Hisperia the Princesse Gentlewoman | Confesses that she secretly	
ore-heard	690

GENTLY = 1

Orl. Speake you so gently? Pardon me I pray you,	1083

GESTURE = *1

*so neere the hart, as your gesture cries it out: when your	2471

GET = 3*4

*Well sir, get you in. I will not long be troubled with	76
Oli. Get you with him, you olde dogge.	81
And get you from our Court.	499
And get our Iewels and our wealth together,	599
*Cor. Sir, I am a true Labourer, I earne that I eate: get	1270
*Ewes and the Rammes together, and to offer to get your	1276
*married vnder a bush like a begger? Get you to church,	1690

GETS = 1

and pleas'd with what he gets:	930

GETTING = *1

*of his owne getting; hornes, euen so poore men alone:	1664

GIANT = 1

Could not drop forth such giant rude inuention,	2183

GIDDIE = *1
*to be touch'd with so many giddie offences as hee   1536
GIDDINESSE = *1
*Ol. Neither call the giddinesse of it in question; the   2413
GIDDY = *1
*then an ape, more giddy in my desires, then a mon-|key: 2061
GIFT see also guift = 1
They haue the gift to know it: and in his braine,   1011
GIFTS = 2*2
*from her wheele, that her gifts may henceforth bee | bestowed equally.   201
*mightily misplaced, and the bountifull blinde woman | doth most
mistake in her gifts to women.   204
*Fortune reignes in gifts of the world, not in the | lineaments of Nature.   210
Heauen would that shee these gifts should haue, | and I to liue and die her
slaue.   1351
GILDED see guilded
GIPSIES = 1
2.Pa. I faith, y'faith, and both in a tune like two | gipsies on a horse.   2544
GIRLE = 1*1
Shall we be sundred? shall we part sweete girle?   562
*girle goes before the Priest, and certainely a Womans | thought runs
before her actions.   2049
GIUE = 24*10
*father charg'd you in his will to giue me good educati-|on: 67
*a gentleman, or giue mee the poore allottery my   72
*physicke your ranckenesse, and yet giue no thousand | crownes
neyther: holla Dennis.   86
*come to morrow, Ile giue him his payment: if euer hee   156
Ros. I my Liege, so please you giue vs leaue.   320
and giue ouer this attempt.   342
That could giue more, but that her hand lacks meanes.   412
Wilt thou change Fathers? I will giue thee mine: 553
All this I giue you, let me be your seruant,   750
If he for gold will giue vs any foode,   846
I thinke of as many matters as he, but I giue   923
Iaq. Ile giue you a verse to this note,   933
I wil giue thee leaue to die: but if thou diest   962
Inuest me in my motley: Giue me leaue   1032
And giue it food. There is an old poore man,   1106
Giue vs some Musicke, and good Cozen, sing.   1154
Support him by the arme: giue me your hand,   1177
Cel. Giue me audience, good Madam. | Ros. Proceed.   1432
*If I could meet that Fancie-monger, I would giue him   1549
*which women stil giue the lie to their consciences. But   1573
Aud. Wel, the Gods giue vs ioy.   1656
Ol. Is there none heere to giue the woman?   1676
Iaq. Proceed, proceede: Ile giue her.   1680
*marrie vs: giue me your hand Orlando: What doe you | say sister?   2034
My gentle Phebe, did bid me giue you this: 2155
Made him giue battell to the Lyonnesse: 2282
His broken promise, and to giue this napkin   2308
Clo. Giue me your hand: Art thou Learned? | Will. No sir.   2380
*Du Se. That would I, had I kingdoms to giue with hir.   2583
You'l giue your selfe to this most faithfull Shepheard.   2589
*Keepe you your word, O Duke, to giue your daughter,   2595
*nor he durst not giue me the lye direct: and so wee mea-|sur'd swords,
and parted.   2660

GIUE *cont*.

Ros. To you I giue my selfe, for I am yours.   2691
To you I giue my selfe, for I am yours.   2692
GIUEN = 1*5
*with a matter: I am giuen sir secretly to vnderstand, that   123
*hath giuen vs wit to flout at Fortune, hath not Fortune   215
I should haue giuen him teares vnto entreaties,   401
*me thinkes I haue giuen him a penie, and he renders me   915
*and Louers are giuen to Poetrie: and what they   1631
*Ol. Truly she must be giuen, or the marriage is not | lawfull.   1678
GIUES = 1*1
*that he so plentifully giues me, the something that   19
therefore he giues them good leaue to wander.   105
GIUING = 2*1
As worldlings doe, giuing thy sum of more   656
*cods, and giuing her them againe, said with weeping   834
By giuing loue your sorrow, and my griefe | Were both extermin'd.   1861
GLAD = *4
*Cha. I am heartily glad I came hither to you: if hee   155
*glad of other mens good content with my harme: 1272
*Orl. I am glad of your departure: Adieu good Mon-|sieur
Melancholly.   1485
*companie, I am verie glad to see you, euen a toy in hand   1683
GLADNESSE = 1
Then thine owne gladnesse, that thou art employd.   1872
GLANCES = 1
Euen by the squandring glances of the foole.   1031
GLASSE = 1*1
'Tis not her glasse, but you that flatters her,   1827
*of a cup into a glasse, by filling the one, doth empty the   2384
GLEANE = 1
To gleane the broken eares after the man   1876
GLIDES = 1
And with indented glides, did slip away   2263
GLOUES = 1
That her old gloues were on, but twas her hands: 2175
GLOWE = 1
And the red glowe of scorne and prowd disdaine,   1762
GO = 14*8
the wrastling might not go forward.   345
*faire eies, and gentle wishes go with mee to my triall;   349
*Ad. Why whether Adam would'st thou haue me go?   733
*Orl. What, would'st thou haue me go & beg my food,   735
Go with me, if you like vpon report,   884
*Ile go sleepe if I can: if I cannot, Ile raile against all | the first borne
of Egypt.   945
Amy. And Ile go seeke the Duke,   947
Adam. Deere Master, I can go no further: 951
Go seeke him, tell him I would speake with him.   979
Whiles (like a Doe) I go to finde my Fawne,   1105
Duke Sen. Go finde him out,   1111
Go to my Caue, and tell mee. Good old man,   1175
*Cel. How now backe friends: Shepheard, go off a lit-|tle: 1356
go with him sirrah.   1357
*go as softly as foot can fall, he thinkes himselfe too soon | there.   1517
*Ros. Go with me to it, and Ile shew it you: and by   1607
Wil you go? | Orl. With all my heart, good youth.   1609

GO *cont*.

*Ros. Nay, you must call mee *Rosalind*: Come sister, | will you go?
Exeunt.   1611
shal we go with you to your Chappell?   1675
Go you, and prepare *Aliena*; for looke you,   2425
If she refuse me, and from hence I go   2600
*Clo. I durst go no further then the lye circumstantial: 2659
GOARD = 1
Haue their round hanches goard.   631
GOATES = *1
**Goates, *Audrey*: and how *Audrey* am I the man yet?   1616
GOATS = *1
*Clo. I am heere with thee, and thy Goats, as the most   1619
GOBLET = 1
concaue as a couered goblet, or a Worme-eaten nut.   1734
GOD = 10*11
**God made, a poore vnworthy brother of yours with | idlenesse.   36
**lost my teeth in your seruice: God be with my olde ma-|ster,   83
so God keepe your worship. *Exit*.   158
*Clo. Wilt thou rest damn'd? God helpe thee shallow   1268
man: God make incision in thee, thou art raw.   1269
*Ros. Why God will send more, if the man will bee   1403
Iaq. God buy you, let's marke as little as we can.   1452
**Lectors against it, and I thanke God, I am not a Wo-|man   1535
*Iaq. Nay then God buy you, and you talke in blanke | verse.   1946
**natiuitie, and almost chide God for making you that   1951
**they will spit, and for louers, lacking (God warne vs)   1989
*Ros. By my troth, and in good earnest, and so God   2094
Read. *Art thou god, to Shepherd turn'd?*   2189
Aud. God ye good eu'n *William*.   2355
Will. I sir, I thanke God. | *Clo*. Thanke God: A good answer: 2364
Aud. Do good *William*. | *Will*. God rest you merry sir. *Exit* 2400
Ros. God saue you brother. | *Ol*. And you faire sister.   2427
**such a foolish song. God buy you, and God mend your | voices. Come
Audrie. *Exeunt*.   2570
To Hymen, *God of euerie Towne*.   2721
GODDES = *1
*Aud. I am not a slut, though I thanke the Goddes I | am foule. 1647
GODDESSES = *1
**to reason of such goddesses, hath sent this Naturall for   222
GODDILD = *1
**Sir, you are verie well met: goddild you for your last   1682
GODHEAD = 1
Ros. Read. *Why, thy godhead laid a part*,   2193
GODILD = *1
*Clo. God'ild you sir, I desire you of the like: I presse   2631
GODS *see also* 'ods = 2*4
*Ros. Is he of Gods making? What manner of man?   1400
**in a little roome: truly, I would the Gods hadde | made thee poeticall. 1626
*Aud. Do you wish then that the Gods had made me | Poeticall? 1633
*Aud. Well, I am not faire, and therefore I pray the | Gods make me
honest.   1643
*Clo. Well, praised be the Gods, for thy foulnesse; slut-|tishnesse 1649
Aud. Wel, the Gods giue vs ioy.   1656
GOE = 22*10
*Orlan. Goe a-part *Adam*, and thou shalt heare how | he will shake me
vp.   30

93

GOE *cont*.

Oli. Let me goe I say. | **Orl*. I will not till I please: you shall heare mee: my	65
*father left me by testament, with that I will goe buy my | fortunes.	73
*goe alone againe, Ile neuer wrastle for prize more: and	157
*cleare all: nothing remaines, but that I kindle the boy | thither, which now Ile goe about. *Exit*.	167
Cel. Gentle Cosen, | Let vs goe thanke him, and encourage him:	403
Shall we goe Coze? | *Cel*. I: fare you well faire Gentleman.	413
Cel. Will you goe Coze? | *Ros*. Haue with you: fare you well. *Exit*.	422
Cel. O my poore *Rosaline*, whether wilt thou goe?	552
Whether to goe, and what to beare with vs,	565
Say what thou canst, Ile goe along with thee.	569
Ros. Why, whether shall we goe? | *Cel*. To seeke my Vncle in the Forrest of *Arden*.	570
Cel. Heele goe along ore the wide world with me,	597
After my flight: now goe in we content	602
Du Sen. Come, shall we goe and kill vs venison?	627
Frostie, but kindely; let me goe with you,	757
But come thy waies, weele goe along together,	770
Ad. Master goe on, and I will follow thee	773
Cel. I pray you beare with me, I cannot goe no fur-|ther.	792
Iaq. Goe thou with mee, | And let me counsel thee.	1699
*told him of as good as he, so he laugh'd and let mee goe.	1744
Goe hence a little, and I shall conduct you | If you will marke it.	1763
Then without Candle may goe darke to bed:	1812
Will you goe Sister? Shepheard ply her hard:	1848
Goe with me *Siluius*. *Exeunt*.	1914
Cel. Goe too: wil you *Orlando*, haue to wife this *Ro-|salind*? | *Orl*. I will.	2039
Ros. I, goe your waies, goe your waies: I knew what	2088
*out of the sight of *Orlando*: Ile goe finde a shadow, and | sigh till he come.	2122
*Well, goe your way to her; (for I see Loue hath	2218
Cel. Come, you looke paler and paler: pray you draw | homewards: good sir, goe with vs.	2332
my counterfeiting to him: will you goe? | *Exeunt*.	2337

GOES = 1 *2

Amy. And Ile sing it. | *Amy*. Thus it goes.	935
*more plentie in it, it goes much against my stomacke.	1220
*girle goes before the Priest, and certainely a Womans | thought runs before her actions.	2049

GOEST = *1

Ros. Nay now thou goest from Fortunes office to Na-|tures:	209

GOING = 2

Do this expediently, and turne him going. *Exeunt*	1198
met your wiues wit going to your neighbours bed.	2077

GOLD = 5

Beautie prouoketh theeues sooner then gold.	574
Be comfort to my age: here is the gold,	749
If he for gold will giue vs any foode,	846
Ros. I prethee Shepheard, if that loue or gold	855
And buy it with your Gold right sodainly. *Exeunt*.	887

GOLDEN = 1

carelesly as they did in the golden world.	119

GOLDENLY = *1

*at schoole, and report speakes goldenly of his profit:	9

GOLDSMITHS = *1
   *with goldsmiths wiues, & cond the(m) out of rings   1465
GONDOLA *see* gundello
GONE = 6
   When she is gone: then open not thy lips   543
   And she beleeues where euer they are gone   695
   1 *Lord*. My Lord, he is but euen now gone hence,   975
   gone I say, I wil not to wedding with thee.   1705
   In parcells as I did, would haue gone neere   1899
   He hath t'ane his bow and arrowes, and is gone forth   2152
GOOD = 44*71
   *father charg'd you in his will to giue me good educati-|on: 67
   Orl. I will no further offend you, then becomes mee | for my good.   79
   Oli. Call him in: 'twill be a good way: and to mor-|row the wrastling is.   94
   Cha. Good morrow to your worship.   97
   Oli. Good Mounsier *Charles*: what's the new newes | at the new Court?   98
   therefore he giues them good leaue to wander.   105
   *emulator of euery mans good parts, a secret & villanous   141
   *Farewell good *Charles*. Now will I stirre this Game-|ster: 159
   *loue no man in good earnest, nor no further in sport ney-|ther,   196
   Cel. Let vs sit and mocke the good houswife *For-|tune*   200
   *they were good Pan-cakes, and swore by his Honor the   231
   *were naught, and the Mustard was good, and yet was   233
   Le Beu. Faire Princesse, | you haue lost much good sport.   264
   *you of good wrastling, which you haue lost the sight of.   275
   Cel. Call him hether good Monsieuer *Le Beu*. | *Duke*. Do so: Ile not be
   by.   326
   Le Beu. Good Sir, I do in friendship counsaile you   429
   And pittie her, for her good Fathers sake;   449
   Cel. O, a good wish vpon you: you will trie in time   482
   *let vs talke in good earnest: Is it possible in such a so-|daine,   484
   Then good my Leige, mistake me not so much,   525
   Sermons in stones, and good in euery thing.   623
   Orl. Oh good old man, how well in thee appeares   760
   *selfe coragious to petty-coate; therefore courage, good | *Aliena*. 790
   Ros. I, be so good *Touchstone*: Look you, who comes   802
   Ros. Peace I say; good euen to your friend.   853
   Cheerely good *Adam*. *Exeunt*   970
   And rail'd on Lady Fortune in good termes,   989
   In good set termes, and yet a motley foole.   990
   Good morrow foole (quoth I:) no Sir, quoth he,   991
   Iaq. What, for a Counter, would I do, but good?   1037
   Or else a rude despiser of good manners,   1068
   If euer sate at any good mans feast: 1092
   And sat at good mens feasts, and wip'd our eies   1099
   Orl. I thanke ye, and be blest for your good comfort.   1113
   In faire round belly, with good Capon lin'd,   1133
   Giue vs some Musicke, and good Cozen, sing.   1154
   Duke Sen. If that you were the good Sir *Rowlands* son,   1169
   Go to my Caue, and tell mee. Good old man,   1175
   *good life; but in respect that it is a shepheards life, it is   1214
   *meanes, and content, is without three good frends. That   1224
   *good pasture makes fat sheepe: and that a great cause of   1226
   *no wit by Nature, nor Art, may complaine of good | breeding, or
   comes of a very dull kindred.   1228
   *saw'st good manners: if thou neuer saw'st good maners,   1239
   Cor. Not a whit *Touchstone*, those that are good ma-|ners   1243

GOOD *cont*.

*of a good peece of flesh indeed: learne of the wise	1263
*glad of other mens good content with my harme:	1272
neuer cri'de, haue patience good people.	1355
*Ros. Good my complection, dost thou think though	1390
*him, and rellish it with good obseruance. I found him	1428
Cel. Giue me audience, good Madam. | Ros. Proceed.	1432
*Iaq. I thanke you for your company, but good faith	1448
*Iaq. Ile tarrie no longer with you, farewell good sig-|nior Loue.	1483
*Orl. I am glad of your departure: Adieu good Mon-|sieur Melancholly.	1485
*some good counsel, for he seemes to haue the Quotidian | of Loue vpon him.	1550
*in good sooth, are you he that hangs the verses on the	1574
Wil you go? | Orl. With all my heart, good youth.	1609
*Clo. Come apace good Audrey, I wil fetch vp your	1615
*a mans good wit seconded with the forward childe, vn-|derstanding:	1624
slut, were to put good meate into an vncleane dish.	1646
*right: Many a man has good Hornes, and knows no end	1662
*Clo. Good euen good Mr what ye cal't: how do you	1681
*and haue a good Priest that can tel you what marriage is,	1691
*me wel: and not being wel married, it wil be a good	1697
*Farewel good Mr Oliuer: Not O sweet Oliuer, O braue	1703
Cel. As good cause as one would desire, | Therefore weepe.	1714
Ros. I'faith his haire is of a good colour.	1720
*told him of as good as he, so he laugh'd and let mee goe.	1744
And thanke heauen, fasting, for a good mans loue;	1831
Iaq. Why, 'tis good to be sad and say nothing.	1924
Ros. Why then 'tis good to be a poste.	1925
Orl. Good day, and happinesse, deere Rosalind.	1945
*to kisse: verie good Orators when they are out,	1988
*(good youth) he went but forth to wash him in the Hel-|lespont,	2014
Ros. Are you not good? | Orl. I hope so.	2030
*good thing: Come sister, you shall be the Priest, and	2033
*Ros. By my troth, and in good earnest, and so God	2094
*Oliu. Good morrow, faire ones: pray you, (if you | know)	2225
Oli. Be of good cheere youth: you a man?	2318
*Oli. Well then, take a good heart, and counterfeit to | be a man.	2328
*Cel. Come, you looke paler and paler: pray you draw | homewards: good sir, goe with vs.	2332
*Awd. Faith the Priest was good enough, for all the | olde gentlemans saying.	2343
*my troth, we that haue good wits, haue much to answer	2352
Will. Good eu'n Audrey.	2354
Aud. God ye good eu'n William.	2355
Will. And good eu'n to you Sir.	2356
*Clo. Good eu'n gentle friend. Couer thy head, couer	2357
Will. I sir, I thanke God. | Clo. Thanke God: A good answer:	2364
*Cle. So, so, is good, very good, very excellent good:	2368
Aud. Do good William. | Will. God rest you merry sir. Exit	2400
*good: for my fathers house, and all the reuennew, that	2418
*that I know you are a Gentleman of good conceit:	2462
*I speake not this, that you should beare a good opinion	2463
*good, and not to grace me. Beleeue then, if you please,	2467
*Phe. Good shepheard, tell this youth what 'tis to loue	2490
But my good Lord, this Boy is Forrest borne,	2606
*Iaq. Good my Lord, bid him welcome: This is the	2617

GOOD *cont*.
Iaq. How seuenth cause? Good my Lord, like this | fellow.	2628
*haue bookes for good manners: I will name you the de-|grees.	2665
Iaq. Is not this a rare fellow my Lord? He's as good	2677
Good Duke receiue thy daughter,	2686
Shal share the good of our returned fortune,	2751
*Lord the Prologue. If it be true, that good wine needs	2778
*no bush, 'tis true, that a good play needes no Epilogue.	2779
*Yet to good wine they do vse good bushes: and good	2780
*playes proue the better by the helpe of good Epilogues:	2781
*What a case am I in then, that am neither a good Epi-|logue,	2782
*good play? I am not furnish'd like a Begger, therefore	2784
*I defi'de not: And I am sure, as many as haue good	2794
*beards, or good faces, or sweet breaths, will for my kind	2795

GOODS = *1
*It is said, many a man knowes no end of his goods;	1661

GOOSE = 1*1
Why then my taxing like a wild-goose flies	1060
*breakes his staffe like a noble goose; but all's braue that	1751

GOTHES = 1
capricious Poet honest *Ouid* was among the Gothes.	1620

GOWT = *1
*that hath not the Gowt: for the one sleepes easily be-|cause	1509

GRACE = 5*5
*grace himselfe on thee, hee will practise against thee by	146
Cha. No, I warrant your Grace you shall not entreat	366
Orl. Yes I beseech your Grace, I am not yet well | breath'd.	378
Ros. I doe beseech your Grace | Let me the knowledge of my fault	
beare with me:	505
They are as innocent as grace it selfe;	515
Amien. I would not change it, happy is your Grace	624
Your Grace was wont to laugh is also missing,	689
Cel. Do I prethee, but yet haue the grace to consider,	1711
And I in such a pouerty of grace,	1874
*good, and not to grace me. Beleeue then, if you please,	2467

GRACES = 4
The parts and graces of the Wrastler	693
Their graces serue them but as enemies,	714
The enemie of all your graces liues	722
With all Graces wide enlarg'd, | *nature presently distill'd*	1341

GRACIOUS = *1
*neuer gracious: if kil'd, but one dead that is willing to	351

GRAFFE = *2
Ros. Ile graffe it with you, and then I shall graffe it	1315

GRANT = 1
and aske me what you will, I will grant it.	2024

GRAPE = *1
*when he had a desire to eate a Grape, would open	2375

GRAPES = *1
*that Grapes were made to eate, and lippes to open.	2377

GRAUE = 1
And measure out my graue. Farwel kinde master.	953

GRAUELD = *1
*were grauel'd, for lacke of matter, you might take oc-|casion	1987

GRAUNT = *1
*And louing woo? and wooing, she should graunt? And | will you	
perseuer to enioy her?	2411

GRAZE = 1*1
And do not sheere the Fleeces that I graze: 864
*and the greatest of my pride, is to see my Ewes graze, & | my Lambes
sucke.   1273
GREASE = *1
*is not the grease of a Mutton, as wholesome as the sweat   1253
GREASIE = 1
*Cor. Why we are still handling our Ewes, and their | Fels you know
are greasie.   1250
GREAT = 5*7
*Cel. How proue you that in the great heape of your | knowledge?   235
*wise men haue makes a great shew; Heere comes Mon- | sieur the Beu.   255
*good pasture makes fat sheepe: and that a great cause of   1226
*'tis a Word too great for any mouth of this Ages size, to   1420
*it strikes a man more dead then a great rec- | koning   1625
*Ros. A Traueller: by my faith you haue great rea- | son   1936
Oli. This was not counterfeit, there is too great te- | stimony   2324
*great matter in the dittie, yet y note was very vntunable   2566
Whom he reports to be a great Magitian.   2609
Song. | Wedding is great Iunos crowne,   2715
Men of great worth resorted to this forrest,   2731
you to your land, and loue, and great allies: 2766
GREATER = 1*2
*Orl. Why how now Adam? No greater heart in thee: 954
Orl. I, and greater wonders then that.   2437
*do I labor for a greater esteeme then may in some   2465
GREATEST = *1
*and the greatest of my pride, is to see my Ewes graze, & | my Lambes
sucke.   1273
GREATNESSE = 1
And in the greatnesse of my word you die. | Exit Duke, &c.   550
GREAZIE = 1
Sweepe on you fat and greazie Citizens,   663
GRECIAN = *1
*Grecian club, yet he did what hee could to die before,   2010
GREEKE = *1
*Iaq. 'Tis a Greeke inuocation, to call fools into a cir- | cle.   944
GREENE = 5
Song. | Vnder the greene wood tree,   890
Heigh ho, sing heigh ho, vnto the greene holly,   1160
and like greene timber, warpe, warpe.   1694
A greene and guilded snake had wreath'd it selfe,   2259
That o're the greene corne feild did passe,   2549
GREET = 1
And neuer staies to greet him: I quoth Iaques,   662
GREETING = 1
Clo. Salutation and greeting to you all.   2616
GREEUE = *1
*youth, greeue, be effeminate, changeable, longing, and   1589
GREEUES = *1
*Ros. Oh my deere Orlando, how it greeues me to see   2429
GRIEFE = 2
If you doe sorrow at my griefe in loue,   1860
By giuing loue your sorrow, and my griefe | Were both extermin'd.   1861
GRIEFES = 1
To beare your griefes your selfe, and leaue me out: 567

98

GRIEUD = 1
I charge thee be not thou more grieu'd then I am.   554
GRIEUES = 1*1
    *grieues me, and the spirit of my Father, which I thinke   24
    1.*Lord*. Indeed my Lord | The melancholy *Iaques* grieues at that,   632
GROANES = 1
    The wretched annimall heau'd forth such groanes   643
GROANING = *1
    *sighing euerie minute, and groaning euerie houre wold   1494
GROOMES = 1
    Play Musicke, and you Brides and Bride-groomes all,   2755
GROSSE = 1*1
    Heere shall he see, grosse fooles as he,   941
    *may bee chosen out of the grosse band of the vnfaith- | full: 2100
GROUND = 2
    Ros. Though it be pittie to see such a sight, it well | becomes the
    ground.   1436
    Lay cowching head on ground, with catlike watch   2266
GROUNDED = 1
    Grounded vpon no other argument,   447
GROW = 1*2
    Oli. Is it euen so, begin you to grow vpon me? I will   85
    Clo. Thus men may grow wiser euery day. It is the   299
    Du Sen. If he compact of iarres, grow Musicall,   977
GROWES = 1*2
    *of my father growes strong in mee, and I will no longer   70
    Clo. And mine, but it growes something stale with | mee.   843
    Of all opinion that growes ranke in them,   1020
GROWNE = 1
    A wretched ragged man, ore-growne with haire   2257
GROWTH = *3
    *him but growth, for the which his Animals on his   17
    Le Beu. Three proper yong men, of excellent growth | and presence.   284
    *thankful: let me stay the growth of his beard, if thou   1404
GUESSE = 3
    Cor. I partly guesse: for I haue lou'd ere now.   806
    Sil. No *Corin*, being old, thou canst not guesse,   807
    I know not the contents, but as I guesse   2156
GUIDES = 1
    youth mounts, and folly guides: who comes heere?   1752
GUIFT = 1
    Clo. I wil not take her on guift of any man.   1677
GUILDED = 1
    A greene and guilded snake had wreath'd it selfe,   2259
GUILTIE = *1
    *thoughts, wherein I confesse me much guiltie to denie   347
GUILTLESSE = 1
    I am but as a guiltlesse messenger.   2160
GUNDELLO = *1
    *swam in a Gundello. Why how now *Orlando*, where   1953
HABIT = *1
    *that habit play the knaue with him, do you hear For- |(rester.   1488
HAD *l*.*61 *136 *143 *179 240 *241 *244 *375 400 529 641 657 *794 *832
    1084 1150 *1363 1449 1450 *1496 *1633 *1742 1838 1898 1903 *1942
    1966 *2009 *2012 *2013 *2074 2259 2294 2301 2302 *2375 *2432 *2583
    *2623 *2792 = 17*25

HADDE = *1
*in a little roome: truly, I would the Gods hadde | made thee poeticall.   1626
HADST *l*.*180 *386 390 392 = 2*2
HAH *l*.1856 = 1
HAIRE = 5
Ros. His very haire | Is of the dissembling colour.   1716
Ros. I'faith his haire is of a good colour.   1720
'Tis not your inkie browes, your blacke silke haire,   1819
He said mine eyes were black, and my haire blacke,   1904
A wretched ragged man, ore-growne with haire   2257
HAIRIE = 1
In pitteous chase: and thus the hairie foole,   647
HALFE = *1
*for you'l be rotten ere you bee halfe ripe, and that's | the right vertue
of the Medler.   1317
HALFEPENCE = *1
*one another, as halfepence are, euerie one fault seeming   1541
HANCHES = 1
Haue their round hanches goard.   631
HAND = 11*6
*not my brother, I would not take this hand from thy   60
*vnder-hand meanes laboured to disswade him from it;   138
That could giue more, but that her hand lacks meanes.   412
A bore-speare in my hand, and in my heart   583
Support him by the arme: giue me your hand,   1177
Orl. I sweare to thee youth, by the white hand of   1576
*companie, I am verie glad to see you, euen a toy in hand   1683
Ros. By this hand, it will not kill a flie: but come,   2022
*marrie vs: giue me your hand *Orlando*: What doe you | say sister?   2034
I saw her hand, she has a leatherne hand,   2173
A freestone coloured hand: I verily did thinke   2174
She has a huswiues hand, but that's no matter: 2176
This is a mans inuention, and his hand. | *Sil*. Sure it is hers.   2178
Left on your right hand, brings you to the place: 2230
Clo. Giue me your hand: Art thou Learned? | *Will*. No sir.   2380
That thou mightst ioyne his hand with his,   2689
HANDKERCHER = 2
What man I am, and how, and why, and where | This handkercher was
stain'd.   2246
to sound, when he shew'd me your handkercher?   2436
HANDLING = *1
Cor. Why we are still handling our Ewes, and their | Fels you know
are greasie.   1250
HANDS = 7*4
Oli. Wilt thou lay hands on me villaine?   56
*chopt hands had milk'd; and I remember the wooing   832
Worth seizure, do we seize into our hands,   1190
*you kisse your hands; that courtesie would be vncleanlie | if Courtiers
were shepheards.   1247
Clo. Why do not your Courtiers hands sweate? and   1252
Cor. Besides, our hands are hard.   1256
Courtiers hands are perfum'd with Ciuet.   1261
nothing, is to haue rich eyes and poore hands.   1939
That her old gloues were on, but twas her hands: 2175
*and they shooke hands, and swore brothers. Your If, is   2675
Here's eight that must take hands,   2702

HANG = 2
  Orl. Hang there my verse, in witnesse of my loue,   1201
  Tonges Ile hang on euerie tree, | that shall ciuill sayings shoe.   1325
HANGD = *1
  *thy name should be hang'd and carued vpon these trees?   1370
HANGS = 1*3
  Orl. What passion hangs these waights vpo(n) my toong?   424
  And thereby hangs a tale. When I did heare   1001
  *barkes; hangs Oades vpon Hauthornes, and Elegies on   1547
  *in good sooth, are you he that hangs the verses on the   1574
HAPPIE = 3
  But iustly as you haue exceeded all promise, | Your Mistris shall be
  happie.   408
  happie, in hauing what he wishes for.   2456
  And after, euery of this happie number   2749
HAPPINES = *1
  *it is, to looke into happines through another mans eies: 2453
HAPPINESSE = 1*1
  *that I weare; owe no man hate, enuie no mans happi-|nesse: 1271
  Orl. Good day, and happinesse, deere *Rosalind*.   1945
HAPPY = 1
  Amien. I would not change it, happy is your Grace   624
HARD = 5*5
  Ros. Indeed there is fortune too hard for nature, when   217
  I haue by hard aduenture found mine owne.   827
  Cor. Besides, our hands are hard.   1256
  Cel. O Lord, Lord, it is a hard matter for friends to   1380
  Ros. Marry he trots hard with a yong maid, between   1503
  *if the interim be but a sennight, Times pace is so hard,   1505
  Clo. No truly, vnlesse thou wert hard fauour'd: for   1639
  Whose heart th'accustom'd sight of death makes hard   1774
  'Tis at the tufft of Oliues, here hard by: 1847
  Will you goe Sister? Shepheard ply her hard: 1848
HARDE = *1
  Orl. I beseech you, punish mee not with your harde   346
HARDLY = 1
  that I was an Irish Rat, which I can hardly remember.   1374
HARE = 1
  Her loue is not the Hare that I doe hunt,   2166
HARME = *1
  *glad of other mens good content with my harme: 1272
HART = 4*1
  If a Hart doe lacke a Hinde, | Let him seeke out Rosalinde: 1299
  Ros. O ominous, he comes to kill my Hart.   1440
  *so neere the hart, as your gesture cries it out: when your   2471
  You and you, are hart in hart: 2706
HARTILY = 1*1
  Sil. Oh thou didst then neuer loue so hartily,   815
  *of two dog-Apes. And when a man thankes me hartily,   914
HARUEST = 1
  That the maine haruest reapes: loose now and then   1877
HAS *l.*1662 2173 2176 = 2*1
HAST *l.*62 556 813 818 819 821 822 824 1039 1042 1863 = 11, 1
  Has't any Philosophie in thee shepheard?   1221
HASTE = 1
  Duk. Mistris, dispatch you with your safest haste,   498

HAT = 1

Is his head worth a hat? Or his chin worth a beard?   1401

HATE = 3*3

*Sonne deerelie? By this kinde of chase, I should hate   489
*him, for my father hated his father deerely; yet I hate | not *Orlando*. 490
Ros. No faith, hate him not for my sake.   492
*that I weare; owe no man hate, enuie no mans happi-|nesse: 1271
I loue him not, nor hate him not: and yet   1901
Haue more cause to hate him then to loue him,   1902

HATED = 1*1

*him, for my father hated his father deerely; yet I hate | not *Orlando*. 490
Siluius; the time was, that I hated thee;   1866

HATES = *2

*I know not why) hates nothing more then he: yet hee's   161
*simpring, none of you hates them) that betweene you,   2790

HATH *l*.*124 *148 *186 *188 *213 *215 *222 *363 446 558 559 560 592
608 635 726 *919 992 *1009 1013 1058 1059 1071 1100 1107 *1227 1307
1375 1402 *1509 1537 *1652 *1665 *1686 *1687 *1725 1791 1881 *1962
*1979 *2109 *2113 2152 2190 *2218 *2348 2576 2607 2619 2758
2760 = 28*24

HAUE *l*.*41 *51 *68 *77 *82 *84 *103 *110 *137 *180 *187 *254 *255
265 274 *275 297 *331 *337 *352 *353 355 *356 *367 370 389 401 402
406 408 420 423 430 433 *460 478 508 530 534 545 555 585 586 *589
631 729 *733 *735 742 771 796 806 814 827 879 *915 921 978 1011 1017
1021 1023 1064 1078 1081 1090 1091 *1097 1098 1102 1120 1170 *1260
1267 *1281 *1319 1350 1351 *1354 1355 *1391 1449 *1464 1467 *1468
1474 *1531 *1534 *1550 *1558 *1559 *1560 *1561 *1636 1638 *1640
*1651 *1658 *1691 *1711 1713 *1737 *1754 1796 1810 1864 1880 1899
1902 *1926 *1936 *1937 *1938 1939 1940 *1943 *1952 *1954 2004 *2012
*2017 *2018 *2020 2027 *2039 *2052 2054 *2069 2078 *2107 *2108
*2131 2137 2200 *2221 *2272 *2330 *2352 2371 *2382 2422 *2446 *2468
*2484 2486 *2525 *2584 2591 *2592 2594 *2618 *2621 *2622 *2623 2624
*2665 2696 2697 2708 2727 2750 2772 *2794 = 81*87, *1

Clo. Then learne this of me, To haue, is to haue. For   2382

HAUING = 3*1

And hauing that do choake their seruice vp,   765
Euen with the hauing, it is not so with thee: 766
*haue not: (but I pardon you for that, for simply your ha-|uing   1561
happie, in hauing what he wishes for.   2456

HAUKING = *1

*1.*Pa*. Shal we clap into't roundly, without hauking,   2541

HAUNT = 1

And this our life exempt from publike haunt,   621

HAUNTS = *1

*that are sicke. There is a man haunts the Forrest, that a-|buses   1545

HAUTHORNES = *1

*barkes; hangs Oades vpon Hauthornes, and Elegies on   1547

HE = 105*79, 3

Rosalind, I am that he, that vnfortunate he.   1577
now you are not *ipse*, for I am he.   2386
Will. Which he sir? | *Clo*. He sir, that must marrie this woman:
Therefore   2387

HEAD = 5*5

Weares yet a precious Iewell in his head: 620
Is his head worth a hat? Or his chin worth a beard?   1401
The matter's in my head, and in my heart,   1912
*carries his house on his head; a better ioyncture I thinke   1969

HEAD *cont.*

*your head, and shew the world what the bird hath done | to her owne
neast.   2109
*horns vpon his head, for a branch of victory; haue you   2131
Who with her head, nimble in threats approach'd | The opening of his
mouth: but sodainly   2260
Lay cowching head on ground, with catlike watch   2266
Clo. Good eu'n gentle friend. Couer thy head, couer   2357
*thy head: Nay prethee bee couer'd. How olde are you | Friend?   2358
HEADED = 1
And all th'imbossed sores, and headed euils,   1041
HEADS = 1
Should in their owne confines with forked heads   630
HEALE = 1
Did make offence, his eye did heale it vp: 1891
HEAPD = 1
With measure heap'd in ioy, to'th Measures fall.   2756
HEAPE = *1
Cel. How proue you that in the great heape of your | knowledge?   235
HEAR = *1
*that habit play the knaue with him, do you hear For- |(rester.   1488
HEARD = 7*5
*first time that euer I heard breaking of ribbes was sport | for Ladies. 300
The Fluxe of companie: anon a carelesse Heard   660
Hisperia the Princesse Gentlewoman | Confesses that she secretly
ore-heard   690
Hath heard your praises, and this night he meanes,   726
Ros. O yes, I heard them all, and more too, for some   1362
*well: for there he fel in loue. I haue heard him read ma- |ny   1534
Ros. You haue heard him sweare downright he was.   1737
Sil. So please you, for I neuer heard it yet: 2186
Yet heard too much of *Phebes* crueltie.   2187
Cel. O I haue heard him speake of that same brother,   2272
Iaq. Sir, by your patience: if I heard you rightly,   2757
There is much matter to be heard, and learn'd: 2762
HEARE *see also* here = 8*4
Orlan. Goe a-part *Adam*, and thou shalt heare how | he will shake me
vp.   30
Oli. Let me goe I say. | *Orl*. I will not till I please: you shall heare
mee: my   65
Cel. Deere Soueraigne heare me speake.   527
1.*Lo*. I cannot heare of any that did see her,   684
And thereby hangs a tale. When I did heare   1001
Cel. Didst thou heare these verses?   1361
Cel. But didst thou heare without wondering, how   1369
When he that speakes them pleases those that heare: 1886
Then in their countenance: will you heare the letter?   2185
Did you euer heare such railing?   2195
Orl. To her, that is not heere, nor doth not heare.   2515
Clo. By my troth yes: I count it but time lost to heare   2569
HEARER = 1
Wearing thy hearer in thy Mistris praise, | Thou hast not lou'd.   820
HEARING = 2
Heere was he merry, hearing of a Song.   976
Duke Frederick hearing how that euerie day   2730
HEART *see also* hart = 19*10
*so much in the heart of the world, and especially of my   164

HEART *cont*.

Sticks me at heart: Sir, you haue well deseru'd,	406
Ros. I could shake them off my coate, these burs are | in my heart.	475
A bore-speare in my hand, and in my heart	583
Ros. I could finde in my heart to disgrace my mans	787
Orl. Why how now *Adam*? No greater heart in thee:	954
Ol. Oh that your Highnesse knew my heart in this:	1193
Helens cheeke, but not his heart, | Cleopatra's *Maiestie:*	1343
Cel. It is yong *Orlando*, that tript vp the Wrastlers | heeles, and your heart, both in an instant.	1406
Iaq. What stature is she of? | *Orl*. Iust as high as my heart.	1462
*as cleane as a sound sheepes heart, that there shal not | be one spot of Loue in't.	1600
Wil you go? | *Orl*. With all my heart, good youth.	1609
Clo. Amen. A man may if he were of a fearful heart,	1657
*them brauely, quite trauers athwart the heart of his lo-|uer,	1749
Whose heart th'accustom'd sight of death makes hard	1774
Now I doe frowne on thee with all my heart,	1786
Sil. *Phebe*, with all my heart.	1910
The matter's in my head, and in my heart,	1912
him oth' shoulder, but Ile warrant him heart hole.	1963
That a maidens heart hath burn'd.	2190
War 'st thou with a womans heart?	2194
And after some small space, being strong at heart,	2305
You lacke a mans heart. | *Ros*. I doe so, I confesse it:	2319
Oli. Well then, take a good heart, and counterfeit to | be a man.	2328
thee weare thy heart in a scarfe. | *Orl*. It is my arme.	2430
Ros. I thought thy heart had beene wounded with | the clawes of a Lion.	2432
*of heart heauinesse, by how much I shal thinke my bro-|ther	2455
Aud. I do desire it with all my heart: and I hope it is	2534
Whose heart within his bosome is.	2690

HEARTILY *see also* hartily = *1

Cha. I am heartily glad I came hither to you: if hee	155

HEARTS = 2

Cel. Your hearts desires be with you.	360
Of manie faces, eyes, and hearts, | *to haue the touches deerest pris'd*.	1349

HEATHEN = *1

*knowes himselfe to be a Foole. The Heathen Philoso-|pher,	2374

HEAUD = 1

The wretched annimall heau'd forth such groanes	643

HEAUEN = 10*1

Ros. Fare you well: praie heauen I be deceiu'd in you.	359
For by this heauen, now at our sorrowes pale;	568
And little wreakes to finde the way to heauen | By doing deeds of hospitalitie.	866
Heauen thankes, and make no boast of them.	924
Call me not foole, till heauen hath sent me fortune,	992
The quintessence of euerie sprite, | *heauen would in little show*.	1337
Therefore heauen Nature charg'd, | *that one bodie should be fill'd*	1339
Heauen would that shee these gifts should haue, | *and I to liue and die her slaue*.	1351
And thanke heauen, fasting, for a good mans loue;	1831
Hymen. *Then is there mirth in heauen*,	2683
Hymen from Heauen brought her,	2687

HEAUENLY = 2

But heauenly *Rosaline*. *Exit*	457

HEAUENLY *cont*.
Thus Rosalinde *of manie parts,* | *by Heauenly Synode was deuis'd,*   1347
HEAUIE = *1
*of heauie tedious penurie. These Time ambles | withal.   1513
HEAUINESSE = *1
*of heart heauinesse, by how much I shal thinke my bro-|ther   2455
HEE *l*.*21 *110 *115 *126 *129 *145 *146 *152 *155 *156 *188 1027
*1223 *1227 *1415 *1434 *1516 *1536 *1586 *1725 *1728 *1747 1851
*1959 *1968 *2010 2242 *2385 *2647 = 3*27
HEELE *l*.597 = 1
HEELES = 1*1
Cel. It is yong *Orlando*, that tript vp the Wrastlers | heeles, and your
heart, both in an instant.   1406
Attalanta's heeles. Will you sitte downe with me, and   1469
HEELL = 1
Hee'll make a proper man: the best thing in him   1889
HEERE = 25*19
*more properly) staies me heere at home vnkept: for call   11
Oli. Now Sir, what make you heere? | *Orl*. Nothing: I am not taught to
make any thing.   32
Oli. Know you where you are sir? | *Orl*. O sir, very well: heere in your
Orchard.   43
Oli. Was not *Charles* the Dukes Wrastler heere to | speake with me?   90
Den. So please you, he is heere at the doore, and im-|portunes accesse
to you.   92
*wise men haue makes a great shew; Heere comes Mon-|sieur the *Beu*.   255
*to doe, and heere where you are, they are comming to | performe it.   279
Le Beu. You must if you stay heere, for heere is the   306
Heere feele we not the penaltie of *Adam*,   611
Cor. That yong Swaine that you saw heere but ere-|while,   874
Heere shall he see no enemie,   896
Come, warble, come. | *Song. Altogether heere.*   925
Heere shall he see. &c.   932
Heere shall he see, grosse fooles as he,   941
O I die for food. Heere lie I downe,   952
At the armes end: I wil heere be with thee presently,   960
Heere was he merry, hearing of a Song.   976
I thought that all things had bin sauage heere,   1084
Cor. Heere comes yong Mr *Ganimed*, my new Mistris-|ses Brother.   1283
*before you came: for looke heere what I found on a   1372
*heere? Did he aske for me? Where remaines he? How   1416
Cel. You bring me out. Soft, comes he not heere?   1446
Ros. With this Shepheardesse my sister: heere in the   1524
Clo. I am heere with thee, and thy Goats, as the most   1619
*stagger in this attempt: for heere wee haue no Temple   1658
*Heere comes Sir *Oliuer*: Sir *Oliuer Mar-text* you are   1673
*wel met. Will you dispatch vs heere vnder this tree, or   1674
Ol. Is there none heere to giue the woman?   1676
heere Sir: Nay, pray be couer'd.   1684
youth mounts, and folly guides: who comes heere?   1752
Ros. How say you now, is it not past two a clock? | And heere much
Orlando.   2148
To sleepe: looke who comes heere.   2153
There stript himselfe, and heere vpon his arme   2300
Mar-text. But *Awdrie*, there is a youth heere in the | Forrest layes
claime to you.   2346
Will. William, sir. | *Clo*. A faire name. Was't borne i'th Forrest heere?   2362

HEERE *cont*.

*was old Sir *Rowlands* will I estate vpon you, and heere | liue and die a
Shepherd. 2419
Heere comes my *Rosalinde*. 2426
Orl. To her, that is not heere, nor doth not heare. 2515
Heere come two of the banish'd Dukes Pages. 2536
You wil bestow her on *Orlando* heere? 2582
*in heere sir, amongst the rest of the Country copulatiues 2632
His brother heere, and put him to the sword: 2734
That heere were well begun, and wel begot: 2748

HEEREAFTER = 1*1

*may come heereafter. But be it, as it may bee, 1650
excuse for me heereafter, to leaue my wife. 1698

HEEREIN = *2

*selfe notice of my Brothers purpose heerein, and haue by 137
Cel. Heerein I see thou lou'st mee not with the full 177

HEES = 2*2

*I know not why) hates nothing more then he: yet hee's 161
Ros. Hees falne in loue with your foulnesse, & shee'll 1839
But sure hee's proud, and yet his pride becomes him; 1888
He is not very tall, yet for his yeeres hee's tall: 1892

HEIGH = 4

Heigh ho, sing heigh ho, vnto the greene holly, 1160
The heigh ho, the holly, | *This Life is most iolly*. 1162
as freind remembred not. | *Heigh ho, sing, &c*. 1167

HEIGHT = *1

*by so much the more shall I to morrow be at the height 2454

HEIGH-HO = 1

*I pray you tell your brother how well I counterfei-|ted: heigh-ho. 2322

HEIRE = 2*1

*be his heire; for what hee hath taken away from thy fa-|ther 188
His yongest sonne, and would not change that calling | To be adopted
heire to *Fredricke*. 396
No, let my Father seeke another heire: 563

HELD = 1

To one his lands with-held, and to the other 2745

HELENS = 1

Helens cheeke, but not his heart, | Cleopatra's *Maiestie:* 1343

HELLESPONT = *1

*(good youth) he went but forth to wash him in the Hel-|lespont, 2014

HELPE = 1*3

And take vpon command, what helpe we haue 1102
Clo. Wilt thou rest damn'd? God helpe thee shallow 1268
*of Irish Wolues against the Moone: I will helpe you 2517
*playes proue the better by the helpe of good Epilogues: 2781

HELPING = *1

Orl. Marry sir, I am helping you to mar that which 35

HEM = 2

Cel. Hem them away. 477
Ros. I would try if I could cry hem, and haue him. 478

HEN = *1

*thee, then a Barbary cocke-pidgeon ouer his hen, more 2059

HENCE = 3*1

1.*Lord*. My Lord, he is but euen now gone hence, 975
Goe hence a little, and I shall conduct you | If you will marke it. 1763
*true louer hence, and not a word; for here comes more | company.
Exit. *Sil*. 2222

HENCE *cont.*
If she refuse me, and from hence I go   2600
HENCEFORTH = *2
  Ros. From henceforth I will Coz, and deuise sports: 193
  *from her wheele, that her gifts may henceforth bee | bestowed equally.   201
HER *see also* hir *l.*107 *108 *109 *110 *111 *112 *201 *203 205 412 425
442 448 449 528 529 530 532 533 *538 539 540 545 547 684 685 686 692
804 805 *831 *833 *834 860 861 862 1051 1052 1352 1459 *1504 *1570
1677 1680 *1687 1822 1827 1828 1829 1836 1842 1848 2003 2004 2021
2050 *2052 2054 *2080 *2081 *2082 2083 *2099 2110 2161 2166 2173
2175 *2218 *2219 *2220 *2221 2238 2260 *2410 2412 *2414 *2416 *2472
*2475 2515 2582 *2584 *2592 2599 2687 2688 = 65*38
HERCULES = 1
  Ros. Now Hercules, be thy speede yong man.   371
HERD *see* heard
HERE = 15*4
  Are all throwne downe, and that which here stands vp   416
  That here was at the Wrastling?   438
  And here detain'd by her vsurping Vncle   442
  Because I doe. Looke, here comes the Duke.   496
  Of old Sir *Rowland*; why, what make you here?   707
  Ad. No matter whether, so you come not here.   734
  Be comfort to my age: here is the gold,   749
  Here liued I, but now liue here no more   776
  here, a yong man and an old in solemne talke.   803
  Vnclaim'd of any man. But who come here?   1061
  Ros. Peace, here comes my sister reading, stand aside.   1322
  *confirmer of false reckonings, he attends here in the for-|rest on the
  Duke your father.   1740
  I had rather here you chide, then this man wooe.   1838
  'Tis at the tufft of Oliues, here hard by: 1847
  *true louer hence, and not a word; for here comes more | company.
  Exit. Sil.   2222
  in the world: here comes the man you meane.   2349
  *Looke, here comes a Louer of mine, and a louer of hers.   2483
  *couples are comming to the Arke. Here comes a payre   2613
HEREAFTER = 1
  Hereafter in a better world then this,   452
HERES = 2
  Here's a yong maid with trauaile much oppressed, | And faints for
  succour.   858
  Here's eight that must take hands,   2702
HERO = *2
  *haue liu'd manie a faire yeere though *Hero* had turn'd   2012
  Hero of Cestos. But these are all lies, men haue died   2017
HERS = 2*1
  Cel. And mine to eeke out hers.   358
  This is a mans inuention, and his hand. | *Sil.* Sure it is hers.   2178
  *Looke, here comes a Louer of mine, and a louer of hers.   2483
HERSELFE *see* selfe
HES = 2*1
  For then he's full of matter.   677
  Clo. Holla; you Clowne. | *Ros.* Peace foole, he's not thy kinsman.   848
  Iaq. Is not this a rare fellow my Lord? He's as good   2677
HETHER = 2
  Cel. Call him hether good Monsieuer *Le Beu.* | *Duke.* Do so: Ile not be
  by.   326

HETHER *cont.*
Yea brought her hether.   2688
HEY = 9
With a hey, and a ho, and a hey nonino,   2548
When Birds do sing, hey ding a ding, ding.   2551
With a hey, & a ho, and a hey nonino,   2554
With a hey, and a ho, & a hey nonino: 2558
With a hey and a ho, & a hey nonino: 2562
HIDDEN = 1
Lye there what hidden womans feare there will,   584
HIDE = 2
To hide vs from pursuite that will be made   601
In the which hope, I blush, and hide my Sword.   1096
HIDING = *1
*hiding from me all gentleman-like qualities: the spirit   69
HIGH = 5
High commendation, true applause, and loue;   431
Iaq. What stature is she of? | *Orl.* Iust as high as my heart.   1462
And high top, bald with drie antiquitie: 2256
High wedlock then be honored: 2719
Honor, high honor and renowne   2720
HIGHNES = *1
Ros. So was I when your highnes took his Dukdome,   520
HIGHNESSE = 3
Did I offend your highnesse.   512
So was I when your highnesse banisht him;   521
Ol. Oh that your Highnesse knew my heart in this: 1193
HIM *l.**17 *18 *22 *46 81 94 *104 *116 *118 *127 *129 *131 *138 *145
*151 *152 *156 *160 *165 *248 *249 *290 *291 *323 *324 325 326 *334
*367 382 388 401 404 419 *490 492 495 521 598 637 661 662 *672 676
678 699 718 724 725 730 *829 *915 921 974 979 988 1055 1058 1111
1149 1177 1181 1186 *1195 1198 1300 1357 *1414 *1417 *1428 1447
1480 *1487 *1488 *1534 *1549 1551 *1587 *1594 *1595 *1599 *1696
1730 *1733 *1737 *1743 *1744 1759 1834 1849 1880 1883 1888 1889
1898 1900 1901 1902 1908 1913 *1962 1963 1971 *1979 *2014 *2120
*2129 2139 2207 2211 *2215 2241 *2272 2273 2277 2282 2283 *2287
2304 2317 2337 2489 2604 *2617 *2620 2630 *2648 2734 2737 2740 2741
2761 = 89*63, 1
Ros. I would try if I could cry hem, and haue him.   478
HIMSELFE = 3*5
*grace himselfe on thee, hee will practise against thee by   146
Then he hath wrong'd himselfe: if he be free,   1059
*diuell himselfe will haue no shepherds, I cannot see else | how thou
shouldst scape.   1281
*go as softly as foot can fall, he thinkes himselfe too soon | there. 1517
Of femall fauour, and bestowes himselfe | Like a ripe sister: the woman
low   2236
There stript himselfe, and heere vpon his arme   2300
*knowes himselfe to be a Foole. The Heathen Philoso-|pher,   2374
*he cut it to please himselfe: this is call'd the quip modest.   2650
HINDE = 1
If a Hart doe lacke a Hinde, | Let him seeke out Rosalinde: 1299
HINDES = *1
*me: hee lets mee feede with his Hindes, barres mee the   21
HIR *l.*1288 *2583 *2584 = 1*2
HIRD = *1
*deerely hir'd: but I (his brother) gaine nothing vnder   16

HIRE = 1
The thriftie hire I saued vnder your Father,   743
HIS *see also* all's *l*.*7 *9 *13 *16 *17 *20 *21 53 *67 *101 *112 *132 *133
   *142 *143 *144 *156 *188 *230 *231 *243 258 *282 *290 294 *304 314
   362 *363 396 398 400 *439 440 443 446 450 *487 *488 *490 497 *520
   558 620 644 646 654 658 *697 698 725 730 868 870 *873 893 938 948
   981 993 1006 1011 1054 1056 1121 1122 1124 1128 1136 1139 1140 1142
   1171 1197 1328 1330 1343 *1377 1401 *1404 1405 *1533 1542 1557
   *1587 *1596 *1661 *1663 *1664 *1686 *1687 1716 1719 1720 1723 *1733
   *1749 *1750 *1751 1758 1834 1888 1890 1891 1892 1893 1894 1896
   *1969 *1970 *1974 1975 *1994 *2008 *2009 *2059 *2120 *2131 2138
   2152 2178 2242 2253 2258 2261 2271 2279 2281 2285 2299 2300 2304
   2308 2310 *2376 *2470 2547 2596 2608 *2647 *2657 *2679 2680 2689
   2690 2707 2733 2734 2738 2739 2745 = 101*64
HISPERIA = 1
Hisperia the Princesse Gentlewoman | Confesses that she secretly
ore-heard   690
HISTORIE = 1
That ends this strange euentfull historie,   1143
HIT = 1
Hee, that a Foole doth very wisely hit,   1027
HITHER *see also* hether = 9*3
*come in: therefore out of my loue to you, I came hither   130
Cha. I am heartily glad I came hither to you: if hee   155
Du. How now daughter, and Cousin: | Are you crept hither to see the
wrastling?   318
Duk. Send to his brother, fetch that gallant hither,   697
Come hither, come hither, come hither: 895
Come hither, come hither, come hither,   931
Be truly welcome hither: I am the Duke   1173
He sent me hither, stranger as I am   2306
HO = 9
Heigh ho, sing heigh ho, vnto the greene holly,   1160
The heigh ho, the holly, | *This Life is most iolly.*   1162
as freind remembred not. | *Heigh ho, sing, &c.*   1167
*I pray you tell your brother how well I counterfei-|ted: heigh-ho. 2322
With a hey, and a ho, and a hey nonino,   2548
With a hey, & a ho, and a hey ñonino,   2554
With a hey, and a ho, & a hey nonino: 2558
With a hey and a ho, & a hey nonino: 2562
HOA = 1
Hy. Peace hoa: I barre confusion,   2699
HOARSE = *1
*or spitting, or saying we are hoarse, which are the onely | prologues to
a bad voice.   2542
HOGS = *1
Orlan. Shall I keepe your hogs, and eat huskes with   40
HOLD = 4
If with my selfe I hold intelligence,   507
*the beggerly thankes. Come sing; and you that wil not | hold your
tongues.   916
For my sake be comfortable, hold death a while   959
for: we shall be flouting: we cannot hold.   2353
HOLDS = 1
If truth holds true contents.   2704
HOLE = 1*1
him oth' shoulder, but Ile warrant him heart hole.   1963

HOLE *cont.*
*'twill out at the key-hole: stop that, 'twill flie with the | smoake out at
the chimney.   2072
HOLIDAY = *1
*in holiday foolerie, if we walke not in the trodden paths   473
HOLLA = 2*1
*physicke your ranckenesse, and yet giue no thousand | crownes
neyther: holla *Dennis*.   86
Clo. Holla; you Clowne. | *Ros*. Peace foole, he's not thy kinsman.   848
Cel. Cry holla, to the tongue, I prethee: it curuettes   1438
HOLLOW = *1
*patheticall breake-promise, and the most hollow louer,   2098
HOLLY = 2
Heigh ho, sing heigh ho, vnto the greene holly,   1160
The heigh ho, the holly, | This Life is most iolly.   1162
HOLY = 4
Are sanctified and holy traitors to you: 716
And haue with holy bell bin knowld to Church,   1098
Ros. And his kissing is as ful of sanctitie, | As the touch of holy bread.   1723
Sil. So holy, and so perfect is my loue,   1873
HOLY-DAY = *1
*holy-day humor, and like enough to consent: What   1982
HOME = 3*3
*for my part, he keepes me rustically at home, or (to speak   10
*more properly) staies me heere at home vnkept: for call   11
Your praise is come too swiftly home before you.   712
*was at home I was in a better place, but Trauellers must | be content.   799
Then sing him home, the rest shall beare this burthen;   2139
Ros. I would I were at home.   2315
HOMEWARDS = 1
Cel. Come, you looke paler and paler: pray you draw | homewards:
good sir, goe with vs.   2332
HOMILIE = *1
Ros. O most gentle Iupiter, what tedious homilie of   1353
HONEST = 4*4
*makes honest, & those that she makes honest, she makes | very
illfauouredly.   207
capricious Poet honest *Ouid* was among the Gothes.   1620
Aud. I do not know what Poetical is: is it honest in | deed and word: is
it a true thing?   1628
Clow. I do truly: for thou swear'st to me thou art ho-|nest: 1635
Aud. Would you not haue me honest?   1638
Aud. Well, I am not faire, and therefore I pray the | Gods make me
honest.   1643
1.*Pa*. Wel met honest Gentleman.   2538
HONESTIE = 2*3
Ros. I pray thee, if it stand with honestie,   877
*honestie coupled to beautie, is to haue Honie a sawce to | Sugar.   1640
Clo. Truly, and to cast away honestie vppon a foule   1645
or I should thinke my honestie ranker then my wit.   1997
*that that no man else will: rich honestie dwels like a mi-|ser   2636
HONIE = *1
*honestie coupled to beautie, is to haue Honie a sawce to | Sugar.   1640
HONOR = 5*6
*mine honor I will, and when I breake that oath, let mee   190
*then with safety of a pure blush, thou maist in ho-|nor come off
againe.   197

HONOR *cont.*
*Clo. No by mine honor, but I was bid to come for you	228
*they were good Pan-cakes, and swore by his Honor the	231
*more was this knight swearing by his Honor, for he ne-|uer	243
*Ros. My Fathers loue is enough to honor him enough;	248
If you out-stay the time, vpon mine honor,	549
Ielous in honor, sodaine, and quicke in quarrell,	1130
Honor, high honor and renowne	2720
you to your former Honor, I bequeath	2763

HONORABLE = *1
*Clo. Come Shepheard, let vs make an honorable re-|treit,	1358

HONORED = 1
High wedlock then be honored:	2719

HONOUR = *2
*loth to foyle him, as I must for my owne honour if hee	129
*Clo. Of a certaine Knight, that swore by his Honour	230

HONOURABLE = 1*1
The world esteem'd thy father honourable,	387
*of a married man, more honourable then the bare	1668

HOOD = *1
*like the old *Robin Hood* of *England*: they say many yong	117

HOOPING = 1
*wonderfull, and yet againe wonderful, and after that out | of all hooping.	1388

HOPE = 5*4
*I hope I shall see an end of him; for my soule (yet	160
*hope of life in him: So he seru'd the second, and so the	291
In the which hope, I blush, and hide my Sword.	1096
Clo. Then thou art damn'd. | Cor. Nay, I hope.	1233
*Now if thou wert a Poet, I might haue some hope | thou didst feigne.	1636
No faith proud Mistresse, hope not after it,	1818
Ros. Are you not good? | Orl. I hope so.	2030
*Aud. I do desire it with all my heart: and I hope it is	2534
As those that feare they hope, and know they feare.	2578

HORNE = 4*1
*then no skill, by so much is a horne more precious | then to want.	1670
Take thou no scorne to weare the horne,	2140
The horne, the horne, the lusty horne,	2144

HORNES = 1*4
*though? Courage. As hornes are odious, they are neces-|sarie.	1660
*right: Many a man has good Hornes, and knows no end	1662
*of his owne getting; hornes, euen so poore men alone:	1664
Orl. What's that? | *Ros. Why hornes: w such as you are faine to be be-|holding	1972
His Leather skin, and hornes to weare:	2138

HORNE-BEASTS = *1
*but the wood, no assembly but horne-beasts. But what	1659

HORNE-MAKER = *1
*Orl. Vertue is no horne-maker: and my *Rosalind* is | vertuous.	1976

HORNS = *1
*horns vpon his head, for a branch of victory; haue you	2131

HORSE = 2*3
*Clo. As the Oxe hath his bow sir, the horse his curb,	1686
*Cel. Yes, I thinke he is not a picke purse, nor a horse-|stealer,	1732
*as a puisny Tilter, y spurs his horse but on one side,	1750
2.Pa. I faith, y'faith, and both in a tune like two | gipsies on a horse.	2544
*Du Se. He vses his folly like a stalking-horse, and vn-|der	2679

HORSES = *1
*not from the stalling of an Oxe? his horses are bred   13
HOSE = 1*5
*the weaker vessell, as doublet and hose ought to show it   789
His youthfull hose well sau'd, a world too wide,   1139
*I am caparison'd like a man, I haue a doublet and hose in   1391
*hose? What did he when thou saw'st him? What sayde   1414
*hose should be vngarter'd, your bonnet vnbanded, your   1563
*we must haue your doublet and hose pluckt ouer   2108
HOSPITALITIE = 1
And little wreakes to finde the way to heauen | By doing deeds of
hospitalitie.   866
HOT = 1*1
For in my youth I neuer did apply | Hot, and rebellious liquors in my
bloud,   752
*Nun; if it had not bin for a hot Midsomer-night, for   2013
HOURE = 10*3
'Tis but an houre agoe, since it was nine,   997
And after one houre more, 'twill be eleuen,   998
And so from houre to houre, we ripe, and ripe,   999
And then from houre to houre, we rot, and rot,   1000
And I did laugh, sans intermission | An houre by his diall. Oh noble
foole,   1005
*sighing euerie minute, and groaning euerie houre wold   1494
*Orl. My faire *Rosalind*, I come within an houre of my | promise.   1957
*minute behinde your houre, I will thinke you the most   2097
Within an houre, and pacing through the Forrest,   2251
This Carroll they began that houre,   2561
Phe. That will I, should I die the houre after.   2587
HOURES = 1*3
Loose, and neglect the creeping houres of time: 1089
*Ros. Breake an houres promise in loue? hee that   1959
*Orl. For these two houres *Rosalinde*, I wil leaue thee.   2084
*Ros. Alas, deere loue, I cannot lacke thee two houres.   2085
HOURS = *1
*and suppers, and sleeping hours excepted: it is the right | Butter-
womens ranke to Market.   1295
HOUSE = 7*4
Hadst thou descended from another house: 390
This is no place, this house is but a butcherie;   731
And let my officers of such a nature | Make an extent vpon his house
and Lands: 1196
*as wel a darke house, and a whip, as madmen do: 1581
*Iaq. O knowledge ill inhabited, worse then Ioue in | a thatch'd house.   1621
Besides, I like you not: if you will know my house,   1846
*carries his house on his head; a better ioyncture I thinke   1969
But at this howre, the house doth keepe it selfe, | There's none within.   2231
The owner of the house I did enquire for?   2239
*good: for my fathers house, and all the reuennew, that   2418
*sir, in a poore house, as your Pearle in your foule oy-|ster.   2637
HOUSEWIUES *see* huswiues
HOUSWIFE = *1
*Cel. Let vs sit and mocke the good houswife *For-|tune*   200
HOW = 28*31
*I will no longer endure it, though yet I know no wise | remedy how to
auoid it.   26

HOW *cont*.
Orlan. Goe a-part *Adam*, and thou shalt heare how | he will shake me
vp.   30
*learne mee how to remember any extraordinary plea-|sure.   175
*the whetstone of the wits. How now Witte, whether | wander you?   224
Cel. How proue you that in the great heape of your | knowledge?   235
Le Beu. What colour Madame? How shall I aun-|swer you?   267
Du. How now daughter, and Cousin: | Are you crept hither to see the
wrastling?   318
Duk. How do'st thou *Charles*?   380
how full of briers is this working day world.   471
Therefore deuise with me how we may flie   564
This I must do, or know not what to do: | Yet this I will not do, do how
I can,   738
Orl. Oh good old man, how well in thee appeares   760
Ros. O *Iupiter*, how merry are my spirits?   784
Sil. Oh *Corin*, that thou knew'st how I do loue her.   805
How many actions most ridiculous,   812
Orl. Why how now *Adam*? No greater heart in thee: 954
Du Sen. Why how now Monsieur, what a life is this   982
Thus we may see (quoth he) how the world wagges: 996
There then, how then, what then, let me see wherein   1057
Co. And how like you this shepherds life Mr *Touchstone*?   1212
*diuell himselfe will haue no shepherds, I cannot see else | how thou
shouldst scape.   1281
Some, how briefe the Life of man | runs his erring pilgrimage,   1327
Cel. How now backe friends: Shepheard, go off a lit-|tle: 1356
Cel. But didst thou heare without wondering, how   1369
*he? How look'd he? Wherein went he? What makes hee   1415
*heere? Did he aske for me? Where remaines he? How   1416
*betweene Terme and Terme, and then they perceiue not | how time
moues.   1521
*he taught me how to know a man in loue: in which cage | of rushes, I
am sure you art not prisoner.   1555
Orl. Neither rime nor reason can expresse how much.   1579
*Goates, *Audrey*: and how *Audrey* am I the man yet?   1616
*brow of a Batcheller: and by how much defence is bet-|ter   1669
Clo. Good euen good Mr what ye cal't: how do you   1681
*swam in a Gundello. Why how now *Orlando*, where   1953
Orl. How if the kisse be denide?   1991
Ros. Now tell me how long you would haue her, af-|ter you haue
possest her?   2052
*didst know how many fathome deepe I am in loue: but   2112
*how deepe I am in loue: ile tell thee *Aliena*, I cannot be   2121
Iaq. Sing it: 'tis no matter how it bee in tune, so it | make noyse
enough.   2134
Ros. How say you now, is it not past two a clock? | And heere much
Orlando.   2148
Ros. She *Phebes* me: marke how the tyrant writes.   2188
How then might your praiers moue?   2204
And then Ile studie how to die.   2212
What man I am, and how, and why, and where | This handkercher was
stain'd.   2246
As how I came into that Desert place.   2295
Cel. Why how now *Ganimed*, sweet *Ganimed*.   2311
*I pray you tell your brother how well I counterfei-|ted: heigh-ho.   2322
How you excuse my brother, *Rosalind*.   2335

HOW *cont*.
    *thy head: Nay prethee bee couer'd. How olde are you | Friend?   2358
    *Ros. Oh my deere *Orlando*, how it greeues me to see   2429
    *Ros. Did your brother tell you how I counterfeyted   2435
    *bid the Duke to the Nuptiall. But O, how bitter a thing   2452
    *of heart heauinesse, by how much I shal thinke my bro-|ther   2455
    How that a life was but a Flower, | *In spring time*, &c.   2563
    Iaq. And how was that tane vp?   2625
    *Iaq. How seuenth cause? Good my Lord, like this | fellow.   2628
    *Iaq. But for the seuenth cause. How did you finde   2642
    *Iaq. And how oft did you say his beard was not well | cut?   2657
    How thus we met, and these things finish.   2714
    Duke Frederick hearing how that euerie day   2730
HOWLING = *1
    *Ros. Pray you no more of this, 'tis like the howling   2516
HOWRE = 2
    *me: 'tis but one cast away, and so come death: two o' | clocke is your
    howre.   2091
    But at this howre, the house doth keepe it selfe, | There's none within.   2231
HUGE = *1
    *No, no, the noblest Deere hath them as huge as the Ras-|call: 1665
HUGELY = 1
    Doth it not flow as hugely as the Sea,   1046
HUMANE = *1
    *to set her before your eyes to morrow, humane as she is, | and without
    any danger.   2475
HUMBLED = 1
    Falls not the axe vpon the humbled neck,   1775
HUMBLENESSE = 1
    All humblenesse, all patience, and impatience,   2504
HUMOR = *4
    *life (looke you) it fits my humor well: but as there is no   1219
    *my Sutor from his mad humor of loue, to a liuing humor   1596
    *holy-day humor, and like enough to consent: What   1982
HUMOROUS = 2*1
    The Duke is humorous, what he is indeede   434
    The bonnie priser of the humorous Duke?   711
    *which by often rumination, wraps me in a most humo-|rous sadnesse.   1934
HUMOUR = *1
    *sir, but mine owne, a poore humour of mine sir, to take   2635
HUNDRED = 1*1
    Ad. But do not so: I haue fiue hundred Crownes,   742
    *will kill thee a hundred and fifty wayes, therefore trem-|ble and
    depart.   2398
HUNGER = 1
    Opprest with two weake euils, age, and hunger,   1109
HUNGRY = 1
    Food to the suck'd and hungry Lyonnesse?   2278
HUNT = 1
    Her loue is not the Hare that I doe hunt,   2166
HUNTER = 1
    vnseasonably. He was furnish'd like a Hunter.   1439
HUNTERS = 1
    That from the Hunters aime had tane a hurt,   641
HUNTRESSE = 1
    Thy Huntresse name, that my full life doth sway.   1204

HURT = 3
    That from the Hunters aime had tane a hurt,   641
    Which I haue darted at thee, hurt thee not,   1796
    Nor I am sure there is no force in eyes | That can doe hurt.   1797
HURTLING = 1
    Who quickly fell before him, in which hurtling   2283
HUSBAND = 1*1
    *But I doe take thee *Orlando* for my husband: there's a   2048
    Ile haue no Husband, if you be not he: 2697
HUSBANDRIE = 1
    In lieu of all thy paines and husbandrie,   769
HUSBANDS = *1
    *make her fault her husbands occasion, let her neuer nurse 2082
HUSKES = *1
    Orlan. Shall I keepe your hogs, and eat huskes with   40
HUSWIUES = 1
    She has a huswiues hand, but that's no matter: 2176
HY = 1
HYEN = *1
    *I will laugh like a Hyen, and that when thou art inclin'd | to sleepe. 2064
HYMEN *see also* Hy. = 5
    Enter Hymen, Rosalind, and Celia. | Still Musicke.   2681
    Hymen. *Then is there mirth in heauen,*   2683
    Hymen from Heauen brought her,   2687
    'Tis Hymen peoples euerie towne,   2718
    To Hymen, God of euerie Towne.   2721
HYMENS = 1
    To ioyne in *Hymens* bands,   2703
HYMNE = 1
    Whiles a Wedlocke Hymne we sing,   2711
I = 334*324, 12*8
    Oli. Know you before whom sir? | *Orl*. I, better then him I am before
    knowes mee: I   45
    Ros. I marry, now vnmuzzle your wisedome.   237
    Ros. I my Liege, so please you giue vs leaue.   320
    Shall we goe Coze? | *Cel*. I: fare you well faire Gentleman. 413
    Duk. I *Celia*, we staid her for your sake,   528
    And neuer staies to greet him: I quoth *Iaques*,   662
    Clo. I, now am I in *Arden*, the more foole I, when I   798
    Ros. I, be so good *Touchstone*: Look you, who comes   802
    Ros. I, but the feet were lame, and could not beare   1366
    *say I and no, to these particulars, is more then to answer | in a
    Catechisme.   1421
    Rosalind, I am that he, that vnfortunate he.   1577
    Ros. I, of a Snaile: for though he comes slowly, hee   1968
    Orl. And wilt thou haue me? | *Ros*. I, and twentie such. 2027
    Ros. I, but when? | *Orl*. Why now, as fast as she can marrie vs. 2042
    Ros. I, goe your waies, goe your waies: I knew what   2088
    Orl. I, sweet *Rosalind*.   2093
    Awd. I, I know who 'tis: he hath no interest in mee   2348
    Will. I sir, I thanke God. | *Clo*. Thanke God: A good answer: 2364
    Art thou wise? | *Will*. I sir, I haue a prettie wit.   2370
    Orl. I, and greater wonders then that.   2437
IA = 1

IANE = *1
*comming a night to *Iane Smile*, and I remember the kis-|sing   830
IAQ = 32*23
IAQUES see also Ia., Iaq. = 13*2
*there begins my sadnesse: My brother *Iaques* he keepes   8
1 *Lord*. Indeed my Lord | The melancholy *Iaques* grieues at that,   632
Much marked of the melancholie *Iaques*,   648
Du Sen. But what said *Iaques*? | Did he not moralize this spectacle?   651
And neuer staies to greet him: I quoth *Iaques*,   662
Enter, Amyens, Iaques, & others.   889
Amy. It will make you melancholly Monsieur *Iaques*   899
Amy. What you wil Monsieur *Iaques*.   908
Enter Iaques.   980
Enter Orlando & Iaques.   1445
Enter Clowne, Audrey, & Iaques.   1614
Enter Rosalind, and Celia, and Iaques.   1916
Enter Iaques and Lords, Forresters.   2126
Enter Duke Senior, Amyens, Iaques, Orlan-|do, Oliuer, Celia.   2573
I am for other, then for dancing meazures. | *Du Se*. Stay, *Iaques*, stay.   2770
IARRES = 1
Du Sen. If he compact of iarres, grow Musicall,   977
ICE *see* yce
ICIE = 1
The seasons difference, as the Icie phange   612
IDLE = *1
Ros. I will wearie you then no longer with idle tal-|king.   2460
IDLENESSE = 1
*God made, a poore vnworthy brother of yours with | idlenesse.   36
IEALOUS = *1
*when they are wiues: I will bee more iealous of   2058
IELOUS = 1
Ielous in honor, sodaine, and quicke in quarrell,   1130
IESTS = *1
*in dispight of a fall: but turning these iests out of seruice,   483
IEWEL = 1
Ros. From the east to westerne Inde, | no iewel is like Rosalinde,   1286
IEWELL = 1
Weares yet a precious Iewell in his head: 620
IEWELS = 1
And get our Iewels and our wealth together,   599
IF *I*.*106 *129 *144 *145 *155 *156 *178 *181 240 *241 *244 272 *277
*306 *324 *338 *350 *351 *375 407 *439 *473 478 502 507 509 514 523
533 549 594 698 728 *785 *795 810 816 819 822 846 855 877 884 *912
937 942 *945 956 961 962 969 977 1010 1029 1035 1058 1059 1090 1091
1092 1093 *1169 *1238 *1239 1248 *1280 1299 1301 *1403 *1404 *1505
*1549 *1603 *1636 *1657 1760 1764 1787 1789 1800 1840 1846 1860
1991 *1996 *2013 *2096 *2103 2199 *2219 *2220 *2221 *2225 2233 2245
*2467 *2470 *2474 *2480 2482 2486 2510 2511 2512 *2518 *2519 *2521
*2522 2527 2581 2586 2588 2591 2600 *2620 *2646 *2648 *2651 *2652
*2654 *2674 *2693 2694 *2695 2696 2697 2698 2704 2757 *2778 *2791 =
70*64, 1*3
*Lye direct: and you may auoide that too, with an If. I   2671
*thought but of an If; as if you saide so, then I saide so: 2674
*and they shooke hands, and swore brothers. Your If, is   2675
the onely peace-maker: much vertue in if.   2676
IFAITH *see also* faith, y'faith = 2
Cel. I'faith (Coz) tis he.   1410

IFAITH *cont.*
Ros. I'faith his haire is of a good colour. 1720
ILE *l.**139 *156 *157 168 *232 327 419 569 575 *589 678 699 758 *912
  *918 933 935 *945 947 965 1206 1267 *1294 *1315 1325 *1483 *1499
  *1607 1680 1768 1841 1870 1878 1908 1911 1963 *2121 *2122 2124 2212
  *2520 *2525 2527 2696 2697 2773 *2786 = 29*19
ILL = 1*2
  *Clo. Truly thou art damn'd, like an ill roasted Egge, | all on one side. 1235
  *Iaq. O knowledge ill inhabited, worse then Ioue in | a thatch'd house. 1621
  Phe. For no ill will I beare you. 1843
ILLFAUOUREDLY = 1
  *makes honest, & those that she makes honest, she makes | very
  illfauouredly. 207
ILL-FAUOURD = 1
  That makes the world full of ill-fauourd children: 1826
ILL-FAUOUREDLY = 1
  *Orl. I pray you marre no moe of my verses with rea- | ding them
  ill-fauouredly. 1456
IL-FAUORD = *1
  *and blood breakes: a poore virgin sir, an il-fauor'd thing 2634
IMAGINE = *1
  *Ros. Yes one, and in this manner. Hee was to ima- | gine 1586
IMBOSSED = 1
  And all th'imbossed sores, and headed euils, 1041
IMPATIENCE = 1
  All humblenesse, all patience, and impatience, 2504
IMPORTUNES = *1
  *Den. So please you, he is heere at the doore, and im- | portunes accesse
  to you. 92
IMPOSSIBLE = *1
  *impossible to me, if it appeare not inconuenient to you, 2474
IMPRESSURE = 1
  The Cicatrice and capable impressure | Thy palme some moment
  keepes: but now mine eyes 1794
IN *see also* i' = 165*150
INACCESSIBLE = 1
  That in this desert inaccessible, 1087
INCH = *1
  *my disposition? One inch of delay more, is a South-sea 1392
INCISION = 1
  man: God make incision in thee, thou art raw. 1269
INCLIND = *1
  *I will laugh like a Hyen, and that when thou art inclin'd | to sleepe. 2064
INCONSTANT = *1
  *liking, proud, fantastical, apish, shallow, inconstant, ful 1590
INCONTINENT = *2
  *which they will climbe incontinent, or else bee inconti- | nent 2447
INCONUENIENT = *1
  *impossible to me, if it appeare not inconuenient to you, 2474
INDE = 1
  Ros. From the east to westerne Inde, | no iewel is like Rosalinde, 1286
INDEED = 2*6
  *deuise, of all sorts enchantingly beloued, and indeed 163
  *Ros. Indeed there is fortune too hard for nature, when 217
  1 *Lord.* Indeed my Lord | The melancholy *Iaques* grieues at that, 632
  Did come to languish; and indeed my Lord 642
  *of a good peece of flesh indeed: learne of the wise 1263

INDEED *cont*.
Ros. I haue bin told so of many: but indeed, an olde   1531
*and indeed the sundrie contemplation of my trauells, in   1933
Orl. With no lesse religion, then if thou wert indeed | my *Rosalind*: so
adieu.   2103
INDEEDE = 2
The Duke is humorous, what he is indeede   434
But yet indeede the taller is his daughter,   440
INDENTED = 1
And with indented glides, did slip away   2263
INDIRECT = *1
*leaue thee till he hath tane thy life by some indirect   148
INFANT = 1
His Acts being seuen ages. At first the Infant,   1122
INFECT = *1
*This is the verie false gallop of Verses, why doe you in-|fect your selfe
with them?   1311
INFECTED = 1
Cleanse the foule bodie of th'infected world,   1034
INGRATITUDE = 1
Thou art not so vnkinde, as mans ingratitude   1157
INHABITED = *1
Iaq. O knowledge ill inhabited, worse then Ioue in | a thatch'd house.   1621
INHERITED = 1
Treason is not inherited my Lord,   522
INIURE = 1
I flye thee, for I would not iniure thee: 1780
INIURIE = *1
*lament me: the world no iniurie, for in it I haue nothing: 353
INKIE = 1
'Tis not your inkie browes, your blacke silke haire,   1819
INLAND *see also* in-land = *1
*in his youth an inland man, one that knew Courtship too   1533
INNOCENT = 2
They are as innocent as grace it selfe;   515
Cours'd one another downe his innocent nose   646
INQUISITION = 1
And let not search and inquisition quaile,   700
INSEPERABLE = 1
Still we went coupled and inseperable.   537
INSINUATE = *1
*nor cannot insinuate with you in the behalfe of a   2783
INSOMUCH = *1
*of my knowledge: insomuch (I say) I know you are: nei-|ther   2464
INSTANCE = 3*2
Clo. Instance, briefly: come, instance.   1249
*of a man? Shallow, shallow: A better instance I say: | Come.   1254
Clo. Your lips wil feele them the sooner. Shallow a-|gen: a more
sounder instance, come.   1257
*verie vncleanly fluxe of a Cat. Mend the instance Shep-|heard.   1265
INSTANCES = 1
Full of wise sawes, and moderne instances,   1135
INSTANT = 2
Rose at an instant, learn'd, plaid, eate together,   535
Cel. It is yong *Orlando*, that tript vp the Wrastlers | heeles, and your
heart, both in an instant.   1406

INSTANTLY = 1
Who led me instantly vnto his Caue,   2299
INSTEAD = *1
*of a peascod instead of her, from whom I tooke two   833
INSTRUMENT = *1
*wilt thou loue such a woman? what to make thee an in-|strument,   2216
INSULT = 1
That you insult, exult, and all at once   1809
INT = 1
*as cleane as a sound sheepes heart, that there shal not | be one spot of
Loue in't.   1600
INTELLIGENCE = 1
If with my selfe I hold intelligence,   507
INTENDMENT = *1
*from his intendment, or brooke such disgrace well as he   132
INTEREST = *1
*Awd. I, I know who 'tis: he hath no interest in mee   2348
INTERIM = *1
*if the interim be but a sennight, Times pace is so hard,   1505
INTERMISSION = 1
And I did laugh, sans intermission | An houre by his diall. Oh noble
foole,   1005
INTO *l.*103 *133 *214 455 *485 626 653 654 814 817 *836 *944 973 1043
1137 1190 1646 *1960 2172 2264 2295 *2376 *2384 *2395 *2453 *2473
2754 2759 = 16*13
INTOT = *1
*1.Pa. Shal we clap into't roundly, without hauking,   2541
INTREAT = 1*1
Cel. I did not then intreat to haue her stay,   530
*neuer haue her, vnlesse thou intreat for her: if you bee a   2221
INTREATED = *1
*Duke. Come on, since the youth will not be intreated   313
INUECTIUELY = 1
Thus most inuectiuely he pierceth through | The body of Countrie,
Citie, Court,   666
INUENT = 1
I say she neuer did inuent this letter,   2177
INUENTION = 3
That I made yesterday in despight of my Inuention.   934
This is a mans inuention, and his hand. | Sil. Sure it is hers.   2178
Could not drop forth such giant rude inuention,   2183
INUEST = 1
Inuest me in my motley: Giue me leaue   1032
INUISIBLE = 1*1
*Cel. I would I were inuisible, to catch the strong fel-|low by the legge.
Wrastle.   372
Then shall you know the wounds inuisible | That Loues keene arrows
make.   1802
INUITE = 1
Inuite the Duke, and all's contented followers: 2424
INUOCATION = *1
*Iaq. 'Tis a Greeke inuocation, to call fools into a cir-|cle.   944
IN-LAND = 1
Of smooth ciuility: yet am I in-land bred,   1072
IOLLY = 1
The heigh ho, the holly, | This Life is most iolly.   1162

119

IOT = *1
*if you breake one iot of your promise, or come one   2096
IOUE = 2*1
Ros. *Ioue*, *Ioue*, this Shepherds passion, | Is much vpon my fashion.   841
Iaq. O knowledge ill inhabited, worse then Ioue in | a thatch'd house.   1621
IOUES = *2
Ros. Ile haue no worse a name then *Ioues* owne Page,   589
Ros. It may wel be cal'd Ioues tree, when it droppes | forth fruite.   1430
IOUR = 1
Boon-iour Monsieur le Beu, what's the newes?   263
IOY = 2*1
Aud. Wel, the Gods giue vs ioy.   1656
Orl. I take some ioy to say you are, because I would | be talking of
her.   2002
With measure heap'd in ioy, to'th Measures fall.   2756
IOYFULL = *1
Clo. To morrow is the ioyfull day *Audrey*, to morow | will we be
married.   2532
IOYNCTURE = *1
*carries his house on his head; a better ioyncture I thinke   1969
IOYNE = 2*2
*this fellow wil but ioyne you together, as they ioyne   1692
That thou mightst ioyne his hand with his,   2689
To ioyne in *Hymens* bands,   2703
IPSE = 1*1
*other. For all your Writers do consent, that *ipse* is hee: 2385
now you are not *ipse*, for I am he.   2386
IRISH = 1*1
that I was an Irish Rat, which I can hardly remember.   1374
*of Irish Wolues against the Moone: I will helpe you   2517
IRKES = 1
And yet it irkes me the poore dapled fooles   628
IRKESOME = 1
Thy company, which erst was irkesome to me   1869
IRREUOCABLE = 1
Firme, and irreuocable is my doombe,   544
IS *see also* hee's, he's, matter's, motley's, 'od's, that's, there's, 'tis, what's,
world's, who's = 130*155, 1*1
Ros. Not true in loue? | *Cel*. Yes, when he is in, but I thinke he is not
in.   1735
Cel. Was, is not is: besides, the oath of Louer is no   1738
IST = 2*1
Cel. Prethee, who is't that thou means't?   246
Ros. I pray you, what i'st a clocke?   1490
Orl. Is't possible, that on so little acquaintance you   2409
IT *see also* cal't, in't, into't, is't, 't, 'tis, to't, was't = 105*106
ITH = 4*1
and loues to liue i'th Sunne: 928
Iaq. A Foole, a foole: I met a foole i'th Forrest,   985
*with a Medler: then it will be the earliest fruit i'th coun-|try: 1316
Will. *William*, sir. | *Clo*. A faire name. Was't borne i'th Forrest heere? 2362
2.Pa. We are for you, sit i'th middle.   2540
ITSELFE *see* selfe
IUDASSES = 2
Cel. Something browner then Iudasses: 1718
Marrie his kisses are Iudasses owne children.   1719

IUDGE = 1*2
Le Beu. Neither his daughter, if we iudge by manners,   439
Clo. You haue said: but whether wisely or no, let the | Forrest iudge.   1319
*ones eyes, because his owne are out, let him bee iudge,   2120
IUDGEMENTS = 1
Prouided that you weed your better iudgements   1019
IUDGMENT = *2
*your selfe with your iudgment, the feare of your aduen- | ture   339
*If againe, it was not well cut, he disabled my iudgment: 2651
IUMPS = 1
Full of the pasture, iumps along by him   661
IUNOS = 2
And wheresoere we went, like *Iunos* Swans,   536
Song. | *Wedding is great Iunos crowne*,   2715
IUPITER = 1*1
Ros. O *Iupiter*, how merry are my spirits?   784
Ros. O most gentle Iupiter, what tedious homilie of   1353
IUST = 5
'Tis iust the fashion; wherefore doe you looke   664
Iaq. *Rosalinde* is your loues name? *Orl*. Yes, Iust.   1458
Iaq. What stature is she of? | *Orl*. Iust as high as my heart.   1462
Then that mixt in his cheeke: 'twas iust the difference   1896
And Nature stronger then his iust occasion,   2281
IUSTICE = 1*1
Seeking the bubble Reputation | Euen in the Canons mouth: And then,
the Iustice   1131
Ros. Well, Time is the olde Iustice that examines all   2105
IUSTICES = *1
*knew when seuen Iustices could not take vp a Quarrell,   2672
IUSTLY = 1
But iustly as you haue exceeded all promise, | Your Mistris shall be
happie.   408
KEENE = 2
Thy tooth is not so keene, because thou art not seene,   1158
Then shall you know the wounds inuisible | That Loues keene arrows
make.   1802
KEEP = *1
*therefore beware my censure, and keep your pro- | mise.   2101
KEEPE = 7*3
Orlan. Shall I keepe your hogs, and eat huskes with   40
so God keepe your worship. *Exit*.   158
Clo. Nay, if I keepe not my ranke. | *Ros*. Thou loosest thy old smell.   272
If you doe keepe your promises in loue;   407
To keepe his daughter companie, whose loues   443
Ros. Nay, you might keepe that checke for it, till you   2076
But at this howre, the house doth keepe it selfe, | There's none within.   2231
*Keepe you your word, O Duke, to giue your daughter,   2595
Keepe you your word *Phebe*, that you'l marrie me,   2597
Keepe your word *Siluius*, that you'l marrie her   2599
KEEPES = 1*2
*there begins my sadnesse: My brother *Iaques* he keepes   8
*for my part, he keepes me rustically at home, or (to speake   10
The Cicatrice and capable impressure | Thy palme some moment
keepes: but now mine eyes   1794
KEEPING = *1
*you that keeping for a gentleman of my birth, that dif- | fers   12

KEPT = 1*1
Let no face bee kept in mind, | but the faire of Rosalinde.   1292
1.Pa. you are deceiu'd Sir, we kept time, we lost not | our time.   2567
KEY-HOLE = *1
*'twill out at the key-hole: stop that, 'twill flie with the | smoake out at
the chimney.   2072
KILD = 1*1
*neuer gracious: if kil'd, but one dead that is willing to   351
Musicke, Song. | *What shall he haue that kild the Deare?*   2136
KILL = 5*4
Du Sen. Come, shall we goe and kill vs venison?   627
To fright the Annimals, and to kill them vp   670
Ros. O ominous, he comes to kill my Hart.   1440
And if mine eyes can wound, now let them kill thee: 1787
for I protest her frowne might kill me.   2021
Ros. By this hand, it will not kill a flie: but come,   2022
Cel. Was't you that did so oft contriue to kill him?   2287
*(to wit) I kill thee, make thee away, translate thy life in- | to   2394
*will kill thee a hundred and fifty wayes, therefore trem- | ble and
depart.   2398
KILLED = 1
Iaq. Which is he that killed the Deare? | *Lord.* Sir, it was I.   2127
KIND = *1
*beards, or good faces, or sweet breaths, will for my kind   2795
KINDE = 8*1
*Sonne deerelie? By this kinde of chase, I should hate   489
And with a kinde of vmber smirch my face,   576
And in that kinde sweares you doe more vsurpe   634
Know you not Master, to seeme kinde of men,   713
The soile, the profit, and this kinde of life,   885
And measure out my graue. Farwel kinde master.   953
Iaq. Of what kinde should this Cocke come of?   1066
If the Cat will after kinde, | so be sure will Rosalinde: 1301
Whether that thy youth and kinde   2208
KINDELY = 2
Frostie, but kindely; let me goe with you,   757
Teares our recountments had most kindely bath'd,   2294
KINDLE = *1
*cleare all: nothing remaines, but that I kindle the boy | thither, which
now Ile goe about. *Exit.*   167
KINDLED = 1
Ros. As the Conie that you see dwell where shee is | kindled.   1527
KINDLY = *1
*thou shalt finde I will most kindly requite: I had my   136
KINDNESSE = 1
But kindnesse, nobler euer then reuenge,   2280
KINDRED = 1
*no wit by Nature, nor Art, may complaine of good | breeding, or
comes of a very dull kindred.   1228
KING = 1
Orl. That would I, were I of all kingdomes King.   2585
KINGDOMES = 1
Orl. That would I, were I of all kingdomes King.   2585
KINGDOMS = *1
Du Se. That would I, had I kingdoms to giue with hir.   2583
KINSMAN = 1
Clo. Holla; you Clowne. | *Ros.* Peace foole, he's not thy kinsman.   848

KISSE = 3*4
  *you kisse your hands; that courtesie would be vncleanlie | if Courtiers
  were shepheards.   1247
  *of our sheepe: and would you haue vs kisse Tarre? The   1260
  Orl. I would kisse before I spoke.   1985
  *to kisse: verie good Orators when they are out,   1988
  matter, the cleanliest shift is to kisse.   1990
  Orl. How if the kisse be denide?   1991
  *I would kisse as many of you as had beards that   2792
KISSES = 1*1
  Marrie his kisses are Iudasses owne children.   1719
  *Nun of winters sisterhood kisses not more religiouslie,   1726
KISSING = 1*1
  *comming a night to Iane Smile, and I remember the kis-|sing   830
  Ros. And his kissing is as ful of sanctitie, | As the touch of holy bread.   1723
KNAUE = 1*2
  and sweare by your beards that I am a knaue.   239
  *that habit play the knaue with him, do yo hear For-|(rester.   1488
  *Ol. 'Tis no matter; Ne're a fantastical knaue of them   1706
KNAUERIE = *1
  *Clo. By my knauerie (if I had it) then I were: but if   241
KNEES = 1
  But Mistris, know your selfe, downe on your knees   1830
KNEW = 1*5
  *strength, if you saw your selfe with your eies, or knew   338
  Ol. Oh that your Highnesse knew my heart in this: 1193
  *in his youth an inland man, one that knew Courtship too   1533
  *Ros. I, goe your waies, goe your waies: I knew what   2088
  *but they ask'd one another the reason: no sooner knew   2444
  *knew when seuen Iustices could not take vp a Quarrell,   2672
KNEWST = 1
  Sil. Oh Corin, that thou knew'st how I do loue her.   805
KNIGHT = 2*2
  *Clo. Of a certaine Knight, that swore by his Honour   230
  not the Knight forsworne.   234
  *more was this knight swearing by his Honor, for he ne-|uer   243
  *Cel. There lay hee stretch'd along like a Wounded | knight.   1434
KNOLLD see also knowld = 1
  If euer beene where bels haue knoll'd to Church: 1091
KNOW = 22*19
  *I will no longer endure it, though yet I know no wise | remedy how to
  auoid it.   26
  Oli. Know you where you are sir? | Orl. O sir, very well: heere in your
  Orchard.   43
  Oli. Know you before whom sir? | *Orl. I, better then him I am before
  knowes mee: I   45
  *know you are my eldest brother, and in the gentle con-|dition   47
  *of bloud you should so know me: -the courtesie of   48
  *I know not why) hates nothing more then he: yet hee's   161
  *owne people, who best know him, that I am altogether   165
  *Cel. You know my Father hath no childe, but I, nor   186
  But now I know her: if she be a Traitor,   533
  Know you not Master, to seeme kinde of men,   713
  This I must do, or know not what to do: | Yet this I will not do, do how
  I can,   738
  *Amy. My voice is ragged, I know I cannot please | you.   903
  They haue the gift to know it: and in his braine,   1011

KNOW *cont.*

And know some nourture: But forbeare, I say,	1073
And know what 'tis to pittie, and be pittied:	1094
Cor. No more, but that I know the more one sickens,	1222
Cor. Why we are still handling our Ewes, and their | Fels you know are greasie.	1250
Will I Rosalinda write, | *teaching all that reade, to know*	1335
Ros. But doth he know that I am in this Forrest, and	1423
Ros. Do you not know I am a woman, when I thinke, | I must speake: sweet, say on.	1443
against whom I know most faults.	1473
*he taught me how to know a man in loue: in which cage | of rushes, I am sure you art not prisoner.	1555
Aud. I do not know what Poetical is: is it honest in | deed and word: is it a true thing?	1628
Then shall you know the wounds inuisible | That Loues keene arrows make.	1802
But Mistris, know your selfe, downe on your knees	1830
Besides, I like you not: if you will know my house,	1846
*didst know how many fathome deepe I am in loue: but	2112
I know not the contents, but as I guesse	2156
Sil. No, I protest, I know not the contents, | *Phebe* did write it.	2169
Oliu. Good morrow, faire ones: pray you, (if you | know)	2225
Then should I know you by description,	2234
Oli. Some of my shame, if you will know of me	2245
Oli. And well he might so doe, | For well I know he was vnnaturall.	2275
Awd. I, I know who 'tis: he hath no interest in mee	2348
Ros. O, I know where you are: nay, tis true: there	2438
*Know of me then (for now I speake to some pur-|pose)	2461
*that I know you are a Gentleman of good conceit:	2462
*of my knowledge: insomuch (I say) I know you are: nei-|ther	2464
*brother marries *Aliena*, shall you marrie her. I know in-|to	2472
As those that feare they hope, and know they feare.	2578
Ile stay to know, at your abandon'd caue. *Exit.*	2773

KNOWES = 1 *3

Oli. Know you before whom sir? | *Orl.* I, better then him I am before knowes mee: I	45
*It is said, many a man knowes no end of his goods;	1661
Little knowes this Loue in me:	2206
*knowes himselfe to be a Foole. The Heathen Philoso-|pher,	2374

KNOWING = *1

*leane and wasteful Learning; the other knowing no bur-|then	1512

KNOWLD = 1

And haue with holy bell bin knowld to Church,	1098

KNOWLEDGE = 4*2

Cel. How proue you that in the great heape of your | knowledge?	235
I shall desire more loue and knowledge of you.	453
Ros. I doe beseech your Grace | Let me the knowledge of my fault beare with me:	505
delay me not the knowledge of his chin.	1405
Iaq. O knowledge ill inhabited, worse then Ioue in | a thatch'd house.	1621
*of my knowledge: insomuch (I say) I know you are: nei-|ther	2464

KNOWNE = 1 *1

Ros. With bils on their neckes: Be it knowne vnto | all men by these presents.	286
Had I before knowne this yong man his sonne,	400

KNOWS = *1
*right: Many a man has good Hornes, and knows no end   1662
KNOWST = 1*1
Prethee be cheerefull; know'st thou not the Duke   557
*Phe. Knowst thou the youth that spoke to mee yere-|(while?   1879
LABOR = 2*1
Before I come, thou art a mocker of my labor.   963
1.Lord. He saues my labor by his owne approach.   981
*do I labor for a greater esteeme then may in some   2465
LABOURED = *1
*vnder-hand meanes laboured to disswade him from it;   138
LABOURER = *1
*Cor. Sir, I am a true Labourer, I earne that I eate: get   1270
LACKE = 4*3
To some shelter, and thou shalt not die | For lacke of a dinner,   967
*the night, is lacke of the Sunne: That hee that hath lear-|ned   1227
If a Hart doe lacke a Hinde, | *Let him seeke out Rosalinde:*   1299
*were grauel'd, for lacke of matter, you might take oc-|casion   1987
*Ros. Alas, deere loue, I cannot lacke thee two houres.   2085
Shee saies I am not faire, that I lacke manners,   2163
You lacke a mans heart. | Ros. I doe so, I confesse it: 2319
LACKE-LUSTRE = 1
And looking on it, with lacke-lustre eye,   994
LACKING = *2
*he feeles no paine: the one lacking the burthen of   1511
*they will spit, and for louers, lacking (God warne vs)   1989
LACKS = 2*1
That could giue more, but that her hand lacks meanes.   412
Cel. No, hath not? Rosaline lacks then the loue   560
*Ros. With a Priest that lacks Latine, and a rich man   1508
LACKY = *1
*Ros. I wil speake to him like a sawcie Lacky, and vn-|der   1487
LADIE = *1
*Ros. It is not the fashion to see the Ladie the Epi-|logue: 2776
LADIES = 4*5
*of her Vncle, then his owne daughter, and neuer two La-|dies loued as
they doe.   112
Le Beu. You amaze me Ladies: I would haue told   274
*Clo. But what is the sport Monsieur, that the Ladies | haue lost?   296
*first time that euer I heard breaking of ribbes was sport | for Ladies.   300
*bee entreated. Speake to him Ladies, see if you can | mooue him.   324
*so faire and excellent Ladies anie thing. But let your   348
The Ladies her attendants of her chamber   685
And sayes, if Ladies be but yong, and faire,   1010
*nor the Ladies, which is nice: nor the Louers, which   1930
LADISHIPS = *1
*your Ladiships, you may see the end, for the best is yet   278
LADY = 3*1
And on my life his malice 'gainst the Lady   450
And rail'd on Lady Fortune in good termes,   989
Orl. Wounded it is, but with the eyes of a Lady.   2434
*purgation, I haue trod a measure, I haue flattred a Lady,   2621
LAID = 4*1
Cel. Well said, that was laid on with a trowell.   271
*Ros. Then there were two Cosens laid vp, when the   466
Who laid him downe, and bask'd him in the Sun,   988
that he laid to the charge of women?   1539

LAID *cont*.
  Ros. Read. *Why, thy godhead laid a part,*   2193
LAMBE = *1
  *and to betray a shee-Lambe of a tweluemonth   1278
LAMBES = 1
  *and the greatest of my pride, is to see my Ewes graze, & | my Lambes
  sucke.   1273
LAMD = *1
  *one should be lam'd with reasons, and the other mad | without any.   467
LAME = 1*2
  *vpon curs, throw some of them at me; come lame mee | with reasons.   464
  When seruice should in my old limbs lie lame,   745
  Ros. I, but the feet were lame, and could not beare   1366
LAMELY = *1
  *themselues without the verse, and therefore stood lame-|ly in the
  verse.   1367
LAMENT = *1
  *lament me: the world no iniurie, for in it I haue nothing: 353
LAND = 3
  Of smooth ciuility: yet am I in-land bred,   1072
  A land it selfe at large, a potent Dukedome.   2746
  you to your land, and loue, and great allies: 2766
LANDS = 4*2
  *him, whose lands and reuenues enrich the new Duke,   104
  Thy Lands and all things that thou dost call thine,   1189
  And let my officers of such a nature | Make an extent vpon his house
  and Lands: 1196
  *to be sad: I feare you haue sold your owne Lands,   1937
  And all their Lands restor'd to him againe   2740
  To one his lands with-held, and to the other   2745
LANGUISH = 1
  Did come to languish; and indeed my Lord   642
LARGE = 2
  Withall, as large a Charter as the winde,   1022
  A land it selfe at large, a potent Dukedome.   2746
LASSE = 1
  Song. | *It was a Louer, and his lasse,*   2546
LAST = 4*1
  To the last gaspe with truth and loyaltie,   774
  And whistles in his sound. Last Scene of all,   1142
  *Sir, you are verie well met: goddild you for your last   1682
  Oli. When last the yong *Orlando* parted from you,   2249
  When from the first to last betwixt vs two,   2293
LATE = 2
  But I can tell you, that of late this Duke   445
  But at fourescore, it is too late a weeke,   778
LATELY = 1
  That did but lately foile the synowie *Charles*,   694
LATINE = *1
  Ros. With a Priest that lacks Latine, and a rich man   1508
LAUGH = 4*1
  Your Grace was wont to laugh is also missing,   689
  And I did laugh, sans intermission | An houre by his diall. Oh noble
  foole,   1005
  They most must laugh: And why sir must they so?   1025
  *I will laugh like a Hyen, and that when thou art inclin'd | to sleepe.   2064
  Is not a thing to laugh to scorne. Exeunt.   2145

LAUGHD = *1
*told him of as good as he, so he laugh'd and let mee goe.   1744
LAUGHING = 1
Iaq. I am so: I doe loue it better then laughing.   1920
LAWES = 1
Enter Duke Sen. & Lord, like Out-lawes.   972
LAWFULL = 1
**Ol*. Truly she must be giuen, or the marriage is not | lawfull.   1678
LAWIERS = *2
**Ros*. With Lawiers in the vacation: for they sleepe   1520
*which is ambitious: nor the Lawiers, which is politick: 1929
LAY = 4*1
Oli. Wilt thou lay hands on me villaine?   56
Did steale behinde him as he lay along   637
**Cel*. There lay hee stretch'd along like a Wounded | knight.   1434
Lay sleeping on his back; about his necke   2258
Lay cowching head on ground, with catlike watch   2266
LAYES = 1
**Mar-text*. But *Awdrie*, there is a youth heere in the | Forrest layes
claime to you.   2346
LAZIE = 1
detect the lazie foot of time, as wel as a clocke.   1495
LE *l*.257 263 326 426 = 4
LE = 6*8
LEAD = 1
Cel. Wee'll lead you thither: 2316
LEANDER = *1
*and he is one of the patternes of loue. *Leander*, he would   2011
LEANE = 2*2
Into the leane and slipper'd Pantaloone,   1137
*leane and wasteful Learning; the other knowing no bur- | then   1512
**Ros*. A leane cheeke, which you haue not: a blew eie   1558
Some scarre of it: Leane vpon a rush   1793
LEARND = 2
Rose at an instant, learn'd, plaid, eate together,   535
There is much matter to be heard, and learn'd: 2762
LEARNE = *3
*learne mee how to remember any extraordinary plea- | sure.   175
*of a good peece of flesh indeed: learne of the wise   1263
**Clo*. Then learne this of me, To haue, is to haue. For   2382
LEARNED = 2*2
*gentle, neuer school'd, and yet learned, full of noble   162
Ros. Where learned you that oath foole?   229
*the night, is lacke of the Sunne: That hee that hath lear- | ned   1227
Clo. Giue me your hand: Art thou Learned? | *Will*. No sir.   2380
LEARNING = *1
*leane and wasteful Learning; the other knowing no bur- | then   1512
LEATHER = 1
His Leather skin, and hornes to weare: 2138
LEATHERNE = 2
That their discharge did stretch his leatherne coat   644
I saw her hand, she has a leatherne hand,   2173
LEAUE = 10*5
*you: you shall haue some part of your will, I pray you | leaue me.   77
therefore he giues them good leaue to wander.   105
*leaue thee till he hath tane thy life by some indirect   148
Ros. I my Liege, so please you giue vs leaue.   320

127

LET *cont*.

Ros. Let me loue him for that, and do you loue him	495
Ros. I doe beseech your Grace | Let me the knowledge of my fault	
beare with me:	505
Let is suffice thee that I trust thee not.	516
No, let my Father seeke another heire:	563
And let not search and inquisition quaile,	700
All this I giue you, let me be your seruant,	750
Frostie, but kindely; let me goe with you,	757
There then, how then, what then, let me see wherein	1057
Orl. I almost die for food, and let me haue it.	1081
Let gentlenesse my strong enforcement be,	1095
*Du Sen. Welcome: set downe your venerable bur-|then, and let him	
feede.	1147
And let me all your fortunes vnderstand. *Exeunt*.	1178
And let my officers of such a nature | Make an extent vpon his house	
and Lands:	1196
Let no face bee kept in mind, | *but the faire of Rosalinde*.	1292
If a Hart doe lacke a Hinde, | *Let him seeke out Rosalinde:*	1299
*Clo. You haue said: but whether wisely or no, let the | Forrest iudge.	1319
*Clo. Come Shepheard, let vs make an honorable re-|treit,	1358
*thankful: let me stay the growth of his beard, if thou	1404
Iaq. Goe thou with mee, | And let me counsel thee.	1699
**told him of as good as he, so he laugh'd and let mee goe.	1744
Ros. O come, let vs remoue,	1765
And if mine eyes can wound, now let them kill thee:	1787
*Iaq. I prethee, pretty youth, let me better acquainted | with thee.	1917
**make her fault her husbands occasion, let her neuer nurse	2082
such offenders, and let time try: adieu. *Exit*.	2106
**ones eyes, because his owne are out, let him bee iudge,	2120
Let your Wedding be to morrow: thither will I	2423
*Clo. If any man doubt that, let him put mee to my	2620
2.Bro. Let me haue audience for a word or two:	2727
First, in this Forrest, let vs do those ends	2747

LETS = 2*2

**me: hee lets mee feede with his Hindes, barres mee the	21
Leaue me alone to woe him; Let's away	598
Iaq. God buy you, let's meet as little as we can.	1452
*Iaq. Let's present him to the Duke like a Romane	2129

LETTER = 6

Ile write to him a very tanting Letter,	1908
Ros. Patience her selfe would startle at this letter,	2161
This is a Letter of your owne deuice.	2168
I say she neuer did inuent this letter,	2177
Then in their countenance: will you heare the letter?	2185
To shew the letter that I writ to you.	2485

LIBERTIE = 1*1

To libertie, and not to banishment. *Exeunt*.	603
**death, thy libertie into bondage: I will deale in poy-|son	2395

LIBERTINE = 1

For thou thy selfe hast bene a Libertine,	1039

LIBERTY = 1

That I am wise. I must haue liberty	1021

LICENSE = 1

That thou with license of free foot hast caught,	1042

LIDS = 1

If euer from your eye-lids wip'd a teare,	1093

LIE *see also* lye = 4*3
*third: yonder they lie, the poore old man their Father,	292
desirous to lie with his mother earth?	362
When seruice should in my old limbs lie lame,	745
O I die for food. Heere lie I downe,	952
*which women stil giue the lie to their consciences. But	1573
These prettie Country folks would lie. | *In spring time*, &c.	2559
*say, I lie: this is call'd the counter-checke quarrelsome:	2655

LIEFE = 2*1
*thy discretion, I had as liefe thou didst breake his necke	143
I had as liefe haue beene my selfe alone.	1449
sight, I had as liefe be woo'd of a Snaile.	1966

LIEGE = 1*1
Ros. I my Liege, so please you giue vs leaue.	320
Orl. Orlando my Liege, the yongest sonne of Sir *Ro-|land de Boys.*	384

LIES = *2
*place of a brother, and as much as in him lies, mines my	22
Hero of Cestos. But these are all lies, men haue died	2017

LIEST = 1
And Ile be with thee quickly: yet thou liest	965

LIEU = 1
In lieu of all thy paines and husbandrie,	769

LIFE = 14*10
*leaue thee till he hath tane thy life by some indirect	148
*hope of life in him: So he seru'd the second, and so the	291
And on my life his malice 'gainst the Lady	450
Hath not old custome made this life more sweete	608
And this our life exempt from publike haunt,	621
Yea, and of this our life, swearing that we	668
The soile, the profit, and this kinde of life,	885
Du Sen. Why how now Monsieur, what a life is this	982
The heigh ho, the holly, | *This Life is most iolly.*	1162
I neuer lou'd my brother in my life.	1194
Thy Huntresse name, that my full life doth sway.	1204
Co. And how like you this shepherds life Mr *Touchstone*?	1212
*good life; but in respect that it is a shepheards life, it is	1214
*but in respect that it is priuate, it is a very vild life. Now	1216
*life (looke you) it fits my humor well: but as there is no	1219
Some, how briefe the Life of man | *runs his erring pilgrimage,*	1327
Of Natures sale-worke? 'ods my little life,	1816
Ros. By my life, she will doe as I doe. | *Orl.* O but she is wise.	2067
*(to wit) I kill thee, make thee away, translate thy life in-|to	2394
Ros. By my life I do, which I tender deerly, though	2478
How that a life was but a Flower, | *In spring time*, &c.	2563
That were with him exil'd. This to be true, | I do engage my life.	2741
The Duke hath put on a Religious life,	2758

LIGHT = 1
Weele light vpon some setled low content.	772

LIKD = *1
*pleas'd me, complexions that lik'd me, and breaths that	2793

LIKE = 32*29
*you haue train'd me like a pezant, obscuring and	68
*hiding from me all gentleman-like qualities: the spirit	69
*like the old *Robin Hood* of *England*: they say many yong	117
*none is like to haue; and truely when he dies, thou shalt	187
And wheresoere we went, like *Iunos* Swans,	536
The like doe you, so shall we passe along, | And neuer stir assailants.	577

LIKE *cont*.

That I did suite me all points like a man,	581
Enter Duke Senior: Amyens, and two or three Lords | like Forresters.	605
Which like the toad, ougly and venemous,	619
*apparell, and to cry like a woman: but I must comfort	788
But if thy loue were euer like to mine,	810
I like this place, and willingly could | Waste my time in it.	881
Go with me, if you like vpon report,	884
*you: but that they cal complement is like th'encounter	913
Enter Duke Sen. & Lord, like Out-lawes.	972
For I can no where finde him, like a man.	974
My Lungs began to crow like Chanticleere,	1003
Why then my taxing like a wild-goose flies	1060
Whiles (like a Doe) I go to finde my Fawne,	1105
And shining morning face, creeping like snaile	1125
Sighing like Furnace, with a wofull ballad	1127
Full of strange oaths, and bearded like the Pard,	1129
*Co. And how like you this shepherds life Mr *Touchstone*?	1212
*naught. In respect that it is solitary, I like it verie well:	1215
*Clo. Truly thou art damn'd, like an ill roasted Egge, | all on one side.	1235
Ros. *From the east to westerne Inde, | no iewel is like Rosalinde,*	1286
*I am caparison'd like a man, I haue a doublet and hose in	1391
vnder a tree like a drop'd Acorne.	1429
*Cel. There lay hee stretch'd along like a Wounded | knight.	1434
vnseasonably. He was furnish'd like a Hunter.	1439
Iaq. I do not like her name.	1459
*Ros. I wil speake to him like a sawcie Lacky, and vn-|der	1487
skirts of the Forrest, like fringe vpon a petticoat.	1525
*Ros. There were none principal, they were all like	1540
*for the most part, cattle of this colour: would now like	1593
*married vnder a bush like a begger? Get you to church,	1690
and like greene timber, warpe, warpe.	1694
*married of him then of another, for he is not like to mar-|rie	1696
*breakes his staffe like a noble goose; but all's braue that	1751
Like foggy South, puffing with winde and raine,	1823
Besides, I like you not: if you will know my house,	1846
*holy-day humor, and like enough to consent: What	1982
*I will weepe for nothing, like *Diana* in the Foun-|taine,	2062
*I will laugh like a Hyen, and that when thou art inclin'd | to sleepe.	2064
her childe her selfe, for she will breed it like a foole.	2083
*it cannot bee sounded: my affection hath an vnknowne | bottome, like	
the Bay of Portugall.	2113
*Iaq. Let's present him to the Duke like a Romane	2129
Like Turke to Christian: womens gentle braine	2182
Of femall fauour, and bestowes himselfe | Like a ripe sister: the woman	
low	2236
*should like her? that, but seeing, you should loue her?	2410
*Ros. Pray you no more of this, 'tis like the howling	2516
2.Pa. I faith, y'faith, and both in a tune like two | gipsies on a horse.	2544
quarrels, and like to haue fought one.	2624
*Iaq. How seuenth cause? Good my Lord, like this | fellow.	2628
Du Se. I like him very well.	2630
*Clo. God'ild you sir, I desire you of the like: I presse	2631
*that that no man else will: rich honestie dwels like a mi-|ser	2636
*Du Se. He vses his folly like a stalking-horse, and vn-|der	2679
*good play? I am not furnish'd like a Begger, therefore	2784
*women) for the loue you beare to men, to like as much	2787

LIKE *cont*.

As you Like it. 2798

LIKELIHOODS = 1

Tell me whereon the likelihoods depends? 518

LIKING = *2

*you should fall into so strong a liking with old Sir | *Roulands* yongest
sonne? 485

*liking, proud, fantastical, apish, shallow, inconstant, ful 1590

LIMBE = *1

*some broken limbe, shall acquit him well: your brother 127

LIMBS = 1

When seruice should in my old limbs lie lame, 745

LIMND = 1

Most truly limn'd, and liuing in your face, 1172

LIMPT = 1

Limpt in pure loue: till he be first suffic'd, 1108

LIND = 1

In faire round belly, with good Capon lin'd, 1133

LINDE = 2

All the pictures fairest Linde, | *are but blacke to Rosalinde:* 1290

Wintred garments must be linde, | *so must slender Rosalinde:* 1303

LINEAMENTS = 2

*Fortune reignes in gifts of the world, not in the | lineaments of Nature. 210

Then any of her lineaments can show her: 1829

LION = 1

Ros. I thought thy heart had beene wounded with | the clawes of a
Lion. 2432

LIONESSE *see* lyonesse

LIP = 1

There was a pretty rednesse in his lip, 1894

LIPPES = *1

*that Grapes were made to eate, and lippes to open. 2377

LIPS = 1*3

When she is gone: then open not thy lips 543

Clo. Your lips wil feele them the sooner. Shallow a-|gen: a more
sounder instance, come. 1257

Cel. Hee hath bought a paire of cast lips of *Diana*: a 1725

*his lips when he put it into his mouth, meaning there-|by, 2376

LIQUORS = 1

For in my youth I neuer did apply | Hot, and rebellious liquors in my
bloud, 752

LISPE = *1

*lispe, and weare strange suites; disable all the benefits 1949

LITTLE = 13*10

Cel. By my troth thou saiest true: For, since the little 253

*wit that fooles haue was silenced, the little foolerie that 254

*him, and broke three of his ribbes, that there is little 290

Du. You wil take little delight in it, I can tell you 321

Ros. The little strength that I haue, I would it were | with you. 356

And little wreakes to finde the way to heauen | By doing deeds of
hospitalitie. 866

That little cares for buying any thing. 876

Liue a little, comfort a little, cheere thy selfe a little. 955

Orl. Then but forbeare your food a little while: 1104

The quintessence of euerie sprite, | *heauen would in little show*. 1337

Cel. How now backe friends: Shepheard, go off a lit-|tle: 1356

Cel. Nay, he hath but a little beard. 1402

LITTLE *cont*.

Iaq. God buy you, let's meet as little as we can.	1452
*in a little roome: truly, I would the Gods hadde | made thee poeticall.	1626
Goe hence a little, and I shall conduct you | If you will marke it.	1763
Of Natures sale-worke? 'ods my little life,	1816
A little riper, and more lustie red	1895
Ros. O coz, coz, coz: my pretty little coz, that thou	2111
Little knowes this Loue in me:	2206
Orl. Is't possible, that on so little acquaintance you	2409
*little measure draw a beleefe from you, to do your selfe	2466

LIUD = 1*1

*haue liu'd manie a faire yeere though *Hero* had turn'd	2012
And he did render him the most vnnaturall | That liu'd amongst men.	2273

LIUE = 12*4

Oli. Where will the old Duke liue? | *Cha*. They say hee is already in the Forrest of *Arden*,	114
*and a many merry men with him; and there they liue	116
I cannot liue out of her companie.	547
Here liued I, but now liue here no more	776
and loues to liue i'th Sunne:	928
Liue a little, comfort a little, cheere thy selfe a little.	955
If there liue any thing in this Desert.	969
As I do liue by foode, I met a foole,	987
Heauen would that shee these gifts should haue, | *and I to liue and die her slaue*.	1351
*and to liue in a nooke meerly Monastick: and thus I cur'd	1598
*the way, you shal tell me, where in the Forrest you liue:	1608
Ol. Come sweete *Audrey*, | We must be married, or we must liue in baudrey:	1701
A scattred smile, and that Ile liue vpon.	1878
*was old Sir *Rowlands* will I estate vpon you, and heere | liue and die a Shepherd.	2419
Orl. I can liue no longer by thinking.	2459
Sil. Ile not faile, if I liue. | *Phe*. Nor I. | *Orl*. Nor I. *Exeunt*.	2527

LIUED = 1

Here liued I, but now liue here no more	776

LIUELESSE = 1

Is but a quintine, a meere liuelesse blocke.	417

LIUELY = 1

Some liuely touches of my daughters fauour.	2603

LIUER = *1

*him, and this way wil I take vpon mee to wash your Li-|uer	1599

LIUES = 2*1

The enemie of all your graces liues	722
*he cannot study, and the other liues merrily, be-|cause	1510
Then he that dies and liues by bloody drops?	1777

LIUING = 4*3

*this day liuing. I speake but brotherly of him,	151
A theeuish liuing on the common rode?	737
Most truly limn'd, and liuing in your face,	1172
Seeke him with Candle: bring him dead, or liuing	1186
To seeke a liuing in our Territorie.	1188
*liuing, by the copulation of Cattle, to be bawd to a Bel-|weather,	1277
*my Sutor from his mad humor of loue, to a liuing humor	1596

LOATH = *1

*him, now loath him: then entertaine him, then forswear	1594

AS YOU LIKE IT

LODGING = 1
To burne the lodging where you vse to lye,　　　　　727
LOE = 1
Loe what befell: he threw his eye aside,　　　　　　2253
LONG = 1*3
*Well sir, get you in. I will not long be troubled with　　76
*misprised: but it shall not be so long, this wrastler shall　166
*Ros. Now tell me how long you would haue her, af-|ter you haue
possest her?　　　　　　　　　　　　　　　　　　　2052
you to a long, and well-deserued bed:　　　　　　　2767
LONGER = 1*5
*I will no longer endure it, though yet I know no wise | remedy how to
auoid it.　　　　　　　　　　　　　　　　　　　　26
*of my father growes strong in mee, and I will no longer　70
Cel. Something that hath a reference to my state: | No longer Celia, but
Aliena.　　　　　　　　　　　　　　　　　　　　　592
*Iaq. Ile tarrie no longer with you, farewell good sig-|nior Loue.　1483
*Orl. I can liue no longer by thinking.　　　　　　　2459
*Ros. I will wearie you then no longer with idle tal-|king.　2460
LONGING = *1
*youth, greeue, be effeminate, changeable, longing, and　1589
LONGS = *1
*Ros. But is there any else longs to see this broken　303
LOOK = *2
*Ros. I, be so good Touchstone: Look you, who comes　802
*Oli. Many will swoon when they do look on bloud.　2312
LOOKD = 1*3
If euer you haue look'd on better dayes:　　　　　　1090
*he? How look'd he? Wherein went he? What makes hee　1415
*met, but they look'd: no sooner look'd, but they　2442
LOOKE = 15*9
*as his finger. And thou wert best looke to't; for if thou　144
*blush, and weepe, and thou must looke pale and | wonder.　153
Because I doe. Looke, here comes the Duke.　　　　496
And therefore looke you call me Ganimed.　　　　　590
'Tis iust the fashion; wherefore doe you looke　　　664
Though I looke old, yet I am strong and lustie;　　　751
*the Duke wil drinke vnder this tree; he hath bin all this | day to looke
you.　　　　　　　　　　　　　　　　　　　　　919
What, you looke merrily.　　　　　　　　　　　　984
Of my reuenge, thou present: but looke to it,　　　1184
*life (looke you) it fits my humor well: but as there is no　1219
*before you came: for looke heere what I found on a　1372
*Orl. He is drown'd in the brooke, looke but in, and | you shall see
him.　　　　　　　　　　　　　　　　　　　　　1479
Why what meanes this? why do you looke on me?　1814
Her with bitter words: why looke you so vpon me?　1842
Come Sister: Shepheardesse, looke on him better　1849
But doe not looke for further recompence　　　　　1871
*Ros. Farewell Mounsieur Trauellor: looke you　　1948
To sleepe: looke who comes heere.　　　　　　　　2153
Oli. Looke, he recouers.　　　　　　　　　　　　2314
*Cel. Come, you looke paler and paler: pray you draw | homewards:
good sir, goe with vs.　　　　　　　　　　　　　　2332
Go you, and prepare Aliena; for looke you,　　　　2425
*it is, to looke into happines through another mans eies:　2453
*Looke, here comes a Louer of mine, and a louer of hers.　2483

134

LOOKE *cont*.
Looke vpon him, loue him: he worships you.   2489
LOOKES = 2
That euerie eye, which in this Forrest lookes,   1207
As she answeres thee with frowning lookes, ile sauce   1841
LOOKING = 1
And looking on it, with lacke-lustre eye,   994
LOOKS = *2
Cel. Alas, he is too yong: yet he looks successefully   317
*in mans apparrell? Looks he as freshly, as he did the day | he
Wrastled?   1424
LOOKST = 1
Wel said, thou look'st cheerely,   964
LOOSE = 2
Loose, and neglect the creeping houres of time: 1089
That the maine haruest reapes: loose now and then   1877
LOOSEST = 1
Clo. Nay, if I keepe not my ranke. | *Ros*. Thou loosest thy old smell.   272
LORD *see also* 1*.Lo*., 1*.Lord*., 2*.Lor*., 2*.Lord*. = 11*8
Le Beu. He cannot speake my Lord.   381
Treason is not inherited my Lord,   522
1*.Lord*. Indeed my Lord | The melancholy *Iaques* grieues at that,   632
To day my Lord of *Amiens*, and my selfe,   636
Did come to languish; and indeed my Lord   642
2*.Lord*. We did my Lord, weeping and commenting | Vpon the sobbing
Deere.   673
2.Lor*. My Lord, the roynish Clown, at whom so oft,   688
Enter Duke Sen. & Lord, like Out-lawes.   972
1*.Lord*. My Lord, he is but euen now gone hence,   975
Cel. O Lord, Lord, it is a hard matter for friends to   1380
Aud. Your features, Lord warrant vs: what features?   1618
Orl. My Lord, the first time that I euer saw him,   2604
But my good Lord, this Boy is Forrest borne,   2606
Iaq. Good my Lord, bid him welcome: This is the   2617
Iaq. How seuenth cause? Good my Lord, like this | fellow.   2628
Iaq. Is not this a rare fellow my Lord? He's as good   2677
Or haue a Woman to your Lord.   2708
*Lord the Prologue. If it be true, that good wine needs   2778
LORD = 2
LORDS = 6*1
*Lords haue put themselues into voluntary exile with   103
Flourish. Enter Duke, Lords, Orlando, Charles, | and Attendants.   311
Enter Duke with Lords.   494
Enter Duke Senior: Amyens, and two or three Lords | like Forresters.   605
Enter Duke, with Lords.   680
Enter Duke, Lords, & Oliuer.   1180
Enter Iaques and Lords, Forresters.   2126
LOSE *see* loose
LOSEST *see* loosest
LOST = 2*4
*lost my teeth in your seruice: God be with my olde ma-|ster,   83
Le Beu. Faire Princesse, | you haue lost much good sport.   264
*you of good wrastling, which you haue lost the sight of.   275
Clo. But what is the sport Monsieur, that the Ladies | haue lost?   296
1.Pa*. you are deceiu'd Sir, we kept time, we lost not | our time.   2567
Clo. By my troth yes: I count it but time lost to heare   2569

LOTH = *1
*loth to foyle him, as I must for my owne honour if hee	129

LOUD = 9*3
Ros. My Father lou'd Sir *Roland* as his soule,	398
Ros. The Duke my Father lou'd his Father deerelie.	487
Cor. I partly guesse: for I haue lou'd ere now.	806
That euer loue did make thee run into, | Thou hast not lou'd.	817
Wearing thy hearer in thy Mistris praise, | Thou hast not lou'd.	820
Abruptly as my passion now makes me, | Thou hast not lou'd.	823
That lou'd your Father, the residue of your fortune,	1174
I neuer lou'd my brother in my life.	1194
Who euer lov'd, that lou'd not at first sight?	1854
*lou'd; no sooner lou'd, but they sigh'd: no sooner sigh'd	2443

LOUE = 66*46
*is but young and tender, and for your loue I would bee	128
*come in: therefore out of my loue to you, I came hither	130
Oli. *Charles*, I thanke thee for thy loue to me, which	135
*waight that I loue thee; if my Vncle thy banished father	178
*hadst beene still with mee, I could haue taught my loue	180
*of thy loue to me were so righteously temper'd, as mine | is to thee.	182
let me see, what thinke you of falling in Loue?	194
*loue no man in good earnest, nor no further in sport ney-|ther,	196
Ros. My Fathers loue is enough to honor him enough;	248
If you doe keepe your promises in loue;	407
High commendation, true applause, and loue;	431
I shall desire more loue and knowledge of you.	453
Cel. Doth it therefore ensue that you should loue his	488
Ros. Let me loue him for that, and do you loue him	495
Cel. No, hath not? *Rosaline* lacks then the loue	560
Du Sen. Show me the place, | I loue to cope him in these sullen fits,	675
Why are you vertuous? Why do people loue you?	708
Sil. Oh *Corin*, that thou knew'st how I do loue her.	805
But if thy loue were euer like to mine,	810
As sure I thinke did neuer man loue so:	811
Sil. Oh thou didst then neuer loue so hartily,	815
That euer loue did make thee run into, | Thou hast not lou'd.	817
Clo. And I mine: I remember when I was in loue, I	828
nature, so is all nature in loue, mortall in folly.	837
Ros. I prethee Shepheard, if that loue or gold	855
Limpt in pure loue: till he be first suffic'd,	1108
Orl. Hang there my verse, in witnesse of my loue,	1201
*Loue haue you wearied your parishioners withall, and	1354
Iaq. The worst fault you haue, is to be in loue.	1474
Iaq. Ile tarrie no longer with you, farewell good sig-|nior Loue.	1483
*well: for there he fel in loue. I haue heard him read ma-|ny	1534
*some good counsel, for he seemes to haue the Quotidian | of Loue vpon him.	1550
*he taught me how to know a man in loue: in which cage | of rushes, I am sure you art not prisoner.	1555
Orl. Faire youth, I would I could make thee beleeue | (I Loue.	1569
*you Loue beleeue it, which I warrant she is apter to do,	1571
Ros. But are you so much in loue, as your rimes speak?	1578
Ros. Loue is meerely a madnesse, and I tel you, de-|serues loue too: yet I professe curing it by counsel.	1580
	1584
*me his Loue, his Mistris: and I set him euerie day	1587
*my Sutor from his mad humor of loue, to a liuing humor	1596

LOUE *cont.*

*as cleane as a sound sheepes heart, that there shal not | be one spot of
Loue in't.   1600
Orlan. Now by the faith of my loue, I will; Tel me | where it is.   1605
*but for his verity in loue, I doe thinke him as   1733
Ros. Not true in loue? | *Cel*. Yes, when he is in, but I thinke he is not
in.   1735
After the Shepheard that complain'd of loue,   1755
Betweene the pale complexion of true Loue,   1761
The sight of Louers feedeth those in loue: 1766
Say that you loue me not, but say not so   1772
And thanke heauen, fasting, for a good mans loue;   1831
Cry the man mercy, loue him, take his offer,   1834
Ros. Hees falne in loue with your foulnesse, & shee'll   1839
Fall in loue with my anger. If it be so, as fast   1840
Ros. I pray you do not fall in loue with mee,   1844
If you doe sorrow at my griefe in loue,   1860
By giuing loue your sorrow, and my griefe | Were both extermin'd.   1861
Phe. Thou hast my loue, is not that neighbourly? | *Sil*. I would haue
you.   1863
And yet it is not, that I beare thee loue,   1867
But since that thou canst talke of loue so well,   1868
Sil. So holy, and so perfect is my loue,   1873
Phe. Thinke not I loue him, though I ask for him,   1883
To fall in loue with him: but for my part   1900
I loue him not, nor hate him not: and yet   1901
Haue more cause to hate him then to loue him,   1902
Iaq. I am so: I doe loue it better then laughing.   1920
*of your owne Countrie: be out of loue with your   1950
Ros. Breake an houres promise in loue? hee that   1959
*of loue, it may be said of him that *Cupid* hath clapt   1962
*a loue cause: *Troilous* had his braines dash'd out with a   2009
*and he is one of the patternes of loue. *Leander*, he would   2011
*from time to time, and wormes haue eaten them, but not | for loue.   2018
Orl. Then loue me *Rosalind*.   2025
Ros. Alas, deere loue, I cannot lacke thee two houres.   2085
*didst know how many fathome deepe I am in loue: but   2112
*how deepe I am in loue: ile tell thee *Aliena*, I cannot be   2121
Cel. I warrant you, with pure loue, & troubled brain,   2150
She calls me proud, and that she could not loue me   2164
Her loue is not the Hare that I doe hunt,   2166
And turn'd into the extremity of loue.   2172
Haue power to raise such loue in mine,   2200
Whiles you chid me, I did loue,   2203
He that brings this loue to thee,   2205
Little knowes this Loue in me: 2206
Or else by him my loue denie,   2211
*wilt thou loue such a woman? what to make thee an in-|strument,   2216
*Well, goe your way to her; (for I see Loue hath   2218
*loue me, I charge her to loue thee: if she will not, I will   2220
Committing me vnto my brothers loue,   2298
You do loue this maid? | *Will*. I do sir.   2378
*should like her? that, but seeing, you should loue her?   2410
*nor sodaine consenting: but say with mee, I loue   2415
*loue, and they will together. Clubbes cannot part | them.   2449
*his Art, and yet not damnable. If you do loue *Rosalinde*   2470
Looke vpon him, loue him: he worships you.   2489

LOUE *cont*.

*Phe. Good shepheard, tell this youth what 'tis to loue — 2490
Phe. If this be so, why blame you me to loue you? — 2510
Sil. If this be so, why blame you me to loue you? — 2511
Orl. If this be so, why blame you me to loue you? — 2512
*Ros. Why do you speake too, Why blame you mee | to loue you. — 2513
**if I can: I would loue you if I could: To morrow meet — 2518
**you, and you shal be married to morrow: As you loue — 2523
*Rosalind meet, as you loue *Phebe* meet, and as I loue no — 2524
Sweet Louers loue the spring, — 2552
For loue is crowned with the prime. | *In spring time*, &c. — 2555
*Phe. If sight & shape be true, why then my loue adieu — 2695
·   You, to his loue must accord, — 2707
you to a loue, that your true faith doth merit: — 2765
you to your land, and loue, and great allies: — 2766
**women) for the loue you beare to men, to like as much — 2787
**for the loue you beare to women (as I perceiue by your — 2789
LOUED = 1
**of her Vncle, then his owne daughter, and neuer two La-|dies loued as
they doe. — 112
LOUEPRATE = *1
*Cel. You haue simply misus'd our sexe in your loue-|prate: — 2107
LOUER = 3*10
Though in thy youth thou wast as true a louer — 808
Vnwillingly to schoole. And then the Louer, — 1126
**propositions of a Louer: but take a taste of my finding — 1427
*Ros. Then there is no true Louer in the Forrest, else — 1493
**as louing your selfe, then seeming the Lo-|uer of any other. — 1567
*Cel. Was, is not is: besides, the oath of Louer is no — 1738
**them brauely, quite trauers athwart the heart of his lo-|uer, — 1749
**haue you bin all this while? you a louer? and you — 1954
**patheticall breake-promise, and the most hollow louer, — 2098
**true louer hence, and not a word; for here comes more | company.
Exit. Sil. — 2222
**Looke, here comes a Louer of mine, and a louer of hers. — 2483
Song. | *It was a Louer, and his lasse*, — 2546
LOUERS = 2*5
**teares, weare these for my sake: wee that are true Lo-|uers, — 835
**and Louers are giuen to Poetrie: and what they — 1631
**sweare in Poetrie, may be said as Louers, they do feigne. — 1632
The sight of Louers feedeth those in loue: — 1766
**nor the Ladies, which is nice: nor the Louers, which — 1930
**they will spit, and for louers, lacking (God warne vs) — 1989
Sweet Louers loue the spring, — 2552
LOUES = 7*2
**loues her, being euer from their Cradles bred together, — 109
Clo. One that old *Fredericke* your Father loues. — 247
To keepe his daughter companie, whose loues — 443
who loues to lye with mee, — 892
and loues to liue i'th Sunne: — 928
He that sweetest rose will finde, | *must finde Loues pricke, & Rosalinde*. — 1309
Iaq. *Rosalinde* is your loues name? *Orl*. Yes, Iust. — 1458
Then shall you know the wounds inuisible | That Loues keene arrows
make. — 1802
*Aliena: say with her, that she loues mee; consent with — 2416
LOUE-SHAKD = *1
*Orl. I am he that is so Loue-shak'd, I pray you tel | me your remedie. — 1552

LOUE-SONGS = 1
*Iaq. I pray you marre no more trees with Writing | Loue-songs in their
barkes. 1454
LOUING = 2*3
*brother the new Duke, and three or foure louing 102
Most frendship, is fayning; most Louing, meere folly: 1161
*as louing your selfe, then seeming the Lo- |uer of any other. 1567
*And louing woo? and wooing, she should graunt? And | will you
perseuer to enioy her? 2411
And you to wrangling, for thy louing voyage 2768
LOUST = *1
*Cel. Heerein I see thou lou'st mee not with the full 177
LOW = 2
Weele. light vpon some setled low content. 772
Of femall fauour, and bestowes himselfe | Like a ripe sister: the woman
low 2236
LOYALTIE = 1
To the last gaspe with truth and loyaltie, 774
LUCRECIAS = 1
Attalanta's *better part,* | *sad* Lucrecia's *Modestie.* 1345
LUNACIE = *1
*that the Lunacie is so ordinarie, that the whippers are in 1583
LUNGS = 1
My Lungs began to crow like Chanticleere, 1003
LUSTIE = 3
Though I looke old, yet I am strong and lustie; 751
Therefore my age is as a lustie winter, 756
A little riper, and more lustie red 1895
LUSTRE = 1
And looking on it, with lacke-lustre eye, 994
LUSTY = 1
The horne, the horne, the lusty horne, 2144
LYE = 7*6
Lye there what hidden womans feare there will, 584
To burne the lodging where you vse to lye, 727
who loues to lye with mee, 892
Lye not, to say mine eyes are murtherers: 1790
*Clo. Vpon a lye, seuen times remoued: (beare your 2644
and so to lye circumstantiall, and the lye direct. 2656
*Clo. I durst go no further then the lye circumstantial: 2659
*nor he durst not giue me the lye direct: and so wee mea- |sur'd swords,
and parted. 2660
*Iaq. Can you nominate in order now, the degrees of | the lye. 2662
*the sixt, the Lye with circumstance: the sea- |uenth, 2669
*the Lye direct: all these you may auoyd, but the 2670
*Lye direct: and you may auoide that too, with an If. I 2671
LYONNESSE = 4
A Lyonnesse, with vdders all drawne drie, 2265
Food to the suck'd and hungry Lyonnesse? 2278
Made him giue battell to the Lyonnesse: 2282
The Lyonnesse had torne some flesh away, 2301
MAD = *2
*one should be lam'd with reasons, and the other mad | without any. 467
*my Sutor from his mad humor of loue, to a liuing humor 1596
MADAM = 2
Ros. Is yonder the man? | *Le Beu.* Euen he, Madam. 315
Cel. Giue me audience, good Madam. | *Ros.* Proceed. 1432

MADAME = *1
*Le Beu. What colour Madame? How shall I aun-|swer you? 267
MADE = 17*7
*God made, a poore vnworthy brother of yours with | idlenesse. 36
*Cel. No; when Nature hath made a faire creature, 213
Cel. Were you made the messenger? 227
*onely in the world I fil vp a place, which may bee better | supplied,
when I haue made it emptie. 354
To hide vs from pursuite that will be made 601
Hath not old custome made this life more sweete 608
That I made yesterday in despight of my Inuention. 934
Made to his Mistresse eye-brow. Then, a Soldier, 1128
But were I not the better part made mercie, 1182
*Iaq. You haue a nimble wit; I thinke 'twas made of 1468
*in a little roome: truly, I would the Gods hadde | made thee poeticall. 1626
*Aud. Do you wish then that the Gods had made me | Poeticall? 1633
Now shew the wound mine eye hath made in thee, 1791
For I am falser then vowes made in wine: 1845
*made thee a tame snake) and say this to her; That if she 2219
Made him giue battell to the Lyonnesse: 2282
*that Grapes were made to eate, and lippes to open. 2377
*degrees, haue they made a paire of staires to marriage, 2446
Sil. It is to be all made of sighes and teares, | And so am I for Phebe. 2491
Sil. It is to be all made of faith and seruice, | And so am I for Phebe. 2496
Sil. It is to be all made of fantasie, 2501
All made of passion, and all made of wishes, 2502
When earthly things made eauen | attone together. 2684
MADMEN = *1
*as wel a darke house, and a whip, as madmen do: 1581
MADNES = *1
*of madnes, w was to forsweare the ful stream of y world, 1597
MADNESSE = *2
*Ros. Loue is meerely a madnesse, and I tel you, de-|serues 1580
*madnesse, that blinde rascally boy, that abuses euery 2119
MAGITIAN = 1*2
*yeare old conuerst with a Magitian, most profound in 2469
*I say I am a Magitian: Therefore put you in your best a-|ray, 2479
Whom he reports to be a great Magitian. 2609
MAID = 3*1
Here's a yong maid with trauaile much oppressed, | And faints for
succour. 858
*Ros. Nay, but the diuell take mocking: speake sadde | brow, and true
maid. 1408
*Ros. Marry he trots hard with a yong maid, between 1503
You do loue this maid? | Will. I do sir. 2378
MAIDENS = 1
That a maidens heart hath burn'd. 2190
MAIDES = 1*2
(Maides as we are) to trauell forth so farre? 573
*Maides are May when they are maides, but the sky chan-|ges 2057
MAIESTIE = 1
Helens cheeke, but not his heart, | Cleopatra's Maiestie: 1343
MAINE = 1
That the maine haruest reapes: loose now and then 1877
MAIST l.*197 = *1

140

MAKE = 21*12

Oli. Now Sir, what make you heere? | *Orl*. Nothing: I am not taught to make any thing.	32
*Cel. Marry I prethee doe, to make sport withall: but	195
**be misprised: we wil make it our suite to the Duke, that	344
Ros. Yet your mistrust cannot make me a Traitor;	517
Ile make him finde him: do this sodainly;	699
Of old Sir *Rowland*; why, what make you here?	707
Cor. That is the way to make her scorne you still.	804
That euer loue did make thee run into, | Thou hast not lou'd.	817
*Amy. It will make you melancholly Monsieur *Iaques*	899
Heauen thankes, and make no boast of them.	924
And let my officers of such a nature | Make an extent vpon his house and Lands:	1196
man: God make incision in thee, thou art raw.	1269
*Clo. Come Shepheard, let vs make an honorable re-|treit,	1358
*Orl. Faire youth, I would I could make thee beleeue | (I Loue.	1569
*Ros. Me beleeue it? You may assoone make her that	1570
*Aud. Well, I am not faire, and therefore I pray the | Gods make me honest.	1643
Then shall you know the wounds inuisible | That Loues keene arrows make.	1802
Hee'll make a proper man: the best thing in him	1889
Did make offence, his eye did heale it vp:	1891
**haue a foole to make me merrie, then experience to	1943
make me sad, and to trauaile for it too.	1944
**then you make a woman: besides, he brings his destinie | with him.	1970
**the wiser, the waywarder: make the doores vpon a wo-|mans	2070
**make her fault her husbands occasion, let her neuer nurse	2082
*Iaq. Sing it: 'tis no matter how it bee in tune, so it | make noyse enough.	2134
Of me, and all that I can make,	2210
**wilt thou loue such a woman? what to make thee an in-|strument,	2216
**(to wit) I kill thee, make thee away, translate thy life in-|to	2394
Ros. I haue promis'd to make all this matter euen:	2594
To makc these doubts all euen. *Exit Ros. and Celia*.	2601
'Tis I must make conclusion | Of these most strange euents:	2700
offer, when I make curt'sie, bid me farewell. *Exit*.	2796

MAKER = 1*1

*Orl. Vertue is no horne-maker: and my *Rosalind* is | vertuous.	1976
the onely peace-maker: much vertue in if.	2676

MAKES = 3*9

*Cel. 'Tis true, for those that she makes faire, she scarce	206
**makes honest, & those that she makes honest, she makes | very illfauouredly.	207
**fortune makes natures naturall, the cutter off of natures | witte.	218
**wise men haue makes a great shew; Heere comes Mon-|sieur the *Beu*.	255
Abruptly as my passion now makes me, | Thou hast not lou'd.	823
**good pasture makes fat sheepe: and that a great cause of	1226
**he? How look'd he? Wherein went he? What makes hee	1415
Whose heart th'accustom'd sight of death makes hard	1774
That makes the world full of ill-fauourd children:	1826
*Ros. And your experience makes you sad: I had ra-|ther	1942

MAKING = *3

**making such pittiful dole ouer them, that all the behol-|ders	293
*Ros. Is he of Gods making? What manner of man?	1400
**natiuitie, and almost chide God for making you that	1951

MAKST = 1

Poore Deere quoth he, thou mak'st a testament 655

MALICE = 2

And on my life his malice 'gainst the Lady 450

I rather will subiect me to the malice 740

MAN = 43*37

*loue no man in good earnest, nor no further in sport ney-|ther, 196

*Le Beu. There comes an old man, and his three sons. 282

*third: yonder they lie, the poore old man their Father, 292

Ros. Is yonder the man? | Le Beu. Euen he, Madam. 315

*there is such oddes in the man: In pitie of the challen-|gers 322

*Ros. Young man, haue you challeng'd Charles the | Wrastler? 331

Ros. Now Hercules, be thy speede yong man. 371

Ros. Oh excellent yong man. 374

Duk. Beare him awaie: | What is thy name yong man? 382

*Duk. I would thou hadst beene son to some man else, 386

Had I before knowne this yong man his sonne, 400

That I did suite me all points like a man, 581

Cel. What shall I call thee when thou art a man? 588

Duk. Can it be possible that no man saw them? 681

Ile doe the seruice of a yonger man 758

Orl. Oh good old man, how well in thee appeares 760

But poore old man, thou prun'st a rotten tree, 767

here, a yong man and an old in solemne talke. 803

As sure I thinke did neuer man loue so: 811

Cel. I pray you, one of you question yon'd man, 845

But I am shepheard to another man, 863

*Iaq. Well then, if euer I thanke any man, Ile thanke 912

*of two dog-Apes. And when a man thankes me hartily, 914

If it do come to passe, that any man turne Asse: 937

For I can no where finde him, like a man. 974

Vnclaim'd of any man. But who come here? 1061

*Du Sen. Art thou thus bolden'd man by thy distres? 1067

And giue it food. There is an old poore man, 1106

And one man in his time playes many parts, 1121

Go to my Caue, and tell mee. Good old man, 1175

*of a man? Shallow, shallow: A better instance I say: | Come. 1254

*Clo. Most shallow man: Thou wormes meate in re-|spect 1262

man: God make incision in thee, thou art raw. 1269

*that I weare; owe no man hate, enuie no mans happi-|nesse: 1271

Some, how briefe the Life of man | runs his erring pilgrimage, 1327

Cel. Tro you, who hath done this? | Ros. Is it a man? 1375

*I am caparison'd like a man, I haue a doublet and hose in 1391

*might'st powre this conceal'd man out of thy mouth, as 1395

Cel. So you may put a man in your belly. 1399

*Ros. Is he of Gods making? What manner of man? 1400

*Ros. Why God will send more, if the man will bee 1403

*Ros. With a Priest that lacks Latine, and a rich man 1508

*in his youth an inland man, one that knew Courtship too 1533

*that are sicke. There is a man haunts the Forrest, that a-|buses 1545

*he taught me how to know a man in loue: in which cage | of rushes, I
am sure you art not prisoner. 1555

*are no such man; you are rather point deuice in your
ac-|coustrements, 1566

*Goates, Audrey: and how Audrey am I the man yet? 1616

*it strikes a man more dead then a great rec-|koning 1625

*Clo. Amen. A man may if he were of a fearful heart, 1657

MAN *cont.*

*It is said, many a man knowes no end of his goods;	1661
*right: Many a man has good Hornes, and knows no end	1662
*Is the single man therefore blessed? No, as a wall'd	1666
*of a married man, more honourable then the bare	1668
Clo. I wil not take her on guilt of any man.	1677
*and the Falcon her bels, so man hath his desires, and as	1687
Iaq. And wil you (being a man of your breeding) be	1689
that teares do not become a man.	1712
*But what talke wee of Fathers, when there is such a man | as *Orlando*?	1745
Cel. O that's a braue man, hee writes braue verses,	1747
You are a thousand times a properer man	1824
Cry the man mercy, loue him, take his offer,	1834
I had rather here you chide, then this man wooe.	1838
To gleane the broken eares after the man	1876
Hee'll make a proper man: the best thing in him	1889
*was not anie man died in his owne person (*videlicet*) in	2008
Orl. A man that had a wife with such a wit, he might | say, wit whether wil't?	2074
Were man as rare as Phenix: 'od's my will,	2165
Whiles the eye of man did wooe me,	2196
What man I am, and how, and why, and where | This handkercher was stain'd.	2246
A wretched ragged man, ore-growne with haire	2257
When that the sleeping man should stirre; for 'tis	2267
This seene, *Orlando* did approach the man,	2270
Oli. Be of good cheere youth: you a man?	2318
Oli. Well then, take a good heart, and counterfeit to | be a man.	2328
in the world: here comes the man you meane.	2349
*if euer I satisfi'd man, and you shall bee married to mor-|row.	2521
Clo. If any man doubt that, let him put mee to my	2620
*that that no man else will: rich honestie dwels like a mi-|ser	2636
Where, meeting with an old Religious man,	2736
Du Se. Welcome yong man:	2743

MANERS = *2

*saw'st good manners: if thou neuer saw'st good maners,	1239
Cor. Not a whit *Touchstone*, those that are good ma-|ners	1243

MANGLED = 1

With obseruation, the which he vents | In mangled formes. O that I were a foole,	1014

MANIE = 3*1

As manie other mannish cowards haue,	586
Thus Rosalinde *of manie parts*, | *by Heauenly Synode was deuis'd*,	1347
Of manie faces, eyes, and hearts, | *to haue the touches deerest pris'd*.	1349
*haue liu'd manie a faire yeere though *Hero* had turn'd	2012

MANLY = 1

For his shrunke shanke, and his bigge manly voice,	1140

MANNAGE = *1

*they are taught their mannage, and to that end Riders	15

MANNER = 1*2

Ros. Yet tell vs the manner of the Wrastling.	276
Ros. Is he of Gods making? What manner of man?	1400
Ros. Yes one, and in this manner. Hee was to ima-|gine	1586

MANNERS = 2*4

Le Beu. Neither his daughter, if we iudge by manners,	439
Or else a rude despiser of good manners,	1068
*saw'st good manners: if thou neuer saw'st good maners,	1239

MANNERS *cont*.

*then thy manners must be wicked, and wickednes is sin,	1240
Shee saies I am not faire, that I lacke manners,	2163
*haue bookes for good manners: I will name you the de-|grees.	2665

MANNISH = 1

As manie other mannish cowards haue,	586

MANS = 6*8

*emulator of euery mans good parts, a secret & villanous	141
*your yeares: you haue seene cruell proofe of this mans	337
*Ros. I could finde in my heart to disgrace my mans	787
The Wise-mans folly is anathomiz'd	1030
If euer sate at any good mans feast:	1092
Thou art not so vnkinde, as mans ingratitude	1157
*that I weare; owe no man hate, enuie no mans happi-|nesse:	1271
*in mans apparrell? Looks he as freshly, as he did the day	he Wrastled?	1424
*Clo. When a mans verses cannot be vnderstood, nor	1623
*a mans good wit seconded with the forward childe, vn-|derstanding:	1624
And thanke heauen, fasting, for a good mans loue;	1831
This is a mans inuention, and his hand.	Sil. Sure it is hers.	2178
You lacke a mans heart.	Ros. I doe so, I confesse it:	2319
*it is, to looke into happines through another mans eies:	2453

MANY = 6*13

*and a many merry men with him; and there they liue	116
*like the old *Robin Hood* of *England*: they say many yong	117
At seauenteene yeeres, many their fortunes seeke	777
How many actions most ridiculous,	812
I thinke of as many matters as he, but I giue	923
Who after me, hath many a weary steppe	1107
And one man in his time playes many parts,	1121
*Ros. I haue bin told so of many: but indeed, an olde	1531
*well: for there he fel in loue. I haue heard him read ma-|ny	1534
*to be touch'd with so many giddie offences as hee	1536
*It is said, many a man knowes no end of his goods;	1661
*right: Many a man has good Hornes, and knows no end	1662
*of many simples, extracted from many obiects,	1932
*didst know how many fathome deepe I am in loue: but	2112
*Oli. Many will swoon when they do look on bloud.	2312
Of many desperate studies, by his vnckle,	2608
*I would kisse as many of you as had beards that	2792
*I defi'de not: And I am sure, as many as haue good	2794

MAR = 1*1

Oli. What mar you then sir?	34
*Orl. Marry sir, I am helping you to mar that which	35

MARIAGE = *1

*to sweare, and to forsweare, according as mariage binds	2633

MARKE = 3

Goe hence a little, and I shall conduct you	If you will marke it.	1763
Ros. She *Phebes* me: marke how the tyrant writes.	2188
And marke what obiect did present it selfe	2254

MARKED = 1

Much marked of the melancholie *Iaques*,	648

MARKES = 1*1

*Ros. There is none of my Vnckles markes vpon you:	1554
Orl. What were his markes?	1557

144

MARKET = 1
*and suppers, and sleeping hours excepted: it is the right | Butter-
womens ranke to Market.   1295
MARKETABLE = *1
*Cel. All the better: we shalbe the more Marketable.   262
MARKETS = 1
Sell when you can, you are not for all markets: 1833
MARKT = 1
There be some women *Siluius*, had they markt him   1898
MARRE = *2
*Iaq. I pray you marre no more trees with Writing | Loue-songs in their
barkes.   1454
*Orl. I pray you marre no moe of my verses with rea-|ding them
ill-fauouredly.   1456
MARRIAGE = *5
*the contract of her marriage, and the day it is solemnizd: 1504
*Ol. Truly she must be giuen, or the marriage is not | lawfull.   1678
*and haue a good Priest that can tel you what marriage is,   1691
*degrees, haue they made a paire of staires to marriage,   2446
*before marriage; they are in the verie wrath of   2448
MARRIE = 7*8
*I wil marrie thee: and to that end, I haue bin with Sir   1651
*married of him then of another, for he is not like to mar-|rie   1696
Marrie his kisses are Iudasses owne children.   1719
*Ros. Marrie that should you if I were your Mistris,   1996
*marrie vs: giue me your hand *Orlando*: What doe you | say sister?   2034
Orl. Pray thee marrie vs. | Cel. I cannot say the words.   2036
Ros. I, but when? | Orl. Why now, as fast as she can marrie vs.   2042
Will. Which he sir? | *Clo. He sir, that must marrie this woman:
Therefore   2387
*brother marries *Aliena*, shall you marrie her. I know in-|to   2472
*me altogether: I wil marrie you, if euer I marrie Wo-|man,   2519
Ros. You say, you'l marrie me, if I be willing.   2586
Ros. But if you do refuse to marrie me,   2588
Keepe you your word *Phebe*, that you'l marrie me,   2597
Keepe your word *Siluius*, that you'l marrie her   2599
MARRIED = 3*9
*of a married man, more honourable then the bare   1668
Iaq. Wil you be married, Motley?   1685
*married vnder a bush like a begger? Get you to church,   1690
*married of him then of another, for he is not like to mar-|rie   1696
*me wel: and not being wel married, it wil be a good   1697
Ol. Come sweete *Audrey*, | We must be married, or we must liue in
baudrey: 1701
*Orl. They shall be married to morrow: and I will   2451
*bid your friends: for if you will be married to mor-|row, you shall: and
to *Rosalind* if you will.   2480
*and Ile be married to morrow: I will satisfie you,   2520
*if euer I satisfi'd man, and you shall bee married to mor-|row.   2521
*you, and you shal be married to morrow: As you loue   2523
*Clo. To morrow is the ioyfull day *Audrey*, to morow | will we be
married.   2532
MARRIES = *1
*brother marries *Aliena*, shall you marrie her. I know in-|to   2472
MARRY = 1*6
*Orl. Marry sir, I am helping you to mar that which   35
*Oliuer. Marry sir be better employed, and be naught | a while.   38

145

MARRY *cont.*

Cha. Marry doe I sir: and I came to acquaint you	122
Cel. Marry I prethee doe, to make sport withall: but	195
Ros. I marry, now vnmuzzle your wisedome.	237
Ros. Marry he trots hard with a yong maid, between	1503
Rosa. Marry to say, she came to seeke you there: you	2079

MARSHALL = 1

Weele haue a swashing and a marshall outside,	585

MARUELL = 1

I maruell why I answer'd not againe,	1906

MAR-TEXT = 1*3

Oliuer Mar-text, the Vicar of the next village, who hath	1652
Enter Sir Oliuer Mar-text.	1672
*Heere comes Sir *Oliuer*: Sir *Oliuer Mar-text* you are	1673
Mar-text. But *Awdrie*, there is a youth heere in the | Forrest layes	
claime to you.	2346

MASTER *see also* Mr = 11*3

Adam. Yonder comes my Master, your brother.	29
*lost my teeth in your seruice: God be with my olde ma-|ster,	83
Orl. Who's there? | *Ad.* What my yong Master, oh my gentle master,	704
Oh my sweet master, O you memorie	706
Know you not Master, to seeme kinde of men,	713
No more doe yours: your vertues gentle Master	715
Ad. Master goe on, and I will follow thee	773
My master is of churlish disposition,	865
Adam. Deere Master, I can go no further:	951
And measure out my graue. Farwel kinde master.	953
Corin. Mistresse and Master, you haue oft enquired	1754
That the old *Carlot* once was Master of.	1882
Cor. Our Master and Mistresse seekes you: come a-|way, away.	2403

MASTERS = 3*1

Adam. Sweet Masters bee patient, for your Fathers | remembrance, be	
at accord.	63
Or Charles, or something weaker masters thee.	428
Then to die well, and not my Masters debter. *Exeunt.*	780
Thou art right welcome, as thy masters is:	1176

MATCH = 2*1

Cel. I could match this beginning with an old tale.	283
*reasonable match. If thou bee'st not damn'd for this, the	1280
monstrous, til his fellow-fault came to match it.	1542

MATERIALL = 1

Iaq. A materiall foole.	1642

MATES = *1

Duk Sen. Now my Coe-mates, and brothers in exile:	607

MATTER = 8*7

*with a matter: I am giuen sir secretly to vnderstand, that	123
For then he's full of matter.	677
Why, what's the matter? | *Ad.* O vnhappie youth,	719
Ad. No matter whether, so you come not here.	734
Cel. That's no matter: the feet might beare y verses.	1365
Cel. O Lord, Lord, it is a hard matter for friends to	1380
Ol. 'Tis no matter; Ne're a fantastical knaue of them	1706
*were grauel'd, for lacke of matter, you might take oc-|casion	1987
matter, the cleanliest shift is to kisse.	1990
Ros. Then she puts you to entreatie, and there begins | new matter.	1992
Iaq. Sing it: 'tis no matter how it bee in tune, so it | make noyse	
enough.	2134

MATTER *cont*.
She has a huswiues hand, but that's no matter:	2176
*great matter in the dittie, yet y note was very vntunable	2566
Ros. I haue promis'd to make all this matter euen:	2594
There is much matter to be heard, and learn'd:	2762

MATTERS = 2
I thinke of as many matters as he, but I giue	923
The matter's in my head, and in my heart,	1912

MAY *l.*71 *201 *214 *251 *278 *299 *354 564 857 996 1103 *1228 *1381 1398 1399 *1430 1453 *1570 *1632 *1650 *1657 1800 1812 *1962 *2100 2233 *2417 *2465 *2670 *2671 2713 *2791 = 11*22, *1
*Maides are May when they are maides, but the sky chan-|ges	2057

ME *l.*5 *10 *11 *19 *21 *24 31 *48 53 56 65 *67 *68 *69 *71 *73 78 *85 91 *126 *135 *174 *182 194 274 *347 *353 *369 370 389 392 406 411 436 *464 495 500 506 517 518 524 525 527 *546 558 564 567 581 590 597 598 617 628 675 698 *733 *735 740 750 757 779 *792 823 884 905 *914 *915 942 992 1032 1057 1071 1081 1083 1107 1177 1178 *1246 1267 1387 *1393 *1404 1405 *1416 1419 1432 1442 1446 *1469 *1491 *1532 1553 *1555 *1570 *1587 *1588 *1603 1604 *1605 *1607 *1608 *1633 *1635 1638 1644 *1653 *1697 1698 1700 *1704 1707 1710 *1743 1756 1771 1772 1781 1805 1806 1814 1842 1857 1869 1903 1905 1914 *1917 *1934 *1943 1944 *1955 1964 *1981 *1983 2021 2024 2025 2027 *2034 *2052 *2091 2155 2159 2164 2167 2181 2188 2196 2197 2198 2201 2203 2206 2210 *2220 2245 2296 2297 2298 2299 2306 *2351 2380 *2382 *2429 2436 *2461 *2467 *2474 *2484 2510 2511 2512 *2519 2586 2588 2597 2598 2600 2605 *2646 *2649 *2660 *2722 2727 *2793 2796 = 121*74

MEANE = 5*1
Orl. You meane to mocke me after: you should not	369
Cel. Ile put my selfe in poore and meane attire,	575
Who can come in, and say that I meane her,	1051
Thinking that I meane him, but therein suites	1055
in the world: here comes the man you meane.	2349
Meane time, forget this new-falne dignitie,	2753

MEANES = 7*4
*vnder-hand meanes laboured to disswade him from it;	138
*meanes or other: for I assure thee, (and almost with	149
That could giue more, but that her hand lacks meanes.	412
Hath heard your praises, and this night he meanes,	726
He will haue other meanes to cut you off;	729
The meanes of weaknesse and debilitie,	755
Till that the wearie verie meanes do ebbe.	1047
*meanes, and content, is without three good frends. That	1224
Ros. By no meanes sir; Time trauels in diuers paces,	1498
Why what meanes this? why do you looke on me?	1814
I thinke she meanes to tangle my eies too:	1817

MEANING = 1*1
Meaning me a beast.	2198
*his lips when he put it into his mouth, meaning there-|by,	2376

MEANINGS = 1
Orl. Speak'st thou in sober meanings?	2477

MEANST = 1
Cel. Prethee, who is't that thou means't?	246

MEANTIME *see* mean
MEASURD = *1
*nor he durst not giue me the lye direct: and so wee mea-|sur'd swords, and parted.	2660

MEASURE = 3*2
And measure out my graue. Farwel kinde master.   953
*little measure draw a beleefe from you, to do your selfe   2466
*purgation, I haue trod a measure, I haue flattred a Lady,   2621
According to the measure of their states.   2752
With measure heap'd in ioy, to'th Measures fall.   2756
MEASURES = 1
With measure heap'd in ioy, to'th Measures fall.   2756
MEAT = *1
*Clo. It is meat and drinke to me to see a Clowne, by   2351
MEATE = 1*1
*Clo. Most shallow man: Thou wormes meate in re-|spect   1262
slut, were to put good meate into an vncleane dish.   1646
MEAZURES = 1
I am for other, then for dancing meazures. | Du Se. Stay, Iaques, stay.   2770
MEDICINE = 1
If they will patiently receiue my medicine.   1035
MEDLER = 1*1
*with a Medler: then it will be the earliest fruit i'th coun-|try: 1316
*for you'l be rotten ere you bee halfe ripe, and that's | the right vertue
of the Medler.   1317
MEE l.*7 *20 *21 *25 *46 *52 *66 *70 *72 *79 *125 *142 *175 *177 *180
*190 *346 *349 *464 844 892 909 1175 *1217 *1599 *1611 1699 *1744
1844 *1879 *1981 *2089 *2095 *2348 *2415 *2416 *2513 *2620
*2785 = 6*34
MEEDE = 1
When seruice sweate for dutie, not for meede: 762
MEERE = 4
Is but a quintine, a meere liuelesse blocke.   417
Are meere vsurpers, tyrants, and whats worse   669
Is second childishnesse, and meere obliuion,   1144
Most frendship, is fayning: most Louing, meere folly: 1161
MEERELY = 1*1
Ia. All the world's a stage, | And all the men and women, meerely
Players;   1118
*Ros. Loue is meerely a madnesse, and I tel you, de-|serues   1580
MEERLY = *1
*and to liue in a nooke meerly Monastick: and thus I cur'd   1598
MEET = 2*5
Iaq. God buy you, let's meet as little as we can.   1452
*If I could meet that Fancie-monger, I would giue him ˙   1549
You meet in some fresh cheeke the power of fancie,   1801
*if I can: I would loue you if I could: To morrow meet   2518
*Rosalind meet, as you loue Phebe meet, and as I loue no   2524
*woman, Ile meet: so fare you wel: I haue left you com-|mands.   2525
MEETE = *2
*meete; but Mountaines may bee remoou'd with Earth-|quakes, and so
encounter.   1381
*promis'd to meete me in this place of the Forrest, and to | couple vs.   1653
MEETING = 2
Iaq. I would faine see this meeting.   1655
Where, meeting with an old Religious man,   2736
MELANCHOLIE = 1
Much marked of the melancholie Iaques,   648
MELANCHOLLY = 4*1
*Amy. It will make you melancholly Monsieur Iaques   899
I can sucke melancholly out of a song,   901

MELANCHOLLY *cont*.
Vnder the shade of melancholly boughes, 1088
Orl. I am glad of your departure: Adieu good Mon-|sieur
Melancholly. 1485
Ros They say you are a melancholly fellow. 1919
MELANCHOLY = 1*2
1.*Lord*. Indeed my Lord | The melancholy *Iaques* grieues at that, 632
Iaq. I haue neither the Schollers melancholy, which 1926
*is all these: but it is a melancholy of mine owne, com-|pounded 1931
MEMORIE = 1
Oh my sweet master, O you memorie 706
MEN = 5*9
*and a many merry men with him; and there they liue 116
*wise men haue makes a great shew; Heere comes Mon-|sieur the *Beu*. 255
Le Beu. Three proper yong men, of excellent growth | and presence. 284
Ros. With bils on their neckes: Be it knowne vnto | all men by these
presents. 286
Clo. Thus men may grow wiser euery day. It is the 299
Know you not Master, to seeme kinde of men, 713
Ia. All the world's a stage, | And all the men and women, meerely
Players; 1118
*of his owne getting; hornes, euen so poore men alone: 1664
Hero of Cestos. But these are all lies, men haue died 2017
Ros. Say a day, without the euer: no, no *Orlando*, men 2055
And he did render him the most vnnaturall | That liu'd amongst men. 2273
Men of great worth resorted to this forrest, 2731
*women) for the loue you beare to men, to like as much 2787
*of this Play, as please you: And I charge you (O men) 2788
MEND = 1*3
Cel. And we will mend thy wages: 880
*verie vncleanly fluxe of a Cat. Mend the instance Shep-|heard. 1265
*mend mee, and by all pretty oathes that are not dange-|rous, 2095
*such a foolish song. God buy you, and God mend your | voices. Come
Audrie. Exeunt. 2570
MENS = 1*2
And sat at good mens feasts, and wip'd our eies 1099
*glad of other mens good content with my harme: 1272
*to see other mens; then to haue seene much, and to haue 1938
MERCIE = 1*1
Cel. Why Cosen, why *Rosaline*: *Cupid* haue mercie, 460
But were I not the better part made mercie, 1182
MERCY = 1
Cry the man mercy, loue him, take his offer, 1834
MERIT = 1
you to a loue, that your true faith doth merit: 2765
MERRIE = 1*1
And turne his merrie Note, 893
*haue a foole to make me merrie, then experience to 1943
MERRIER = *1
*of, and would you yet were merrier: vnlesse you 173
MERRILY = 1*1
What, you looke merrily. 984
*he cannot study, and the other liues merrily, be-|cause 1510
MERRY = 5*2
*and a many merry men with him; and there they liue 116
Cel. I pray thee *Rosalind*, sweet my Coz, be merry. 171
*turne monster: therefore my sweet *Rose*, my deare *Rose*, | be merry. 191

149

MERRY *cont*.

Ros. O *Iupiter*, how merry are my spirits?	784
Heere was he merry, hearing of a Song.	976
*z I wil do that when you are dispos'd to be merry:	2063
Aud. Do good *William*. | *Will*. God rest you merry sir. *Exit*	2400

MESSENGER = 2

Cel. Were you made the messenger?	227
I am but as a guiltlesse messenger.	2160

MET = 6*8

Iaq. A Foole, a foole: I met a foole i'th Forrest,	985
As I do liue by foode, I met a foole,	987
*wel met. Will you dispatch vs heere vnder this tree, or	1674
*Sir, you are verie well met: goddild you for your last	1682
Ros. I met the Duke yesterday, and had much que-|stion	1742
Sil. Not very well, but I haue met him oft,	1880
met your wiues wit going to your neighbours bed.	2077
*met, but they look'd: no sooner look'd, but they	2442
1.*Pa*. Wel met honest Gentleman.	2538
Clo. By my troth well met: come, sit, sit, and a song.	2539
*Motley-minded Gentleman, that I haue so often met in	2618
Clo. 'Faith we met, and found the quarrel was vpon | the seuenth cause.	2626
*but when the parties were met themselues, one of them	2673
How thus we met, and these things finish.	2714

METHINKES *see* thinkes
METHOUGHT *see* thought
METTLE = 1

His folly to the mettle of my speech,	1056

MEWLING = 1

Mewling, and puking in the Nurses armes:	1123

MIDDLE = 1

2.*Pa*. We are for you, sit i'th middle.	2540

MIDNIGHT = 1

As euer sigh'd vpon a midnight pillow:	809

MIDSOMER-NIGHT = *1

*Nun; if it had not bin for a hot Midsomer-night, for	2013

MIGHT *l*.*131 345 *1365 *1636 *1808 *1987 2021 2047 *2074 *2076 2204 2275 2307 = 6*7, *1

Phe. Dead Shepheard, now I find thy saw of might,	1853

MIGHTIE = 1

Addrest a mightie power, which were on foote	2732

MIGHTILIE = *2

*dost him any slight disgrace, or if hee doe not mightilie	145
*him to a second, that haue so mightilie perswaded him | from a first.	367

MIGHTILY = *1

*mightily misplaced, and the bountifull blinde woman | doth most mistake in her gifts to women.	204

MIGHTST *l*.*1395 2689 = 1*1
MILDE = 1

Would they worke in milde aspect?	2202

MILES = 1

So neere our publike Court as twentie miles, | Thou diest for it.	503

MILKD = *1

*chopt hands had milk'd; and I remember the wooing	832

MIND = 1*1

Let no face bee kept in mind, | but the faire of Rosalinde.	1292
Orl. I would not haue my right *Rosalind* of this mind,	2020

MINDE = 3*2
And all the world was of my Fathers minde,   399
To speake my minde, and I will through and through   1033
*Clo. I am not in the minde, but I were better to bee   1695
And by him seale vp thy minde,   2207
*said his beard was not cut well, hee was in the minde it   2647
MINDED = *1
*Motley-minded Gentleman, that I haue so often met in   2618
MINE l.*181 *182 *190 *228 358 *375 388 508 549 553 810 827 *828 *839
    *843 861 1171 1481 *1532 1781 1787 1790 1791 1795 1904 *1931 2005
    2200 *2483 *2622 *2635 2724 = 19*14
MINES = *1
*place of a brother, and as much as in him lies, mines my   22
MINGLED = 1
Betwixt the constant red, and mingled Damaske.   1897
MINISTRED = 1
That to your wanting may be ministred.   1103
MINUTE = *4
*sighing euerie minute, and groaning euerie houre wold   1494
*will diuide a minute into a thousand parts, and breake   1960
*but a part of the thousand part of a minute in the affairs   1961
*minute behinde your houre, I will thinke you the most   2097
MIRTH = 1*1
*Ros. Deere Cellia; I show more mirth then I am mi-|stresse   172
Hymen. Then is there mirth in heauen,   2683
MISCHEEUOUS = 1
Du Sen. Most mischeeuous foule sin, in chiding sin: 1038
MISCONSTERS = 1
That he misconsters all that you haue done: 433
MISER = *1
*that that no man else will: rich honestie dwels like a mi-|ser   2636
MISERABLE = 2
A motley Foole (a miserable world:)   986
From miserable slumber I awaked.   2284
MISERIE = 2
'Tis right quoth he, thus miserie doth part   659
*wee two, will raile against our Mistris the world, and all | our miserie.   1470
MISPLACED = *1
*mightily misplaced, and the bountifull blinde woman | doth most
mistake in her gifts to women.   204
MISPRISED = *2
*misprised: but it shall not be so long, this wrastler shall   166
*be misprised: we wil make it our suite to the Duke, that   344
MISSING = 1
Your Grace was wont to laugh is also missing,   689
MISTAKE = 2
*mightily misplaced, and the bountifull blinde woman | doth most
mistake in her gifts to women.   204
Then good my Leige, mistake me not so much,   525
MISTRESSE = 3*4
*Ros. Deere Cellia; I show more mirth then I am mi-|stresse   172
*Clow. Mistresse, you must come away to your father.   226
Made to his Mistresse eye-brow. Then, a Soldier,   1128
*Corin. Mistresse and Master, you haue oft enquired   1754
Praising the proud disdainfull Shepherdesse | That was his Mistresse.   1757
No faith proud Mistresse, hope not after it,   1818
*Cor. Our Master and Mistresse seekes you: come a-|way, away.   2403

MISTRIS = 6*3
But iustly as you haue exceeded all promise, | Your Mistris shall be
happie.   408
Duk. Mistris, dispatch you with your safest haste,   498
They found the bed vntreasur'd of their Mistris.   687
Wearing thy hearer in thy Mistris praise, | Thou hast not lou'd.   820
*wee two, will raile against our Mistris the world, and all | our miserie.   1470
*me his Loue, his Mistris: and I set him euerie day   1587
But Mistris, know your selfe, downe on your knees   1830
Orl. Who could be out, being before his beloued | Mistris?   1994
Ros. Marrie that should you if I were your Mistris,   1996
MISTRISSES = *1
Cor. Heere comes yong Mr *Ganimed*, my new Mistris-|ses Brother.   1283
MISTRUST = 1
Ros. Yet your mistrust cannot make me a Traitor;   517
MISUSD = *1
Cel. You haue simply misus'd our sexe in your loue-|prate: 2107
MIXT = 1
Then that mixt in his cheeke: 'twas iust the difference   1896
MOCKE = *2
Cel. Let vs sit and mocke the good houswife *For-|tune*   200
Orl. You meane to mocke me after: you should not   369
MOCKEABLE = *1
*the behauiour of the Countrie is most mockeable at the   1245
MOCKER = 1
Before I come, thou art a mocker of my labor.   963
MOCKES = 1
Afflict me with thy mockes, pitty me not,   1806
MOCKING = *1
Ros. Nay, but the diuell take mocking: speake sadde | brow, and true
maid.   1408
MOCKT = 1
haue mockt me before: but come your waies.   370
MODERNE = 1*1
Full of wise sawes, and moderne instances,   1135
*fellowes, and betray themselues to euery mo-|derne censure, worse
then drunkards.   1922
MODEST = *3
Orl. Readie Sir, but his will hath in it a more modest | working.   363
*he cut it to please himselfe: this is call'd the quip modest.   2650
*Quip-modest: the third, the reply Churlish: the fourth,   2667
MODESTIE = 1
Attalanta's *better part*, | *sad* Lucrecia's *Modestie*.   1345
MOE = *1
Orl. I pray you marre no moe of my verses with rea-|ding them
ill-fauouredly.   1456
MOMENT = 1*1
*the Dukes Wrastler, which *Charles* in a moment threw   289
The Cicatrice and capable impressure | Thy palme some moment
keepes: but now mine eyes   1794
MONASTICK = *1
*and to liue in a nooke meerly Monastick: and thus I cur'd   1598
MONETHS = *1
*Is but for two moneths victuall'd: So to your pleasures,   2769
MONEY = 1*1
you, for I thinke you haue no money in your purse.   796
*the worse at ease he is: and that hee that wants money,   1223

MONGER = *1
*If I could meet that Fancie-monger, I would giue him 1549
MONKEY = *1
*then an ape, more giddy in my desires, then a mon-|key: 2061
MONSIEUER = 1
Cel. Call him hether good Monsieuer *Le Beu*. | *Duke*. Do so: Ile not be
by. 326
MONSIEUR = 2*6
*wise men haue makes a great shew; Heere comes Mon-|sieur the *Beu*. 255
. *Boon-iour Monsieur le Beu*, what's the newes? 263
Clo. But what is the sport Monsieur, that the Ladies | haue lost? 296
Le Beu. Monsieur the Challenger, the Princesse cals | for you. 328
Amy. It will make you melancholly Monsieur *Iaques* 899
Amy. What you wil Monsieur *Iaques*. 908
Du Sen. Why how now Monsieur, what a life is this 982
Orl. I am glad of your departure: Adieu good Mon-|sieur
Melancholly. 1485
MONSTER = *1
*turne monster: therefore my sweet *Rose*, my deare *Rose*, | be merry. 191
MONSTROUS = 1
monstrous, til his fellow-fault came to match it. 1542
MOONE = *1
*of Irish Wolues against the Moone: I will helpe you 2517
MOONISH = *1
*to woe me. At which time would I, being but a moonish 1588
MOOUE = 1
*bee entreated. Speake to him Ladies, see if you can | mooue him. 324
MORALIZE = 1
Du Sen. But what said *Iaques*? | Did he not moralize this spectacle? 651
MORALL = 1
The motley Foole, thus morall on the time, 1002
MORE *see also* moe = 40*40
*more properly) staies me heere at home vnkept: for call 11
*goe alone againe, Ile neuer wrastle for prize more: and 157
*I know not why) hates nothing more then he: yet hee's 161
Ros. Deere *Cellia*; I show more mirth then I am mi-|stresse 172
*more was this knight swearing by his Honor, for he ne-|uer 243
*speake no more of him, you'l be whipt for taxation one | of these
daies. 249
Clo. The more pittie that fooles may not speak wise-|ly, what
Wisemen do foolishly. 251
Cel. All the better: we shalbe the more Marketable. 262
*would counsel you to a more equall enterprise. We 340
Orl. Readie Sir, but his will hath in it a more modest | working. 363
Duk. No more, no more. 377
Orl. I am more proud to be Sir *Rolands* sonne, 395
That could giue more, but that her hand lacks meanes. 412
Sir, you haue wrastled well, and ouerthrowne | More then your enemies. 420
More suites you to conceiue, then I to speake of. 435
I shall desire more loue and knowledge of you. 453
*And thou wilt show more bright, & seem more vertuous 542
I charge thee be not thou more grieu'd then I am. 554
Ros. I haue more cause. | *Cel*. Thou hast not Cosen, 555
Ros. Were it not better, | Because that I am more then common tall, 579
Hath not old custome made this life more sweete 608
More free from perill then the enuious Court? 610
And in that kinde sweares you doe more vsurpe 634

MORE *cont*.

As worldlings doe, giuing thy sum of more	656
No more doe yours: your vertues gentle Master	715
Here liued I, but now liue here no more	776
Clo. I, now am I in *Arden*, the more foole I, when I	798
And wish for her sake more then for mine owne,	861
My fortunes were more able to releeue her:	862
Iaq. More, more, I pre'thee more.	898
Iaq. I thanke it: More, I prethee more,	900
As a Weazel suckes egges: More, I pre'thee more.	902
Come, more, another stanzo: Cal you'em stanzo's?	907
Amy. More at your request, then to please my selfe.	911
And after one houre more, 'twill be eleuen,	998
Orl. Forbeare, and eate no more.	1063
Du Sen. What would you haue? | Your gentlenesse shall force, more then your force	1078
Presents more wofull Pageants then the Sceane | Wherein we play in.	1116
Within this tweluemonth, or turne thou no more	1187
Duke. More villaine thou. Well push him out of dores	1195
*more plentie in it, it goes much against my stomacke.	1220
Cor. No more, but that I know the more one sickens,	1222
Clo. Your lips wil feele them the sooner. Shallow a-|gen: a more sounder instance, come.	1257
Ros. O yes, I heard them all, and more too, for some	1362
*of them had in them more feete then the Verses would | beare.	1363
*my disposition? One inch of delay more, is a South-sea	1392
Ros. Why God will send more, if the man will bee	1403
*say I and no, to these particulars, is more then to answer | in a Catechisme.	1421
Iaq. I pray you marre no more trees with Writing | Loue-songs in their barkes.	1454
*it strikes a man more dead then a great rec-|koning	1625
*Towne is more worthier then a village, so is the fore-|head	1667
*of a married man, more honourable then the bare	1668
*then no skill, by so much is a horne more precious | then to want.	1670
*Nun of winters sisterhood kisses not more religiouslie,	1726
As by my faith, I see no more in you	1811
I see no more in you then in the ordinary	1815
And out of you she sees her selfe more proper	1828
A little riper, and more lustie red	1895
Haue more cause to hate him then to loue him,	1902
*serue me such another tricke, neuer come in my sight | more.	1955
Ros. Nay, and you be so tardie, come no more in my	1965
*now I will be your *Rosalind* in a more comming-on dis-|position:	2023
*when they are wiues: I will bee more iealous of	2058
*thee, then a Barbary cocke-pidgeon ouer his hen, more	2059
*clamorous then a Parrat against raine, more new-fang-|led	2060
*then an ape, more giddy in my desires, then a mon-|key:	2061
*true louer hence, and not a word; for here comes more | company. *Exit. Sil.*	2222
Cel. There is more in it; Cosen *Ganimed*.	2313
*by so much the more shall I to morrow be at the height	2454
Ros. Pray you no more of this, 'tis like the howling	2516
Ros. Patience once more, whiles our co(m)pact is vrg'd:	2580
*bodie more seeming *Audry*) as thus sir: I did dislike the	2645
*but it is no more vnhandsome, then to see the	2777

MORNING = 3
Saw her a bed, and in the morning early,   686
And shining morning face, creeping like snaile   1125
*Rosa. But why did hee sweare hee would come this | morning, and
comes not?   1728
MOROW = *1
*Clo. To morrow is the ioyfull day Audrey, to morow | will we be
married.   2532
MORROW = 4*14
Oli. Call him in: 'twill be a good way: and to mor-|row the wrastling is. 94
Cha. Good morrow to your worship.   97
*Oli. What, you wrastle to morrow before the new | Duke.   120
*in disguis'd against mee to try a fall: to morrow sir I   125
*come to morrow, Ile giue him his payment: if euer hee   156
Good morrow foole (quoth I:) no Sir, quoth he,   991
*Oliu. Good morrow, faire ones: pray you, (if you | know)   2225
Let your Wedding be to morrow: thither will I   2423
*Orl. They shall be married to morrow: and I will   2451
*by so much the more shall I to morrow be at the height   2454
*Ros. Why then to morrow, I cannot serue your turne | for Rosalind? 2457
*to set her before your eyes to morrow, humane as she is, | and without
any danger.   2475
*bid your friends: for if you will be married to mor-|row, you shall: and
to Rosalind if you will.   2480
*if I can: I would loue you if I could: To morrow meet   2518
*and Ile be married to morrow: I will satisfie you,   2520
*if euer I satisfi'd man, and you shall bee married to mor-|row.   2521
*you, and you shal be married to morrow: As you loue   2523
*Clo. To morrow is the ioyfull day Audrey, to morow | will we be
married.   2532
MORTALL = 1*1
*runne into strange capers; but as all is mortall in   836
nature, so is all nature in loue, mortall in folly.   837
MOSSD = *1
*Vnder an old Oake, whose bows were moss'd with age   2255
MOST = 19*17
*Adam. Is old dogge my reward: most true, I haue   82
*thou shalt finde I will most kindly requite: I had my   136
*mightily misplaced, and the bountifull blinde woman | doth most
mistake in her gifts to women.   204
Thus most inuectiuely he pierceth through | The body of Countrie,
Citie, Court,   666
How many actions most ridiculous,   812
And in my voice most welcome shall you be.   872
And they that are most gauled with my folly,   1024
They most must laugh: And why sir must they so?   1025
Du Sen. Most mischeeuous foule sin, in chiding sin: 1038
Orl. I thanke you most for him. | Ad. So had you neede,   1149
Most frendship, is fayning; most Louing, meere folly: 1161
The heigh ho, the holly, | This Life is most iolly.   1162
Most truly limn'd, and liuing in your face,   1172
*the behauiour of the Countrie is most mockeable at the   1245
*Clo. Most shallow man: Thou wormes meate in re-|spect   1262
*Ros. O most gentle Iupiter, what tedious homilie of   1353
*Ros. Nay, I pre'thee now, with most petitionary ve-|hemence, tell me
who it is.   1385
*Cel. O wonderfull, wonderfull, and most wonderfull   1387

MOST *cont*.
against whom I know most faults.	1473
*for the most part, cattle of this colour: would now like	1593
Clo. I am heere with thee, and thy Goats, as the most	1619
Clo. No trulie: for the truest poetrie is the most fai-|ning,	1630
Foule is most foule, being foule to be a scoffer.	1835
That I shall thinke it a most plenteous crop	1875
*which by often rumination, wraps me in a most humo-|rous sadnesse.	1934
*minute behinde your houre, I will thinke you the most	2097
*patheticall breake-promise, and the most hollow louer,	2098
*and the most vnworthy of her you call *Rosalinde*, that	2099
And he did render him the most vnnaturall | That liu'd amongst men.	2273
Teares our recountments had most kindely bath'd,	2294
Clow. A most wicked Sir *Oliuer*, *Awdrie*, a most vile	2345
*yeare old conuerst with a Magitian, most profound in	2469
You'l giue your selfe to this most faithfull Shepheard.	2589
'Tis I must make conclusion | Of these most strange euents:	2700

MOTHER = 1*1
desirous to lie with his mother earth?	362
Ros. And why I pray you? who might be your mother	1808

MOTLEY = 6
A motley Foole (a miserable world:)	986
In good set termes, and yet a motley foole.	990
The motley Foole, thus morall on the time,	1002
I am ambitious for a motley coat. | *Du Sen*. Thou shalt haue one.	1016
Inuest me in my motley: Giue me leaue	1032
Iaq. Wil you be married, Motley?	1685

MOTLEYS = 1
A worthy foole: Motley's the onely weare.	1007

MOTLEY-MINDED = *1
*Motley-minded Gentleman, that I haue so often met in	2618

MOUE = 2
Moue vs to gentlenesse.	1080
How then might your praiers moue?	2204

MOUES = 1
*betweene Terme and Terme, and then they perceiue not | how time moues.	1521

MOUNSIER = *1
Oli. Good Mounsier *Charles*: what's the new newes | at the new Court?	98

MOUNSIEUR = *1
Ros. Farewell Mounsieur Trauellor: looke you	1948

MOUNTAINES = *1
*meete; but Mountaines may bee remoou'd with Earth-|quakes, and so encounter.	1381

MOUNTED = 1
Hir worth being mounted on the winde, | *through all the world beares Rosalinde*.	1288

MOUNTS = 1
youth mounts, and folly guides: who comes heere?	1752

MOUTH = 5*4
Enter le Beau. | *Ros*. With his mouth full of newes.	257
Seeking the bubble Reputation | Euen in the Canons mouth: And then, the Iustice	1131
Till thou canst quit thee by thy brothers mouth,	1191
*might'st powre this conceal'd man out of thy mouth, as	1395
out of thy mouth, that I may drinke thy tydings.	1398
Cel. You must borrow me Gargantuas mouth first:	1419

MOUTH *cont*.
*'tis a Word too great for any mouth of this Ages size, to	1420
Who with her head, nimble in threats approach'd | The opening of his mouth: but sodainly	2260
*his lips when he put it into his mouth, meaning there-|by,	2376

MOUTHD = *1
*Wine comes out of a narrow-mouth'd bottle: either too	1396

MR = *4
*Co. And how like you this shepherds life Mr *Touchstone*?	1212
*Cor. Heere comes yong Mr *Ganimed*, my new Mistris-|ses Brother.	1283
*Clo. Good euen good Mr what ye cal't: how do you	1681
*Farewel good Mr *Oliuer*: Not O sweet *Oliuer*, O braue	1703

MUCH = 14*20
*dunghils are as much bound to him as I: besides this no-|thing	18
*place of a brother, and as much as in him lies, mines my	22
*were there twenty brothers betwixt vs: I haue as much	51
*so much in the heart of the world, and especially of my	164
Le Beu. Faire Princesse, | you haue lost much good sport.	264
*thoughts, wherein I confesse me much guiltie to denie	347
Orl. I rest much bounden to you: fare you well.	454
Neuer so much as in a thought vnborne,	511
Then good my Leige, mistake me not so much,	525
Much marked of the melancholie *Iaques*,	648
To that which had too much: then being there alone,	657
Your daughter and her Cosen much commend	692
That cannot so much as a blossome yeelde,	768
Ros. *Ioue*, *Ioue*, this Shepherds passion, | Is much vpon my fashion.	841
Here's a yong maid with trauaile much oppressed, | And faints for succour.	858
*more plentie in it, it goes much against my stomacke.	1220
*much at once, or none at all. I pre'thee take the Corke	1397
Ros. But are you so much in loue, as your rimes speak?	1578
Orl. Neither rime nor reason can expresse how much.	1579
*brow of a Batcheller: and by how much defence is bet-|ter	1669
*then no skill, by so much is a horne more precious | then to want.	1670
Ros. I met the Duke yesterday, and had much que-|stion	1742
*to see other mens; then to haue seene much, and to haue	1938
Rosalind. Why then, can one desire too much of a	2032
*you would proue, my friends told mee as much, and I	2089
Ros. How say you now, is it not past two a clock? | And heere much *Orlando*.	2148
Yet heard too much of *Phebes* crueltie.	2187
*my troth, we that haue good wits, haue much to answer	2352
*by so much the more shall I to morrow be at the height	2454
*of heart heauinesse, by how much I shal thinke my bro-|ther	2455
Phe. Youth, you haue done me much vngentlenesse,	2484
the onely peace-maker: much vertue in if.	2676
There is much matter to be heard, and learn'd:	2762
*women) for the loue you beare to men, to like as much	2787

MURDER = 1
Thou tellst me there is murder in mine eye,	1781

MURMURING = 1
The ranke of Oziers, by the murmuring streame	2229

MURTHERERS = 2
Should be called tyrants, butchers, murtherers.	1785
Lye not, to say mine eyes are murtherers:	1790

MUSICALL = 1
Du Sen. If he compact of iarres, grow Musicall,   977
MUSICKE = 4*1
  *Musicke in his sides? Is there yet another doates vpon   304
  Giue vs some Musicke, and good Cozen, sing.   1154
  Musicke, Song. | *What shall he haue that kild the Deare?*   2136
  Enter Hymen, Rosalind, and Celia. | Still Musicke.   2681
  Play Musicke, and you Brides and Bride-groomes all,   2755
MUSITIANS = *1
  *is emulation: nor the Musitians, which is fantasticall;   1927
MUST = 22*16
  *loth to foyle him, as I must for my owne honour if hee   129
  *but should I anathomize him to thee, as hee is, I must   152
  *blush, and weepe, and thou must looke pale and | wonder.   153
  *could teach me to forget a banished father, you must not   174
  Clow. Mistresse, you must come away to your father.   226
  Le Beu. You must if you stay heere, for heere is the   306
  Thus must I from the smoake into the smother,   455
  This I must do, or know not what to do: | Yet this I will not do, do how
  I can,   738
  *apparell, and to cry like a woman: but I must comfort   788
  *was at home I was in a better place, but Trauellers must | be content.   799
  That your poore friends must woe your companie,   983
  That I am wise. I must haue liberty   1021
  They most must laugh: And why sir must they so?   1025
  Iaq. And you will not be answer'd with reason, | I must dye.   1076
  *then thy manners must be wicked, and wickednes is sin,   1240
  Wintred garments must be linde, | so must slender Rosalinde: 1303
  They that reap must sheafe and binde, | then to cart with Rosalinde.   1305
  He that sweetest rose will finde, | must finde Loues pricke, & Rosalinde.   1309
  Cel. You must borrow me Gargantuas mouth first: 1419
  Ros. Do you not know I am a woman, when I thinke, | I must speake:
  sweet, say on.   1443
  Ros. Nay, you must call mee *Rosalind*: Come sister, | will you go?
  Exeunt.   1611
  Ol. Truly she must be giuen, or the marriage is not | lawfull.   1678
  Ol. Come sweete *Audrey*, | We must be married, or we must liue in
  baudrey: 1701
  Must you be therefore prowd and pittilesse?   1813
  For I must tell you friendly in your eare,   1832
  Ros. You must begin, will you *Orlando*.   2038
  Ros. Then you must say, I take thee *Rosalind* for | wife.   2044
  Orl. I must attend the Duke at dinner, by two a clock | I will be with
  thee againe.   2086
  *we must haue your doublet and hose pluckt ouer   2108
  Ros. I am: what must we vnderstand by this?   2244
  Oli. That will I: for I must beare answere backe   2334
  Will. Which he sir? | *Clo*. He sir, that must marrie this woman:
  Therefore   2387
  'Tis I must make conclusion | Of these most strange euents: 2700
  Here's eight that must take hands,   2702
  You, to his loue must accord,   2707
MUSTARD = 1*2
  *Mustard was naught: Now Ile stand to it, the Pancakes   232
  *were naught, and the Mustard was good, and yet was   233
  euer he saw those Pancakes, or that Mustard.   245

MUTINIE = *1
*is within mee, begins to mutinie against this seruitude.   25
MUTTON = *1
*is not the grease of a Mutton, as wholesome as the sweat   1253
MY *l*.*6 *8 *10 *12 *22 *23 *24 29 *47 *49 *50 *52 *58 *60 *66 *70 *72
*73 80 *82 *83 *126 *129 *130 134 *136 *137 *160 *164 171 *178 *179
*180 *184 *186 *191 *241 *248 *253 272 320 335 *349 *352 381 *384
394 398 399 405 415 *418 *424 450 *470 *475 476 481 *487 *490 492
506 507 522 524 525 526 544 *546 550 552 563 571 575 576 582 583 592
602 *607 614 632 636 642 673 682 *688 705 706 *735 744 745 749 752
753 756 780 784 *785 *787 *794 823 *829 *835 840 842 862 865 872 882
*903 911 922 934 953 959 963 975 981 1003 1018 1024 1032 1033 1035
1054 1056 1058 1060 1070 1075 1095 1096 1105 1151 1175 1184 1193
1194 1196 1201 1204 1205 1206 *1219 *1220 *1272 *1273 1274 *1283
1322 *1390 *1392 *1413 *1427 1440 *1441 1449 *1456 1463 *1472 *1477
*1524 *1544 *1554 *1596 1604 *1605 1610 1617 1698 1707 1786 1811
1816 1817 1821 1840 1846 1860 1861 1863 1873 1900 1904 1910 1912
*1933 *1936 1940 *1955 *1957 *1965 *1976 1997 1998 *2020 *2048
*2061 2066 2067 *2089 *2094 *2101 2104 *2111 *2113 2154 2155 2165
2211 2245 2289 2298 2335 2337 *2352 *2414 *2418 2422 2426 *2429
2431 *2441 *2455 *2464 *2478 2486 *2534 *2539 *2569 2603 2604 2606
*2617 *2620 *2622 *2628 *2639 *2651 *2677 2691 2692 *2693 2694
*2695 2722 2724 2725 2742 *2785 *2795 = 150*117
MYSELFE *see* selfe
NAME = 8*4
Duk. Beare him awaie: | What is thy name yong man?   382
Thou art a foole, she robs thee of thy name,   541
Ros. Ile haue no worse a name then *Ioues* owne Page,   589
What woman in the Citie do I name,   1048
Thy Huntresse name, that my full life doth sway.   1204
*thy name should be hang'd and carued vpon these trees?   1370
Iaq. *Rosalinde* is your loues name? *Orl*. Yes, Iust.   1458
Iaq. I do not like her name.   1459
*brambles; all (forsooth) defying the name of *Rosalinde*.   1548
Will. Fiue and twentie Sir. | *Clo*. A ripe age: Is thy name *William*?   2360
Will. *William*, sir. | *Clo*. A faire name. Was't borne i'th Forrest heere?   2362
*haue bookes for good manners: I will name you the de- | grees.   2665
NAMES = 1
Iaq. Nay, I care not for their names, they owe mee | nothing. Wil you
sing?   909
NAPKIN = 3
He sends this bloudy napkin; are you he?   2243
Ros. But for the bloody napkin? | *Oli*. By and by: 2291
His broken promise, and to giue this napkin   2308
NARROW-MOUTHD = *1
*Wine comes out of a narrow-mouth'd bottle: either too   1396
NATIONS = *1
*nations allowes you my better, in that you are the first   49
NATIUE = 3
Being natiue Burgers of this desert City,   629
In their assign'd and natiue dwelling place.   671
Orl. Are you natiue of this place?   1526
NATIUITIE = *1
*natiuitie, and almost chide God for making you that   1951
NATURALL = 2*4
*contriuer against mee his naturall brother: therefore vse   142
*fortune makes natures naturall, the cutter off of natures | witte.   218

NATURALL *cont.*
 *but Natures, who perceiueth our naturall wits too dull 221
 *to reason of such goddesses, hath sent this Naturall for 222
 Are deerer then the naturall bond of Sisters: 444
 Clo. Such a one is a naturall Philosopher: 1230
NATURE = 7*5
 *nature gaue mee, his countenance seemes to take from 20
 *Fortune reignes in gifts of the world, not in the | lineaments of Nature. 210
 Cel. No; when Nature hath made a faire creature, 213
 *may she not by Fortune fall into the fire? though nature 214
 Ros. Indeed there is fortune too hard for nature, when 217
 nature, so is all nature in loue, mortall in folly. 837
 And let my officers of such a nature | Make an extent vpon his house
 and Lands: 1196
 *no wit by Nature, nor Art, may complaine of good | breeding, or
 comes of a very dull kindred. 1228
 Therefore heauen Nature charg'd, | that one bodie should be fill'd 1339
 With all Graces wide enlarg'd, | nature presently distill'd 1341
 And Nature stronger then his iust occasion, 2281
NATURES = 1*4
 Ros. Nay now thou goest from Fortunes office to Na- |tures: 209
 *fortune makes natures naturall, the cutter off of natures | witte. 218
 *but Natures, who perceiueth our naturall wits too dull 221
 Of Natures sale-worke? 'ods my little life, 1816
NAUGHT = *4
 Oliuer. Marry sir be better employed, and be naught | a while. 38
 *Mustard was naught: Now Ile stand to it, the Pancakes 232
 *were naught, and the Mustard was good, and yet was 233
 *naught. In respect that it is solitary, I like it verie well: 1215
NAY = 7*11
 Ros. Nay now thou goest from Fortunes office to Na- |tures: 209
 Clo. Nay, if I keepe not my ranke. | *Ros.* Thou loosest thy old smell. 272
 Clo. Nay, I shall nere be ware of mine owne wit, till 839
 Iaq. Nay, I care not for their names, they owe mee | nothing. Wil you
 sing? 909
 Clo. Then thou art damn'd. | *Cor.* Nay, I hope. 1233
 Ros. Nay, but who is it? | *Cel.* Is it possible? 1383
 Ros. Nay, I pre'thee now, with most petitionary ve- |hemence, tell me
 who it is. 1385
 Cel. Nay, he hath but a little beard. 1402
 Ros. Nay, but the diuell take mocking: speake sadde | brow, and true
 maid. 1408
 Ros. Nay, you must call mee *Rosalind*: Come sister, | will you go?
 Exeunt. 1611
 heere Sir: Nay, pray be couer'd. 1684
 Cel. Nay certainly there is no truth in him. | *Ros.* Doe you thinke so? 1730
 Iaq. Nay then God buy you, and you talke in blanke | verse. 1946
 Ros. Nay, and you be so tardie, come no more in my 1965
 Ros. Nay, you were better speake first, and when you 1986
 Ros. Nay, you might keepe that checke for it, till you 2076
 *thy head: Nay prethee bee couer'd. How olde are you | Friend? 2358
 Ros. O, I know where you are: nay, tis true: there 2438
NEAST = 1
 *your head, and shew the world what the bird hath done | to her owne
 neast. 2109
NECESSARIE = *1
 *though? Courage. As hornes are odious, they are neces- |sarie. 1660

NECESSITIES = 1
In all your businesse and necessities. 759
NECESSITY = 1
Orl. Nor shalt not, till necessity be seru'd. 1065
NECK = 1*1
Cel. And a chaine that you once wore about his neck: 1377
Falls not the axe vpon the humbled neck, 1775
NECKE = 1*1
*thy discretion, I had as liefe thou didst breake his necke 143
Lay sleeping on his back; about his necke 2258
NECKES = *1
Ros. With bils on their neckes: Be it knowne vnto | all men by these
presents. 286
NEECE = 1*1
Hath tane displeasure 'gainst his gentle Neece, 446
Du Se. O my deere Neece, welcome thou art to me, 2722
NEEDE = 1
Orl. I thanke you most for him. | *Ad*. So had you neede, 1149
NEEDES = *1
*no bush, 'tis true, that a good play needes no Epilogue. 2779
NEEDLESSE = 1
First, for his weeping into the needlesse streame; 654
NEEDS = *1
*Lord the Prologue. If it be true, that good wine needs 2778
NEERE = 4*1
So neere our publike Court as twentie miles, | Thou diest for it. 503
Sil. O deere *Phebe*, | If euer (as that euer may be neere) 1799
Phe. But till that time | Come not thou neere me: and when that time
comes, 1804
In parcells as I did, would haue gone neere 1899
*so neere the hart, as your gesture cries it out: when your 2471
NEERER = 2
before me is neerer to his reuerence. | *Oli*. What Boy. 53
Thy conceite is neerer death, then thy powers. 958
NEGLECT = 2
Loose, and neglect the creeping houres of time: 1089
And throwne into neglect the pompous Court. | *2.Bro*. He hath. 2759
NEGLECTED = *1
*which you haue not: a beard neglected, which you 1560
NEICE = *1
Duk. You are a foole: you Neice prouide your selfe, 548
NEIGHBOR = 1*1
When such a one as shee, such is her neighbor? 1052
Cel. West of this place, down in the neighbor bottom 2228
NEIGHBOURLY = 1
Phe. Thou hast my loue, is not that neighbourly? | *Sil*. I would haue
you. 1863
NEIGHBOURS = 1
met your wiues wit going to your neighbours bed. 2077
NEITHER *see also* neyther = *7
Cel. Peraduenture this is not Fortunes work neither, 220
Le Beu. Neither his daughter, if we iudge by manners, 439
Orl. Neither rime nor reason can expresse how much. 1579
Iaq. I haue neither the Schollers melancholy, which 1926
Ol. Neither call the giddinesse of it in question; the 2413
*of my knowledge: insomuch (I say) I know you are: nei-|ther 2464
*What a case am I in then, that am neither a good Epi-|logue, 2782

NERE = 1*2

Clo. Nay, I shall nere be ware of mine owne wit, till   839
Ol. 'Tis no matter; Ne're a fantastical knaue of them   1706
Nor ne're wed woman, if you be not shee.   2698

NEUER *see also* nere = 11*15

*of her Vncle, then his owne daughter, and neuer two La-|dies loued as
they doe.   112
*poyson, entrap thee by some treacherous deuise, and ne-|uer   147
*goe alone againe, Ile neuer wrastle for prize more: and   157
*gentle, neuer school'd, and yet learned, full of noble   162
*more was this knight swearing by his Honor, for he ne-|uer   243
*neuer gracious: if kil'd, but one dead that is willing to   351
Neuer so much as in a thought vnborne,   511
The like doe you, so shall we passe along, | And neuer stir assailants.   577
And neuer staies to greet him: I quoth *Iaques*,   662
For in my youth I neuer did apply | Hot, and rebellious liquors in my
bloud,   752
As sure I thinke did neuer man loue so: 811
Sil. Oh thou didst then neuer loue so hartily,   815
I neuer lou'd my brother in my life.   1194
Clo. Why, if thou neuer was't at Court, thou neuer   1238
*saw'st good manners: if thou neuer saw'st good maners,   1239
neuer cri'de, haue patience good people.   1355
*Palme tree; I was neuer so berim'd since *Pythagoras* time   1373
Ros. Neuer talke to me, I wil weepe.   1710
*serue me such another tricke, neuer come in my sight | more.   1955
*shall neuer take her without her answer, vnlesse you take   2080
*make her fault her husbands occasion, let her neuer nurse   2082
I say she neuer did inuent this letter,   2177
Sil. So please you, for I neuer heard it yet: 2186
*neuer haue her, vnlesse thou intreat for her: if you bee a   2221
*was neuer any thing so sodaine, but the sight of two   2439

NEW = 2*5

Oli. Good Mounsier *Charles*: what's the new newes | at the new Court?   98
*brother the new Duke, and three or foure louing   102
*him, whose lands and reuenues enrich the new Duke,   104
Oli. What, you wrastle to morrow before the new | Duke.   120
Cor. Heere comes yong Mr *Ganimed*, my new Mistris-|ses Brother.   1283
Ros. Then she puts you to entreatie, and there begins | new matter.   1992

NEWES = 2*3

Oli. Good Mounsier *Charles*: what's the new newes | at the new Court?   98
Charles. There's no newes at the Court Sir, but the   100
*olde newes: that is, the old Duke is banished by his yon-|ger   101
Enter le Beau. | *Ros*. With his mouth full of newes.   257
Boon-iour Monsieur le Beu, what's the newes?   263

NEWES-CRAMD = 1

Ros. Then shal we be newes-cram'd.   261

NEW-FALNE = 1

Meane time, forget this new-falne dignitie,   2753

NEW-FANGLED = 1

*clamorous then a Parrat against raine, more new-fang-|led   2060

NEXT = *1

Oliuer Mar-text, the Vicar of the next village, who hath   1652

NEYTHER = 1*1

*physicke your ranckenesse, and yet giue no thousand | crownes
neyther: holla *Dennis*.   86
*loue no man in good earnest, nor no further in sport ney-|ther,   196

NIBLING = 1
Pigeons bill, so wedlocke would be nibling.   1688
NICE = *1
*nor the Ladies, which is nice: nor the Louers, which   1930
NIECE *see* neece, neice
NIGH = 1
Freize, freize, thou bitter skie that dost not bight so nigh | as benefitts
forgot: 1164
NIGHT = 2*3
Hath heard your praises, and this night he meanes,   726
*comming a night to *Iane Smile*, and I remember the kis- | sing   830
And thou thrice crowned Queene of night suruey   1202
*the night, is lacke of the Sunne: That hee that hath lear- | ned   1227
*Nun; if it had not bin for a hot Midsomer-night, for   2013
NIGHTS = 1
That haue endur'd shrew'd daies, and nights with vs,   2750
NIMBLE = 1*1
Iaq. You haue a nimble wit; I thinke 'twas made of   1468
Who with her head, nimble in threats approach'd | The opening of his
mouth: but sodainly   2260
NINE = 1*1
'Tis but an houre agoe, since it was nine,   997
Ros. I was seuen out of the nine daies out of the wonder,   1371
NO *l*.*26 *57 *70 *79 *86 *100 *108 *111 *186 *196 *213 *228 *242 *249
*333 *352 *353 *366 377 447 *463 *470 492 524 560 563 *589 593 616
681 715 723 731 734 776 *792 *795 796 807 896 924 951 *954 974 991
1063 1187 *1219 *1222 *1228 1232 *1271 *1281 1287 1292 *1319 *1365
*1421 *1454 *1456 *1460 *1472 *1483 *1491 *1493 *1498 *1511 *1512
*1544 *1566 *1592 *1630 *1639 *1658 *1659 *1661 *1662 *1665 *1666
*1670 *1706 1730 *1738 1797 1810 1811 1815 1818 1843 1907 *1965
*1976 *2006 *2055 *2090 *2103 *2117 2132 *2134 2140 2169 2176 2197
*2215 2240 *2348 2381 *2441 *2442 *2443 *2444 *2459 *2460 2495 2500
2509 *2516 *2524 *2535 *2565 *2636 *2659 2696 2697 2705 2723 2772
*2777 *2779 = 51*88
NOBLE = 1*2
*gentle, neuer school'd, and yet learned, full of noble   162
And I did laugh, sans intermission | An houre by his diall. Oh noble
foole,   1005
*breakes his staffe like a noble goose; but all's braue that   1751
NOBLER = 1
But kindnesse, nobler euer then reuenge,   2280
NOBLEST = *1
*No, no, the noblest Deere hath them as huge as the Ras- | call: 1665
NOE *l*.1324 = 1
NOMINATE = *1
Iaq. Can you nominate in order now, the degrees of | the lye.   2662
NONE = 5*7
*none is like to haue; and truely when he dies, thou shalt   187
*be so: I shall do my friends no wrong, for I haue none to   352
Where none will sweate, but for promotion,   764
Iaq. Why I haue eate none yet.   1064
*much at once, or none at all. I pre'thee take the Corke   1397
Ros. There were none principal, they were all like   1540
Ros. There is none of my Vnckles markes vpon you: 1554
*of them. Well, that is the dowrie of his wife, 'tis none   1663
Ol. Is there none heere to giue the woman?   1676
None could be so abus'd in sight as hee.   1851

NONE *cont*.

But at this howre, the house doth keepe it selfe, | There's none within. 2231
*simpring, none of you hates them) that betweene you, 2790

NONINO = 4

With a hey, and a ho, and a hey nonino, 2548
With a hey, & a ho, and a hey nonino, 2554
With a hey, and a ho, & a hey nonino: 2558
With a hey and a ho, & a hey nonino: 2562

NOOKE = *1

*and to liue in a nooke meerly Monastick: and thus I cur'd 1598

NOR *l*.*186 *196 754 1065 *1228 *1579 *1623 *1732 1797 1820 1901
*1927 *1928 *1929 *1930 *2415 2515 2528 2529 *2660 2698
*2783 = 9*15

NOSE = 2

Cours'd one another downe his innocent nose 646
With spectacles on nose, and pouch on side, 1138

NOT *l*.*13 33 *50 *60 *66 *76 *84 *90 *145 *150 *161 *166 *174 *177
*210 *214 *215 *220 234 *242 *251 272 *313 *323 327 *343 345 *346
*366 *369 *378 396 415 461 462 *473 491 492 493 509 510 516 522 525
530 543 554 556 557 559 560 566 579 596 603 608 609 611 624 652 700
713 721 724 732 734 738 739 742 754 762 763 766 780 *785 807 816 818
819 821 822 824 849 864 905 909 *916 961 967 992 1029 1046 1054 1065
1076 1110 1114 *1152 1157 1158 1164 1166 1167 1181 1182 1183 *1218
1237 *1243 *1246 *1252 *1253 *1280 1343 *1359 *1366 1405 *1443 1446
1459 *1464 *1466 1475 *1496 *1509 *1521 *1535 *1544 1556 *1558
*1559 *1560 *1561 *1582 *1600 1602 *1628 1638 *1643 *1647 1677
*1678 *1695 *1696 *1697 *1703 *1704 1705 1712 1713 *1726 1729 *1732
1735 1736 *1738 1771 1772 1775 1779 1780 1789 1790 1796 1805 1806
1807 1818 1819 1827 1833 1844 1846 1850 1854 1863 1867 1871 1880
1883 1887 1892 1901 1906 *1999 2001 2004 *2008 *2013 *2018 *2020
*2022 2030 *2069 *2095 2145 2148 2156 2163 2164 2166 2169 2183
*2217 *2220 *2222 2238 2288 2324 2369 2386 *2463 *2467 *2470 *2473
*2474 2486 2515 2527 *2567 *2577 *2647 *2649 *2651 *2652 *2653
*2654 *2657 *2660 *2672 *2677 2696 2697 2698 2724 *2776 *2784 *2785
*2794 = 152*100

NOTE = 3*1

And turne his merrie Note, 893
Iaq. Ile giue you a verse to this note, 933
Ros. 'Tis he, slinke by, and note him. 1447
*great matter in the dittie, yet y note was very vntunable 2566

NOTHING = 7*6

*deerely hir'd: but I (his brother) gaine nothing vnder 16
*dunghils are as much bound to him as I: besides this no- | thing 18
Oli. Now Sir, what make you heere? | *Orl*. Nothing: I am not taught to
make any thing. 32
*I know not why) hates nothing more then he: yet hee's 161
*cleare all: nothing remaines, but that I kindle the boy | thither, which
now Ile goe about. *Exit*. 167
*lament me: the world no iniurie, for in it I haue nothing: 353
By reason of his absence there is nothing 870
Iaq. Nay, I care not for their names, they owe mee | nothing. Wil you
sing? 909
And we will nothing waste till you returne. 1112
Iaq. Why, 'tis good to be sad and say nothing. 1924
nothing, is to haue rich eyes and poore hands. 1939
*I will weepe for nothing, like *Diana* in the Foun- | taine, 2062

NOTHING *cont.*
The royall disposition of that beast | To prey on nothing, that doth
seeme as dead: 2268
NOTICE = *1
*selfe notice of my Brothers purpose heerein, and haue by   137
NOURTURE = 1
And know some nourture: But forbeare, I say,   1073
NOW = 31*27
Oli. Now Sir, what make you heere? | *Orl.* Nothing: I am not taught to
make any thing.   32
*Farewell good *Charles.* Now will I stirre this Game- |ster: 159
*cleare all: nothing remaines, but that I kindle the boy | thither, which
now Ile goe about. *Exit.*   167
Ros. Nay now thou goest from Fortunes office to Na- |tures: 209
*the whetstone of the wits. How now Witte, whether | wander you?   224
*Mustard was naught: Now Ile stand to it, the Pancakes   232
Ros. I marry, now vnmuzzle your wisedome.   237
Clo. Stand you both forth now: stroke your chinnes,   238
Cel. Yonder sure they are comming. Let vs now stay | and see it.   309
Du. How now daughter, and Cousin: | Are you crept hither to see the
wrastling?   318
Ros. Now Hercules, be thy speede yong man.   371
Yet such is now the Dukes condition,   432
But now I know her: if she be a Traitor,   533
For by this heauen, now at our sorrowes pale;   568
After my flight: now goe in we content   602
Duk.Sen. Now my Coe-mates, and brothers in exile: 607
From seauentie yeeres, till now almost fourescore   775
Here liued I, but now liue here no more   776
Clo. I, now am I in *Arden*, the more foole I, when I   798
Cor. I partly guesse: for I haue lou'd ere now.   806
Or if thou hast not sat as I doe now,   819
Abruptly as my passion now makes me, | Thou hast not lou'd.   823
Are now on sale, and at our sheep-coat now   869
Orl. Why how now *Adam*? No greater heart in thee: 954
1 *Lord.* My Lord, he is but euen now gone hence,   975
Du Sen. Why how now Monsieur, what a life is this   982
*but in respect that it is priuate, it is a very vild life. Now   1216
Cel. How now backe friends: Shepheard, go off a lit- |tle: 1356
Ros. Nay, I pre'thee now, with most petitionary ve- |hemence, tell me
who it is.   1385
*for the most part, cattle of this colour: would now like   1593
*him, now loath him: then entertaine him, then forswear   1594
*him: now weepe for him, then spit at him; that I draue   1595
Orlan. Now by the faith of my loue, I will; Tel me | where it is.   1605
*Now if thou wert a Poet, I might haue some hope | thou didst feigne. 1636
Now I doe frowne on thee with all my heart,   1786
And if mine eyes can wound, now let them kill thee: 1787
Now counterfeit to swound, why now fall downe,   1788
Now shew the wound mine eye hath made in thee,   1791
The Cicatrice and capable impressure | Thy palme some moment
keepes: but now mine eyes   1794
Phe. Dead Shepheard, now I find thy saw of might,   1853
That the maine haruest reapes: loose now and then   1877
And now I am remembred, scorn'd at me: 1905
*swam in a Gundello. Why how now *Orlando*, where   1953
Ros. Come, wooe me, wooe mee: for now I am in a   1981

NOW *cont*.

*would you say to me now, and I were your verie, verie | *Rosalind*?	1983
*now I will be your *Rosalind* in a more comming-on dis- |position:	2023
Ros. I, but when? | *Orl*. Why now, as fast as she can marrie vs.	2042
Ros. Now tell me how long you would haue her, af- |ter you haue possess her?	2052
Ros. How say you now, is it not past two a clock? | And heere much *Orlando*.	2148
Which all this while had bled: and now he fainted,	2302
Cel. Why how now *Ganimed*, sweet *Ganimed*.	2311
Clo. Why, thou saist well. I do now remember a say- |ing:	2372
now you are not *ipse*, for I am he.	2386
*Know of me then (for now I speake to some pur- |pose)	2461
Iaq. Can you nominate in order now, the degrees of | the lye.	2662
Phe. I wil not eate my word, now thou art mine,	2724

NOWHERE *see* where

NOYSE = 1

Iaq. Sing it: 'tis no matter how it bee in tune, so it | make noyse enough.	2134

NUMBER = 1

And after, euery of this happie number	2749

NUN = *2

*Nun of winters sisterhood kisses not more religiouslie,	1726
*Nun; if it had not bin for a hot Midsomer-night, for	2013

NUPTIALL = *1

*bid the Duke to the Nuptiall. But O, how bitter a thing	2452

NURSE = 1*1

Which I did store to be my foster Nurse,	744
*make her fault her husbands occasion, let her neuer nurse	2082

NURSES = 1

Mewling, and puking in the Nurses armes:	1123

NURTURE *see* nourture

NUT = 3

Sweetest nut, hath sowrest rinde, | such a nut is Rosalinde.	1307
concaue as a couered goblet, or a Worme-eaten nut.	1734

O *l*.44 *108 427 *480 *482 552 653 706 720 784 825 952 *1009 1015 1205 *1353 *1362 *1380 *1387 1440 *1491 *1621 *1703 *1747 1765 1799 2068 *2081 *2111 *2272 *2438 *2452 *2595 *2664 2717 *2722 *2786 *2788 = 16*23, *1

*me: 'tis but one cast away, and so come death: two o' | clocke is your howre.	2091

OADES = *1

*barkes; hangs Oades vpon Hauthornes, and Elegies on	1547

OAKE = 1*1

Vnder an oake, whose anticke roote peepes out	638
*Vnder an old Oake, whose bows were moss'd with age	2255

OATH = 1*2

*mine honor I will, and when I breake that oath, let mee	190
Ros. Where learned you that oath foole?	229
Cel. Was, is not is: besides, the oath of Louer is no	1738

OATHES = *2

*speakes braue words, sweares braue oathes, and breakes	1748
*mend mee, and by all pretty oathes that are not dange- |rous,	2095

OATHS = 1

Full of strange oaths, and bearded like the Pard,	1129

OBIECT = 1

And marke what obiect did present it selfe	2254

OBIECTS = *1
*of many simples, extracted from many obiects,   1932
OBLIUION = 1
Is second childishnesse, and meere obliuion,   1144
OBSCURED = 1
Obscured in the circle of this Forrest.   2611
OBSCURING = *1
*you haue train'd me like a pezant, obscuring and   68
OBSERUANCE = 2*1
*him, and rellish it with good obseruance. I found him   1428
All adoration, dutie, and obseruance,   2503
All puritie, all triall, all obseruance: | And so am I for *Phebe*.   2505
OBSERUATION = 1
With obseruation, the which he vents | In mangled formes. O that I
were a foole,   1014
OCCASION = 1*2
*were grauel'd, for lacke of matter, you might take oc- |casion   1987
*make her fault her husbands occasion, let her neuer nurse   2082
And Nature stronger then his iust occasion,   2281
OCLOCKE *see* clocke
ODDES = *1
*there is such oddes in the man: In pitie of the challen- |gers   322
ODES *see* oades
ODIOUS = *1
*though? Courage. As hornes are odious, they are neces- |sarie.   1660
ODS = 2
Of Natures sale-worke? 'ods my little life,   1816
Were man as rare as Phenix: 'od's my will,   2165
OF *see also* a, o' = 206*216
OFF *l*.199 216 *218 *475 729 *1356 = 3*3
OFFENCE = 1
Did make offence, his eye did heale it vp: 1891
OFFENCES = *1
*to be touch'd with so many giddie offences as hee   1536
OFFEND = 1*1
Orl. I will no further offend you, then becomes mee | for my good.   79
Did I offend your highnesse.   512
OFFENDERS = 1
such offenders, and let time try: adieu. *Exit*.   2106
OFFER = 3*1
*Ewes and the Rammes together, and to offer to get your   1276
Cry the man mercy, loue him, take his offer,   1834
Will the faithfull offer take   2209
offer, when I make curt'sie, bid me farewell. *Exit*.   2796
OFFERST = 1
Thou offer'st fairely to thy brothers wedding: 2744
OFFICE = *1
Ros. Nay now thou goest from Fortunes office to Na- |tures: 209
OFFICERS = 1
And let my officers of such a nature | Make an extent vpon his house
and Lands: 1196
OFT = 1*4
*2 *Lor*. My Lord, the roynish Clown, at whom so oft,   688
Corin. Mistresse and Master, you haue oft enquired   1754
Sil. Not very well, but I haue met him oft,   1880
Cel. Was't you that did so oft contriue to kill him?   2287
Iaq. And how oft did you say his beard was not well | cut?   2657

OFTEN = *3
  Cor. And they are often tarr'd ouer, with the surgery   1259
  *which by often rumination, wraps me in a most humo- |rous sadnesse.   1934
  *Motley-minded Gentleman, that I haue so often met in   2618
OH *see also* O *l*.374 *470 705 706 717 760 805 815 1006 1193 1789
  *2429 = 10*2
OL = 4*3
OLD = 18*10
  Adam. Is old dogge my reward: most true, I haue   82
  *olde newes: that is, the old Duke is banished by his yon- |ger   101
  Oli. Where will the old Duke liue? | *Cha*. They say hee is already in
  the Forrest of *Arden*,   114
  *like the old *Robin Hood* of *England*: they say many yong   117
  Clo. One that old *Fredericke* your Father loues.   247
  Clo. Nay, if I keepe not my ranke. | *Ros*. Thou loosest thy old smell.   272
  Le Beu. There comes an old man, and his three sons.   282
  Cel. I could match this beginning with an old tale.   283
  *third: yonder they lie, the poore old man their Father,   292
  *you should fall into so strong a liking with old Sir | *Roulands* yongest
  sonne?   485
  Hath not old custome made this life more sweete   608
  Of old Sir *Rowland*; why, what make you here?   707
  When seruice should in my old limbs lie lame,   745
  Though I looke old, yet I am strong and lustie;   751
  Orl. Oh good old man, how well in thee appeares   760
  But poore old man, thou prun'st a rotten tree,   767
  here, a yong man and an old in solemne talke.   803
  Sil. No *Corin*, being old, thou canst not guesse,   807
  And giue it food. There is an old poore man,   1106
  Go to my Caue, and tell mee. Good old man,   1175
  That the old *Carlot* once was Master of.   1882
  *almost six thousand yeeres old, and in all this time there   2007
  That her old gloues were on, but twas her hands: 2175
  *Vnder an old Oake, whose bows were moss'd with age   2255
  *was old Sir *Rowlands* will I estate vpon you, and heere | liue and die a
  Shepherd.   2419
  *yeare old conuerst with a Magitian, most profound in   2469
  I am the second sonne of old *Sir Rowland*,   2728
  Where, meeting with an old Religious man,   2736
OLDE = 2*6
  Oli. Get you with him, you olde dogge.   81
  *lost my teeth in your seruice: God be with my olde ma- |ster,   83
  *olde newes: that is, the old Duke is banished by his yon- |ger   101
  *to a crooked-pated olde Cuckoldly Ramme, out of all   1279
  Ros. I haue bin told so of many: but indeed, an olde   1531
  Ros. Well, Time is the olde Iustice that examines all   2105
  Awd. Faith the Priest was good enough, for all the | olde gentlemans
  saying.   2343
  *thy head: Nay prethee bee couer'd. How olde are you | Friend?   2358
OLI = 22*9
OLIU = *1
OLIUER *see also* Ol*., Oli*., Oliu*. = 6*7
  Enter Oliuer.   28
  Enter Duke, Lords, & Oliuer.   1180
  Oliuer Mar-text, the Vicar of the next village, who hath   1652
  Enter Sir Oliuer Mar-text.   1672

OLIUER *cont.*
   *Heere comes Sir *Oliuer*: Sir *Oliuer Mar-text* you are   1673
   *Farewel good Mr *Oliuer*: Not O sweet *Oliuer*, O braue   1703
   *Oliuer leaue me not behind thee: But winde away, bee   1704
   Enter *Oliuer*.   2224
   **Clow.* A most wicked Sir *Oliuer*, *Awdrie*, a most vile   2345
   Enter *Orlando* & *Oliuer*.   2408
   Enter *Duke Senior*, *Amyens*, *Iaques*, *Orlan-|do*, *Oliuer*, *Celia*.   2573
OLIUER = *1
OLIUES = 1
   'Tis at the tufft of Oliues, here hard by: 1847
OLIUE-TREES = 1
   A sheep-coat, fenc'd about with Oliue-trees.   2227
OMINOUS = 1
   Ros. O ominous, he comes to kill my Hart.   1440
OMITTANCE = 1
   But that's all one: omittance is no quittance: 1907
ON *see also* comming-on = 46*18
ONCE = 2*3
   **Cel.* And a chaine that you once wore about his neck: 1377
   *much at once, or none at all. I pre'thee take the Corke   1397
   That you insult, exult, and all at once   1809
   That the old *Carlot* once was Master of.   1882
   **Ros.* Patience once more, whiles our co(m)pact is vrg'd: 2580
ONE = 20*26
   *teares I speake it) there is not one so young, and so vil-|lanous   150
   Clo. One that old *Fredericke* your Father loues.   247
   *speake no more of him, you'l be whipt for taxation one | of these
   daies.   249
   *wherein if I bee foil'd, there is but one sham'd that was   350
   *neuer gracious: if kil'd, but one dead that is willing to   351
   Duk. You shall trie but one fall.   365
   Ros. Gentleman, | Weare this for me: one out of suites with fortune   410
   Not a word? | *Ros.* Not one to throw at a dog.   461
   *one should be lam'd with reasons, and the other mad | without any.   467
   Which teacheth thee that thou and I am one,   561
   Cours'd one another downe his innocent nose   646
   Cel. I pray you, one of you question yon'd man,   845
   And after one houre more, 'twill be eleuen,   998
   **Iaq.* O worthie Foole: One that hath bin a Courtier   1009
   I am ambitious for a motley coat. | *Du Sen.* Thou shalt haue one.   1016
   When such a one as shee, such is her neighbor?   1052
   And one man in his time playes many parts,   1121
   **Cor.* No more, but that I know the more one sickens,   1222
   Clo. Such a one is a naturall Philosopher: 1230
   **Clo.* Truly thou art damn'd, like an ill roasted Egge, | all on one side.   1235
   Therefore heauen Nature charg'd, | that one bodie should be fill'd   1339
   *my disposition? One inch of delay more, is a South-sea   1392
   *parted he with thee? And when shalt thou see him a-|gaine? Answer
   me in one word.   1417
   *that hath not the Gowt: for the one sleepes easily be-|cause   1509
   *he feeles no paine: the one lacking the burthen of   1511
   *in his youth an inland man, one that knew Courtship too   1533
   *one another, as halfepence are, euerie one fault seeming   1541
   *then to confesse she do's: that is one of the points, in the   1572
   **Ros.* Yes one, and in this manner. Hee was to ima-|gine   1586

ONE *cont.*
*as cleane as a sound sheepes heart, that there shal not | be one spot of
Loue in't.   1600
*Wainscot, then one of you wil proue a shrunke pannell,   1693
Cel. As good cause as one would desire, | Therefore weepe.   1714
*as a puisny Tilter, y spurs his horse but on one side,   1750
But that's all one: omittance is no quittance: 1907
*and he is one of the patternes of loue. *Leander*, he would   2011
Rosalind. Why then, can one desire too much of a   2032
*me: 'tis but one cast away, and so come death: two o' | clocke is your
howre.   2091
*if you breake one iot of your promise, or come one   2096
*of a cup into a glasse, by filling the one, doth empty the   2384
*but they ask'd one another the reason: no sooner knew   2444
Sil. Though to haue her and death, were both one | thing.   2592
quarrels, and like to haue fought one.   2624
*but when the parties were met themselues, one of them   2673
To one his lands with-held, and to the other   2745
ONELY = 5*2
*onely in the world I fil vp a place, which may bee better | supplied,
when I haue made it emptie.   354
A worthy foole: Motley's the onely weare.   1007
Iaq. It is my onely suite,   1018
Your Chessenut was euer the onely colour: 1722
*or spitting, or saying we are hoarse, which are the onely | prologues to
a bad voice.   2542
In the spring time, the onely pretty rang time.   2550
the onely peace-maker: much vertue in if.   2676
ONES = *2
*ones eyes, because his owne are out, let him bee iudge,   2120
Oliu. Good morrow, faire ones: pray you, (if you | know)   2225
OPEN = 1*2
When she is gone: then open not thy lips   543
*when he had a desire to eate a Grape, would open   2375
*that Grapes were made to eate, and lippes to open.   2377
OPENING = 1
Who with her head, nimble in threats approach'd | The opening of his
mouth: but sodainly   2260
OPINION = 1*1
Of all opinion that growes ranke in them,   1020
*I speake not this, that you should beare a good opinion   2463
OPPRESSED = 1
Here's a yong maid with trauaile much oppressed, | And faints for
succour.   858
OPPREST = 1
Opprest with two weake euils, age, and hunger,   1109
OR *l.**10 *72 *102 *110 *132 *145 *149 *244 245 270 302 *338 428 508
509 523 605 736 738 819 822 855 957 1053 1068 1186 1187 1229 *1319
1334 *1397 1401 1482 *1674 *1678 1702 1734 1789 *1952 1997 *2069
*2096 *2115 2211 *2392 *2393 *2396 *2447 *2542 2598 2708 2727
*2795 = 31*27
ORATORS = *1
*to kisse: verie good Orators when they are out,   1988
ORCHARD = 1
Oli. Know you where you are sir? | *Orl.* O sir, very well: heere in your
Orchard.   43

ORDER = *1
  Iaq. Can you nominate in order now, the degrees of | the lye.   2662
ORDINARIE = *1
  *that the Lunacie is so ordinarie, that the whippers are in   1583
ORDINARY = 1
  I see no more in you then in the ordinary   1815
ORE = 2
  Cel. Heele goe along ore the wide world with me,   597
  That o're the greene corne feild did passe,   2549
ORE-GROWNE = 1
  A wretched ragged man, ore-growne with haire   2257
ORE-HEARD = 1
  Hisperia the Princesse Gentlewoman | Confesses that she secretly
  ore-heard   690
ORE-RUN = *1
  *with thee in faction, I will ore-run thee with policie: I   2397
ORL = *1
  *he would not haue spoke such a word. *Ex*. *Orl*. *Ad*.   84
ORL = 71*43
ORLAN = *3
ORLANDO see also Orl., Orlan. = 27*10
  Enter Orlando and Adam.   2
  *your yonger brother *Orlando* hath a disposition to come   124
  Flourish. Enter Duke, Lords, Orlando, Charles, | *and Attendants*.   311
  Orl. Orlando my Liege, the yongest sonne of Sir *Ro-*|*land de Boys*.   384
  O poore *Orlando*! thou art ouerthrowne   427
  *him, for my father hated his father deerely; yet I hate | not *Orlando*.   490
  Enter Orlando and Adam.   703
  Enter Orlando, & Adam.   950
  Enter Orlando.   1062
  Enter Orlando with Adam.   1146
  Enter Orlando.   1200
  Run, run *Orlando*, carue on euery Tree,   1209
  Cel. It is yong *Orlando*, that tript vp the Wrastlers | heeles, and your
  heart, both in an instant.   1406
  Ros. Orlando? | *Cel. Orlando*.   1411
  Enter Orlando & Iaques.   1445
  *But what talke wee of Fathers, when there is such a man | as *Orlando*?   1745
  Enter Orlando.   1941
  *swam in a Gundello. Why how now *Orlando*, where   1953
  *marrie vs: giue me your hand *Orlando*: What doe you | say sister?   2034
  Ros. You must begin, will you *Orlando*.   2038
  Cel. Goe too: wil you *Orlando*, haue to wife this *Ro-*|*salind?* | *Orl*. I
  will.   2039
  *But I doe take thee *Orlando* for my husband: there's a   2048
  Ros. Say a day, without the euer: no, no *Orlando*, men   2055
  *out of the sight of *Orlando*: Ile goe finde a shadow, and | sigh till he
  come.   2122
  Ros. How say you now, is it not past two a clock? | And heere much
  Orlando.   2148
  Oli. Orlando doth commend him to you both,   2241
  Oli. When last the yong *Orlando* parted from you,   2249
  Seeing *Orlando*, it vnlink'd it selfe,   2262
  This seene, *Orlando* did approach the man,   2270
  Ros. But to *Orlando*: did he leaue him there   2277
  Enter Orlando & Oliuer.   2408
  Ros. Oh my deere *Orlando*, how it greeues me to see   2429

ORLANDO cont.
Enter Duke Senior, Amyens, Iaques, Orlan-|do, Oliuer, Celia.	2573
Du Sen. Dost thou beleeue *Orlando*, that the boy	2575
You wil bestow her on *Orlando* heere?	2582
You yours *Orlando*, to receiue his daughter.	2596

ORLANDO = 1
OSIERS *see* oziers
OTH = 1
him oth' shoulder, but Ile warrant him heart hole.	1963

OTHER = 7*9
*throat, till this other had puld out thy tongue for saying	61
*meanes or other. for I assure thee, (and almost with	149
The other is daughter to the banish'd Duke,	441
Grounded vpon no other argument,	447
*one should be lam'd with reasons, and the other mad | without any.	467
As manie other mannish cowards haue,	586
He will haue other meanes to cut you off;	729
*glad of other mens good content with my harme:	1272
*he cannot study, and the other liues merrily, be-|cause	1510
*leane and wasteful Learning; the other knowing no bur-|then	1512
*as louing your selfe, then seeming the Lo-|uer of any other.	1567
*to see other mens; then to haue seene much, and to haue	1938
*other. For all your Writers do consent, that *ipse* is hee:	2385
*both, that we may enioy each other. it shall be to your	2417
To one his lands with-held, and to the other	2745
I am for other, then for dancing meazures. | *Du Se.* Stay, *Iaques*, stay.	2770

OTHERS = 1*1
*I come but in as others do, to try with him the strength | of my youth.	334
Enter, Amyens, Iaques, & others.	889

OUER *see also* ore = 2*4
*making such pittiful dole ouer them, that all the behol-|ders	293
and giue ouer this attempt.	342
Cor. And they are often tarr'd ouer, with the surgery	1259
Ouer the wretched? what though you haue no beauty	1810
*thee, then a Barbary cocke-pidgeon ouer his hen, more	2059
*we must haue your doublet and hose pluckt ouer	2108

OUERCOME = 1*1
Why would you be so fond to ouercome	710
*and ouercome. For your brother, and my sister, no soo-|ner	2441

OUERHEARD = 1
I ouerheard him: and his practises:	730

OUERTHROWNE = 2
Sir, you haue wrastled well, and ouerthrowne | More then your enemies.	420
O poore *Orlando*! thou art ouerthrowne	427

OUGHT = *1
*the weaker vessell, as doublet and hose ought to show it	789

OUGLY = 1
Which like the toad, ougly and venemous,	619

OUID = 1
capricious Poet honest *Ouid* was among the Gothes.	1620

OUR *l.*199 *221 *223 240 *344 474 499 503 523 568 596 599 621 668 857
869 *1082 1099 1188 1190 *1250 1256 *1260 *1470 1471 *1546 1852
*2107 2294 *2403 2568 *2580 2751 2754 = 24*11
OURSELUES *see* selues
OUT *l.*61 *130 358 411 *483 547 567 595 638 901 953 1044 1111 1185
*1195 *1279 1297 1300 *1371 *1388 *1395 *1396 1398 1442 1446 *1465

OUT *cont.*
1707 1828 *1950 *1988 *1994 *1999 *2009 *2071 *2072 2073 *2100 2116
*2120 *2122 *2383 *2471 2761 = 21*23
OUTFACE = 1
That doe outface it with their semblances.   587
OUTSIDE = 1
Weele haue a swashing and a marshall outside,   585
OUT-LAWES = 1
Enter Duke Sen. & Lord, like Out-lawes.   972
OUT-STAY = 1
If you out-stay the time, vpon mine honor,   549
OWE = 1*1
Iaq. Nay, I care not for their names, they owe mee | nothing. Wil you
sing?   909
*that I weare; owe no man hate, enuie no mans happi-|nesse: 1271
OWN = *1
*pray you for your owne sake to embrace your own safe-|tie,   341
OWNE = 14*14
*of her Vncle, then his owne daughter, and neuer two La-|dies loued as
they doe.   112
*loth to foyle him, as I must for my owne honour if hee   129
*shall runne into, in that it is a thing of his owne search, | and
altogether against my will.   133
*owne people, who best know him, that I am altogether   165
His owne perill on his forwardnesse.   314
*pray you for your owne sake to embrace your own safe-|tie,   341
Or haue acquaintance with mine owne desires,   508
It was your pleasure, and your owne remorse,   531
Ros. Ile haue no worse a name then *Ioues* owne Page,   589
Should in their owne confines with forked heads   630
I haue by hard aduenture found mine owne.   827
Clo. Nay, I shall nere be ware of mine owne wit, till   839
And wish for her sake more then for mine owne,   861
1 *Lord.* He saues my labor by his owne approach.   981
Iaq. There I shal see mine owne figure.   1481
*of his owne getting; hornes, euen so poore men alone: 1664
Marrie his kisses are Iudasses owne children.   1719
Then thine owne gladnesse, that thou art employd.   1872
*is all these: but it is a melancholy of mine owne, com-|pounded   1931
*to be sad: I feare you haue sold your owne Lands,   1937
*of your owne Countrie: be out of loue with your   1950
Orl. Then in mine owne person, I die.   2005
*was not anie man died in his owne person (*videlicet*) in   2008
*your head, and shew the world what the bird hath done | to her owne
neast.   2109
*ones eyes, because his owne are out, let him bee iudge,   2120
This is a Letter of your owne deuice.   2168
*sir, but mine owne, a poore humour of mine sir, to take   2635
In his owne conduct, purposely to take   2733
OWNER = 1
The owner of the house I did enquire for?   2239
OXE = *2
*not from the stalling of an Oxe? his horses are bred   13
Clo. As the Oxe hath his bow sir, the horse his curb,   1686
OYSTER = *1
*sir, in a poore house, as your Pearle in your foule oy-|ster.   2637

OZIERS = 1
The ranke of Oziers, by the murmuring streame   2229
PACE = *1
*if the interim be but a sennight, Times pace is so hard,   1505
PACES = *1
*Ros. By no meanes sir; Time trauels in diuers paces,   1498
PACING = 1
Within an houre, and pacing through the Forrest,   2251
PAGE see also 1.Pa., 2.Pa. = *1
*Ros. Ile haue no worse a name then *Ioues* owne Page,   589
PAGEANT = 1
Cor. If you will see a pageant truely plaid   1760
PAGEANTS = 1
Presents more wofull Pageants then the Sceane | Wherein we play in. 1116
PAGES = 2
Heere come two of the banish'd Dukes Pages.   2536
Enter two Pages.   2537
PAINE = *1
*he feeles no paine: the one lacking the burthen of   1511
PAINES = 1
In lieu of all thy paines and husbandrie,   769
PAINTED = 1*1
Then that of painted pompe? Are not these woods   609
*Orl. Not so: but I answer you right painted cloath,   1466
PAIRE = *2
*Cel. Hee hath bought a paire of cast lips of *Diana*: a   1725
*degrees, haue they made a paire of staires to marriage,   2446
PALE = 3*1
*blush, and weepe, and thou must looke pale and | wonder.   153
For by this heauen, now at our sorrowes pale;   568
With thy chaste eye, from thy pale spheare aboue   1203
Betweene the pale complexion of true Loue,   1761
PALER = *2
*Cel. Come, you looke paler and paler: pray you draw | homewards:
good sir, goe with vs.   2332
PALME = 1*1
*Palme tree; I was neuer so berim'd since *Pythagoras* time   1373
The Cicatrice and capable impressure | Thy palme some moment
keepes: but now mine eyes   1794
PANCAKES see also pan-cakes = 1*1
*Mustard was naught: Now Ile stand to it, the Pancakes   232
euer he saw those Pancakes, or that Mustard.   245
PANNELL = *1
*Wainscot, then one of you wil proue a shrunke pannell,   1693
PANTALOONE = 1
Into the leane and slipper'd Pantaloone,   1137
PAN-CAKES = *1
*they were good Pan-cakes, and swore by his Honor the   231
PARCELLS = 1
In parcells as I did, would haue gone neere   1899
PARD = 1
Full of strange oaths, and bearded like the Pard,   1129
PARDON = 4*1
Orl. Speake you so gently? Pardon me I pray you,   1083
*haue not: (but I pardon you for that, for simply your ha-|uing   1561
But first begs pardon: will you sterner be   1776
Orl. Pardon me deere *Rosalind*.   1964

PARDON *cont.*
It beares an angry tenure; pardon me,   2159
PARENTAGE = *1
*with him: he askt me of what parentage I was; I   1743
PARISH = 1
The why is plaine, as way to Parish Church: 1026
PARISHIONERS = *1
*Loue haue you wearied your parishioners withall, and   1354
PARLOUS = *1
*and sinne is damnation: Thou art in a parlous state shep- | heard.   1241
PARRAT = *1
*clamorous then a Parrat against raine, more new-fang- | led   2060
PART = 9*9
*for my part, he keepes me rustically at home, or (to speak   10
Orlan. Goe a-part *Adam,* and thou shalt heare how | he will shake me
vp.   30
*you: you shall haue some part of your will, I pray you | leaue me.   77
take his part with weeping. | *Ros.* Alas.   294
Ros. O they take the part of a better wrastler then | my selfe.   480
Shall we be sundred? shall we part sweete girle?   562
'Tis right quoth he, thus miserie doth part   659
Clo. For my part, I had rather beare with you, then   794
And so he playes his part. The sixt age shifts   1136
But were I not the better part made mercie,   1182
Attalanta's *better part,* | *sad* Lucrecia's *Modestie.*   1345
*for the most part, cattle of this colour: would now like   1593
To fall in loue with him: but for my part   1900
*but a part of the thousand part of a minute in the affairs   1961
Ros. Read. *Why, thy godhead laid a part,*   2193
*loue, and they will together. Clubbes cannot part | them.   2449
You and you, no crosse shall part;   2705
PARTED = 2*1
*parted he with thee? And when shalt thou see him a- | gaine? Answer
me in one word.   1417
Oli. When last the yong *Orlando* parted from you,   2249
*nor he durst not giue me the lye direct: and so wee mea- | sur'd swords,
and parted.   2660
PARTICULARS = *1
*say I and no, to these particulars, is more then to answer | in a
Catechisme.   1421
PARTIES = *1
*but when the parties were met themselues, one of them   2673
PARTLY = 1
Cor. I partly guesse: for I haue lou'd ere now.   806
PARTS = 4*2
*emulator of euery mans good parts, a secret & villanous   141
Orl. Can I not say, I thanke you? My better parts   415
The parts and graces of the Wrastler   693
And one man in his time playes many parts,   1121
Thus Rosalinde *of manie parts,* | *by Heauenly Synode was deuis'd,*   1347
*will diuide a minute into a thousand parts, and breake   1960
PARTY = 1
That can therein taxe any priuate party: 1045
PASSD *see* past
PASSE = 3
The like doe you, so shall we passe along, | And neuer stir assailants.   577
If it do come to passe, that any man turne Asse: 937

175

PASSE *cont.*
That o're the greene corne feild did passe,   2549
PASSING = 1
I will be bitter with him, and passing short;   1913
PASSION = 3*4
Orl. What passion hangs these waights vpo(n) my toong?   424
Abruptly as my passion now makes me, | Thou hast not lou'd.   823
Ros. Ioue, Ioue, this Shepherds passion, | Is much vpon my fashion.   841
*of teares, full of smiles; for euerie passion something, and 1591
*for no passion truly any thing; as boyes and women are   1592
*in your complexion, that it was a passion of ear- | nest.   2325
All made of passion, and all made of wishes,   2502
PAST = 2
Which I haue past vpon her, she is banish'd.   545
Ros. How say you now, is it not past two a clock? | And heere much
Orlando.   2148
PASTIME = 1
Iaq. To see no pastime, I: what you would haue,   2772
PASTURE = 2*2
Full of the pasture, iumps along by him   661
Ros. What is he that shall buy his flocke and pasture?   873
Buy thou the Cottage, pasture, and the flocke,   878
*good pasture makes fat sheepe: and that a great cause of   1226
PATED = *1
*to a crooked-pated olde Cuckoldly Ramme, out of all   1279
PATHETICALL = *1
*patheticall breake-promise, and the most hollow louer,   2098
PATHS = *1
*in holiday foolerie, if we walke not in the trodden paths   473
PATIENCE = 6*2
Her verie silence, and her patience, | Speake to the people, and they
pittie her: 539
neuer cri'de, haue patience good people.   1355
Ros. Patience her selfe would startle at this letter,   2161
Clow. We shall finde a time *Awdrie*, patience gen- | tle *Awdrie*.   2341
All humblenesse, all patience, and impatience,   2504
Ros. Patience once more, whiles our co(m)pact is vrg'd: 2580
Iaq. Sir, by your patience: if I heard you rightly,   2757
your patience, and your vertue, well deserues it.   2764
PATIENT = *1
Adam. Sweet Masters bee patient, for your Fathers | remembrance, be
at accord.   63
PATIENTLY = 1
If they will patiently receiue my medicine.   1035
PATTERNES = *1
*and he is one of the patternes of loue. *Leander*, he would   2011
PAY = 1
And thou shalt haue to pay for it of vs.   879
PAYMENT = *1
*come to morrow, Ile giue him his payment: if euer hee   156
PAYRE = *1
*couples are comming to the Arke. Here comes a payre   2613
PEACE = 5
Clo. Holla; you Clowne. | *Ros*. Peace foole, he's not thy kinsman.   848
Ros. Peace I say; good euen to your friend.   853
Ros. Peace you dull foole, I found them on a tree.   1313
Ros. Peace, here comes my sister reading, stand aside.   1322

PEACE *cont*.
Hy. Peace hoa: I barre confusion,   2699
PEACE-MAKER = 1
   the onely peace-maker: much vertue in if.   2676
PEARLE = *1
   *sir, in a poore house, as your Pearle in your foule oy-|ster. 2637
PEASANT *see* pezant
PEASCOD = *1
   *of a peascod instead of her, from whom I tooke two   833
PEECE = *1
   *of a good peece of flesh indeed: learne of the wise   1263
PEEPES = 1
   Vnder an oake, whose anticke roote peepes out   638
PEEUISH = 1
   'Tis but a peeuish boy, yet he talkes well,   1884
PENALTIE = 1
   Heere feele we not the penaltie of *Adam*,   611
PENIE = *1
   *me thinkes I haue giuen him a penie, and he renders me   915
PENURIE = *1
   *of heauie tedious penurie. These Time ambles | withal.   1513
PENURY = 1
   *them? what prodigall portion haue I spent, that I should | come to such
   penury?   41
PEOPLE = 4*1
   *owne people, who best know him, that I am altogether   165
   But that the people praise her for her vertues,   448
   Her verie silence, and her patience, | Speake to the people, and they
   pittie her.   539
   Why are you vertuous? Why do people loue you?   708
   neuer cri'de, haue patience good people.   1355
PEOPLES = 1
   Tis Hymen peoples euerie towne,   2718
PERADUENTURE = *1
   Cel. Peraduenture this is not Fortunes work neither,   220
PERCEIUE = *2
   *betweene Terme and Terme, and then they perceiue not | how time
   moues.   1521
   *for the loue you beare to women (as I perceiue by your   2789
PERCEIUETH = *1
   *but Natures, who perceiueth our naturall wits too dull   221
PERFECT = 1
   Sil. So holy, and so perfect is my loue,   1873
PERFORCE = *1
   *perforce, I will render thee againe in affection: by   189
PERFORME = 2
   *to doe, and heere where you are, they are comming to | performe it. 279
   *place appointed for the wrastling, and they are ready to | performe it. 307
PERFUMD = 1
   Courtiers hands are perfum'd with Ciuet.   1261
PERILL = 2
   His owne perill on his forwardnesse.   314
   More free from perill then the enuious Court?   610
PERISHEST = *1
   *thou perishest: or to thy better vnderstanding, dyest; or   2393
PERPEND = *1
   *and perpend: Ciuet is of a baser birth then Tarre, the   1264

PERSEUER = 1
*And louing woo? and wooing, she should graunt? And | will you
perseuer to enioy her?   2411
PERSON = 2*1
Ros. Well, in her person, I say I will not haue you.   2004
Orl. Then in mine owne person, I die.   2005
*was not anie man died in his owne person (videlicet) in   2008
PERSONS = *1
*with diuers persons: Ile tel you who Time ambles with- | all,   1499
PERSWADE = 1
That feelingly perswade me what I am: 617
PERSWADED = *1
*him to a second, that haue so mightilie perswaded him | from a first. 367
PETITIONARY = *1
*Ros. Nay, I pre'thee now, with most petitionary ve- | hemence, tell me
who it is.   1385
PETTICOAT = 1
skirts of the Forrest, like fringe vpon a petticoat.   1525
PETTY-COATE = *1
*selfe coragious to petty-coate; therefore courage, good | Aliena.   790
PETTY-COATES = 1
our very petty-coates will catch them.   474
PEZANT = *1
*you haue train'd me like a pezant, obscuring and   68
PHANGE = 1
The seasons difference, as the Icie phange   612
PHE = 17*6
PHEBE see also Phe. = 19*1
O Phebe, Phebe, Phebe. Exit.   825
Enter Siluius and Phebe.   1770
Sil. Sweet Phebe doe not scorne me, do not Phebe   1771
Sil. O deere Phebe, | If euer (as that euer may be neere)   1799
Sil. Sweet Phebe. | Phe. Hah: what saist thou Siluius?   1855
Sil. Sweet Phebe pitty me.   1857
Sil. Phebe, with all my heart.   1910
My gentle Phebe, did bid me giue you this: 2155
Sil. No, I protest, I know not the contents, | Phebe did write it.   2169
Enter Siluius & Phebe.   2482
Sil. It is to be all made of sighes and teares, | And so am I for Phebe. 2491
Sil. It is to be all made of faith and seruice, | And so am I for Phebe. 2496
All puritie, all triall, all obseruance: | And so am I for Phebe. 2505
*Rosalind meet, as you loue Phebe meet, and as I loue no   2524
Enter Rosalinde, Siluius, & Phebe.   2579
Ros. You say that you'l haue Phebe if she will.   2591
Keepe you your word Phebe, that you'l marrie me,   2597
PHEBES = 2
Yet heard too much of Phebes crueltie.   2187
Ros. She Phebes me: marke how the tyrant writes.   2188
PHENIX = 1
Were man as rare as Phenix: 'od's my will,   2165
PHILOSOPHER = 1*1
Clo. Such a one is a naturall Philosopher.   1230
*knowes himselfe to be a Foole. The Heathen Philoso- | pher,   2374
PHILOSOPHIE = 1
Has't any Philosophie in thee shepheard?   1221
PHYSICK = *1
*Ros. No: I wil not cast away my physick, but on those   1544

PHYSICKE = *1
*physicke your ranckenesse, and yet giue no thousand | crownes
neyther: holla *Dennis*.   86
PICKE = *1
*Cel. Yes, I thinke he is not a picke purse, nor a horse- |stealer,   1732
PICTURES = 1
All the pictures fairest Linde, | are but blacke to Rosalinde: 1290
PIDGEON = *1
*thee, then a Barbary cocke-pidgeon ouer his hen, more   2059
PIERCETH = 1
Thus most inuectiuely he pierceth through | The body of Countrie,
Citie, Court,   666
PIGEONS = 1*1
*Cel. Which he will put on vs, as Pigeons feed their | young.   259
Pigeons bill, so wedlocke would be nibling.   1688
PILGRIMAGE = 1
Some, how briefe the Life of man | runs his erring pilgrimage,   1327
PILLOW = 1
As euer sigh'd vpon a midnight pillow: 809
PIN = 1
Scratch thee but with a pin, and there remaines   1792
PIPES = 1
Turning againe toward childish trebble pipes,   1141
PITIE = *1
*there is such oddes in the man: In pitie of the challen- |gers   322
PITTEOUS = 1
In pitteous chase: and thus the hairie foole,   647
PITTIE = 4*2
*Clo. The more pittie that fooles may not speak wise- |ly, what
Wisemen do foolishly.   251
And pittie her, for her good Fathers sake;   449
Her verie silence, and her patience, | Speake to the people, and they
pittie her: 539
Cor. Faire Sir, I pittie her,   860
And know what 'tis to pittie, and be pittied: 1094
*Ros. Though it be pittie to see such a sight, it well | becomes the
ground.   1436
PITTIED = 1
And know what 'tis to pittie, and be pittied: 1094
PITTIFUL = *1
*making such pittiful dole ouer them, that all the behol- |ders   293
PITTILESSE = 1
Must you be therefore prowd and pittilesse?   1813
PITTY = 3*2
Afflict me with thy mockes, pitty me not,   1806
As till that time I shall not pitty thee.   1807
Sil. Sweet *Phebe* pitty me.   1857
*Ros. Doe you pitty him? No, he deserues no pitty: 2215
PITY = 1
Of drops, that sacred pity hath engendred: 1100
PLACE = 10*6
*place of a brother, and as much as in him lies, mines my   22
*place appointed for the wrastling, and they are ready to | performe it. 307
*onely in the world I fil vp a place, which may bee better | supplied,
when I haue made it emptie.   354
To leaue this place; Albeit you haue deseru'd   430
To the which place a poore sequestred Stag   640

PLACE *cont.*

In their assign'd and natiue dwelling place.	671
Du Sen. Show me the place, | I loue to cope him in these sullen fits,	675
This is no place, this house is but a butcherie;	731
*was at home I was in a better place, but Trauellers must | be content.	799
Can in this desert place buy entertainment,	856
I like this place, and willingly could | Waste my time in it.	881
Orl. Are you natiue of this place?	1526
*promis'd to meete me in this place of the Forrest, and to | couple vs.	1653
Cel. West of this place, down in the neighbor bottom	2228
Left on your right hand, brings you to the place:	2230
As how I came into that Desert place.	2295

PLACES = 1

After a voyage: He hath strange places cram'd	1013

PLAID = 2

Rose at an instant, learn'd, plaid, eate together,	535
Cor. If you will see a pageant truely plaid	1760

PLAINE = 1

The why is plaine, as way to Parish Church:	1026

PLANTS = *1

*our yong plants with caruing *Rosalinde* on their	1546

PLAY = 4*6

Presents more wofull Pageants then the Sceane | Wherein we play in.	1116
*that habit play the knaue with him, do you hear For- |(rester.	1488
Ile proue a busie actor in their play. *Exeunt.*	1768
And play the swaggerer, beare this, beare all:	2162
*and play false straines vpon thee? not to be en- |dur'd.	2217
Play Musicke, and you Brides and Bride-groomes all,	2755
*no bush, 'tis true, that a good play needes no Epilogue.	2779
*good play? I am not furnish'd like a Begger, therefore	2784
*of this Play, as please you: And I charge you (O men)	2788
*and the women, the play may please. If I were a Wo- |man,	2791

PLAYERS = 1

Ia. All the world's a stage, | And all the men and women, meerely Players;	1118

PLAYES = 2*1

And one man in his time playes many parts,	1121
And so he playes his part. The sixt age shifts	1136
*playes proue the better by the helpe of good Epilogues:	2781

PLEASD = 2*1

Thou should'st haue better pleas'd me with this deede,	389
and pleas'd with what he gets:	930
*pleas'd me, complexions that lik'd me, and breaths that	2793

PLEASE = 6*8

Oli. Let me goe I say. | *Orl.* I will not till I please: you shall heare mee: my	65
Den. So please you, he is heere at the doore, and im- |portunes accesse to you.	92
Le Beu. I wil tell you the beginning: and if it please	277
Ros. I my Liege, so please you giue vs leaue.	320
Amy. My voice is ragged, I know I cannot please | you.	903
Iaq. I do not desire you to please me,	905
Amy. More at your request, then to please my selfe.	911
A stubborne will to please,	939
To blow on whom I please, for so fooles haue:	1023
Sil. So please you, for I neuer heard it yet:	2186
*good, and not to grace me. Beleeue then, if you please,	2467

PLEASE *cont*.
*he cut it to please himselfe: this is call'd the quip modest.	2650
*of this Play, as please you: And I charge you (O men)	2788
*and the women, the play may please. If I were a Wo- |man,	2791

PLEASES = 1 *2
When he that speakes them pleases those that heare:	1886
*Cel. It pleases him to call you so: but he hath a Rosa- |lind of a better leere then you.	1979
*I wil content you, if what pleases you contents	2522

PLEASETH = *1
*in respect it is in the fields, it pleaseth mee well: but in	1217

PLEASING = *1
*Orl. There was no thought of pleasing you when she | was christen'd.	1460

PLEASURE = 1 *1
*learne mee how to remember any extraordinary plea- |sure.	175
It was your pleasure, and your owne remorse,	531

PLEASURES = *1
*Is but for two moneths victuall'd: So to your pleasures,	2769

PLENTEOUS = 1
That I shall thinke it a most plenteous crop	1875

PLENTIE = *1
*more plentie in it, it goes much against my stomacke.	1220

PLENTIFULLY = *1
*that he so plentifully giues me, the something that	19

PLUCKT = *1
*we must haue your doublet and hose pluckt ouer	2108

PLY = 1
Will you goe Sister? Shepheard ply her hard:	1848

POAKE = 1
And then he drew a diall from his poake,	993

POET = 1 *1
capricious Poet honest Ouid was among the Gothes.	1620
*Now if thou wert a Poet, I might haue some hope | thou didst feigne.	1636

POETICAL = *1
*Aud. I do not know what Poetical is: is it honest in | deed and word: is it a true thing?	1628

POETICALL = 2
*in a little roome: truly, I would the Gods hadde | made thee poeticall.	1626
*Aud. Do you wish then that the Gods had made me | Poeticall?	1633

POETRIE = *3
*Clo. No trulie: for the truest poetrie is the most fai- |ning,	1630
*and Louers are giuen to Poetrie: and what they	1631
*sweare in Poetrie, may be said as Louers, they do feigne.	1632

POINT = 1 *1
Orl. You touch'd my veine at first, the thorny point	1070
*are no such man; you are rather point deuice in your ac- |coustrements,	1566

POINTS = 1 *1
That I did suite me all points like a man,	581
*then to confesse she do's: that is one of the points, in the	1572

POLICIE = *1
*with thee in faction, I will ore-run thee with policie: I	2397

POLITICK = *1
*which is ambitious: nor the Lawiers, which is politick:	1929

POLITICKE = *1
*I haue bin politicke with my friend, smooth with mine	2622

POMPE = 1
Then that of painted pompe? Are not these woods 609
POMPOUS = 1
And throwne into neglect the pompous Court. | 2.*Bro*. He hath. 2759
POORE = 12*10
*bequeathed me by will, but poore a thousand 5
*God made, a poore vnworthy brother of yours with | idlenesse. 36
*a gentleman, or giue mee the poore allottery my 72
*third: yonder they lie, the poore old man their Father, 292
O poore *Orlando*! thou art ouerthrowne 427
Cel. O my poore *Rosaline*, whether wilt thou goe? 552
Cel. Ile put my selfe in poore and meane attire, 575
And yet it irkes me the poore dapled fooles 628
To the which place a poore sequestred Stag 640
Poore Deere quoth he, thou mak'st a testament 655
Vpon that poore and broken bankrupt there? 665
But poore old man, thou prun'st a rotten tree, 767
Ros. Alas poore Shepheard searching of they would, 826
That your poore friends must woe your companie, 983
And giue it food. There is an old poore man, 1106
*of his owne getting; hornes, euen so poore men alone: 1664
nothing, is to haue rich eyes and poore hands. 1939
Ros. No faith, die by Attorney: the poore world is 2006
Sil. Call you this chiding? | *Cel*. Alas poore Shepheard. 2213
*and blood breakes: a poore virgin sir, an il-fauor'd thing 2634
*sir, but mine owne, a poore humour of mine sir, to take 2635
*sir, in a poore house, as your Pearle in your foule oy- | ster. 2637
PORTION = *1
*them? what prodigall portion haue I spent, that I should | come to such
penury? 41
PORTUGALL = 1
*it cannot bee sounded: my affection hath an vnknowne | bottome, like
the Bay of Portugall. 2113
POSSEST = 1
Ros. Now tell me how long you would haue her, af- | ter you haue
possest her? 2052
POSSIBLE = 2*2
*let vs talke in good earnest: Is it possible in such a so- | daine, 484
Duk. Can it be possible that no man saw them? 681
Ros. Nay, but who is it? | *Cel*. Is it possible? 1383
**Orl*. Is't possible, that on so little acquaintance you 2409
POSTE = 1
Ros. Why then 'tis good to be a poste. 1925
POTENT = 1
A land it selfe at large, a potent Dukedome. 2746
POUCH = 1
With spectacles on nose, and pouch on side, 1138
POUERTIE = 1*1
To thinke my pouertie is treacherous. 526
*pouertie of her, the small acquaintance, my sodaine wo- | ing, 2414
POUERTY = 1
And I in such a pouerty of grace, 1874
POURE = *1
**Cel*. Or rather bottomlesse, that as fast as you poure | affection in, it
runs out. 2115
POWER = 3
You meet in some fresh cheeke the power of fancie, 1801

POWER *cont*.

Haue power to raise such loue in mine,	2200
Addrest a mightie power, which were on foote	2732

POWERS = 1

Thy conceite is neerer death, then thy powers.	958

POWRD = *1

*it is a figure in Rhetoricke, that drink being powr'd out	2383

POWRE = *1

*might'st powre this conceal'd man out of thy mouth, as	1395

POYSON = *2

*poyson, entrap thee by some treacherous deuise, and ne-|uer	147
*death, thy libertie into bondage: I will deale in poy-|son	2395

PRACTISE = *1

*grace himselfe on thee, hee will practise against thee by	146

PRACTISES = 1

I ouerheard him: and his practises:	730

PRAIE = *1

*Ros. Fare you well: praie heauen I be deceiu'd in you.	359

PRAIERS = 1

How then might your praiers moue?	2204

PRAISE = 3

But that the people praise her for her vertues,	448
Your praise is come too swiftly home before you.	712
Wearing thy hearer in thy Mistris praise, | Thou hast not lou'd.	820

PRAISED = *1

*Clo. Well, praised be the Gods, for thy foulnesse; slut-|tishnesse	1649

PRAISES = 1

Hath heard your praises, and this night he meanes,	726

PRAISING = 1

Praising the proud disdainfull Shepherdesse | That was his Mistresse.	1757

PRAY = 11*14

*you: you shall haue some part of your will, I pray you | leaue me.	77
Cel. I pray thee *Rosalind*, sweet my Coz, be merry.	171
*pray you for your owne sake to embrace your own safe-|tie,	341
Orl. I thanke you Sir; and pray you tell me this,	436
Cel. I pray you beare with me, I cannot goe no fur-|ther.	792
Cel. I pray you, one of you question yon'd man,	845
Ros. I pray thee, if it stand with honestie,	877
Orl. Speake you so gently? Pardon me I pray you,	1083
Iaq. I pray you marre no more trees with Writing | Loue-songs in their barkes.	1454
Orl. I pray you marre no moe of my verses with rea-|ding them ill-fauouredly.	1456
Ros. I pray you, what i'st a clocke?	1490
Orl. I am he that is so Loue-shak'd, I pray you tel | me your remedie.	1552
Aud. Well, I am not faire, and therefore I pray the | Gods make me honest.	1643
heere Sir: Nay, pray be couer'd.	1684
Ros. And why I pray you? who might be your mother	1808
Phe. Sweet youth, I pray you chide a yere together,	1837
Ros. I pray you do not fall in loue with mee,	1844
Orl. Pray thee marrie vs. | *Cel*. I cannot say the words.	2036
Oliu. Good morrow, faire ones: pray you, (if you | know)	2225
Cel. I pray you tell it.	2248
I pray you will you take him by the arme.	2317
*I pray you tell your brother how well I counterfei-|ted: heigh-ho.	2322

PRAY *cont*.

*Cel. Come, you looke paler and paler: pray you draw | homewards: good sir, goe with vs.	2332
*Ros. I shall deuise something: but I pray you com-|mend	2336
*Ros. Pray you no more of this, 'tis like the howling	2516

PRECIOUS = 1*2

*Cel. No, thy words are too precious to be cast away	463
Weares yet a precious Iewell in his head:	620
*then no skill, by so much is a horne more precious | then to want.	1670

PREPARD = 1

His banket is prepar'd. *Exeunt*	948

PREPARE = 1

Go you, and prepare *Aliena*; for looke you,	2425

PRESENCE = 1

*Le Beu. Three proper yong men, of excellent growth | and presence.	284

PRESENT = 3*1

Of my reuenge, thou present: but looke to it,	1184
*Iaq. Let's present him to the Duke like a Romane	2129
And marke what obiect did present it selfe	2254
And therefore take the present time.	2553

PRESENTATION = 1

the presentation of that he shoots his wit.	2680

PRESENTLY = 2

At the armes end: I wil heere be with thee presently,	960
With all Graces wide enlarg'd, | nature presently distill'd	1341

PRESENTS = 2

*Ros. With bils on their neckes: Be it knowne vnto | all men by these presents.	286
Presents more wofull Pageants then the Sceane | Wherein we play in.	1116

PRESSE = *1

*Clo. God'ild you sir, I desire you of the like: I presse	2631

PRETHEE = 9*8

*Cel. Marry I prethee doe, to make sport withall: but	195
Cel. Prethee, who is't that thou means't?	246
Prethee be cheerefull; know'st thou not the Duke	557
Ros. I prethee Shepheard, if that loue or gold	855
Iaq. More, more, I pre'thee more.	898
Iaq. I thanke it: More, I prethee more,	900
As a Weazel suckes egges: More, I pre'thee more.	902
change you colour? | *Ros.* I pre'thee who?	1378
*Ros. Nay, I pre'thee now, with most petitionary ve-|hemence, tell me who it is.	1385
*of discouerie. I pre'thee tell me, who is it quickely, and	1393
*much at once, or none at all. I pre'thee take the Corke	1397
*Cel. Cry holla, to the tongue, I prethee: it curuettes	1438
Orl. I prethee, who doth he trot withal?	1502
Orl. I prethee recount some of them.	1543
*Cel. Do I prethee, but yet haue the grace to consider,	1711
*Iaq. I prethee, pretty youth, let me better acquainted | with thee.	1917
*thy head: Nay prethee bee couer'd. How olde are you | Friend?	2358

PRETTIE = 4*1

*of her batler, and the Cowes dugs that her prettie	831
Orl. Where dwel you prettie youth?	1523
It is a pretty youth, not very prettie,	1887
Art thou wise? | *Will.* I sir, I haue a prettie wit.	2370
These prettie Country folks would lie. | In spring time, &c.	2559

PRETTY = 4*3
  'Tis pretty sure, and very probable,   1782
  It is a pretty youth, not very prettie,   1887
  There was a pretty rednesse in his lip,   1894
  *Iaq. I prethee, pretty youth, let me better acquainted | with thee.   1917
  *mend mee, and by all pretty oathes that are not dange- | rous,   2095
  *Ros. O coz, coz, coz: my pretty little coz, that thou   2111
  In the spring time, the onely pretty rang time.   2550
PRETY = *1
  *Iaq. You are ful of prety answers: haue you not bin ac- | quainted   1464
PREUENTS = 1
  fortune, and preuents the slander of his wife.   1975
PREY = 1
  The royall disposition of that beast | To prey on nothing, that doth
  seeme as dead: 2268
PRICKE = 1
  He that sweetest rose will finde, | must finde Loues pricke, & Rosalinde. 1309
PRIDE = 2*2
  *Ros. He cals vs back: my pride fell with my fortunes,   418
  *Iaq. Why who cries out on pride,   1044
  *and the greatest of my pride, is to see my Ewes graze, & | my Lambes
  sucke.   1273
  But sure hee's proud, and yet his pride becomes him;   1888
PRIEST = *5
  *Ros. With a Priest that lacks Latine, and a rich man   1508
  *and haue a good Priest that can tel you what marriage is,   1691
  *good thing: Come sister, you shall be the Priest, and   2033
  *girle goes before the Priest, and certainely a Womans | thought runs
  before her actions.   2049
  *Awd. Faith the Priest was good enough, for all the | olde gentlemans
  saying.   2343
PRIMA *l*.1 604 1179 1915 2339 = 5
PRIME = 1
  For loue is crowned with the prime. | In spring time, &c.   2555
PRIMUS *l*.1 = 1
PRINCES = 1
  The cost of Princes on vnworthy shoulders?   1050
PRINCESSE = 2*2
  Le Beu. Faire Princesse, | you haue lost much good sport.   264
  *Le Beu. Monsieur the Challenger, the Princesse cals | for you.   328
  *Orl. No faire Princesse: he is the generall challenger,   333
  Hisperia the Princesse Gentlewoman | Confesses that she secretly
  ore-heard   690
PRINCIPAL = *1
  *Ros. There were none principal, they were all like   1540
PRINCIPALL = *1
  *Orl. Can you remember any of the principall euils,   1538
PRINT = *1
  *Clo. O sir, we quarrel in print, by the booke: as you   2664
PRISD = 1
  Of manie faces, eyes, and hearts, | to haue the touches deerest pris'd. 1349
PRISER = 1
  The bonnie priser of the humorous Duke?   711
PRISONER = 1
  *he taught me how to know a man in loue: in which cage | of rushes, I
  am sure you art not prisoner.   1555

PRIUATE = 1*1
    That can therein taxe any priuate party: 1045
    *but in respect that it is priuate, it is a very vild life. Now   1216
PRIZE = *1
    *goe alone againe, Ile neuer wrastle for prize more: and   157
PROBABLE = 1
    'Tis pretty sure, and very probable,   1782
PROCEED = 2*2
    Cel. Giue me audience, good Madam. | *Ros*. Proceed.   1432
    Iaq. Proceed, proceede: Ile giue her.   1680
    Du Se. Proceed, proceed: wee'l begin these rights,   2774
PROCEEDE = 1
    Iaq. Proceed, proceede: Ile giue her.   1680
PRODIGALL = *1
    *them? what prodigall portion haue I spent, that I should | come to such
    penury?   41
PROFESSE = 1
    loue too: yet I professe curing it by counsel.   1584
PROFIT = 2*1
    *at schoole, and report speakes goldenly of his profit: 9
    The soile, the profit, and this kinde of life,   885
    Oli. If that an eye may profit by a tongue,   2233
PROFOUND = *1
    *yeare old conuerst with a Magitian, most profound in   2469
PROLOGUE = *1
    *Lord the Prologue. If it be true, that good wine needs   2778
PROLOGUES = 1
    *or spitting, or saying we are hoarse, which are the onely | prologues to
    a bad voice.   2542
PROMISD = 1*1
    *promis'd to meete me in this place of the Forrest, and to | couple vs.   1653
    Ros. I haue promis'd to make all this matter euen: 2594
PROMISE = 5*4
    Cel. Or I, I promise thee.   302
    But iustly as you haue exceeded all promise, | Your Mistris shall be
    happie.   408
    Orl. My faire *Rosalind*, I come within an houre of my | promise.   1957
    Ros. Breake an houres promise in loue? hee that   1959
    *if you breake one iot of your promise, or come one   2096
    *patheticall breake-promise, and the most hollow louer,   2098
    *therefore beware my censure, and keep your pro-|mise.   2101
    He left a promise to returne againe   2250
    His broken promise, and to giue this napkin   2308
PROMISED = 1
    Can do all this that he hath promised?   2576
PROMISES = 1
    If you doe keepe your promises in loue;   407
PROMOTION = 1
    Where none will sweate, but for promotion,   764
PRONOUNCE = *1
    Cel. Pronounce that sentence then on me my Leige,   546
PROOFE = *1
    *your yeares: you haue seene cruell proofe of this mans   337
PROPER = 3*1
    Le Beu. Three proper yong men, of excellent growth | and presence.   284
    Orl. And why not the swift foote of time? Had not | that bin as
    proper?   1496

PROPER *cont*.
And out of you she sees her selfe more proper   1828
Hee'll make a proper man: the best thing in him   1889
PROPERER = 1
You are a thousand times a properer man   1824
PROPERLY = *1
*more properly) staies me heere at home vnkept: for call   11
PROPERTIE = *1
*the propertie of raine is to wet, and fire to burne: That   1225
PROPOSITIONS = *1
*propositions of a Louer: but take a taste of my finding   1427
PROTEST = 2
for I protest her frowne might kill me.   2021
Sil. No, I protest, I know not the contents, | *Phebe* did write it.   2169
PROUD = 6*2
Orl. I am more proud to be Sir *Rolands* sonne,   395
*liking, proud, fantastical, apish, shallow, inconstant, ful   1590
Praising the proud disdainfull Shepherdesse | That was his Mistresse.   1757
No faith proud Mistresse, hope not after it,   1818
And be not proud, though all the world could see,   1850
But sure hee's proud, and yet his pride becomes him;   1888
*nor the Courtiers, which is proud: nor the Souldiers,   1928
She calls me proud, and that she could not loue me   2164
PROUE = 1*4
Cel. How proue you that in the great heape of your | knowledge?   235
*Wainscot, then one of you wil proue a shrunke pannell,   1693
Ile proue a busie actor in their play. *Exeunt*.   1768
*you would proue, my friends told mee as much, and I   2089
*playes proue the better by the helpe of good Epilogues: 2781
PROUIDE = *1
Duk. You are a foole: you Neice prouide your selfe,   548
PROUIDED = 1
Prouided that you weed your better iudgements   1019
PROUIDENTLY = 1
Yea prouidently caters for the Sparrow,   748
PROUOKETH = 1
Beautie prouoketh theeues sooner then gold.   574
PROWD = 2
And the red glowe of scorne and prowd disdaine,   1762
Must you be therefore prowd and pittilesse?   1813
PRUNST = 1
But poore old man, thou prun'st a rotten tree,   767
PUBLIKE = 2
So neere our publike Court as twentie miles, | Thou diest for it.   503
And this our life exempt from publike haunt,   621
PUFFING = 1
Like foggy South, puffing with winde and raine,   1823
PUISNY = *1
*as a puisny Tilter, y spurs his horse but on one side,   1750
PUKING = 1
Mewling, and puking in the Nurses armes: 1123
PULD = *1
*throat, till this other had puld out thy tongue for saying   61
PUNISH = *1
Orl. I beseech you, punish mee not with your harde   346
PUNISHD = *1
*and the reason why they are not so punish'd and cured, is   1582

PURCHASE = 1
Orl. Your accent is something finer, then you could | purchase in so
remoued a dwelling. 1529
PURE = 1*2
*then with safety of a pure blush, thou maist in ho-|nor come off
againe. 197
Limpt in pure loue: till he be first suffic'd, 1108
Cel. I warrant you, with pure loue, & troubled brain, 2150
PURGATION = 1*1
If their purgation did consist in words, 514
*purgation, I haue trod a measure, I haue flattred a Lady, 2621
PURITIE = 1
All puritie, all triall, all obseruance: | And so am I for *Phebe*. 2505
PURLEWS = 1
Where in the Purlews of this Forrest, stands 2226
PURPOSD = 1
Oli. Twice did he turne his backe, and purpos'd so: 2279
PURPOSE = 1*2
*selfe notice of my Brothers purpose heerein, and haue by 137
no song Forrester for this purpose? | *Lord*. Yes Sir. 2132
*Know of me then (for now I speake to some pur-|pose) 2461
PURPOSELY = 1
In his owne conduct, purposely to take 2733
PURSE = 1*1
you, for I thinke you haue no money in your purse. 796
Cel. Yes, I thinke he is not a picke purse, nor a horse-|stealer, 1732
PURSUITE = 1
To hide vs from pursuite that will be made 601
PUSH = *1
Duke. More villaine thou. Well push him out of dores 1195
PUT = 6*5
*Lords haue put themselues into voluntary exile with 103
Cel. Which he will put on vs, as Pigeons feed their | young. 259
Cel. Ile put my selfe in poore and meane attire, 575
And therefore put I on the countenance 1085
Cel. So you may put a man in your belly. 1399
slut, were to put good meate into an vncleane dish. 1646
*his lips when he put it into his mouth, meaning there-|by, 2376
*I say I am a Magitian: Therefore put you in your best a-|ray, 2479
Clo. If any man doubt that, let him put mee to my 2620
His brother heere, and put him to the sword: 2734
The Duke hath put on a Religious life, 2758
PUTS = *1
Ros. Then she puts you to entreatie, and there begins | new matter. 1992
PYTHAGORAS = *1
*Palme tree; I was neuer so berim'd since *Pythagoras* time 1373
QUAILE = 1
And let not search and inquisition quaile, 700
QUALITIES = *1
*hiding from me all gentleman-like qualities: the spirit 69
QUARREL = *2
Clo. 'Faith we met, and found the quarrel was vpon | the seuenth
cause. 2626
Clo. O sir, we quarrel in print, by the booke: as you 2664
QUARRELL = 2*1
Ielous in honor, sodaine, and quicke in quarrell, 1130
the quarrell on the seuenth cause? 2643

QUARRELL *cont*.

*knew when seuen Iustices could not take vp a Quarrell,   2672
QUARRELS = 1
quarrels, and like to haue fought one.   2624
QUARRELSOME = *2
*say, I lie: this is call'd the counter-checke quarrelsome: 2655
*the Reproofe valiant: the fift, the Counterchecke quar- | relsome: 2668
QUARTA *l*.781 1708 2572 = 3
QUARTUS *l*.1915 = 1
QUEENE = 1
And thou thrice crowned Queene of night suruey   1202
QUESTION = 3*2
Cel. I pray you, one of you question yon'd man,   845
As yet to question you about your fortunes: 1153
Ros. I met the Duke yesterday, and had much que- | stion   1742
Ol. Neither call the giddinesse of it in question; the   2413
After some question with him, was conuerted   2737
QUESTIONING = 1
Feede your selues with questioning: 2712
QUESTIONS = 1
from whence you haue studied your questions.   1467
QUICKE = 1
Ielous in honor, sodaine, and quicke in quarrell,   1130
QUICKELY = *1
*of discouerie. I pre'thee tell me, who is it quickely, and   1393
QUICKLY = 2
And Ile be with thee quickly: yet thou liest   965
Who quickly fell before him, in which hurtling   2283
QUIET = 1
That can translate the stubbornnesse of fortune | Into so quiet and so
sweet a stile.   625
QUINTA *l*.888 1769 = 2
QUINTESSENCE = 1
The quintessence of euerie sprite, | heauen would in little show.   1337
QUINTINE – 1
Is but a quintine, a meere liuelesse blocke.   417
QUINTUS *l*.2339 = 1
QUIP = *1
*he cut it to please himselfe: this is call'd the quip modest.   2650
QUIP-MODEST = *1
*Quip-modest: the third, the reply Churlish: the fourth,   2667
QUIT = 1
Till thou canst quit thee by thy brothers mouth,   1191
QUITE = *1
*them brauely, quite trauers athwart the heart of his lo- | uer,   1749
QUITTANCE = 1
But that's all one: omittance is no quittance: 1907
QUOTH = 6
Poore Deere quoth he, thou mak'st a testament   655
'Tis right quoth he, thus miserie doth part   659
And neuer staies to greet him: I quoth *Iaques*,   662
Good morrow foole (quoth I:) no Sir, quoth he,   991
Thus we may see (quoth he) how the world wagges: 996
QUOTIDIAN = *1
*some good counsel, for he seemes to haue the Quotidian | of Loue
vpon him.   1550

RAGGED = 1*1
Amy. My voice is ragged, I know I cannot please | you.   903
A wretched ragged man, ore-growne with haire   2257
RAILD = 2
so, thou hast raild on thy selfe.   62
And rail'd on Lady Fortune in good termes,   989
RAILE = 1*2
*Ile go sleepe if I can: if I cannot, Ile raile against all | the first borne
of Egypt.   945
*wee two, will raile against our Mistris the world, and all | our miserie.   1470
Can a woman raile thus?   2191
RAILING = 2
Sil. Call you this railing?   2192
Did you euer heare such railing?   2195
RAINE = 1*2
*the propertie of raine is to wet, and fire to burne: That   1225
Like foggy South, puffing with winde and raine,   1823
*clamorous then a Parrat against raine, more new-fang- | led   2060
RAISE = 1
Haue power to raise such loue in mine,   2200
RAMME = *1
*to a crooked-pated olde Cuckoldly Ramme, out of all   1279
RAMMES = *2
*Ewes and the Rammes together, and to offer to get your   1276
*Rammes, and *Cesars* Thrasonicall bragge of I came, saw,   2440
RANCKENESSE = *1
*physicke your ranckenesse, and yet giue no thousand | crownes
neyther: holla *Dennis*.   86
RANG = 1
In the spring time, the onely pretty rang time.   2550
RANGD = 1
Else had she with her Father rang'd along.   529
RANKE = 4
Clo. Nay, if I keepe not my ranke. | *Ros*. Thou loosest thy old smell.   272
Of all opinion that growes ranke in them,   1020
*and suppers, and sleeping hours excepted: it is the right | Butter-
womens ranke to Market.   1295
The ranke of Oziers, by the murmuring streame   2229
RANKER = 1
or I should thinke my honestie ranker then my wit.   1997
RARE = 1*1
Were man as rare as Phenix: 'od's my will,   2165
Iaq. Is not this a rare fellow my Lord? He's as good   2677
RASCALL = *1
*No, no, the noblest Deere hath them as huge as the Ras- | call: 1665
RASCALLY = *1
*madnesse, that blinde rascally boy, that abuses euery   2119
RAT = 1
that I was an Irish Rat, which I can hardly remember.   1374
RATHER = 2*4
I rather will subiect me to the malice   740
Clo. For my part, I had rather beare with you, then   794
*are no such man; you are rather point deuice in your
ac- | coustrements,   1566
I had rather here you chide, then this man wooe.   1838
Ros. And your experience makes you sad: I had ra- | ther   1942

RATHER *cont.*
Cel. Or rather bottomlesse, that as fast as you poure | affection in, it
runs out.   2115
RAUENS = 1
Take that, and he that doth the Rauens feede,   747
RAW = 1
man: God make incision in thee, thou art raw.   1269
READ = 2*1
*well: for there he fel in loue. I haue heard him read ma- | ny   1534
Read. *Art thou god, to Shepherd turn'd?*   2189
Ros. Read. *Why, thy godhead laid a part,*   2193
READE = 1
Will I Rosalinda write, | teaching all that reade, to know   1335
READIE = *1
Orl. Readie Sir, but his will hath in it a more modest | working.   363
READING = 1*1
Ros. Peace, here comes my sister reading, stand aside.   1322
Orl. I pray you marre no moe of my verses with rea- | ding them
ill-fauouredly.   1456
READY = *1
*place appointed for the wrastling, and they are ready to | performe it.   307
REAP = 1
They that reap must sheafe and binde, | then to cart with Rosalinde.   1305
REAPES = 1
That the maine haruest reapes: loose now and then   1877
REASON = 4*6
*to reason of such goddesses, hath sent this Naturall for   222
By reason of his absence there is nothing   870
Iaq. And you will not be answer'd with reason, | I must dye.   1076
Cor. For not being at Court? your reason.   1237
Orl. Neither rime nor reason can expresse how much.   1579
*and the reason why they are not so punish'd and cured, is   1582
Ros. A Traueller: by my faith you haue great rea- | son   1936
*but they ask'd one another the reason: no sooner knew   2444
*the reason, but they sought the remedie: and in these   2445
That reason, wonder may diminish   2713
REASONABLE = *1
*reasonable match. If thou bee'st not damn'd for this, the   1280
REASONS = 1*1
*vpon curs, throw some of them at me; come lame mee | with reasons.   464
*one should be lam'd with reasons, and the other mad | without any.   467
REBELLIOUS = 1
For in my youth I neuer did apply | Hot, and rebellious liquors in my
bloud,   752
RECEIUE = 3
If they will patiently receiue my medicine.   1035
You yours *Orlando*, to receiue his daughter: 2596
Good Duke receiue thy daughter,   2686
RECKONING = *1
*it strikes a man more dead then a great rec- | koning   1625
RECKONINGS = *1
*confirmer of false reckonings, he attends here in the for- | rest on the
Duke your father.   1740
RECOMPENCE = 2
Yet fortune cannot recompence me better   779
But doe not looke for further recompence   1871

RECOUERD = 1
Briefe, I recouer'd him, bound vp his wound,   2304
RECOUERS = 1
Oli. Looke, he recouers.   2314
RECOUNT = 1
Orl. I prethee recount some of them.   1543
RECOUNTMENTS = 1
Teares our recountments had most kindely bath'd,   2294
RED = 3
And the red glowe of scorne and prowd disdaine,   1762
A little riper, and more lustie red   1895
Betwixt the constant red, and mingled Damaske.   1897
REDNESSE = 1
There was a pretty rednesse in his lip,   1894
REFERENCE = 1
Cel. Something that hath a reference to my state: | No longer *Celia*, but
Aliena.   592
REFUSE = 2
Ros. But if you do refuse to marrie me,   2588
If she refuse me, and from hence I go   2600
REFUSING = 1
Or else refusing me to wed this shepheard: 2598
REIGNES = *1
*Fortune reignes in gifts of the world, not in the | lineaments of Nature.   210
REIOYCE = 1
Ros. Well, I will forget the condition of my estate, | to reioyce in
yours.   184
RELEEUE = 1
My fortunes were more able to releeue her.   862
RELIEFE = 1
Sil. Where euer sorrow is, reliefe would be: 1859
RELIGION = *1
Orl. With no lesse religion, then if thou wert indeed | my *Rosalind*: so
adieu.   2103
RELIGIOUS = 2*1
*religious Vnckle of mine taught me to speake, who was   1532
Where, meeting with an old Religious man,   2736
The Duke hath put on a Religious life,   2758
RELIGIOUSLIE = *1
*Nun of winters sisterhood kisses not more religiouslie,   1726
RELLISH = *1
*him, and rellish it with good obseruance. I found him   1428
REMAINDER = 1
Which is as drie as the remainder bisket   1012
REMAINES = 1*2
*cleare all: nothing remaines, but that I kindle the boy | thither, which
now Ile goe about. *Exit*.   167
*heere? Did he aske for me? Where remaines he? How   1416
Scratch thee but with a pin, and there remaines   1792
REMEDIE = 1*1
Orl. I am he that is so Loue-shak'd, I pray you tel | me your remedie.   1552
*the reason, but they sought the remedie: and in these   2445
REMEDY = 1
*I will no longer endure it, though yet I know no wise | remedy how to
auoid it.   26
REMEMBER = 2*7
Orlando. | *As I remember *Adam*, it was vpon this fashion   3

REMEMBER *cont*.
 *learne mee how to remember any extraordinary plea-|sure.   175
 Clo. And I mine: I remember when I was in loue, I   828
 *comming a night to *Iane Smile*, and I remember the kis-|sing   830
 *chopt hands had milk'd; and I remember the wooing   832
 that I was an Irish Rat, which I can hardly remember.   1374
 Orl. Can you remember any of the principall euils,   1538
 Clo. Why, thou saist well. I do now remember a say-|ing: 2372
 Du Sen. I do remember in this shepheard boy,   2602
REMEMBRANCE = 1
 Adam. Sweet Masters bee patient, for your Fathers | remembrance, be
 at accord.   63
REMEMBRED = 2
 as freind remembred not. | *Heigh ho, sing*, &*c*.   1167
 And now I am remembred, scorn'd at me: 1905
REMEMBREST = 1
 If thou remembrest not the slightest folly,   816
REMOOUD = *1
 *meete; but Mountaines may bee remoou'd with Earth-|quakes, and so
 encounter.   1381
REMORSE = 1
 It was your pleasure, and your owne remorse,   531
REMOUE = 1
 Ros. O come, let vs remoue,   1765
REMOUED = 1*1
 Orl. Your accent is something finer, then you could | purchase in so
 remoued a dwelling.   1529
 Clo. Vpon a lye, seuen times remoued: (beare your   2644
RENDER = 1*1
 *perforce, I will render thee againe in affection: by   189
 And he did render him the most vnnaturall | That liu'd amongst men.   2273
RENDERS = *1
 *me thinkes I haue giuen him a penie, and he renders me   915
RENOWNE = 1
 Honor, high honor and renowne   2720
REPLY = *2
 *this is called, the reply churlish. If againe it was not well   2652
 *Quip-modest: the third, the reply Churlish: the fourth,   2667
REPORT = 1*1
 *at schoole, and report speakes goldenly of his profit: 9
 Go with me, if you like vpon report,   884
REPORTS = 1
 Whom he reports to be a great Magitian.   2609
REPROOFE = *2
 *reproofe valiant. If againe, it was not well cut, he wold   2654
 *the Reproofe valiant: the fift, the Counterchecke quar-|relsome: 2668
REPUTATION = 1*1
 Ros. Do yong Sir, your reputation shall not therefore   343
 Seeking the bubble Reputation | Euen in the Canons mouth: And then,
 the Iustice   1131
REQUEST = 1
 Amy. More at your request, then to please my selfe.   911
REQUITE = *1
 *thou shalt finde I will most kindly requite: I had my   136
RESCUD = 1
 Ros. Was't you he rescu'd?   2286

RESIDUE = 1
That lou'd your Father, the residue of your fortune,   1174
RESOLUE = *1
*Cel. It is as easie to count Atomies as to resolue the   1426
RESOLUTE = *1
*but he is resolute. Ile tell thee Charles, it is the stubbor-|nest   139
RESORTED = 1
Men of great worth resorted to this forrest,   2731
RESPECT = 1*7
Orl. I attend them with all respect and dutie.   330
*Clow. Truely Shepheard, in respect of it selfe, it is a   1213
*good life; but in respect that it is a shepheards life, it is   1214
*naught. In respect that it is solitary, I like it verie well: 1215
*but in respect that it is priuate, it is a very vild life. Now   1216
*in respect it is in the fields, it pleaseth mee well: but in   1217
*respect it is not in the Court, it is tedious. As it is a spare   1218
*Clo. Most shallow man: Thou wormes meate in re-|spect   1262
REST = 5*2
Orl. I rest much bounden to you: fare you well.   454
Bring vs where we may rest our selues, and feed: 857
Cor. You haue too Courtly a wit, for me, Ile rest.   1267
*Clo. Wilt thou rest damn'd? God helpe thee shallow   1268
Then sing him home, the rest shall beare this burthen;   2139
Aud. Do good William. | Will. God rest you merry sir. Exit   2400
*in heere sir, amongst the rest of the Country copulatiues   2632
RESTORD = 1
And all their Lands restor'd to him againe   2740
RETORT = *2
*was: this is call'd the retort courteous. If I sent him   2648
*The first, the Retort courteous: the second, the   2666
RETREIT = *1
*Clo. Come Shepheard, let vs make an honorable re-|treit,   1358
RETURNE = 2
And we will nothing waste till you returne.   1112
He left a promise to returne againe   2250
RETURNED = 1
Shal share the good of our returned fortune,   2751
REUELRIE = 1
And fall into our Rusticke Reuelrie: 2754
REUENGE = 2
Of my reuenge, thou present: but looke to it,   1184
But kindnesse, nobler euer then reuenge,   2280
REUENNEW = *2
*in beard, is a yonger brothers reuennew) then your   1562
*good: for my fathers house, and all the reuennew, that   2418
REUENUES = *1
*him, whose lands and reuenues enrich the new Duke,   104
REUERENCE = 1
before me is neerer to his reuerence. | Oli. What Boy.   53
REWARD = *1
*Adam. Is old dogge my reward: most true, I haue   82
RHETORICKE = *1
*it is a figure in Rhetoricke, that drink being powr'd out   2383
RHYME see rime
RHYMES see rimes
RIBBES = *2
*him, and broke three of his ribbes, that there is little   290

RIBBES *cont*.
　*first time that euer I heard breaking of ribbes was sport | for Ladies.　300
RIB-BREAKING = 1
　rib-breaking? Shall we see this wrastling Cosin?　305
RICH = 2*2
　Ros. With a Priest that lacks Latine, and a rich man　1508
　nothing, is to haue rich eyes and poore hands.　1939
　Art rich? | *Will*. 'Faith sir, so, so.　2366
　*that that no man else will: rich honestie dwels like a mi-|ser　2636
RIDERS = *1
　*they are taught their mannage, and to that end Riders　15
RIDICULOUS = 1*1
　How many actions most ridiculous,　812
　*at the Court, are as ridiculous in the Countrey, as　1244
RIE = 1
　Betweene the acres of the Rie,　2557
RIGHT = 7*4
　'Tis right quoth he, thus miserie doth part　659
　And buy it with your Gold right sodainly. *Exeunt*.　887
　My tongue hath wrong'd him: if it do him right,　1058
　Thou art right welcome, as thy masters is:　1176
　*and suppers, and sleeping hours excepted: it is the right | Butter-
　womens ranke to Market.　1295
　*for you'l be rotten ere you bee halfe ripe, and that's | the right vertue
　of the Medler.　1317
　Orl. Not so: but I answer you right painted cloath,　1466
　*right: Many a man has good Hornes, and knows no end　1662
　Orl. I would not haue my right *Rosalind* of this mind,　2020
　Left on your right hand, brings you to the place:　2230
　Ros. So I doe: but yfaith, I should haue beene a wo-|man by right.　2330
RIGHTEOUSLY = *1
　*of thy loue to me were so righteously temper'd, as mine | is to thee.　182
RIGHTLY = 1
　Iaq. Sir, by your patience: if I heard you rightly,　2757
RIGHTS = *1
　Du Se. Proceed, proceed: wee'l begin these rights,　2774
RIME = *2
　Clo. Ile rime you so, eight yeares together; dinners,　1294
　Orl. Neither rime nor reason can expresse how much.　1579
RIMES = *1
　Ros. But are you so much in loue, as your rimes speak?　1578
RINDE = 1
　Sweetest nut, *hath sowrest rinde*, | *such a nut is Rosalinde*.　1307
RINGS = *1
　*with goldsmiths wiues, & cond the(m) out of rings　1465
RIPE = 4*1
　And so from houre to houre, we ripe, and ripe,　999
　*for you'l be rotten ere you bee halfe ripe, and that's | the right vertue
　of the Medler.　1317
　Of femall fauour, and bestowes himselfe | Like a ripe sister: the woman
　low　2236
　Will. Fiue and twentie Sir. | *Clo*. A ripe age: Is thy name *William*?　2360
RIPER = 1
　A little riper, and more lustie red　1895
ROADE *see* rode
ROASTED = *1
　Clo. Truly thou art damn'd, like an ill roasted Egge, | all on one side.　1235

ROBIN = *1
*like the old *Robin Hood* of *England*: they say many yong   117
ROBS = 1
Thou art a foole, she robs thee of thy name,   541
RODE = 1
A theeuish liuing on the common rode?   737
ROLAND = 1*1
Orl. *Orlando* my Liege, the yongest sonne of Sir *Ro-|land de Boys*.   384
Ros. My Father lou'd Sir *Roland* as his soule,   398
ROLANDS = 1
Orl. I am more proud to be Sir *Rolands* sonne,   395
ROMANE = *1
Iaq. Let's present him to the Duke like a Romane   2129
ROOFE = 1
Come not within these doores: within this roofe   721
ROOME = *1
*in a little roome: truly, I would the Gods hadde | made thee poeticall.   1626
ROOTE = 1
Vnder an oake, whose anticke roote peepes out   638
ROS = 1
To make these doubts all euen. *Exit Ros. and Celia.*   2601
ROS = 93*106
ROSA = *2
ROSALIND see also Ros., Rosa. = 28*11
Oli. Can you tell if *Rosalind* the Dukes daughter bee | banished with
her Father?   106
Enter Rosalind, and Cellia.   170
Cel. I pray thee *Rosalind*, sweet my Coz, be merry.   171
O *Rosalind*, these Trees shall be my Bookes,   1205
Enter Rosalind.   1285
Ros. I would cure you, if you would but call me *Rosa-|lind*,   1603
Ros. Nay, you must call mee *Rosalind*: Come sister, | will you go?
Exeunt.   1611
Enter Rosalind & Celia.   1709
Enter Rosalind, Celia, and Corin.   1778
Enter Rosalind, and Celia, and Iaques.   1916
Orl. Good day, and happinesse, deere *Rosalind*.   1945
Orl. My faire *Rosalind*, I come within an houre of my | promise.   1957
Orl. Pardon me deere *Rosalind*.   1964
Orl. Vertue is no horne-maker: and my *Rosalind* is | vertuous.   1976
Ros. And I am your *Rosalind*.   1978
Cel. It pleases him to call you so: but he hath a *Rosa-|lind* of a better
leere then you.   1979
Am not I your *Rosalind*?   2001
Orl. I would not haue my right *Rosalind* of this mind,   2020
*now I will be your *Rosalind* in a more comming-on dis-|position: 2023
Orl. Then loue me *Rosalind*.   2025
Cel. Goe too: wil you *Orlando*, haue to wife this *Ro-|salind*? | *Orl*. I
will.   2039
Ros. Then you must say, I take thee *Rosalind* for | wife.   2044
Orl. I take thee *Rosalind* for wife.   2046
Orl. But will my *Rosalind* doe so?   2066
Orl. I, sweet *Rosalind*.   2093
Orl. With no lesse religion, then if thou wert indeed | my *Rosalind*: so
adieu.   2103
Enter Rosalind and Celia.   2147
And to that youth hee calls his *Rosalind*,   2242

196

ROSALIND cont.
That he in sport doth call his *Rosalind*. 2310
How you excuse my brother, *Rosalind*. 2335
Enter Rosalind. 2421
*Ros. Why then to morrow, I cannot serue your turne | for *Rosalind*? 2457
*bid your friends: for if you will be married to mor-|row, you shall: and
to *Rosalind* if you will. 2480
Orl. And I for *Rosalind*. | *Ros*. And I for no woman. 2494
Orl. And I for *Rosalind*. | *Ros*. And I for no woman. 2499
Orl. And so am I for *Rosalind*. | *Ros*. And so am I for no woman. 2508
*Rosalind meet, as you loue *Phebe* meet, and as I loue no 2524
Enter Hymen, Rosalind, and Celia. | *Still Musicke*. 2681
Orl. If there be truth in sight, you are my *Rosalind*. 2694
ROSALIND = 3*1
ROSALINDA = 1
Will I Rosalinda write, | teaching all that reade, to know 1335
ROSALINDE = 16*5
Ros. From the east to westerne Inde, | no iewel is like Rosalinde, 1286
Hir worth being mounted on the winde, | through all the world beares
Rosalinde. 1288
All the pictures fairest Linde, | are but blacke to Rosalinde: 1290
Let no face bee kept in mind, | but the faire of Rosalinde. 1292
If a Hart doe lacke a Hinde, | Let him seeke out Rosalinde: 1299
If the Cat will after kinde, | so be sure will Rosalinde: 1301
Wintred garments must be linde, | so must slender Rosalinde: 1303
They that reap must sheafe and binde, | then to cart with Rosalinde. 1305
Sweetest nut, hath sowrest rinde, | such a nut is Rosalinde. 1307
He that sweetest rose will finde, | must finde Loues pricke, & Rosalinde. 1309
Thus Rosalinde *of manie parts, | by Heauenly Synode was deuis'd,* 1347
Iaq. Rosalinde is your loues name? Orl. Yes, Iust. 1458
*our yong plants with caruing *Rosalinde* on their 1546
*brambles; all (forsooth) defying the name of *Rosalinde*. 1548
*Orl. For these two houres *Rosalinde*, I wil leaue thee. 2084
*and the most vnworthy of her you call *Rosalinde*, that 2099
And cride in fainting vpon *Rosalinde*. 2303
Heere comes my *Rosalinde*. 2426
*his Art, and yet not damnable. If you do loue *Rosalinde* 2470
Enter Rosalinde, Siluius, & Phebe. 2579
You say, if I bring in your *Rosalinde*, 2581
ROSALINE = 5*1
But heauenly *Rosaline. Exit* 457
Enter Celia and Rosaline. 459
*Cel. Why Cosen, why *Rosaline: Cupid* haue mercie, 460
Cel. O my poore *Rosaline*, whether wilt thou goe? 552
Cel. No, hath not? *Rosaline* lacks then the loue 560
Enter Rosaline for Ganimed, Celia for Aliena, and | Clowne, alias
Touchstone. 782
ROSE = 2*2
*turne monster: therefore my sweet *Rose*, my deare *Rose*, | be merry. 191
Rose at an instant, learn'd, plaid, eate together, 535
He that sweetest rose will finde, | must finde Loues pricke, & Rosalinde. 1309
ROT = 2
And then from houre to houre, we rot, and rot, 1000
ROTTEN = 1*1
But poore old man, thou prun'st a rotten tree, 767
*for you'l be rotten ere you bee halfe ripe, and that's | the right vertue
of the Medler. 1317

ROUGH = 2
My Fathers rough and enuious disposition 405
But Winter and rough Weather. 897
ROULANDS = 1
*you should fall into so strong a liking with old Sir | *Roulands* yongest
sonne? 485
ROUND = 3
Haue their round hanches goard. 631
Almost to bursting, and the big round teares 645
In faire round belly, with good Capon lin'd, 1133
ROUNDLY = *1
*1.*Pa.* Shal we clap into't roundly, without hauking, 2541
ROWLAND = 2*1
Rowland de Boys, he was my father, and he is thrice a vil- | laine 58
Of old Sir *Rowland*; why, what make you here? 707
I am the second sonne of old *Sir Rowland*, 2728
ROWLANDS = *2
Duke Sen. If that you were the good Sir *Rowlands* son, 1169
*was old Sir *Rowlands* will I estate vpon you, and heere | liue and die a
Shepherd. 2419
ROYALL = 1
The royall disposition of that beast | To prey on nothing, that doth
seeme as dead: 2268
ROYNISH = *1
*2.*Lor.* My Lord, the roynish Clown, at whom so oft, 688
RUDE = 3
Or else a rude despiser of good manners, 1068
although thy breath be rude. 1159
Could not drop forth such giant rude inuention, 2183
RUDIMENTS = 1
And hath bin tutor'd in the rudiments 2607
RUMINATION = *1
*which by often rumination, wraps me in a most humo- | rous sadnesse. 1934
RUN = 3*1
That euer loue did make thee run into, | Thou hast not lou'd. 817
Run, run *Orlando*, carue on euery Tree, 1209
*with thee in faction, I will ore-run thee with policie: I 2397
RUNAWAIES = 1
To bring againe these foolish runawaies. *Exeunt.* 701
RUNNE = *2
*shall runne into, in that it is a thing of his owne search, | and
altogether against my will. 133
*runne into strange capers; but as all is mortall in 836
RUNNING = *1
*Findes tongues in trees, bookes in the running brookes, 622
RUNS = 3
Some, how briefe the Life of man | runs his erring pilgrimage, 1327
*girle goes before the Priest, and certainely a Womans | thought runs
before her actions. 2049
Cel. Or rather bottomlesse, that as fast as you poure | affection in, it
runs out. 2115
RUSH = 1
Some scarre of it: Leane vpon a rush 1793
RUSHES = 1
*he taught me how to know a man in loue: in which cage | of rushes, I
am sure you art not prisoner. 1555

RUSTICALLY = *1
*for my part, he keepes me rustically at home, or (to speak   10
RUSTICKE = 1
And fall into our Rusticke Reuelrie: 2754
RYE *see* rie
SACRED = 1
Of drops, that sacred pity hath engendred: 1100
SAD = 3*2
Attalanta's *better part*, | *sad* Lucrecia's *Modestie*.   1345
Iaq. Why, 'tis good to be sad and say nothing.   1924
*to be sad: I feare you haue sold your owne Lands,   1937
Ros. And your experience makes you sad: I had ra- | ther   1942
make me sad, and to trauaile for it too.   1944
SADDE = *1
Ros. Nay, but the diuell take mocking: speake sadde | brow, and true
maid.   1408
SADNESSE = 1*1
*there begins my sadnesse: My brother *Iaques* he keepes   8
*which by often rumination, wraps me in a most humo- | rous sadnesse.   1934
SAFEST = 2
Duk. Mistris, dispatch you with your safest haste,   498
Deuise the fittest time, and safest way   600
SAFETIE = *1
*pray you for your owne sake to embrace your own safe- | tie,   341
SAFETY = *1
*then with safety of a pure blush, thou maist in ho- | nor come off
againe.   197
SAID = 4*6
Cel. Well said, that was laid on with a trowell.   271
Du Sen. But what said *Iaques*? | Did he not moralize this spectacle?   651
*cods, and giuing her them againe, said with weeping   834
Wel said, thou look'st cheerely,   964
Clo. You haue said: but whether wisely or no, let the | Forrest iudge.   1319
*sweare in Poetrie, may be said as Louers, they do feigne.   1632
*It is said, many a man knowes no end of his goods;   1661
He said mine eyes were black, and my haire blacke,   1904
*of loue, it may be said of him that *Cupid* hath clapt   1962
*said his beard was not cut well, hee was in the minde it   2647
SAIDE = *2
*thought but of an If; as if you saide so, then I saide so: 2674
SAIES = 1*1
*that saies such a father begot villaines: wert thou   59
Shee saies I am not faire, that I lacke manners,   2163
SAIEST = 1*1
Cel. By my troth thou saiest true: For, since the little   253
Orl. What saiest thou?   2029
SAIST = 1*2
*Crownes, and as thou saist, charged my bro- | ther   6
Sil. Sweet *Phebe*. | *Phe*. Hah: what saist thou *Siluius*?   1855
Clo. Why, thou saist well. I do now remember a say- | ing: 2372
SAKE = 6*2
*pray you for your owne sake to embrace your own safe- | tie,   341
And pittie her, for her good Fathers sake;   449
Ros. No faith, hate him not for my sake.   492
Duk. I *Celia*, we staid her for your sake,   528
*teares, weare these for my sake: wee that are true Lo- | uers,   835
And wish for her sake more then for mine owne,   861

SAKE *cont*.

For my sake be comfortable, hold death a while	959
Orl. And so had I: but yet for fashion sake	1450

SALE = 1

Are now on sale, and at our sheep-coat now	869

SALE-WORKE = 1

Of Natures sale-worke? 'ods my little life,	1816

SALUTATION = 1

Clo. Salutation and greeting to you all.	2616

SALUTE = *1

*Court. You told me, you salute not at the Court, but	1246

SAME = *3

*borne, but the same tradition takes not away my bloud,	50
Ros. No, that same wicked Bastard of *Venus*, that was	2117
Cel. O I haue heard him speake of that same brother,	2272

SANCTIFIED = 1

Are sanctified and holy traitors to you:	716

SANCTITIE = 1

Ros. And his kissing is as ful of sanctitie, | As the touch of holy bread.	1723

SANS = 5

And I did laugh, sans intermission | An houre by his diall. Oh noble foole,	1005
Sans teeth, sans eyes, sans taste, sans euery thing.	1145

SAT = 2

Or if thou hast not sat as I doe now,	819
And sat at good mens feasts, and wip'd our eies	1099

SATCHELL = 1

Then, the whining Schoole-boy with his Satchell	1124

SATE = 1

If euer sate at any good mans feast:	1092

SATERDAIES = 1

Ros. Yes faith will I, fridaies and saterdaies, and all.	2026

SATISFID = *1

*if euer I satisfi'd man, and you shall bee married to mor-|row.	2521

SATISFIE = *1

*and Ile be married to morrow: I will satisfie you,	2520

SAUAGE = 2

If this vncouth Forrest yeeld any thing sauage,	956
I thought that all things had bin sauage heere,	1084

SAUCE = 1

As she answeres thee with frowning lookes, ile sauce	1841

SAUD = 1

His youthfull hose well sau'd, a world too wide,	1139

SAUE = 1

Ros. God saue you brother. | *Ol*. And you faire sister.	2427

SAUED = 1

The thriftie hire I saued vnder your Father,	743

SAUES = 1

1 *Lord*. He saues my labor by his owne approach.	981

SAW = 6*4

euer he saw those Pancakes, or that Mustard.	245
*strength, if you saw your selfe with your eies, or knew	338
Duk. Can it be possible that no man saw them?	681
Saw her a bed, and in the morning early,	686
Cor. That yong Swaine that you saw heere but ere-|while,	874
Who you saw sitting by me on the Turph,	1756
Phe. Dead Shepheard, now I find thy saw of might,	1853

SAW *cont*.

I saw her hand, she has a leatherne hand,	2173
*Rammes, and *Cesars* Thrasonicall bragge of I came, saw,	2440
Orl. My Lord, the first time that I euer saw him,	2604

SAWCE = *1

*honestie coupled to beautie, is to haue Honie a sawce to | Sugar.	1640

SAWCIE = *1

Ros. I wil speake to him like a sawcie Lacky, and vn-|der	1487

SAWES = 1

Full of wise sawes, and moderne instances,	1135

SAWST = *3

*saw'st good manners: if thou neuer saw'st good maners,	1239
*hose? What did he when thou saw'st him? What sayde	1414

SAY = 26*17

Oli. Let me goe I say. | *Orl*. I will not till I please: you shall heare mee: my	65
Oli. Where will the old Duke liue? | *Cha*. They say hee is already in the Forrest of *Arden*,	114
*like the old *Robin Hood* of *England*: they say many yong	117
Orl. Can I not say, I thanke you? My better parts	415
Say what thou canst, Ile goe along with thee.	569
Euen till I shrinke with cold, I smile, and say	615
Ros. Peace I say; good euen to your friend.	853
When that I say the City woman beares	1049
Who can come in, and say that I meane her,	1051
And know some nourture: But forbeare, I say,	1073
*of a man? Shallow, shallow: A better instance I say: | Come.	1254
*say I and no, to these particulars, is more then to answer | in a Catechisme.	1421
Ros. Do you not know I am a woman, when I thinke, | I must speake: sweet, say on.	1443
gone I say, I wil not to wedding with thee.	1705
Bring vs to this sight, and you shall say	1767
Say that you loue me not, but say not so	1772
Lye not, to say mine eyes are murtherers:	1790
Ros They say you are a melancholly fellow.	1919
Iaq. Why, 'tis good to be sad and say nothing.	1924
*would you say to me now, and I were your verie, verie | *Rosalind*?	1983
Orl. I take some ioy to say you are, because I would | be talking of her.	2002
Ros. Well, in her person, I say I will not haue you.	2004
*marrie vs: giue me your hand *Orlando*: What doe you | say sister?	2034
Orl. Pray thee marrie vs. | *Cel*. I cannot say the words.	2036
Ros. Then you must say, I take thee *Rosalind* for | wife.	2044
Ros. Say a day, without the euer: no, no *Orlando*, men	2055
Orl. A man that had a wife with such a wit, he might | say, wit whether wil't?	2074
Rosa. Marry to say, she came to seeke you there: you	2079
Ros. How say you now, is it not past two a clock? | And heere much *Orlando*.	2148
I say she neuer did inuent this letter,	2177
*made thee a tame snake) and say this to her; That if she	2219
Cel. It is no boast, being ask'd, to say we are.	2240
*nor sodaine consenting: but say with mee, I loue	2415
Aliena: say with her, that she loues mee; consent with	2416
*of my knowledge: insomuch (I say) I know you are: nei-|ther	2464
*I say I am a Magitian: Therefore put you in your best a-|ray,	2479

SAY *cont*.
You say, if I bring in your *Rosalinde*,	2581
Ros. And you say you wil haue her, when I bring hir?	2584
Ros. You say, you'l marrie me, if I be willing.	2586
Ros. You say that you'l haue *Phebe* if she will.	2591
*say, I lie: this is call'd the counter-checke quarrelsome:	2655
Iaq. And how oft did you say his beard was not well | cut?	2657

SAYDE = *1
*hose? What did he when thou saw'st him? What sayde	1414

SAYES = 3
Sayes, very wisely, it is ten a clocke:	995
And sayes, if Ladies be but yong, and faire,	1010
That sayes his brauerie is not on my cost,	1054

SAYING = 1*3
*throat, till this other had puld out thy tongue for saying	61
Awd. Faith the Priest was good enough, for all the | olde gentlemans saying.	2343
Clo. Why, thou saist well. I do now remember a say-|ing:	2372
*or spitting, or saying we are hoarse, which are the onely | prologues to a bad voice.	2542

SAYINGS = 1
Tonges Ile hang on euerie tree, | *that shall ciuill sayings shoe*.	1325

SCAPE = 1
*diuell himselfe will haue no shepherds, I cannot see else | how thou shouldst scape.	1281

SCARCE = 1*2
Cel. 'Tis true, for those that she makes faire, she scarce	206
I scarce can speake to thanke you for my selfe.	1151
*countenance you are; or I will scarce thinke you haue	1952

SCARFE = 1
thee weare thy heart in a scarfe. | *Orl*. It is my arme.	2430

SCARRE = 1
Some scarre of it: Leane vpon a rush	1793

SCATTRED = 1
A scattred smile, and that Ile liue vpon.	1878

SCEANE = 1
Presents more wofull Pageants then the Sceane | Wherein we play in.	1116

SCENA *l*.458 679 702 781 888 949 971 1179 1199 1769 1915 2125 2339 2572 = 14

SCENE = 1
And whistles in his sound. Last Scene of all,	1142

SCHOLLERS = *1
Iaq. I haue neither the Schollers melancholy, which	1926

SCHOOLD = *1
*gentle, neuer school'd, and yet learned, full of noble	162

SCHOOLE = 1*1
*at schoole, and report speakes goldenly of his profit:	9
Vnwillingly to schoole. And then the Louer,	1126

SCHOOLE-BOY = 1
Then, the whining Schoole-boy with his Satchell	1124

SCOENA *l*.1 169 604 1613 1708 2146 2407 2530 = 8

SCOFFER = 1
Foule is most foule, being foule to be a scoffer.	1835

SCORND = 1
And now I am remembred, scorn'd at me:	1905

SCORNE = 6
Cor. That is the way to make her scorne you still.	804

SCORNE *cont*.
And the red glowe of scorne and prowd disdaine,	1762
Sil. Sweet *Phebe* doe not scorne me, do not *Phebe*	1771
Take thou no scorne to weare the horne,	2140
Is not a thing to laugh to scorne. Exeunt.	2145
If the scorne of your bright eine	2199

SCRATCH = 1
Scratch thee but with a pin, and there remaines	1792

SCRIP = 1
*though not with bagge and baggage, yet with	scrip and scrippage. *Exit.*	1359

SCRIPPAGE = 1
*though not with bagge and baggage, yet with	scrip and scrippage. *Exit.*	1359

SEA = 1*1
Doth it not flow as hugely as the Sea,	1046
*my disposition? One inch of delay more, is a South-sea	1392

SEALE = 1
And by him seale vp thy minde,	2207

SEARCH = 1*1
*shall runne into, in that it is a thing of his owne search,	and altogether against my will.	133
And let not search and inquisition quaile,	700

SEARCHING = *1
Ros. Alas poore Shepheard searching of they would,	826

SEASONS = 1
The seasons difference, as the Icie phange	612

SEAUENTEENE = 1
At seauenteene yeeres, many their fortunes seeke	777

SEAUENTH = *1
*the sixt, the Lye with circumstance: the sea-|uenth,	2669

SEAUENTIE = 1
From seauentie yeeres, till now almost fourescore	775

SECOND = 3*3
*hope of life in him: So he seru'd the second, and so the	291
*him to a second, that haue so mightilie perswaded him	from a first.	367
Is second childishnesse, and meere obliuion,	1144
*The first, the Retort courteous: the second, the	2666
Enter Second Brother.	2726
I am the second sonne of old *Sir Rowland,*	2728

SECONDED = *1
*a mans good wit seconded with the forward childe, vn-|derstanding:	1624

SECRET = *1
*emulator of euery mans good parts, a secret & villanous	141

SECRETLY = 1*1
*with a matter: I am giuen sir secretly to vnderstand, that	123
Hisperia the Princesse Gentlewoman	Confesses that she secretly ore-heard	690

SECUNDA *l.*169 679 1199 2125 2407 = 5
SECUNDUS *l.*604 = 1
SEE = 21*17
*I hope I shall see an end of him; for my soule (yet	160
Cel. Heerein I see thou lou'st mee not with the full	177
let me see, what thinke you of falling in Loue?	194
*your Ladiships, you may see the end, for the best is yet	278
Ros. But is there any else longs to see this broken	303
rib-breaking? Shall we see this wrastling Cosin?	305

SEE *cont*.

Cel. Yonder sure they are comming. Let vs now stay | and see it.	309
Du. How now daughter, and Cousin: | Are you crept hither to see the wrastling?	318
*bee entreated. Speake to him Ladies, see if you can | mooue him.	324
1 *Lo*. I cannot heare of any that did see her,	684
That you will feed on: but what is, come see,	871
Heere shall he see no enemie,	896
Heere shall he see. &c.	932
Heere shall he see, grosse fooles as he,	941
Thus we may see (quoth he) how the world wagges:	996
There then, how then, what then, let me see wherein	1057
Du. Not see him since? Sir, sir, that cannot be:	1181
Shall see thy vertue witnest euery where.	1208
*and the greatest of my pride, is to see my Ewes graze, & | my Lambes sucke.	1273
*diuell himselfe will haue no shepherds, I cannot see else | how thou shouldst scape.	1281
*parted he with thee? And when shalt thou see him a- | gaine? Answer me in one word.	1417
Ros. Though it be pittie to see such a sight, it well | becomes the ground.	1436
Orl. He is drown'd in the brooke, looke but in, and | you shall see him.	1479
Iaq. There I shal see mine owne figure.	1481
Ros. As the Conie that you see dwell where shee is | kindled.	1527
Iaq. I would faine see this meeting.	1655
*companie, I am verie glad to see you, euen a toy in hand	1683
Cor. If you will see a pageant truely plaid	1760
As by my faith, I see no more in you	1811
I see no more in you then in the ordinary	1815
And be not proud, though all the world could see,	1850
*to see other mens; then to haue seene much, and to haue	1938
*Well, goe your way to her; (for I see Loue hath	2218
Clo. It is meat and drinke to me to see a Clowne, by	2351
Ros. Oh my deere *Orlando*, how it greeues me to see	2429
Iaq. To see no pastime, I: what you would haue,	2772
Ros. It is not the fashion to see the Ladie the Epi- | logue:	2776
*but it is no more vnhandsome, then to see the	2777
SEEING = 1 *1	
Seeing *Orlando*, it vnlink'd it selfe,	2262
*should like her? that, but seeing, you should loue her?	2410
SEEKE = 10 *1	
No, let my Father seeke another heire:	563
And doe not seeke to take your change vpon you,	566
Ros. Why, whether shall we goe? | *Cel*. To seeke my Vncle in the Forrest of *Arden*.	570
At seauenteene yeeres, many their fortunes seeke	777
Amy. And Ile go seeke the Duke,	947
Go seeke him, tell him I would speake with him.	979
I should not seeke an absent argument	1183
Seeke him with Candle: bring him dead, or liuing	1186
To seeke a liuing in our Territorie.	1188
If a Hart doe lacke a Hinde, | *Let him seeke out Rosalinde:*	1299
Rosa. Marry to say, she came to seeke you there: you	2079
SEEKES = *1	
Cor. Our Master and Mistresse seekes you: come a- | way, away.	2403

204

SEEKING = 2*1
  Seeking the food he eates,   929
  Seeking the bubble Reputation | Euen in the Canons mouth: And then,
  the Iustice   1131
  Iaq. By my troth, I was seeking for a Foole, when I | found you.   1477
SEEM = *1
  *And thou wilt show more bright, & seem more vertuous   542
SEEME = 4
  Know you not Master, to seeme kinde of men,   713
  Seeme senselesse of the bob. If not,   1029
  The royall disposition of that beast | To prey on nothing, that doth
  seeme as dead: 2268
  To seeme despightfull and vngentle to you: 2487
SEEMES = 1*2
  *nature gaue mee, his countenance seemes to take from   20
  that it seemes the length of seuen yeare.   1506
  *some good counsel, for he seemes to haue the Quotidian | of Loue
  vpon him.   1550
SEEMING = *3
  *one another, as halfepence are, euerie one fault seeming   1541
  *as louing your selfe, then seeming the Lo- |uer of any other.   1567
  *bodie more seeming *Audry*) as thus sir: I did dislike the   2645
SEEMST = 1
  That in ciuility thou seem'st so emptie?   1069
SEENE = 2*3
  *your yeares: you haue seene cruell proofe of this mans   337
  *Du Sen. True is it, that we haue seene better dayes,   1097
  Thy tooth is not so keene, because thou art not seene,   1158
  *to see other mens; then to haue seene much, and to haue   1938
  This seene, *Orlando* did approach the man,   2270
SEES = 1
  And out of you she sees her selfe more proper   1828
SEEST = 1
  Du Sen. Thou seest, we are not all alone vnhappie: 1114
SEIZE = 1
  Worth seizure, do we seize into our hands,   1190
SEIZURE = 1
  Worth seizure, do we seize into our hands,   1190
SELFE = 26*9
  so, thou hast raild on thy selfe.   62
  *selfe notice of my Brothers purpose heerein, and haue by   137
  *strength, if you saw your selfe with your eies, or knew   338
  *your selfe with your iudgment, the feare of your aduen- |ture   339
  Ros. O they take the part of a better wrastler then | my selfe.   480
  If with my selfe I hold intelligence,   507
  They are as innocent as grace it selfe;   515
  Duk. You are a foole: you Neice prouide your selfe,   548
  To beare your griefes your selfe, and leaue me out: 567
  Cel. Ile put my selfe in poore and meane attire,   575
  To day my Lord of *Amiens*, and my selfe,   636
  *selfe coragious to petty-coate; therefore courage, good | *Aliena*.   790
  Amy. More at your request, then to please my selfe.   911
  Liue a little, comfort a little, cheere thy selfe a little.   955
  For thou thy selfe hast bene a Libertine,   1039
  As sensuall as the brutish sting it selfe,   1040
  I scarce can speake to thanke you for my selfe.   1151
  Clow. Truely Shepheard, in respect of it selfe, it is a   1213

SELFE *cont*.
*This is the verie false gallop of Verses, why doe you in- | fect your selfe
with them? 1311
I had as liefe haue beene my selfe alone. 1449
Orl. I wil chide no breather in the world but my selfe 1472
*as louing your selfe, then seeming the Lo- | uer of any other. 1567
And out of you she sees her selfe more proper 1828
But Mistris, know your selfe, downe on your knees 1830
her childe her selfe, for she will breed it like a foole. 2083
Ros. Patience her selfe would startle at this letter, 2161
But at this howre, the house doth keepe it selfe, | There's none within. 2231
And marke what obiect did present it selfe 2254
A greene and guilded snake had wreath'd it selfe, 2259
Seeing *Orlando*, it vnlink'd it selfe, 2262
*little measure draw a beleefe from you, to do your selfe 2466
You'l giue your selfe to this most faithfull Shepheard. 2589
Ros. To you I giue my selfe, for I am yours. 2691
To you I giue my selfe, for I am yours. 2692
A land it selfe at large, a potent Dukedome. 2746
SELL = 1
Sell when you can, you are not for all markets: 1833
SELUES = 2
Bring vs where we may rest our selues, and feed: 857
Feede your selues with questioning: 2712
SEMBLANCES = 1
That doe outface it with their semblances. 587
SEN = 1
Enter Duke Sen. & Lord, like Out-lawes. 972
SEN = 1*1
SEND = *3
Duk. Send to his brother, fetch that gallant hither, 697
Ros. Why God will send more, if the man will bee 1403
*word againe, it was not well cut, he wold send me word 2649
SENDS = 1
He sends this bloudy napkin; are you he? 2243
SENIOR see also D Sen., Du Se., Du Sen., Sen., Duk Sen. = 2
Enter Duke Senior: Amyens, and two or three Lords | like Forresters. 605
Enter Duke Senior, Amyens, Iaques, Orlan- | do, Oliuer, Celia. 2573
SENNIGHT = *1
*if the interim be but a sennight, Times pace is so hard, 1505
SENSELESSE = 1
Seeme senselesse of the bob. If not, 1029
SENSUALL = 1
As sensuall as the brutish sting it selfe, 1040
SENT = 3*3
sent in this foole to cut off the argument? 216
*to reason of such goddesses, hath sent this Naturall for 222
Call me not foole, till heauen hath sent me fortune, 992
He sent me hither, stranger as I am 2306
*cut of a certaine Courtiers beard: he sent me word, if I 2646
*was: this is call'd the retort courteous. If I sent him 2648
SENTENCE = 1*1
Cel. Pronounce that sentence then on me my Leige, 546
But vpon the fairest bowes, | or at euerie sentence end; 1333
SENTENTIOUS = *1
Du Se. By my faith, he is very swift, and sententious 2639

SEPTIMA *l*.971 = 1
SEQUESTRED = 1
    To the which place a poore sequestred Stag   640
SERMONS = 1
    Sermons in stones, and good in euery thing.   623
SERUANT = 1
    All this I giue you, let me be your seruant,   750
SERUD = 1*1
    *hope of life in him: So he seru'd the second, and so the   291
    Orl. Nor shalt not, till necessity be seru'd.   1065
SERUE = 1*2
    Their graces serue them but as enemies,   714
    *serue me such another tricke, neuer come in my sight | more.   1955
    Ros. Why then to morrow, I cannot serue your turne | for *Rosalind?*   2457
SERUICE = 6*2
    *lost my teeth in your seruice: God be with my olde ma- | ster,   83
    *in dispight of a fall: but turning these iests out of seruice,   483
    When seruice should in my old limbs lie lame,   745
    Ile doe the seruice of a yonger man   758
    The constant seruice of the antique world,   761
    When seruice sweate for dutie, not for meede: 762
    And hauing that do choake their seruice vp,   765
    Sil. It is to be all made of faith and seruice, | And so am I for *Phebe*.   2496
SERUITUDE = *1
    *is within mee, begins to mutinie against this seruitude.   25
SET = 1*4
    In good set termes, and yet a motley foole.   990
    Du Sen. Welcome: set downe your venerable bur- | then, and let him
    feede.   1147
    *me his Loue, his Mistris: and I set him euerie day   1587
    *Conquerour, and it would doe well to set the Deares   2130
    *to set her before your eyes to morrow, humane as she is, | and without
    any danger.   2475
SETLED = 1
    Weele light vpon some setled low content.   772
SEUEN – 2*3
    His Acts being seuen ages. At first the Infant,   1122
    Ros. I was seuen of the nine daies out of the wonder,   1371
    that it seemes the length of seuen yeare.   1506
    Clo. Vpon a lye, seuen times remoued: (beare your   2644
    *knew when seuen Iustices could not take vp a Quarrell,   2672
SEUENTH = 2*2
    Clo. 'Faith we met, and found the quarrel was vpon | the seuenth
    cause.   2626
    Iaq. How seuenth cause? Good my Lord, like this | fellow.   2628
    Iaq. But for the seuenth cause. How did you finde   2642
    the quarrell on the seuenth cause?   2643
SEUERE = 1
    With eyes seuere, and beard of formall cut,   1134
SEX = 1
    hath generally tax'd their whole sex withal.   1537
SEXE = *1
    Cel. You haue simply misus'd our sexe in your loue- | prate: 2107
SEXTA *l*.949 = 1
SHADE = 2
    Vnder the shade of melancholly boughes,   1088
    Into a bush, vnder which bushes shade   2264

SHADOW = *1
*out of the sight of *Orlando*: Ile goe finde a shadow, and | sigh till he
come.   2122
SHAKD = *1
Orl. I am he that is so Loue-shak'd, I pray you tel | me your remedie.   1552
SHAKE = 1*1
Orlan. Goe a-part *Adam*, and thou shalt heare how | he will shake me
vp.   30
Ros. I could shake them off my coate, these burs are | in my heart.   475
SHAL *l*.261 1481 *1600 *1608 1675 1707 *2455 *2523 *2541 2751 = 5*5
SHALBE = *1
Cel. All the better: we shalbe the more Marketable.   262
SHALL *l*.*40 *66 *77 *127 *133 *160 *166 199 *267 305 *343 *352 365
   *366 409 413 453 562 570 577 588 627 *839 872 *873 896 932 941 978
   1079 1205 1208 *1315 1326 *1413 1480 1763 1767 1802 1807 1875 *2033
   *2080 2137 2139 *2336 *2341 2353 *2417 *2451 2454 *2472 2482 *2521
   2705 = 32*25
SHALLOW = *6
*of a man? Shallow, shallow: A better instance I say: | Come.   1254
Clo. Your lips wil feele them the sooner. Shallow a-|gen: a more
sounder instance, come.   1257
Clo. Most shallow man: Thou wormes meate in re-|spect   1262
Clo. Wilt thou rest damn'd? God helpe thee shallow   1268
*liking, proud, fantastical, apish, shallow, inconstant, ful   1590
SHALT *l*.*30 *136 *187 879 967 1017 1065 *1417 1909 = 5*4
SHAMD = *1
*wherein if I bee foil'd, there is but one sham'd that was   350
SHAME = 4
Or if thou canst not, oh for shame, for shame,   1789
Oli. Some of my shame, if you will know of me   2245
Oli. 'Twas I: but 'tis not I: I doe not shame   2288
SHANKE = 1
For his shrunke shanke, and his bigge manly voice,   1140
SHAPE = *1
Phe. If sight & shape be true, why then my loue adieu   2695
SHARE = 1
Shal share the good of our returned fortune,   2751
SHARPE = 1
Though thou the waters warpe, thy sting is not so sharpe,   1166
SHE = 29*19
SHEAFE = 1
They that reap must sheafe and binde, | then to cart with Rosalinde.   1305
SHEE *l*.1052 1210 1351 *1527 *2069 2163 2698 = 5*2
SHEELL = *1
Ros. Hees falne in loue with your foulnesse, & shee'll   1839
SHEEPE = *2
*good pasture makes fat sheepe: and that a great cause of   1226
*of our sheepe: and would you haue vs kisse Tarre? The   1260
SHEEPES = *1
*as cleane as a sound sheepes heart, that there shal not | be one spot of
Loue in 't.   1600
SHEEP-COAT = 2
Are now on sale, and at our sheep-coat now   869
A sheep-coat, fenc'd about with Oliue-trees.   2227
SHEERE = 1
And do not sheere the Fleeces that I graze: 864

SHEE-LAMBE = *1
*and to betray a shee-Lambe of a tweluemonth   1278
SHELTER = 1
To some shelter, and thou shalt not die | For lacke of a dinner,   967
SHEPHEARD = 15*8
*Ros. Alas poore Shepheard searching of they would,   826
Ros. I prethee Shepheard, if that loue or gold   855
But I am shepheard to another man,   863
*Clow. Truely Shepheard, in respect of it selfe, it is a   1213
Has't any Philosophie in thee shepheard?   1221
Was't euer in Court, Shepheard? | Cor. No truly.   1231
*and sinne is damnation: Thou art in a parlous state shep-|heard.   1241
*verie vncleanly fluxe of a Cat. Mend the instance Shep-|heard.   1265
*Cel. How now backe friends: Shepheard, go off a lit-|tle: 1356
*Clo. Come Shepheard, let vs make an honorable re-|treit,   1358
After the Shepheard that complain'd of loue,   1755
You foolish Shepheard, wherefore do you follow her   1822
So take her to thee Shepheard, fareyouwell.   1836
Will you goe Sister? Shepheard ply her hard: 1848
*Phe. Dead Shepheard, now I find thy saw of might,   1853
Why writes she so to me? well Shepheard, well,   2167
Sil. Call you this chiding? | Cel. Alas poore Shepheard.   2213
Died in this bloud, vnto the Shepheard youth,   2309
you are there followed by a faithful shepheard,   2488
*Phe. Good shepheard, tell this youth what 'tis to loue   2490
You'l giue your selfe to this most faithfull Shepheard.   2589
Or else refusing me to wed this shepheard: 2598
Du Sen. I do remember in this shepheard boy,   2602
SHEPHEARDESSE = 1*1
*Ros. With this Shepheardesse my sister: heere in the   1524
Come Sister: Shepheardesse, looke on him better   1849
SHEPHEARDS = 1*1
*good life; but in respect that it is a shepheards life, it is   1214
*you kisse your hands; that courtesie would be vncleanlie | if Courtiers
were shepheards.   1247
SHEPHERD = 2
Read. Art thou god, to Shepherd turn'd?   2189
*was old Sir Rowlands will I estate vpon you, and heere | liue and die a
Shepherd.   2419
SHEPHERDESSE = 1
Praising the proud disdainfull Shepherdesse | That was his Mistresse.   1757
SHEPHERDS = 1*2
Ros. Ioue, Ioue, this Shepherds passion, | Is much vpon my fashion.   841
*Co. And how like you this shepherds life Mr Touchstone?   1212
*diuell himselfe will haue no shepherds, I cannot see else | how thou
shouldst scape.   1281
SHEW = 3*3
*wise men haue makes a great shew; Heere comes Mon-|sieur the Beu.   255
Of bare distresse, hath tane from me the shew   1071
*Ros. Go with me to it, and Ile shew it you: and by   1607
Now shew the wound mine eye hath made in thee,   1791
*your head, and shew the world what the bird hath done | to her owne
neast.   2109
To shew the letter that I writ to you.   2485
SHEWD = 1
to sound, when he shew'd me your handkercher?   2436

SHIFT = 1
matter, the cleanliest shift is to kisse.   1990
SHIFTS = 1
And so he playes his part. The sixt age shifts   1136
SHINING = 1
And shining morning face, creeping like snaile   1125
SHINS = 1
I breake my shins against it.   840
SHOE = 1
Tonges Ile hang on euerie tree, | that shall ciuill sayings shoe. 1325
SHOO = *1
*sleeue vnbutton'd, your shoo vnti'de, and euerie thing   1564
SHOOKE = *1
*and they shooke hands, and swore brothers. Your If, is   2675
SHOOTS = 1
the presentation of that he shoots his wit.   2680
SHORT = 1
I will be bitter with him, and passing short;   1913
SHORTLY = 1
We shall haue shortly discord in the Spheares: 978
SHOULD *l.**41 *48 *152 *369 376 401 402 *467 *485 *488 *489 493 630
745 *795 1004 1066 1183 1323 1340 1351 *1370 *1491 *1563 1785 *1996
1997 2234 2267 *2330 *2410 *2411 *2463 2587 = 17*18
SHOULDER = 1
him oth' shoulder, but Ile warrant him heart hole.   1963
SHOULDERS = 1
The cost of Princes on vnworthy shoulders?   1050
SHOULDST *l.*389 1282 = 2
SHOUT = 1
Cel. If I had a thunderbolt in mine eie, I can tell who | should downe.
Shout.   375
SHOW *see also* shew, shoe = 3*3
Ros. Deere *Cellia*; I show more mirth then I am mi-|stresse   172
*And thou wilt show more bright, & seem more vertuous   542
Du Sen. Show me the place, | I loue to cope him in these sullen fits, 675
*the weaker vessell, as doublet and hose ought to show it   789
The quintessence of euerie sprite, | heauen would in little show. 1337
Then any of her lineaments can show her: 1829
SHREWD = 1
That haue endur'd shrew'd daies, and nights with vs,   2750
SHRINKE = 1
Euen till I shrinke with cold, I smile, and say   615
SHRUNKE = 1*1
For his shrunke shanke, and his bigge manly voice,   1140
*Wainscot, then one of you wil proue a shrunke pannell,   1693
SHUNNE = 1
Who doth ambition shunne,   927
SHUT = 1*1
Who shut their coward gates on atomyes,   1784
*wit, and it will out at the casement: shut that, and   2071
SICKE = *1
*that are sicke. There is a man haunts the Forrest, that a-|buses 1545
SICKENS = *1
Cor. No more, but that I know the more one sickens,   1222
SIDE = 2*1
With spectacles on nose, and pouch on side,   1138
Clo. Truly thou art damn'd, like an ill roasted Egge, | all on one side. 1235

SIDE *cont.*
*as a puisny Tilter, y spurs his horse but on one side,   1750
SIDES = *1
*Musicke in his sides? Is there yet another doates vpon   304
SIGH = 1
*out of the sight of *Orlando*: Ile goe finde a shadow, and | sigh till he
come.   2122
SIGHD = 1*2
As euer sigh'd vpon a midnight pillow: 809
*lou'd; no sooner lou'd, but they sigh'd: no sooner sigh'd   2443
SIGHES = 1
Sil. It is to be all made of sighes and teares, | And so am I for *Phebe*. 2491
SIGHING = 1*1
Sighing like Furnace, with a wofull ballad   1127
*sighing euerie minute, and groaning euerie houre wold   1494
SIGHT = 7*7
*you of good wrastling, which you haue lost the sight of.   275
Ros. Though it be pittie to see such a sight, it well | becomes the
ground.   1436
The sight of Louers feedeth those in loue: 1766
Bring vs to this sight, and you shall say   1767
Whose heart th'accustom'd sight of death makes hard   1774
None could be so abus'd in sight as hee.   1851
Who euer lov'd, that lou'd not at first sight?   1854
*serue me such another tricke, neuer come in my sight | more.   1955
sight, I had as liefe be woo'd of a Snaile.   1966
*out of the sight of *Orlando*: Ile goe finde a shadow, and | sigh till he
come.   2122
*was neuer any thing so sodaine, but the sight of two   2439
Du Se. If there be truth in sight, you are my daughter.   2693
Orl. If there be truth in sight, you are my *Rosalind*.   2694
Phe. If sight & shape be true, why then my loue adieu   2695
SIGNIOR = *1
Iaq. Ile tarrie no longer with you, farewell good sig-|nior Loue.   1483
SIL = 1
*true louer hence, and not a word; for here comes more | company.
Exit. Sil.   2222
SIL = 23*1
SILENCE = 1
Her verie silence, and her patience, | Speake to the people, and they
pittie her.   539
SILENCED = *1
*wit that fooles haue was silenced, the little foolerie that   254
SILKE = 1
'Tis not your inkie browes, your blacke silke haire,   1819
SILUIUS see also Sil. = 12
Enter Corin and Siluius.   801
Enter Siluius and Phebe.   1770
Sil. Sweet *Phebe.* | *Phe.* Hah: what saist thou *Siluius*?   1855
Phe. Why I am sorry for thee gentle *Siluius*.   1858
Siluius; the time was, that I hated thee;   1866
There be some women *Siluius*, had they markt him   1898
And thou shalt beare it, wilt thou *Siluius*?   1909
Goe with me *Siluius. Exeunt.*   1914
Enter Siluius.   2151
Enter Siluius & Phebe.   2482
Enter Rosalinde, Siluius, & Phebe.   2579

SILUIUS cont.

Keepe your word *Siluius*, that you'l marrie her	2599

SIMILIES = 1

1.*Lord*. O yes, into a thousand similies.	653

SIMPLE = 1 *1

Clo. That is another simple sinne in you, to bring the	1275
Doth my simple feature content you?	1617

SIMPLES = *1

*of many simples, extracted from many obiects,	1932

SIMPLY = *2

*haue not: (but I pardon you for that, for simply your ha- | uing	1561
Cel. You haue simply misus'd our sexe in your loue- | prate:	2107

SIMPRING = *1

*simpring, none of you hates them) that betweene you,	2790

SIN = 2 *1

Du Sen. Most mischeeuous foule sin, in chiding sin:	1038
*then thy manners must be wicked, and wickednes is sin,	1240

SINCE = 4 *4

Cel. By my troth thou saiest true: For, since the little	253
Duke. Come on, since the youth will not be intreated	313
'Tis but an houre agoe, since it was nine,	997
Du. Not see him since? Sir, sir, that cannot be:	1181
*Palme tree; I was neuer so berim'd since *Pythagoras* time	1373
But since that thou canst talke of loue so well,	1868
To tell you what I was, since my conuersion	2289
*that I can do strange things: I haue since I was three	2468

SINEWIE *see* synowie

SING = 9 *3

I do desire you to sing:	906
Iaq. Nay, I care not for their names, they owe mee | nothing. Wil you sing?	909
*the beggerly thankes. Come sing; and you that wil not | hold your tongues.	916
Amy. And Ile sing it. | *Amy*. Thus it goes.	935
Giue vs some Musicke, and good Cozen, sing.	1154
Heigh ho, sing heigh ho, vnto the greene holly,	1160
as freind remembred not. | *Heigh ho, sing, &c.*	1167
Cel. I would sing my song without a burthen, thou | bring'st me out of tune.	1441
Iaq. Sing it: 'tis no matter how it bee in tune, so it | make noyse enough.	2134
Then sing him home, the rest shall beare this burthen;	2139
When Birds do sing, hey ding a ding, ding.	2551
Whiles a Wedlocke Hymne we sing,	2711

SINGLE = *1

*Is the single man therefore blessed? No, as a wall'd	1666

SINNE = *2

*and sinne is damnation: Thou art in a parlous state shep- | heard.	1241
Clo. That is another simple sinne in you, to bring the	1275

SIR *l*.32 34 *35 *38 43 44 45 *57 *76 *100 *122 *123 *125 *343 *363 *384 395 398 406 419 420 429 436 451 *485 707 851 854 860 991 1025 *1169 1181 *1270 *1498 *1651 1672 *1673 *1682 1684 *1686 2128 2133 2333 *2345 2356 2360 2362 2364 2367 2371 2379 2381 2387 *2388 2401 *2419 *2567 *2631 *2632 *2634 *2635 *2637 *2640 *2645 *2664 2728 2757 = 38 *33

SIRRA = *1

*Ah, sirra, a body would thinke this was well counterfei- | ted,	2321

SIRRAH = 1
go with him sirrah.   1357
SIRS = *1
*Amy. Wel, Ile end the song. Sirs, couer the while,   918
SISTER = 6*4
Ros. Peace, here comes my sister reading, stand aside.   1322
*Ros. With this Shepheardesse my sister: heere in the   1524
*Ros. Nay, you must call mee *Rosalind*: Come sister, | will you go?
Exeunt.   1611
Will you goe Sister? Shepheard ply her hard: 1848
Come Sister: Shepheardesse, looke on him better   1849
*good thing: Come sister, you shall be the Priest, and   2033
*marrie vs: giue me your hand *Orlando*: What doe you | say sister?   2034
Of femall fauour, and bestowes himselfe | Like a ripe sister: the woman
low   2236
Ros. God saue you brother. | Ol. And you faire sister.   2427
*and ouercome. For your brother, and my sister, no soo-|ner   2441
SISTERHOOD = *1
*Nun of winters sisterhood kisses not more religiouslie,   1726
SISTERS = 1
Are deerer then the naturall bond of Sisters: 444
SIT = 2*4
*Cel. Let vs sit and mocke the good houswife *For-|tune*   200
*Du Sen. Sit downe and feed, & welcom to our table   1082
And therefore sit you downe in gentlenesse,   1101
*Clo. By my troth well met: come, sit, sit, and a song.   2539
2.Pa. We are for you, sit i'th middle.   2540
SITTE = *1
*Attalanta's heeles. Will you sitte downe with me, and   1469
SITTING = 1
Who you saw sitting by me on the Turph,   1756
SIX = *1
*almost six thousand yeeres old, and in all this time there   2007
SIXT = 1*1
And so he plays his part. The sixt age shifts   1136
*the sixt, the Lye with circumstance: the sea-|uenth,   2669
SIZE = *1
*'tis a Word too great for any mouth of this Ages size, to   1420
SKIE = 1
*Freize, freize, thou bitter skie that dost not bight so nigh | as benefitts
forgot:*   1164
SKILL = *1
*then no skill, by so much is a horne more precious | then to want.   1670
SKIN = 1
His Leather skin, and hornes to weare: 2138
SKIRTS = 2
skirts of the Forrest, like fringe vpon a petticoat.   1525
And to the skirts of this wilde Wood he came;   2735
SKY = *1
*Maides are May when they are maides, but the sky chan-|ges   2057
SLANDER = 1
fortune, and preuents the slander of his wife.   1975
SLAUE = 1
*Heauen would that shee these gifts should haue, | and I to liue and die her
slaue.*   1351

SLEEPE = 3*2
*Ile go sleepe if I can: if I cannot, Ile raile against all | the first borne
of Egypt.   945
*Ros. With Lawiers in the vacation: for they sleepe   1520
*I will laugh like a Hyen, and that when thou art inclin'd | to sleepe. 2064
Cel. And Ile sleepe. Exeunt.   2124
To sleepe: looke who comes heere.   2153
SLEEPES = *1
*that hath not the Gowt: for the one sleepes easily be- | cause   1509
SLEEPING = 2*1
*and suppers, and sleeping hours excepted: it is the right | Butter-
womens ranke to Market.   1295
Lay sleeping on his back; about his necke   2258
When that the sleeping man should stirre; for 'tis   2267
SLEEUE = *1
*sleeue vnbutton'd, your shoo vnti'de, and euerie thing   1564
SLENDER = 1
Wintred garments must be linde, | so must slender Rosalinde: 1303
SLEPT = 1
Why so am I: we still haue slept together,   534
SLIGHT = *1
*dost him any slight disgrace, or if hee doe not mightilie   145
SLIGHTEST = 1
If thou remembrest not the slightest folly,   816
SLINKE = 1
Ros. 'Tis he, slinke by, and note him.   1447
SLIP = 1
And with indented glides, did slip away   2263
SLIPPERD = 1
Into the leane and slipper'd Pantaloone,   1137
SLOWLY = *1
*Ros. I, of a Snaile: for though he comes slowly, hee   1968
SLUMBER = 1
From miserable slumber I awaked.   2284
SLUT = 1*1
slut, were to put good meate into an vncleane dish.   1646
*Aud. I am not a slut, though I thanke the Goddes I | am foule.   1647
SLUTTISHNESSE = *1
*Clo. Well, praised be the Gods, for thy foulnesse; slut- | tishnesse   1649
SMALL = 1*1
And after some small space, being strong at heart,   2305
*pouertie of her, the small acquaintance, my sodaine wo- | ing,   2414
SMART = 1
Doth very foolishly, although he smart   1028
SMELL = 1
Clo. Nay, if I keepe not my ranke. | Ros. Thou loosest thy old smell.   272
SMILE = 2*1
Euen till I shrinke with cold, I smile, and say   615
*comming a night to *Iane Smile*, and I remember the kis- | sing   830
A scattred smile, and that Ile liue vpon.   1878
SMILES = *1
*of teares, full of smiles; for euerie passion something, and   1591
SMIRCH = 1
And with a kinde of vmber smirch my face,   576
SMOAKE = 2
Thus must I from the smoake into the smother,   455

SMOAKE *cont.*
  *'twill out at the key-hole: stop that, 'twill flie with the | smoake out at
  the chimney.   2072
SMOOTH = 1*1
  Of smooth ciuility: yet am I in-land bred,   1072
  *I haue bin politicke with my friend, smooth with mine   2622
SMOOTHNES = *1
  *Duk. She is too subtile for thee, and her smoothnes;   538
SMOTHER = 1
  Thus must I from the smoake into the smother,   455
SNAILE = 3*1
  And shining morning face, creeping like snaile   1125
  sight, I had as liefe be woo'd of a Snaile.   1966
  Orl. Of a Snaile?   1967
  *Ros. I, of a Snaile: for though he comes slowly, hee   1968
SNAKE = 1*1
  *made thee a tame snake) and say this to her; That if she   2219
  A greene and guilded snake had wreath'd it selfe,   2259
SO *l*.*19 *48 62 *85 *92 *108 *150 158 *164 *166 *179 *181 *182 *203
  *291 320 327 *348 *352 *361 *367 *485 503 511 *520 521 525 534 573
  577 626 *688 710 734 742 766 768 *802 811 815 837 999 1004 1023 1025
  1069 1083 1136 1150 1157 1158 1164 1166 *1294 1302 1304 *1373 1383
  1399 1450 *1466 *1505 1530 *1531 *1536 *1552 1575 *1578 *1582 *1583
  1585 *1664 *1667 *1670 *1687 1688 1731 *1744 1772 1836 1840 1842
  1851 1868 1873 1893 1920 *1965 *1979 2031 2051 2066 *2091 *2094
  2104 *2134 2167 2186 2275 2279 *2287 2290 2320 *2330 2367 *2368
  2369 *2409 *2439 *2454 *2471 2492 2497 2506 2507 2508 2509 2510
  2511 2512 *2525 2590 *2618 2656 *2660 *2674 *2769 = 76*56, 3*1
  His leg is but so so, and yet 'tis well: 1893
  Art rich? | *Will.* 'Faith sir, so, so.   2366
  *Cle. So, so; is good, very good, very excellent good: 2368
  and yet it is not, it is but so, so: 2369
SOBBING = 1
  2.*Lord.* We did my Lord, weeping and commenting | Vpon the sobbing
  Deere.   673
SOBER = 1
  Orl. Speak'st thou in sober meanings?   2477
SOCIETIE = 1*1
  I thanke you too, for your societie.   1451
  *societie: which in the boorish, is companie, of this fe-|male: 2390
SOCIETY = *1
  *is, abandon the society of this Female, or Clowne   2392
SODAINE = 1*4
  *let vs talke in good earnest: Is it possible in such a so-|daine,   484
  Ielous in honor, sodaine, and quicke in quarrell,   1130
  *pouertie of her, the small acquaintance, my sodaine wo-|ing,   2414
  *nor sodaine consenting: but say with mee, I loue   2415
  *was neuer any thing so sodaine, but the sight of two   2439
SODAINLY = 4
  Will sodainly breake forth: Sir, fare you well,   451
  Ile make him finde him: do this sodainly;   699
  And buy it with your Gold right sodainly. *Exeunt.*   887
  Who with her head, nimble in threats approach'd | The opening of his
  mouth: but sodainly   2260
SOFT = 1
  Cel. You bring me out. Soft, comes he not heere?   1446

SOFTEST = 1
| That eyes that are the frailst, and softest things, | 1783 |

SOFTLY = *1
| *go as softly as foot can fall, he thinkes himselfe too soon | there. | 1517 |

SOILE = 1
| The soile, the profit, and this kinde of life, | 885 |

SOLD = 1*1
| Cor. Assuredly the thing is to be sold: | 883 |
| *to be sad: I feare you haue sold your owne Lands, | 1937 |

SOLDIER = 1
| Made to his Mistresse eye-brow. Then, a Soldier, | 1128 |

SOLEMNE = 1
| here, a yong man and an old in solemne talke. | 803 |

SOLEMNIZD = *1
| *the contract of her marriage, and the day it is solemnizd: | 1504 |

SOLITARY = *1
| *naught. In respect that it is solitary, I like it verie well: | 1215 |

SOME = 17*13
*you: you shall haue some part of your will, I pray you	leaue me.	77
*some broken limbe, shall acquit him well: your brother	127
*poyson, entrap thee by some treacherous deuise, and ne-	uer	147
*leaue thee till he hath tane thy life by some indirect	148
*Duk. I would thou hadst beene son to some man else,	386
*vpon curs, throw some of them at me; come lame mee	with reasons.	464
*Ros. No, some of it is for my childes Father: Oh	470

It cannot be, some villaines of my Court | Are of consent and sufferance
in this.	682
Weele light vpon some setled low content.	772
To some shelter, and thou shalt not die	For lacke of a dinner,	967
And know some nourture: But forbeare, I say,	1073
Giue vs some Musicke, and good Cozen, sing.	1154
Some, *how briefe the Life of man*	*runs his erring pilgrimage*,	1327
Some of violated vowes,	*twixt the soules of friend*, *and friend*:	1331
*Ros. O yes, I heard them all, and more too, for some	1362
Orl. I prethee recount some of them.	1543

*some good counsel, for he seemes to haue the Quotidian | of Loue
vpon him.	1550
*Now if thou wert a Poet, I might haue some hope	thou didst feigne.	1636
Some scarre of it: Leane vpon a rush	1793

The Cicatrice and capable impressure | Thy palme some moment
keepes: but now mine eyes	1794
You meet in some fresh cheeke the power of fancie,	1801
There be some women *Siluius*, had they markt him	1898

*Orl. I take some ioy to say you are, because I would | be talking of
her.	2002
Oli. Some of my shame, if you will know of me	2245
The Lyonnesse had torne some flesh away,	2301
And after some small space, being strong at heart,	2305
*Know of me then (for now I speake to some pur-|pose)	2461
*do I labor for a greater esteeme then may in some	2465
Some liuely touches of my daughters fauour.	2603
After some question with him, was conuerted	2737

SOMETHING = 4*5
| *that he so plentifully giues me, the something that | 19 |
| Or Charles, or something weaker masters thee. | 428 |

Cel. Something that hath a reference to my state: | No longer *Celia*, but
| Aliena. | 592 |

SOMETHING *cont.*
*Clo. And mine, but it growes something stale with | mee.	843
And if I bring thee not something to eate,	961
*Orl. Your accent is something finer, then you could | purchase in so	
remoued a dwelling.	1529
*of teares, full of smiles; for euerie passion something, and	1591
Cel. Something browner then Iudasses:	1718
*Ros. I shall deuise something: but I pray you com- |mend	2336

SOMETIMES = *1
*Orl. I sometimes do beleeue, and somtimes do not,	2577

SOMTIMES = *1
*Orl. I sometimes do beleeue, and somtimes do not,	2577

SON = 2*2
*Duk. I would thou hadst beene son to some man else,	386
(Yet not the son, I will not call him son)	724
*Duke Sen. If that you were the good Sir *Rowlands* son,	1169

SONG = 9*4
Song. | *Vnder the greene wood tree*,	890
I can sucke melancholly out of a song,	901
*Amy. Wel, Ile end the song. Sirs, couer the while,	918
Come, warble, come. | *Song. Altogether heere.*	925
Heere was he merry, hearing of a Song.	976
Song. | *Blow, blow, thou winter winde*,	1155
*Cel. I would sing my song without a burthen, thou | bring'st me out of	
tune.	1441
no song Forrester for this purpose? | *Lord.* Yes Sir.	2132
Musicke, Song. | *What shall he haue that kild the Deare?*	2136
*Clo. By my troth well met: come, sit, sit, and a song.	2539
Song. | *It was a Louer, and his lasse*,	2546
*such a foolish song. God buy you, and God mend your | voices. Come	
Audrie. Exeunt.	2570
Song. | Wedding is great Iunos crowne,	2715

SONGS = 1
*Iaq. I pray you marre no more trees with Writing | Loue-songs in their	
barkes.	1454

SONNE = 6*3
*Orl. I am no villaine: I am the yongest sonne of Sir	57
*Orl. Orlando my Liege, the yongest sonne of Sir *Ro-|land de Boys.*	384
Orl. I am more proud to be Sir *Rolands* sonne,	395
His yongest sonne, and would not change that calling | To be adopted	
heire to *Fredricke.*	396
Had I before knowne this yong man his sonne,	400
*you should fall into so strong a liking with old Sir | *Roulands* yongest	
sonne?	485
*Sonne deerelie? By this kinde of chase, I should hate	489
Your brother, no, no brother, yet the sonne	723
I am the second sonne of old *Sir Rowland,*	2728

SONS = *1
*Le Beu. There comes an old man, and his three sons.	282

SOON *see also* assoone = *1
*go as softly as foot can fall, he thinkes himselfe too soon | there.	1517

SOONER = 1*6
Beautie prouoketh theeues sooner then gold.	574
*Clo. Your lips wil feele them the sooner. Shallow a-|gen: a more	
sounder instance, come.	1257
*and ouercome. For your brother, and my sister, no soo-|ner	2441
*met, but they look'd: no sooner look'd, but they	2442

SOONER *cont*.

*lou'd; no sooner lou'd, but they sigh'd: no sooner sigh'd   2443
*but they ask'd one another the reason: no sooner knew   2444
SOOTH = *1
*in good sooth, are you he that hangs the verses on the   1574
SORES = 1
And all th'imbossed sores, and headed euils,   1041
SORROW = 3
Sil. Where euer sorrow is, reliefe would be: 1859
If you doe sorrow at my griefe in loue,   1860
By giuing loue your sorrow, and my griefe | Were both extermin'd.   1861
SORROWES = 1
For by this heauen, now at our sorrowes pale;   568
SORRY = 1
Phe. Why I am sorry for thee gentle *Siluius*.   1858
SORTS = *1
*deuise, of all sorts enchantingly beloued, and indeed   163
SOUERAIGNE = 1
Cel. Deere Soueraigne heare me speake.   527
SOUGHT = *1
*the reason, but they sought the remedie: and in these   2445
SOULDIERS = *1
*nor the Courtiers, which is proud: nor the Souldiers,   1928
SOULE = 1*1
*I hope I shall see an end of him; for my soule (yet   160
Ros. My Father lou'd Sir *Roland* as his soule,   398
SOULES = 1
Some of violated vowes, | *twixt the soules of friend, and friend:*   1331
SOUND = 2*1
And whistles in his sound. Last Scene of all,   1142
*as cleane as a sound sheepes heart, that there shal not | be one spot of
Loue in't.   1600
to sound, when he shew'd me your handkercher?   2436
SOUNDED = *1
*it cannot bee sounded: my affection hath an vnknowne | bottome, like
the Bay of Portugall.   2113
SOUNDER = 1
Clo. Your lips wil feele them the sooner. Shallow a-|gen: a more
sounder instance, come.   1257
SOUTH = 1
Like foggy South, puffing with winde and raine,   1823
SOUTH-SEA = *1
*my disposition? One inch of delay more, is a South-sea   1392
SOWREST = 1
Sweetest nut, hath sowrest rinde, | *such a nut is Rosalinde*.   1307
SPACE = 1
And after some small space, being strong at heart,   2305
SPAKE = *1
*cut, he would answer I spake not true: this is call'd the   2653
SPAN = 1
That the stretching of a span, | *buckles in his summe of age*.   1329
SPARE = *1
*respect it is not in the Court, it is tedious. As it is a spare   1218
SPARROW = 1
Yea prouidently caters for the Sparrow,   748
SPEAK = *3
*for my part, he keepes me rustically at home, or (to speak   10

SPEAK *cont*.

*Clo. The more pittie that fooles may not speak wise-|ly, what
Wisemen do foolishly.   251

*Ros. But are you so much in loue, as your rimes speak?   1578

SPEAKE = 12*13

*Oli. Was not *Charles* the Dukes Wrastler heere to | speake with me?   90

**teares I speake it) there is not one so young, and so vil-|lanous   150

**this day liuing. I speake but brotherly of him,   151

**speake no more of him, you'l be whipt for taxation one | of these
daies.   249

Le Beu. Why this that I speake of.   298

**bee entreated. Speake to him Ladies, see if you can | mooue him.   324

Le Beu. He cannot speake my Lord.   381

I cannot speake to her, yet she vrg'd conference.   425

More suites you to conceiue, then I to speake of.   435

Cel. Deere Soueraigne heare me speake.   527

Her verie silence, and her patience, | Speake to the people, and they
pittie her.   539

Go seeke him, tell him I would speake with him.   979

To speake my minde, and I will through and through   1033

Orl. Speake you so gently? Pardon me I pray you,   1083

I scarce can speake to thanke you for my selfe.   1151

**speake apace: I would thou couldst stammer, that thou   1394

*Ros. Nay, but the diuell take mocking: speake sadde | brow, and true
maid.   1408

*Ros. Do you not know I am a woman, when I thinke, | I must speake:
sweet, say on.   1443

*Ros. I wil speake to him like a sawcie Lacky, and vn-|der   1487

**religious Vnckle of mine taught me to speake, who was   1532

*Ros. Nay, you were better speake first, and when you   1986

*Cel. O I haue heard him speake of that same brother,   2272

**Know of me then (for now I speake to some pur-|pose)   2461

**I speake not this, that you should beare a good opinion   2463

*Ros. Why do you speake too, Why blame you mee | to loue you.   2513

SPEAKES = 1*2

**at schoole, and report speakes goldenly of his profit: 9

**speakes braue words, sweares braue oathes, and breakes   1748

When he that speakes them pleases those that heare: 1886

SPEAKST = 2

Ros. Thou speak'st wiser then thou art ware of.   838

Orl. Speak'st thou in sober meanings?   2477

SPEARE = 1

A bore-speare in my hand, and in my heart   583

SPECTACLE = 1

Du Sen. But what said *Iaques*? | Did he not moralize this spectacle?   651

SPECTACLES = 1

With spectacles on nose, and pouch on side,   1138

SPEECH = 1

His folly to the mettle of my speech,   1056

SPEEDE = 1

Ros. Now Hercules, be thy speede yong man.   371

SPENT = 1*2

**them? what prodigall portion haue I spent, that I should | come to such
penury?   41

*Oli. And what wilt thou do? beg when that is spent?   75

And ere we haue thy youthfull wages spent,   771

SPHEARE = 1
With thy chaste eye, from thy pale spheare aboue   1203
SPHEARES = 1
We shall haue shortly discord in the Spheares: 978
SPIRIT = *3
*grieues me, and the spirit of my Father, which I thinke   24
*hiding from me all gentleman-like qualities: the spirit   69
*and sunken, which you haue not: an vnquestionable spi-|rit,   1559
SPIRITS = 2*2
*Cel. Yong Gentleman, your spirits are too bold for   336
Ros. O Iupiter, how merry are my spirits?   784
*Clo. I care not for my spirits, if my legges were not | wearie.   785
That can entame my spirits to your worship: 1821
SPIT = *2
*him: now weepe for him, then spit at him; that I draue   1595
*they will spit, and for louers, lacking (God warne vs)   1989
SPITTING = *1
*or spitting, or saying we are hoarse, which are the onely | prologues to
a bad voice.   2542
SPLEENE = *1
*begot of thought, conceiu'd of spleene, and borne of   2118
SPOKE = 1*2
*he would not haue spoke such a word. Ex. Orl. Ad.   84
*Phe. Knowst thou the youth that spoke to mee yere-|(while?   1879
Orl. I would kisse before I spoke.   1985
SPORT = 4*4
*Cel. Marry I prethee doe, to make sport withall: but   195
*loue no man in good earnest, nor no further in sport ney-|ther,   196
Ros. What shall be our sport then?   199
Le Beu. Faire Princesse, | you haue lost much good sport.   264
Cel. Sport: of what colour?   266
*Clo. But what is the sport Monsieur, that the Ladies | haue lost?   296
*first time that euer I heard breaking of ribbes was sport | for Ladies.   300
That he in sport doth call his Rosalind.   2310
SPORTS = *1
*Ros. From henceforth I will Coz, and deuise sports: 193
SPOT = 1
*as cleane as a sound sheepes heart, that there shal not | be one spot of
Loue in't.   1600
SPRING = 5
In the spring time, the onely pretty rang time.   2550
Sweet Louers loue the spring,   2552
For loue is crowned with the prime. | In spring time, &c.   2555
These prettie Country folks would lie. | In spring time, &c.   2559
How that a life was but a Flower, | In spring time, &c.   2563
SPRITE = 1
The quintessence of euerie sprite, | heauen would in little show.   1337
SPURS = *1
*as a puisny Tilter, y spurs his horse but on one side,   1750
SQUANDRING = 1
Euen by the squandring glances of the foole.   1031
STAFFE = *1
*breakes his staffe like a noble goose; but all's braue that   1751
STAG = 1
To the which place a poore sequestred Stag   640

220

STAGE = 1
Ia. All the world's a stage, | And all the men and women, meerely
Players;   1118
STAGGER = *1
*stagger in this attempt: for heere wee haue no Temple   1658
STAID = 1
Duk. I *Celia*, we staid her for your sake,   528
STAIES = 2*1
*more properly) staies me heere at home vnkept: for call   11
And neuer staies to greet him: I quoth *Iaques*,   662
Orl. Who staies it stil withal?   1519
STAIND = 1
What man I am, and how, and why, and where | This handkercher was
stain'd.   2246
STAIRES = *1
*degrees, haue they made a paire of staires to marriage,   2446
STALE = *1
Clo. And mine, but it growes something stale with | mee.   843
STALKING-HORSE = *1
Du Se. He vses his folly like a stalking-horse, and vn-|der   2679
STALLING = *1
*not from the stalling of an Oxe? his horses are bred   13
STAMMER = *1
*speake apace: I would thou couldst stammer, that thou   1394
STAND = 2*2
*Mustard was naught: Now Ile stand to it, the Pancakes   232
Clo. Stand you both forth now: stroke your chinnes,   238
Ros. I pray thee, if it stand with honestie,   877
Ros. Peace, here comes my sister reading, stand aside.   1322
STANDS = 3
Are all throwne downe, and that which here stands vp   416
and who he stands stil withall.   1501
Where in the Purlews of this Forrest, stands   2226
STANZO = 1
Come, more, another stanzo: Cal you 'em stanzo's?   907
STANZOS = 1
Come, more, another stanzo: Cal you 'em stanzo's?   907
STARTLE = 1
Ros. Patience her selfe would startle at this letter,   2161
STATE = 1*1
Cel. Something that hath a reference to my state: | No longer *Celia*, but
Aliena.   592
*and sinne is damnation: Thou art in a parlous state shep-|heard.   1241
STATES = 1
According to the measure of their states.   2752
STATURE = 1
Iaq. What stature is she of? | *Orl*. Iust as high as my heart.   1462
STAY = 5*5
*stay behind her; she is at the Court, and no lesse beloued   111
*to acquaint you withall, that either you might stay him   131
Le Beu. You must if you stay heere, for heere is the   306
Cel. Yonder sure they are comming. Let vs now stay | and see it.   309
Cel. I did not then intreat to haue her stay,   530
If you out-stay the time, vpon mine honor,   549
*thankful: let me stay the growth of his beard, if thou   1404
I am for other, then for dancing meazures. | *Du Se*. Stay, *Iaques*, stay. 2770
Ile stay to know, at your abandon'd caue. *Exit*.   2773

STEALE = 2
>*Ros*. But Cosen, what if we assaid to steale   594
>Did steale behinde him as he lay along   637

STEALER = 1
>**Cel*. Yes, I thinke he is not a picke purse, nor a horse-|stealer,   1732

STEELE = *1
>*with thee, or in bastinado, or in steele: I will bandy   2396

STEPPE = 1
>Who after me, hath many a weary steppe   1107

STERNE = 2
>Of sterne command'ment. But what ere you are   1086
>By the sterne brow, and waspish action   2157

STERNER = 1
>But first begs pardon: will you sterner be   1776

STICKS = 1
>Sticks me at heart: Sir, you haue well deseru'd,   406

STIL = 2*1
>and who he stands stil withall.   1501
>*Orl*. Who staies it stil withal?   1519
>*which women stil giue the lie to their consciences. But   1573

STILE = 3
>That can translate the stubbornnesse of fortune | Into so quiet and so
>sweet a stile.   625
>*Ros*. Why, tis a boysterous and a cruell stile,   2180
>A stile for challengers: why, she defies me,   2181

STILL = 5*2
>*hadst beene still with mee, I could haue taught my loue   180
>But I did finde him still mine enemie: 388
>Why so am I: we still haue slept together,   534
>Still we went coupled and inseperable.   537
>*Cor*. That is the way to make her scorne you still.   804
>**Cor*. Why we are still handling our Ewes, and their | Fels you know
>are greasie.   1250
>*Enter Hymen, Rosalind, and Celia. | Still Musicke.*   2681

STING = 2
>As sensuall as the brutish sting it selfe,   1040
>*Though thou the waters warpe, thy sting is not so sharpe*,   1166

STIR = 1
>The like doe you, so shall we passe along, | And neuer stir assailants.   577

STIRRE = 1*1
>*Farewell good *Charles*. Now will I stirre this Game-|ster: 159
>When that the sleeping man should stirre; for 'tis   2267

STOMACKE = *1
>*more plentie in it, it goes much against my stomacke.   1220

STONE = *1
>*broke my sword vpon a stone, and bid him take that for   829

STONES = 1
>Sermons in stones, and good in euery thing.   623

STOOD = 1*1
>Stood on th'extremest verge of the swift brooke, | Augmenting it with
>teares.   649
>*themselues without the verse, and therefore stood lame-|ly in the
>verse.   1367

STOP = *1
>* 'twill out at the key-hole: stop that, 'twill flie with the | smoake out at
>the chimney.   2072

STORE = 1

Which I did store to be my foster Nurse,   744

STORY = 1

To tell this story, that you might excuse   2307
STRAIGHTS = *1

*what straights of Fortune she is driuen, and it is not   2473
STRAINES = *1

*and play false straines vpon thee? not to be en-|dur'd.   2217
STRAIT = 2

1 *Lor*. Ile bring you to him strait. *Exeunt*.   678

Phe. Ile write it strait: 1911
STRANGE = 5*4

*runne into strange capers; but as all is mortall in   836

After a voyage: He hath strange places cram'd   1013

Full of strange oaths, and bearded like the Pard,   1129

That ends this strange euentfull historie,   1143

*lispe, and weare strange suites; disable all the benefits   1949

Alacke, in me, what strange effect   2201

*that I can do strange things: I haue since I was three   2468

*of verie strange beasts, which in all tongues, are call'd | Fooles.   2614

'Tis I must make conclusion | Of these most strange euents: 2700
STRANGER = 1

He sent me hither, stranger as I am   2306
STRANGERS = 1

Orl. I do desire we may be better strangers.   1453
STREAM = *1

*of madnes, w was to forsweare the ful stream of y world,   1597
STREAME = 2

First, for his weeping into the needlesse streame;   654

The ranke of Oziers, by the murmuring streame   2229
STRENGTH = *3

*I come but in as others do, to try with him the strength | of my youth.   334

*strength, if you saw your selfe with your eies, or knew   338

Ros. The little strength that I haue, I would it were | with you.   356
STRETCH = 1

That their discharge did stretch his leatherne coat   644
STRETCHD = *1

Cel. There lay hee stretch'd along like a Wounded | knight.   1434
STRETCHING = 1

That the stretching of a span, | buckles in his summe of age.   1329
STRIKES = *1

*it strikes a man more dead then a great rec-|koning   1625
STRIPT = 1

There stript himselfe, and heere vpon his arme   2300
STROKE = *1

Clo. Stand you both forth now: stroke your chinnes,   238
STRONG = 4*3

*of my father growes strong in mee, and I will no longer   70

Cel. I would I were inuisible, to catch the strong fel-|low by the legge.
Wrastle.   372

*you should fall into so strong a liking with old Sir | *Roulands* yongest
sonne?   485

And wherefore are you gentle, strong, and valiant?   709

Though I looke old, yet I am strong and lustie;   751

Let gentlenesse my strong enforcement be,   1095

And after some small space, being strong at heart,   2305

STRONGER = 1*1
*stronger then the word of a Tapster, they are both the 1739
And Nature stronger then his iust occasion, 2281
STUBBORNE = 1
A stubborne will to please, 939
STUBBORNEST = *1
*but he is resolute. Ile tell thee *Charles*, it is the stubbor-|nest 139
STUBBORNNESSE = 1
That can translate the stubbornnesse of fortune | Into so quiet and so
sweet a stile. 625
STUDIE = 2
And then Ile studie how to die. 2212
Ros. I care not if I haue: it is my studie 2486
STUDIED = 1
from whence you haue studied your questions. 1467
STUDIES = 1
Of many desperate studies, by his vnckle, 2608
STUDY = *1
*he cannot study, and the other liues merrily, be-|cause 1510
SUBIECT = 1
I rather will subiect me to the malice 740
SUBTILE = *1
Duk. She is too subtile for thee, and her smoothnes; 538
SUCCESSEFULLY = *1
Cel. Alas, he is too yong: yet he looks successefully 317
SUCCOUR = 1
Here's a yong maid with trauaile much oppressed, | And faints for
succour. 858
SUCH = 18*17
*them? what prodigall portion haue I spent, that I should | come to such
penury? 41
*that saies such a father begot villaines: wert thou 59
*endure it: therefore allow me such exercises as may be-|come 71
*he would not haue spoke such a word. *Ex. Orl. Ad*. 84
*from his intendment, or brooke such disgrace well as he 132
*to reason of such goddesses, hath sent this Naturall for 222
*making such pittiful dole ouer them, that all the behol-|ders 293
*there is such oddes in the man: In pitie of the challen-|gers 322
Yet such is now the Dukes condition, 432
*let vs talke in good earnest: Is it possible in such a so-|daine, 484
The wretched annimall heau'd forth such groanes 643
When such a one as shee, such is her neighbor? 1052
And let my officers of such a nature | Make an extent vpon his house
and Lands: 1196
Clo. Such a one is a naturall Philosopher: 1230
Sweetest nut, hath sowrest rinde, | such a nut is Rosalinde. 1307
Ros. Though it be pittie to see such a sight, it well | becomes the
ground. 1436
*are no such man; you are rather point deuice in your
ac-|coustrements, 1566
*But what talke wee of Fathers, when there is such a man | as *Orlando*? · 1745
Then she a woman. 'Tis such fooles as you 1825
And I in such a pouerty of grace, 1874
*serue me such another tricke, neuer come in my sight | more. 1955
Orl. What's that? | *Ros*. Why hornes: w such as you are faine to be
be-|holding 1972
Orl. And wilt thou haue me? | *Ros*. I, and twentie such. 2027

SUCH *cont.*
*Orl. A man that had a wife with such a wit, he might | say, wit
whether wil't?   2074
such offenders, and let time try: adieu. *Exit.*   2106
Could not drop forth such giant rude inuention,   2183
Such Ethiop words, blacker in their effect   2184
Did you euer heare such railing?   2195
Haue power to raise such loue in mine,   2200
*wilt thou loue such a woman? what to make thee an in-|strument, 2216
Such garments, and such yeeres: the boy is faire,   2235
*such a foolish song. God buy you, and God mend your | voices. Come
Audrie. Exeunt.   2570
*Clo. According to the fooles bolt sir, and such dulcet | diseases. 2640
SUCKD = 1
Food to the suck'd and hungry Lyonnesse?   2278
SUCKE = 2
I can sucke melancholly out of a song,   901
*and the greatest of my pride, is to see my Ewes graze, & | my Lambes
sucke.   1273
SUCKES = 1
As a Weazel suckes egges: More, I pre'thee more.   902
SUDDEN *see* sodaine
SUFFERANCE = 1
It cannot be, some villaines of my Court | Are of consent and sufferance
in this.   682
SUFFICD = 1
Limpt in pure loue: till he be first suffic'd,   1108
SUFFICE = 1
Let is suffice thee that I trust thee not.   516
SUGAR = 1
*honestie coupled to beautie, is to haue Honie a sawce to | Sugar. 1640
SUITE = 4*1
*be misprised: we wil make it our suite to the Duke, that   344
That I did suite me all points like a man,   581
Iaq. It is my onely suite,   1018
Orl. What, of my suite?   1998
*Ros. Not out of your apparrell, and yet out of your | suite: 1999
SUITES = 3*1
Ros. Gentleman, | Weare this for me: one out of suites with fortune 410
More suites you to conceiue, then I to speake of.   435
Thinking that I meane him, but therein suites   1055
*lispe, and weare strange suites; disable all the benefits   1949
SULLEN = 1
Du Sen. Show me the place, | I loue to cope him in these sullen fits, 675
SUM = 1
As worldlings doe, giuing thy sum of more   656
SUMME = 1
That the stretching of a span, | buckles in his summe of age.   1329
SUN = 1
Who laid him downe, and bask'd him in the Sun,   988
SUNDRED = 1
Shall we be sundred? shall we part sweete girle?   562
SUNDRIE = *1
*and indeed the sundrie contemplation of my trauells, in   1933
SUNKEN = *1
*and sunken, which you haue not: an vnquestionable spi-|rit,   1559

SUNNE = 1*1
and loues to liue i'th Sunne: 928
*the night, is lacke of the Sunne: That hee that hath lear-|ned 1227
SUPPERS = *1
*and suppers, and sleeping hours excepted: it is the right | Butter-
womens ranke to Market. 1295
SUPPLIED = 1
*onely in the world I fil vp a place, which may bee better | supplied,
when I haue made it emptie. 354
SUPPORT = 1
Support him by the arme: giue me your hand, 1177
SURE = 8*3
Cel. Yonder sure they are comming. Let vs now stay | and see it. 309
As sure I thinke did neuer man loue so: 811
If the Cat will after kinde, | so be sure will Rosalinde: 1301
*he taught me how to know a man in loue: in which cage | of rushes, I
am sure you art not prisoner. 1555
'Tis pretty sure, and very probable, 1782
Nor I am sure there is no force in eyes | That can doe hurt. 1797
But sure hee's proud, and yet his pride becomes him; 1888
This is a mans inuention, and his hand. | *Sil.* Sure it is hers. 2178
Iaq. There is sure another flood toward, and these 2612
You and you, are sure together, 2709
*I defi'de not: And I am sure, as many as haue good 2794
SURELY = 1
That youth is surely in their companie. 696
SURGERY = *1
Cor. And they are often tarr'd ouer, with the surgery 1259
SURUEY = 1
And thou thrice crowned Queene of night suruey 1202
SUTOR = *1
*my Sutor from his mad humor of loue, to a liuing humor 1596
SWAGGERER = 1
And play the swaggerer, beare this, beare all: 2162
SWAINE = *1
Cor. That yong Swaine that you saw heere but ere-|while, 874
SWAM = *1
*swam in a Gundello. Why how now *Orlando*, where 1953
SWANS = 1
And wheresoere we went, like *Iunos* Swans, 536
SWASHING = 1
Weele haue a swashing and a marshall outside, 585
SWAY = 1
Thy Huntresse name, that my full life doth sway. 1204
SWEARE = 1*6
and sweare by your beards that I am a knaue. 239
*you sweare by that that is not, you are not forsworn: no 242
Orl. I sweare to thee youth, by the white hand of 1576
*sweare in Poetrie, may be said as Louers, they do feigne. 1632
Rosa. But why did hee sweare hee would come this | morning, and
comes not? 1728
Ros. You haue heard him sweare downright he was. 1737
*to sweare, and to forsweare, according as mariage binds 2633
SWEARES = 2*1
And in that kinde sweares you doe more vsurpe 634
*speakes braue words, sweares braue oathes, and breakes 1748
the Forrest: he hath bin a Courtier he sweares. 2619

SWEARING = 1*1
*more was this knight swearing by his Honor, for he ne-|uer 243
Yea, and of this our life, swearing that we 668
SWEARST = *1
*Clow. I do truly: for thou swear'st to me thou art ho-|nest: 1635
SWEAT = *1
*is not the grease of a Mutton, as wholesome as the sweat 1253
SWEATE = 2*1
When seruice sweate for dutie, not for meede: 762
Where none will sweate, but for promotion, 764
*Clo. Why do not your Courtiers hands sweate? and 1252
SWEEPE = 1
Sweepe on you fat and greazie Citizens, 663
SWEET = 13*5
*Adam. Sweet Masters bee patient, for your Fathers | remembrance, be
at accord. 63
Cel. I pray thee Rosalind, sweet my Coz, be merry. 171
*turne monster: therefore my sweet Rose, my deare Rose, | be merry. 191
Sweet are the vses of aduersitie 618
That can translate the stubbornnesse of fortune | Into so quiet and so
sweet a stile. 625
Oh my sweet master, O you memorie 706
vnto the sweet Birds throte: 894
*Ros. Do you not know I am a woman, when I thinke, | I must speake:
sweet, say on. 1443
*Farewel good Mr Oliuer: Not O sweet Oliuer, O braue 1703
Sil. Sweet Phebe doe not scorne me, do not Phebe 1771
*Phe. Sweet youth, I pray you chide a yere together, 1837
Sil. Sweet Phebe. | Phe. Hah: what saist thou Siluius? 1855
Sil. Sweet Phebe pitty me. 1857
Orl. I, sweet Rosalind. 2093
Chewing the food of sweet and bitter fancie, 2252
Cel. Why how now Ganimed, sweet Ganimed. 2311
Sweet Louers loue the spring, 2552
*beards, or good faces, or sweet breaths, will for my kind 2795
SWEETE = 3
Shall we be sundred? shall we part sweete girle? 562
Hath not old custome made this life more sweete 608
Ol. Come sweete Audrey, | We must be married, or we must liue in
baudrey: 1701
SWEETEST = 2
Sweetest nut, hath sowrest rinde, | such a nut is Rosalinde. 1307
He that sweetest rose will finde, | must finde Loues pricke, & Rosalinde. 1309
SWEETLY = 1
So sweetly tastes, being the thing I am. 2290
SWIFT = 1*2
Stood on th'extremest verge of the swift brooke, | Augmenting it with
teares. 649
*Orl. And why not the swift foote of time? Had not | that bin as
proper? 1496
*Du.Se. By my faith, he is very swift, and sententious 2639
SWIFTLY = 1
Your praise is come too swiftly home before you. 712
SWOON = *1
*Oli. Many will swoon when they do look on bloud. 2312
SWORD = 3*1
Or with a base and boistrous Sword enforce 736

SWORD *cont*.

*broke my sword vpon a stone, and bid him take that for	829
In the which hope, I blush, and hide my Sword.	1096
His brother heere, and put him to the sword:	2734

SWORDS = 1

*nor he durst not giue me the lye direct: and so wee mea- | sur'd swords, and parted.	2660

SWORE = *3

*Clo. Of a certaine Knight, that swore by his Honour	230
*they were good Pan-cakes, and swore by his Honor the	231
*and they shooke hands, and swore brothers. Your If, is	2675

SWORNE = *1

*had anie; or if he had, he had sworne it away, before	244

SWOUND *see also* sound = 1

Now counterfeit to swound, why now fall downe,	1788

SYNODE = 1

Thus Rosalinde *of manie parts*, | *by Heauenly Synode was deuis'd*,	1347

SYNOWIE = 1

That did but lately foile the synowie *Charles*,	694

TABLE = *1

*Du Sen. Sit downe and feed, & welcom to our table	1082

TAILORS = *1

*enemie, I haue vndone three Tailors, I haue had foure	2623

TAKE = 15*19

*nature gaue mee, his countenance seemes to take from	20
*not my brother, I would not take this hand from thy	60
*to take thy father for mine; so wouldst thou, if the truth	181
take his part with weeping. | Ros. Alas.	294
*Du. You wil take little delight in it, I can tell you	321
*Ros. O they take the part of a better wrastler then | my selfe.	480
And doe not seeke to take your change vpon you,	566
Take that, and he that doth the Rauens feede,	747
*broke my sword vpon a stone, and bid him take that for	829
And take vpon command, what helpe we haue	1102
*much at once, or none at all. I pre'thee take the Corke	1397
*Ros. Nay, but the diuell take mocking: speake sadde | brow, and true maid.	1408
*propositions of a Louer: but take a taste of my finding	1427
Orl. Which I take to be either a foole, or a Cipher.	1482
*him, and this way wil I take vpon mee to wash your Li- | uer	1599
Clo. I wil not take her on guift of any man.	1677
Cry the man mercy, loue him, take his offer,	1834
So take her to thee Shepheard, fareyouwell.	1836
*were grauel'd, for lacke of matter, you might take oc- | casion	1987
*Orl. I take some ioy to say you are, because I would | be talking of her.	2002
*Ros. Then you must say, I take thee *Rosalind* for | wife.	2044
Orl. I take thee *Rosalind* for wife.	2046
*But I doe take thee *Orlando* for my husband: there's a	2048
*shall neuer take her without her answer, vnlesse you take	2080
Take thou no scòrne to weare the horne,	2140
Will the faithfull offer take	2209
I pray you will you take him by the arme.	2317
*Oli. Well then, take a good heart, and counterfeit to | be a man.	2328
And therefore take the present time.	2553
*sir, but mine owne, a poore humour of mine sir, to take	2635
*knew when seuen Iustices could not take vp a Quarrell,	2672

TAKE *cont.*

Here's eight that must take hands,	2702
In his owne conduct, purposely to take	2733

TAKEN *see also* tane = *2

*be his heire; for what hee hath taken away from thy fa-|ther	188
*and being taken with the crampe, was droun'd,	2015

TAKES = *1

*borne, but the same tradition takes not away my bloud,	50

TALE = 2

Cel. I could match this beginning with an old tale.	283
And thereby hangs a tale. When I did heare	1001

TALKE = 3*3

*let vs talke in good earnest: Is it possible in such a so-|daine,	484
here, a yong man and an old in solemne talke.	803
Ros. Neuer talke to me, I wil weepe.	1710
*But what talke wee of Fathers, when there is such a man | as *Orlando?*	1745
But since that thou canst talke of loue so well,	1868
Iaq. Nay then God buy you, and you talke in blanke | verse.	1946

TALKES = 1

'Tis but a peeuish boy, yet he talkes well,	1884

TALKING = 1*1

Orl. I take some ioy to say you are, because I would | be talking of her.	2002
Ros. I will wearie you then no longer with idle tal-|king.	2460

TALL = 3

Ros. Were it not better, | Because that I am more then common tall,	579
He is not very tall, yet for his yeeres hee's tall:	1892

TALLER = 1

But yet indeede the taller is his daughter,	440

TAME = *1

*made thee a tame snake) and say this to her; That if she	2219

TANE = 5*1

*leaue thee till he hath tane thy life by some indirect	148
Hath tane displeasure 'gainst his gentle Neece,	446
That from the Hunters aime had tane a hurt,	641
Of bare distresse, hath tane from me the shew	1071
He hath t'ane his bow and arrowes, and is gone forth	2152
Iaq. And how was that tane vp?	2625

TANGLE = 1

I thinke she meanes to tangle my eies too:	1817

TANTING = 1

Ile write to him a very tanting Letter,	1908

TAPSTER = *1

*stronger then the word of a Tapster, they are both the	1739

TARDIE = *1

Ros. Nay, and you be so tardie, come no more in my	1965

TARRD = *1

Cor. And they are often tarr'd ouer, with the surgery	1259

TARRE = *2

*of our sheepe: and would you haue vs kisse Tarre? The	1260
*and perpend: Ciuet is of a baser birth then Tarre, the	1264

TARRIE = *1

Iaq. Ile tarrie no longer with you, farewell good sig-|nior Loue.	1483

TASTE = 2*1

Sans teeth, sans eyes, sans taste, sans euery thing.	1145
Ros. Out Foole. | *Clo.* For a taste.	1297
*propositions of a Louer: but take a taste of my finding	1427

TASTES = 1
So sweetly tastes, being the thing I am. 2290
TAUGHT = 1*4
*they are taught their mannage, and to that end Riders 15
Oli. Now Sir, what make you heere? | *Orl*. Nothing: I am not taught to
make any thing. 32
*hadst beene still with mee, I could haue taught my loue 180
*religious Vnckle of mine taught me to speake, who was 1532
*he taught me how to know a man in loue: in which cage | of rushes, I
am sure you art not prisoner. 1555
TAXATION = *1
*speake no more of him, you'l be whipt for taxation one | of these
daies. 249
TAXD = 1
hath generally tax'd their whole sex withal. 1537
TAXE = 1
That can therein taxe any priuate party: 1045
TAXING = 1
Why then my taxing like a wild-goose flies 1060
TEACH = *1
*could teach me to forget a banished father, you must not 174
TEACHETH = 1
Which teacheth thee that thou and I am one, 561
TEACHING = 1
Will I Rosalinda write, | teaching all that reade, to know 1335
TEARE = 1
If euer from your eye-lids wip'd a teare, 1093
TEARES = 6*3
*teares I speake it) there is not one so young, and so vil- |lanous 150
I should haue giuen him teares vnto entreaties, 401
Almost to bursting, and the big round teares 645
Stood on th'extremest verge of the swift brooke, | Augmenting it with
teares. 649
*teares, weare these for my sake: wee that are true Lo- |uers, 835
*of teares, full of smiles; for euerie passion something, and 1591
that teares do not become a man. 1712
Teares our recountments had most kindely bath'd, 2294
Sil. It is to be all made of sighes and teares, | And so am I for *Phebe*. 2491
TEDIOUS = *3
*respect it is not in the Court, it is tedious. As it is a spare 1218
Ros. O most gentle Iupiter, what tedious homilie of 1353
*of heauie tedious penurie. These Time ambles | withal. 1513
TEETH = 1*1
*lost my teeth in your seruice: God be with my olde ma- |ster, 83
Sans teeth, sans eyes, sans taste, sans euery thing. 1145
TEL = *5
*with diuers persons: Ile tel you who Time ambles with- |all, 1499
Orl. I am he that is so Loue-shak'd, I pray you tel | me your remedie. 1552
Ros. Loue is meerely a madnesse, and I tel you, de- |serues 1580
Orlan. Now by the faith of my loue, I will; Tel me | where it is. 1605
*and haue a good Priest that can tel you what marriage is, 1691
TELL = 11*13
Oli. Can you tell if *Rosalind* the Dukes daughter bee | banished with
her Father? 106
*but he is resolute. Ile tell thee *Charles*, it is the stubbor- |nest 139
Ros. Yet tell vs the manner of the Wrastling. 276
Le Beu. I wil tell you the beginning: and if it please 277

230

TELL *cont*.
Du. You wil take little delight in it, I can tell you   321
Cel. If I had a thunderbolt in mine eie, I can tell who | should downe.
Shout.   375
Orl. I thanke you Sir; and pray you tell me this,   436
But I can tell you, that of late this Duke   445
Tell me whereon the likelihoods depends?   518
Go seeke him, tell him I would speake with him.   979
Du Sen. Fie on thee. I can tell what thou wouldst do.   1036
Go to my Caue, and tell mee. Good old man,   1175
Ros. Nay, I pre'thee now, with most petitionary ve-|hemence, tell me
who it is.   1385
*of discouerie. I pre'thee tell me, who is it quickely, and   1393
*the way, you shal tell me, where in the Forrest you liue: 1608
For I must tell you friendly in your eare,   1832
Ros. Now tell me how long you would haue her, af-|ter you haue
possest her?   2052
*how deepe I am in loue: ile tell thee *Aliena*, I cannot be   2121
Cel. I pray you tell it.   2248
To tell you what I was, since my conuersion   2289
To tell this story, that you might excuse   2307
*I pray you tell your brother how well I counterfei-|ted: heigh-ho.   2322
Ros. Did your brother tell you how I counterfeyted   2435
Phe. Good shepheard, tell this youth what 'tis to loue   2490
TELLST = 1
Thou tellst me there is murder in mine eye,   1781
TEMPERD = *1
*of thy loue to me were so righteously temper'd, as mine | is to thee.   182
TEMPLE = *1
*stagger in this attempt: for heere wee haue no Temple   1658
TEN = 2
Within these ten daies if that thou beest found   502
Sayes, very wisely, it is ten a clocke: 995
TENDER = *2
*is but young and tender, and for your loue I would bee   128
Ros. By my life I do, which I tender deerly, though   2478
TENURE = 1
It beares an angry tenure; pardon me,   2159
TERME = *2
*betweene Terme and Terme, and then they perceiue not | how time
moues.   1521
TERMES = 2
And rail'd on Lady Fortune in good termes,   989
In good set termes, and yet a motley foole.   990
TERRITORIE = 1
To seeke a liuing in our Territorie.   1188
TERTIA *l*.702 1613 2146 2530 = 4
TERTIUS *l*.458 1179 = 2
TESTAMENT = 1 *1
*father left me by testament, with that I will goe buy my | fortunes.   73
Poore Deere quoth he, thou mak'st a testament   655
TESTIMONY = 1
Oli. This was not counterfeit, there is too great te-|stimony   2324
TEXT = 1 *3
Oliuer Mar-text, the Vicar of the next village, who hath   1652
Enter Sir Oliuer Mar-text.   1672
*Heere comes Sir *Oliuer*: Sir *Oliuer Mar-text* you are   1673

TEXT *cont*.
Mar-text. But *Awdrie*, there is a youth heere in the | Forrest layes
claime to you.   2346
TH *see also* i'th, oth', to'th = 4*1
Stood on th'extremest verge of the swift brooke, | Augmenting it with
teares.   649
*you: but that they cal complement is like th'encounter   913
Cleanse the foule bodie of th'infected world,   1034
And all th'imbossed sores, and headed euils,   1041
Whose heart th'accustom'd sight of death makes hard   1774
THAN *see* then
THANKE = 10*7
Oli. *Charles*, I thanke thee for thy loue to me, which   135
Cel. Gentle Cosen, | Let vs goe thanke him, and encourage him: 403
Orl. Can I not say, I thanke you? My better parts   415
Orl. I thanke you Sir; and pray you tell me this,   436
Iaq. I thanke it: More, I prethee more,   900
Iaq. Well then, if euer I thanke any man, Ile thanke   912
Orl. I thanke ye, and be blest for your good comfort.   1113
Orl. I thanke you most for him. | *Ad*. So had you neede,   1149
I scarce can speake to thanke you for my selfe.   1151
Iaq. I thanke you for your company, but good faith   1448
I thanke you too, for your societie.   1451
*Lectors against it, and I thanke God, I am not a Wo-|man   1535
Aud. I am not a slut, though I thanke the Goddes I | am foule.   1647
And thanke heauen, fasting, for a good mans loue;   1831
Will. I sir, I thanke God. | *Clo*. Thanke God: A good answer: 2364
THANKES = 1 *2
*of two dog-Apes. And when a man thankes me hartily,   914
*the beggerly thankes. Come sing; and you that wil not | hold your
tongues.   916
Heauen thankes, and make no boast of them.   924
THANKFUL = *1
*thankful: let me stay the growth of his beard, if thou   1404
THAT *see also* y *l*.*12 *14 *15 *19 *23 *35 *41 *49 *59 *73 *75 *101 *110
*123 *126 *131 *133 *165 *167 *178 *190 *201 *206 *207 229 *230
*235 239 *242 245 246 247 *251 *254 271 281 *290 *293 *296 298 *300
*344 *350 *351 *356 *361 *367 396 412 416 433 438 445 448 *488 495
502 509 516 524 532 *546 559 561 580 581 587 592 601 609 617 625 633
634 635 639 641 644 657 665 668 681 684 691 694 696 *697 718 728 747
765 768 804 805 814 817 *829 *831 *835 855 864 871 *873 *874 876
*913 *916 934 937 943 983 1004 *1009 1015 1019 1020 1021 1024 1027
1042 1045 1047 1049 1051 1054 1055 1069 1074 1084 1087 *1097 1100
1103 1143 1164 *1169 1174 1181 1189 1193 1204 1207 *1214 *1215
*1216 *1222 *1223 *1224 *1225 *1226 *1227 *1243 *1247 *1270 *1271
*1275 1305 1309 1326 1329 1336 1340 1351 1374 *1377 *1388 *1394
1398 *1406 *1423 *1488 1497 1506 *1508 *1509 *1527 *1533 1539 *1545
*1549 *1552 *1561 *1570 *1572 *1574 1577 *1583 *1595 *1600 *1633
*1651 *1663 *1691 1712 *1751 1755 1758 1772 1777 1783 1798 1800
1803 1804 1805 1807 1809 1821 1826 1827 1854 1863 1865 1866 1867
1868 1872 1875 1877 1878 *1879 1882 1886 1896 *1921 *1951 *1959
*1962 1972 *1996 *2016 *2063 *2064 *2071 *2072 *2074 *2076 2078
*2081 *2090 *2095 *2099 *2105 *2111 *2115 *2117 *2119 2127 2137
2163 2164 2166 2175 2190 2197 2205 2208 2210 *2219 2233 2242 2267
2268 2269 *2272 2274 *2287 2295 2307 2310 *2325 2334 *2352 *2377
*2383 *2385 *2388 *2409 *2410 *2416 *2417 *2418 2437 *2462 *2463
*2468 2485 2515 2549 2561 2563 2575 2576 2578 *2583 2585 2587 2591

THAT *cont*.
2597 2599 2604 *2618 *2620 2625 *2636 *2671 2680 2689 2702 2713
2729 2730 2741 2748 2750 2765 *2778 *2779 *2782 *2790 *2792
*2793 = 187*155
THATCHD = 1
Iaq. O knowledge ill inhabited, worse then Ioue in | a thatch'd house.   1621
THATS = 2*3
*for you'l be rotten ere you bee halfe ripe, and that's | the right vertue
of the Medler.   1317
Cel. That's no matter: the feet might beare y verses.   1365
Cel. O that's a braue man, hee writes braue verses,   1747
But that's all one: omittance is no quittance: 1907
She has a huswiues hand, but that's no matter: 2176
THE *see also* th', y = 320*340
THEATER = 1
This wide and vniuersall Theater   1115
THEE *see also* pre'thee *l*.*135 *139 *146 *147 *148 *149 *152 171 *178
183 *189 302 391 428 *472 516 *538 541 553 554 561 569 588 760 766
773 817 877 *954 957 960 961 962 965 966 *1036 1191 1192 1221 *1268
1269 *1417 *1569 *1576 *1619 1627 *1651 1700 *1704 1705 1780 1786
1787 1791 1792 1796 1807 1836 1841 1858 1866 1867 1870 1918 2036
*2044 2046 *2048 *2059 *2084 *2085 2087 *2121 2205 *2216 *2217
*2219 *2220 *2394 *2396 *2397 *2398 2430 2725 = 53*37
THEEFE = *1
Ros. With a theefe to the gallowes: for though hee   1516
THEEUES = 1
Beautie prouoketh theeues sooner then gold.   574
THEEUISH = 1
A theeuish liuing on the common rode?   737
THEIR *l*.*14 *15 *109 *259 *286 *292 514 587 630 631 644 671 687 696
714 765 777 909 1120 1206 *1250 1455 1537 *1546 *1573 1768 1784
2184 2185 2740 2752 = 23*9
THEM *see also* 'em *l*.*41 105 240 *293 330 *464 474 *475 477 670 681 714
*834 924 1020 *1257 1313 *1362 *1363 1458 *1465 1543 *1663 *1665
*1706 1727 *1749 1787 1886 *2018 2450 *2673 *2790 = 18*17
THEMSELUES = *4
*Lords haue put themselues into voluntary exile with   103
*themselues without the verse, and therefore stood lame-|ly in the
verse.   1367
*fellowes, and betray themselues to euery mo-|derne censure, worse
then drunkards.   1922
*but when the parties were met themselues, one of them   2673
THEN *l*.34 *46 *79 *112 *161 *172 *197 199 *241 261 421 435 444 452
*466 *480 510 525 530 543 *546 554 560 574 580 *589 609 610 635 657
677 780 *794 815 838 861 911 *912 958 993 1000 1057 1059 1060 1079
1104 1116 1124 1126 1128 1132 1233 *1240 *1264 1306 *1315 *1316
*1363 *1421 *1493 *1521 *1529 *1562 *1567 *1572 *1594 *1595 *1621
*1625 *1633 *1667 *1668 *1670 1671 *1693 *1696 1718 *1739 1777 1802
1812 1815 1825 1829 1838 1845 1872 1877 1890 1896 1902 1920 1924
1925 *1938 *1943 *1946 *1970 1981 *1992 1997 2005 2025 *2032 *2044
*2059 *2060 *2061 *2103 2139 2185 2204 2212 2234 2238 2280 2281
*2328 *2382 2437 *2457 *2460 *2461 *2465 *2467 *2659 *2674 2683
*2695 2719 2770 *2777 *2782 = 76*61
THERE *l*.*8 *51 *116 *150 *217 *282 *290 *303 *304 *322 *350 *466 584
657 665 704 870 969 1057 1106 1201 *1219 *1434 *1460 1481 *1493
1518 *1534 *1540 *1545 *1554 *1600 1676 1730 *1745 1781 1792 1797

THERE cont.
1894 1898 *1992 *2007 *2079 2277 2300 2313 2324 *2346 *2438 2488
*2565 *2612 2683 *2693 2694 2762 = 27*30
THEREBY = 1*1
| And thereby hangs a tale. When I did heare | 1001 |
| *his lips when he put it into his mouth, meaning there-\|by, | 2376 |

THEREFORE = 10*15
*endure it: therefore allow me such exercises as may be-|come	71
therefore he giues them good leaue to wander.	105
*come in: therefore out of my loue to you, I came hither	130
*contriuer against mee his naturall brother: therefore vse	142
*turne monster: therefore my sweet *Rose*, my deare *Rose*, | be merry.	191
Ros. Do yong Sir, your reputation shall not therefore	343
Cel. Doth it therefore ensue that you should loue his	488
Therefore deuise with me how we may flie	564
And therefore looke you call me *Ganimed*.	590
Therefore my age is as a lustie winter,	756
*selfe coragious to petty-coate; therefore courage, good | *Aliena*.	790
And therefore put I on the countenance	1085
And therefore sit you downe in gentlenesse,	1101
Therefore heauen Nature charg'd, | that one bodie should be fill'd	1339
*themselues without the verse, and therefore stood lame-|ly in the verse.	1367
Aud. Well, I am not faire, and therefore I pray the | Gods make me honest.	1643
*Is the single man therefore blessed? No, as a wall'd	1666
Cel. As good cause as one would desire, | Therefore weepe.	1714
Must you be therefore prowd and pittilesse?	1813
*therefore beware my censure, and keep your pro-|mise.	2101
Will. Which he sir? | *Clo*. He sir, that must marrie this woman: Therefore	2387
*will kill thee a hundred and fifty wayes, therefore trem-|ble and depart.	2398
*I say I am a Magitian: Therefore put you in your best a-|ray,	2479
And therefore take the present time.	2553
*good play? I am not furnish'd like a Begger, therefore	2784

THEREIN = 2
| That can therein taxe any priuate party: | 1045 |
| Thinking that I meane him, but therein suites | 1055 |

THERES = 1*4
Charles. There's no newes at the Court Sir, but the	100
Duk. Thou art thy Fathers daughter, there's enough.	519
Orl. You should aske me what time o'day: there's no | clocke in the Forrest.	1491
*But I doe take thee *Orlando* for my husband: there's a	2048
But at this howre, the house doth keepe it selfe, | There's none within.	2231

THESE *l*.250 287 *424 *475 *483 502 609 616 676 701 721 763 *835 1205
1351 1361 *1370 *1421 *1513 *1931 *2017 *2084 *2445 2559 2601 *2612
*2670 2701 2714 2729 2761 *2774 = 18*14
THEY = 22*43
THEYL = 1
| As we do trust, they'l end in true delights. *Exit* | 2775 |

THIGH = 1
| A gallant curtelax vpon my thigh, | 582 |

THINE = 2
| Thy Lands and all things that thou dost call thine, | 1189 |
| Then thine owne gladnesse, that thou art employd. | 1872 |

THING = 13*8

Oli. Now Sir, what make you heere? | *Orl*. Nothing: I am not taught to
make any thing. | 32
*shall runne into, in that it is a thing of his owne search, | and
altogether against my will. | 133
*so faire and excellent Ladies anie thing. But let your | 348
Sermons in stones, and good in euery thing. | 623
That little cares for buying any thing. | 876
Cor. Assuredly the thing is to be sold: | 883
If this vncouth Forrest yeeld any thing sauage, | 956
If there liue any thing in this Desert. | 969
Sans teeth, sans eyes, sans taste, sans euery thing. | 1145
*sleeue vnbutton'd, your shoo vnti'de, and euerie thing | 1564
*for no passion truly any thing; as boyes and women are | 1592
Aud. I do not know what Poetical is: is it honest in | deed and word: is
it a true thing? | 1628
Hee'll make a proper man: the best thing in him | 1889
*good thing: Come sister, you shall be the Priest, and | 2033
Is not a thing to laugh to scorne. Exeunt. | 2145
So sweetly tastes, being the thing I am. | 2290
*was neuer any thing so sodaine, but the sight of two | 2439
*bid the Duke to the Nuptiall. But O, how bitter a thing | 2452
Sil. Though to haue her and death, were both one | thing. | 2592
*and blood breakes: a poore virgin sir, an il-fauor'd thing | 2634
at any thing, and yet a foole. | 2678

THINGS = 5*1

I thought that all things had bin sauage heere, | 1084
Thy Lands and all things that thou dost call thine, | 1189
That eyes that are the frailst, and softest things, | 1783
*that I can do strange things: I haue since I was three | 2468
When earthly things made eauen | attone together. | 2684
How thus we met, and these things finish. | 2714

THINK = *1

Ros. Good my complection, dost thou think though | 1390

THINKE = 14*11

*grieues me, and the spirit of my Father, which I thinke | 24
let me see, what thinke you of falling in Loue? | 194
To thinke my pouertie is treacherous. | 526
you, for I thinke you haue no money in your purse. | 796
As sure I thinke did neuer man loue so: | 811
I thinke of as many matters as he, but I giue | 923
Du Sen. I thinke he be transform'd into a beast, | 973
Of what we thinke against thee. | 1192
Ros. Do you not know I am a woman, when I thinke, | I must speake:
sweet, say on. | 1443
Iaq. You haue a nimble wit; I thinke 'twas made of | 1468
Cel. Nay certainly there is no truth in him. | *Ros*. Doe you thinke so? | 1730
Cel. Yes, I thinke he is not a picke purse, nor a horse-|stealer, | 1732
*but for his verity in loue, I doe thinke him as | 1733
Ros. Not true in loue? | *Cel*. Yes, when he is in, but I thinke he is not
in. | 1735
I thinke she meanes to tangle my eies too: | 1817
That I shall thinke it a most plenteous crop | 1875
Phe. Thinke not I loue him, though I ask for him, | 1883
*countenance you are; or I will scarce thinke you haue | 1952
*carries his house on his head; a better ioyncture I thinke | 1969
or I should thinke my honestie ranker then my wit. | 1997

THINKE *cont.*
*minute behinde your houre, I will thinke you the most	2097
A freestone coloured hand: I verily did thinke	2174
*Ah, sirra, a body would thinke this was well counterfei-|ted,	2321
*The Foole doth thinke he is wise, but the wiseman	2373
*of heart heauinesse, by how much I shal thinke my bro-|ther	2455

THINKES = *2
*me thinkes I haue giuen him a penie, and he renders me	915
*go as softly as foot can fall, he thinkes himselfe too soon | there.	1517

THINKING = 1*1
Thinking that I meane him, but therein suites	1055
*Orl. I can liue no longer by thinking.	2459

THIRD = *2
*third: yonder they lie, the poore old man their Father,	292
*Quip-modest: the third, the reply Churlish: the fourth,	2667

THIS *l.**4 *18 *23 *25 56 *60 *61 *151 *159 *166 216 *220 *222 *243 283 298 *303 305 *337 342 *361 389 394 400 411 430 436 445 452 469 471 *489 568 608 616 621 629 639 652 668 *672 683 699 717 721 726 731 738 739 750 797 841 856 881 885 *919 921 933 956 969 *982 1008 1066 1074 1087 1115 1143 1163 1187 1193 1198 1207 *1212 *1280 *1311 1323 1375 *1395 *1420 *1423 *1524 1526 *1586 *1593 *1599 *1653 1655 *1658 *1674 *1692 *1728 1767 1814 1838 *1954 *2007 *2020 *2022 *2039 *2069 2132 2139 2155 2161 2162 2168 2177 2178 2192 2205 2206 2213 *2219 2226 *2228 2231 2243 2244 2247 2270 2302 2307 2308 2309 *2321 2324 2378 *2382 *2388 *2390 *2392 *2463 *2490 2510 2511 2512 *2516 2561 2576 2589 2594 2598 2602 2606 2611 *2617 *2628 *2648 *2650 *2652 *2653 *2655 *2677 2729 2731 2735 2741 2747 2749 2753 *2788 = 103*60

THITHER = 3
*cleare all: nothing remaines, but that I kindle the boy | thither, which now Ile goe about. *Exit*.	167
Cel. Wee'll lead you thither:	2316
Let your Wedding be to morrow: thither will I	2423

THORNY = 1
Orl. You touch'd my veine at first, the thorny point	1070

THOSE *l.**206 *207 245 *1243 *1544 1766 1886 *1921 2578 2747 = 5*5

THOU *l.**6 *30 56 *59 62 *75 *136 *143 *144 *153 *177 *179 *181 *187 *197 *209 240 246 *253 273 380 *386 389 390 391 392 427 502 504 *519 541 *542 552 553 554 556 557 561 569 588 655 *733 *735 763 767 805 807 808 813 815 816 818 819 821 822 824 838 878 879 962 963 964 965 967 1017 *1036 1039 1042 1043 *1067 1069 1114 1156 1157 1158 1164 1166 1176 1184 1187 1189 1191 *1195 1202 1233 *1235 *1238 *1239 *1241 *1262 *1268 1269 *1280 1282 1361 *1369 *1390 *1394 *1404 *1414 *1417 *1441 *1635 *1636 1637 *1639 1699 1781 1789 1805 1856 1863 1868 1872 *1879 1909 2027 2029 *2064 *2103 *2111 2140 2141 2189 2194 *2216 *2221 2370 *2372 2380 *2393 2477 2575 2689 *2722 2724 2744 = 90*53

THOUGH = 6*13
*I will no longer endure it, though yet I know no wise | remedy how to auoid it.	26
*may she not by Fortune fall into the fire? though nature	214
Though I looke old, yet I am strong and lustie;	751
Though in thy youth thou wast as true a louer	808
Though thou the waters warpe, thy sting is not so sharpe,	1166
*though not with bagge and baggage, yet with | scrip and scrippage. *Exit*.	1359
Ros. Good my complection, dost thou think though	1390

THOUGH *cont*.

Ros. Though it be pittie to see such a sight, it well | becomes the ground.	1436
Ros. With a theefe to the gallowes: for though hee	1516
Aud. I am not a slut, though I thanke the Goddes I | am foule.	1647
*though? Courage. As hornes are odious, they are neces-|sarie.	1660
Ouer the wretched? what though you haue no beauty	1810
And be not proud, though all the world could see,	1850
Phe. Thinke not I loue him, though I ask for him,	1883
Ros. I, of a Snaile: for though he comes slowly, hee	1968
*haue liu'd manie a faire yeere though *Hero* had turn'd	2012
Ros. By my life I do, which I tender deerly, though	2478
Clo. Truly yong Gentlemen, though there was no	2565
Sil. Though to haue her and death, were both one | thing.	2592

THOUGHT = 4*5

Neuer so much as in a thought vnborne,	511
I thought that all things had bin sauage heere,	1084
Orl. There was no thought of pleasing you when she | was christen'd.	1460
*girle goes before the Priest, and certainely a Womans | thought runs before her actions.	2049
*thought no lesse: that flattering tongue of yours wonne	2090
*begot of thought, conceiu'd of spleene, and borne of	2118
Ros. I thought thy heart had beene wounded with | the clawes of a Lion.	2432
Me thought he was a brother to your daughter:	2605
*thought but of an If; as if you saide so, then I saide so:	2674

THOUGHTS = 2*1

*thoughts, wherein I confesse me much guiltie to denie	347
And in their barkes my thoughts Ile charracter,	1206
Orl. So do all thoughts, they are wing'd.	2051

THOUSAND = 3*5

*bequeathed me by will, but poore a thousand	5
*physicke your ranckenesse, and yet giue no thousand | crownes neyther: holla *Dennis*.	86
1.*Lord*. O yes, into a thousand similies.	653
Cor. Into a thousand that I haue forgotten.	814
You are a thousand times a properer man	1824
*will diuide a minute into a thousand parts, and breake	1960
*but a part of the thousand part of a minute in the affairs	1961
*almost six thousand yeeres old, and in all this time there	2007

THRASONICALL = *1

*Rammes, and *Cesars* Thrasonicall bragge of I came, saw,	2440

THREATS = 1

Who with her head, nimble in threats approach'd | The opening of his mouth: but sodainly	2260

THREE = 1*8

*brother the new Duke, and three or foure louing	102
Le Beu. There comes an old man, and his three sons.	282
Le Beu. Three proper yong men, of excellent growth | and presence.	284
Le Beu. The eldest of the three, wrastled with *Charles*	288
*him, and broke three of his ribbes, that there is little	290
Enter Duke Senior: Amyens, and two or three Lords | like Forresters.	605
*meanes, and content, is without three good frends. That	1224
*that I can do strange things: I haue since I was three	2468
*enemie, I haue vndone three Tailors, I haue had foure	2623

THREW = 1*1

*the Dukes Wrastler, which *Charles* in a moment threw	289

THREW *cont*.
  Loe what befell: he threw his eye aside,   2253
THRICE = 1*1
  Rowland de Boys, he was my father, and he is thrice a vil-|laine   58
  And thou thrice crowned Queene of night suruey   1202
THRIFTIE = 1
  The thriftie hire I saued vnder your Father,   743
THROAT = *1
  *throat, till this other had puld out thy tongue for saying   61
THROTE = 1
  vnto the sweet Birds throte: 894
THROUGH = 5*1
  Thus most inuectiuely he pierceth through | The body of Countrie,
  Citie, Court,   666
  To speake my minde, and I will through and through   1033
  Hir worth being mounted on the winde, | *through all the world beares*
  Rosalinde.   1288
  Within an houre, and pacing through the Forrest,   2251
  *it is, to looke into happines through another mans eies: 2453
THROW = 1*1
  Not a word? | *Ros*. Not one to throw at a dog.   461
  *vpon curs, throw some of them at me; come lame mee | with reasons. 464
THROWNE = 3*1
  Are all throwne downe, and that which here stands vp   416
  Cel. They are but burs, Cosen, throwne vpon thee   472
  And vnregarded age in corners throwne,   746
  And throwne into neglect the pompous Court. | 2.*Bro*. He hath. 2759
THUNDERBOLT = *1
  Cel. If I had a thunderbolt in mine eie, I can tell who | should downe.
  Shout.   375
THUS = 12*4
  Clo. Thus men may grow wiser euery day. It is the   299
  Ere he should thus haue ventur'd.   402
  Thus must I from the smoake into the smother,   455
  Duk. Thus doe all Traitors,   513
  In pitteous chase: and thus the hairie foole,   647
  'Tis right quoth he, thus miserie doth part   659
  Thus most inuectiuely he pierceth through | The body of Countrie,
  Citie, Court,   666
  Amy. And Ile sing it. | *Amy*. Thus it goes.   935
  Thus we may see (quoth he) how the world wagges: 996
  The motley Foole, thus morall on the time,   1002
  Du Sen. Art thou thus bolden'd man by thy distres?   1067
  Thus Rosalinde *of manie parts*, | *by Heauenly Synode was deuis'd*, 1347
  *and to liue in a nooke meerly Monastick: and thus I cur'd   1598
  Can a woman raile thus?   2191
  *bodie more seeming *Audry*) as thus sir: I did dislike the   2645
  How thus we met, and these things finish.   2714
THY *l*.*60 *61 62 *135 *143 *148 *178 *179 *181 *182 *188 273 371 383
  387 *463 479 *519 541 543 656 769 770 771 808 810 813 820 849 880
  955 958 1039 *1067 1158 1159 1166 1176 1185 1189 1191 1203 1204
  1208 *1240 *1370 *1395 1398 *1619 *1649 1779 1795 1806 *1853 1869
  2142 2143 2193 2207 2208 *2357 *2358 2361 *2393 *2394 *2395 2430
  *2432 2686 2725 2744 2768 = 51*25
THYSELFE *see* selfe
TIDINGS *see also* tydings = 1
  That bring these tidings to this faire assembly.   2729

TIL = 1
monstrous, til his fellow-fault came to match it. 1542
TILL = 12*5
*throat, till this other had puld out thy tongue for saying 61
Oli. Let me goe I say. | *Orl*. I will not till I please: you shall heare
mee: my 65
*leaue thee till he hath tane thy life by some indirect 148
Euen till I shrinke with cold, I smile, and say 615
From seauentie yeeres, till now almost fourescore 775
Clo. Nay, I shall nere be ware of mine owne wit, till 839
Call me not foole, till heauen hath sent me fortune, 992
Till that the wearie verie meanes do ebbe. 1047
Orl. Nor shalt not, till necessity be seru'd. 1065
He dies that touches any of this fruite, | Till I, and my affaires are
answered. 1074
Limpt in pure loue: till he be first suffic'd, 1108
And we will nothing waste till you returne. 1112
Till thou canst quit thee by thy brothers mouth, 1191
Phe. But till that time | Come not thou neere me: and when that time
comes, 1804
As till that time I shall not pitty thee. 1807
Ros. Nay, you might keepe that checke for it, till you 2076
*out of the sight of *Orlando*: Ile goe finde a shadow, and | sigh till he
come. 2122
TILTER = *1
*as a puisny Tilter, y spurs his horse but on one side, 1750
TIMBER = 1
and like greene timber, warpe, warpe. 1694
TIME = 24*19
*Gentlemen flocke to him euery day, and fleet the time 118
*first time that euer I heard breaking of ribbes was sport | for Ladies. 300
Cel. O, a good wish vpon you: you will trie in time 482
I was too yong that time to value her, 532
If you out-stay the time, vpon mine honor, 549
Deuise the fittest time, and safest way 600
I like this place, and willingly could | Waste my time in it. 881
The motley Foole, thus morall on the time, 1002
Loose, and neglect the creeping houres of time: 1089
And one man in his time playes many parts, 1121
*Palme tree; I was neuer so berim'd since *Pythagoras* time 1373
Orl. You should aske me what time o'day: there's no | clocke in the
Forrest. 1491
detect the lazie foot of time, as wel as a clocke. 1495
Orl. And why not the swift foote of time? Had not | that bin as
proper? 1496
Ros. By no meanes sir; Time trauels in diuers paces, 1498
*with diuers persons: Ile tel you who Time ambles with- | all, 1499
*who Time trots withal, who Time gallops withal, 1500
Orl. Who ambles Time withal? 1507
*of heauie tedious penurie. These Time ambles | withal. 1513
*betweene Terme and Terme, and then they perceiue not | how time
moues. 1521
*to woe me. At which time would I, being but a moonish 1588
Phe. But till that time | Come not thou neere me: and when that time
comes, 1804
As till that time I shall not pitty thee. 1807
Siluius; the time was, that I hated thee; 1866

TIME *cont*.
*almost six thousand yeeres old, and in all this time there	2007
*from time to time, and wormes haue eaten them, but not | for loue.	2018
Ros. Well, Time is the olde Iustice that examines all	2105
such offenders, and let time try: adieu. *Exit*.	2106
Clow. We shall finde a time *Awdrie*, patience gen-|tle *Awdrie*.	2341
In the spring time, the onely pretty rang time.	2550
And therefore take the present time.	2553
For loue is crowned with the prime. | *In spring time*, &c.	2555
These prettie Country folks would lie. | *In spring time*, &c.	2559
How that a life was but a Flower, | *In spring time*, &c.	2563
1.Pa. you are deceiu'd Sir, we kept time, we lost not | our time.	2567
Clo. By my troth yes: I count it but time lost to heare	2569
Orl. My Lord, the first time that I euer saw him,	2604
Meane time, forget this new-falne dignitie,	2753

TIMES = 2*2
Thou art not for the fashion of these times,	763
*if the interim be but a sennight, Times pace is so hard,	1505
You are a thousand times a properer man	1824
Clo. Vpon a lye, seuen times remoued: (beare your	2644

TIS *l*.*206 659 664 *944 997 1094 1410 *1420 1447 1475 *1663 *1706 1782 1819 1825 1827 1847 1884 1893 1924 1925 *2091 *2134 2180 2267 2288 *2348 *2438 *2490 *2516 2700 2718 *2779 = 21*12

TO *see also* a, too = 254*204

TOAD = 1
Which like the toad, ougly and venemous,	619

TODAY *see* day

TOGETHER = 6*7
*loues her, being euer from their Cradles bred together,	109
Why so am I: we still haue slept together,	534
Rose at an instant, learn'd, plaid, eate together,	535
And get our Iewels and our wealth together,	599
But come thy waies, weele goe along together,	770
*Ewes and the Rammes together, and to offer to get your	1276
Clo. Ile rime you so, eight yeares together; dinners,	1294
*this fellow wil but ioyne you together, as they ioyne	1692
Phe. Sweet youth, I pray you chide a yere together,	1837
*which in the common, is woman: which toge-|ther,	2391
*loue, and they will together. Clubbes cannot part | them.	2449
When earthly things made eauen | attone together.	2684
You and you, are sure together,	2709

TOLD = 2*4
Le Beu. You amaze me Ladies: I would haue told	274
I would thou had'st told me of another Father. | *Exit Duke*.	392
*Court. You told me, you salute not at the Court, but	1246
Ros. I haue bin told so of many: but indeed, an olde	1531
*told him of as good as he, so he laugh'd and let mee goe.	1744
*you would proue, my friends told mee as much, and I	2089

TOMORROW *see* morrow

TONGES = 1
Tonges Ile hang on euerie tree, | *that shall ciuill sayings shoe*.	1325

TONGUE *see also* toong = 3*4
*throat, till this other had puld out thy tongue for saying	61
My tongue hath wrong'd him: if it do him right,	1058
Cel. Cry holla, to the tongue, I prethee: it curuettes	1438
Is his complexion: and faster then his tongue	1890
*her without her tongue: o that woman that cannot	2081

TONGUE *cont*.
*thought no lesse: that flattering tongue of yours wonne	2090
Oli. If that an eye may profit by a tongue,	2233

TONGUES = 1*2
*Findes tongues in trees, bookes in the running brookes,	622
*the beggerly thankes. Come sing; and you that wil not | hold your	
tongues.	916
*of verie strange beasts, which in all tongues, are call'd | Fooles.	2614

TOO = 14*17
Orl. Come, come elder brother, you are too yong in | (this.	55
Ros. Indeed there is fortune too hard for nature, when	217
*but Natures, who perceiueth our naturall wits too dull	221
Cel. Alas, he is too yong: yet he looks successefully	317
Cel. Yong Gentleman, your spirits are too bold for	336
Cel. No, thy words are too precious to be cast away	463
I was too yong that time to value her,	532
Duk. She is too subtile for thee, and her smoothnes;	538
To that which had too much: then being there alone,	657
Your praise is come too swiftly home before you.	712
But at fourescore, it is too late a weeke,	778
He is too disputeable for my companie:	922
His youthfull hose well sau'd, a world too wide,	1139
Du Sen. Welcome, fall too: I wil not trouble you,	1152
Cor. You haue too Courtly a wit, for me, Ile rest.	1267
Ros. O yes, I heard them all, and more too, for some	1362
*Wine comes out of a narrow-mouth'd bottle: either too	1396
*'tis a Word too great for any mouth of this Ages size, to	1420
I thanke you too, for your societie.	1451
*go as softly as foot can fall, he thinkes himselfe too soon | there.	1517
*in his youth an inland man, one that knew Courtship too	1533
loue too: yet I professe curing it by counsel.	1584
I thinke she meanes to tangle my eies too:	1817
I will endure; and Ile employ thee too:	1870
make me sad, and to trauaile for it too.	1944
Rosalind. Why then, can one desire too much of a	2032
Cel. Goe too: wil you *Orlando*, haue to wife this *Ro-|salind*? | *Orl*. I	
will.	2039
Yet heard too much of *Phebes* crueltie.	2187
Oli. This was not counterfeit, there is too great te-|stimony	2324
Ros. Why do you speake too, Why blame you mee | to loue you.	2513
*Lye direct: and you may auoide that too, with an If. I	2671

TOOK = *1
Ros. So was I when your highnes took his Dukdome,	520

TOOKE = *1
*of a peascod instead of her, from whom I tooke two	833

TOONG = *1
Orl. What passion hangs these waights vpo(n) my toong?	424

TOOTH = 1
Thy tooth is not so keene, because thou art not seene,	1158

TOP = 1
And high top, bald with drie antiquitie:	2256

TORNE = 1
The Lyonnesse had torne some flesh away,	2301

TOT = *1
*as his finger. And thou wert best looke to't; for if thou	144

TOTH = 1
With measure heap'd in ioy, to'th Measures fall.	2756

TOUCH = 2
I will not touch a bit. 1110
Ros. And his kissing is as ful of sanctitie, | As the touch of holy bread. 1723
TOUCHD = 1*1
Orl. You touch'd my veine at first, the thorny point 1070
*to be touch'd with so many giddie offences as hee 1536
TOUCHES = 3
He dies that touches any of this fruite, | Till I, and my affaires are
answered. 1074
Of manie faces, eyes, and hearts, | *to haue the touches deerest pris'd.* 1349
Some liuely touches of my daughters fauour. 2603
TOUCHSTONE = 1*3
Enter Rosaline for Ganimed, Celia for Aliena, and | *Clowne,* alias
Touchstone. 782
Ros. I, be so good *Touchstone*: Look you, who comes 802
Co. And how like you this shepherds life Mr *Touchstone*? 1212
Cor. Not a whit *Touchstone*, those that are good ma- | ners 1243
TOWARD = 1*1
Turning againe toward childish trebble pipes, 1141
Iaq. There is sure another flood toward, and these 2612
TOWNE = 2*1
*Towne is more worthier then a village, so is the fore- | head 1667
'Tis Hymen peoples euerie towne, 2718
To Hymen, God of euerie Towne. 2721
TOY = *1
*companie, I am verie glad to see you, euen a toy in hand 1683
TRADITION = *1
*borne, but the same tradition takes not away my bloud, 50
TRAIND = *1
*you haue train'd me like a pezant, obscuring and 68
TRAITOR = 3
Ros. Yet your mistrust cannot make me a Traitor, 517
What's that to me, my Father was no Traitor, 524
But now I know her: if she be a Traitor, 533
TRAITORS = 2
Duk. Thus doe all Traitors, 513
Are sanctified and holy traitors to you: 716
TRANSFORMD = 1
Du Sen. I thinke he be transform'd into a beast, 973
TRANSLATE = 1*1
That can translate the stubbornnesse of fortune | Into so quiet and so
sweet a stile. 625
*(to wit) I kill thee, make thee away, translate thy life in- | to 2394
TRAUAILE = 3
Would he not be a comfort to our trauaile? 596
Here's a yong maid with trauaile much oppressed, | And faints for
succour. 858
make me sad, and to trauaile for it too. 1944
TRAUELL = 1
(Maides as we are) to trauell forth so farre? 573
TRAUELLER = *1
Ros. A Traueller: by my faith you haue great rea- | son 1936
TRAUELLERS = *1
*was at home I was in a better place, but Trauellers must | be content. 799
TRAUELLOR = *1
Ros. Farewell Mounsieur Trauellor: looke you 1948

TRAUELLS = *1
*and indeed the sundrie contemplation of my trauells, in   1933
TRAUELS = *1
*Ros. By no meanes sir; Time trauels in diuers paces,   1498
TRAUERS = *1
*them brauely, quite trauers athwart the heart of his lo-|uer,   1749
TREACHEROUS = 1*1
*poyson, entrap thee by some treacherous deuise, and ne-|uer   147
To thinke my pouertie is treacherous.   526
TREASON = 1
Treason is not inherited my Lord,   522
TREBBLE = 1
Turning againe toward childish trebble pipes,   1141
TREE = 7*4
But poore old man, thou prun'st a rotten tree,   767
Song. | *Vnder the greene wood tree*,   890
*the Duke wil drinke vnder this tree; he hath bin all this | day to looke
you.   919
Run, run *Orlando*, carue on euery Tree,   1209
Ros. Peace you dull foole, I found them on a tree.   1313
Clo. Truely the tree yeelds bad fruite.   1314
Tonges Ile hang on euerie tree, | that shall ciuill sayings shoe.   1325
*Palme tree; I was neuer so berim'd since *Pythagoras* time   1373
vnder a tree like a drop'd Acorne.   1429
Ros. It may wel be cal'd loues tree, when it droppes | forth fruite.   1430
*wel met. Will you dispatch vs heere vnder this tree, or   1674
TREES = 3*3
*Findes tongues in trees, bookes in the running brookes,   622
O *Rosalind*, these Trees shall be my Bookes,   1205
*thy name should be hang'd and carued vpon these trees?   1370
Iaq. I pray you marre no more trees with Writing | Loue-songs in their
barkes.   1454
Trees, wherein *Rosalind* is so admired?   1575
A sheep-coat, fenc'd about with Oliue-trees.   2227
TREMBLE = *1
*will kill thee a hundred and fifty wayes, therefore trem-|ble and
depart.   2398
TRIALL = 1*1
*faire eies, and gentle wishes go with mee to my triall;   349
All puritie, all triall, all obseruance: | And so am I for *Phebe*.   2505
TRICKE = *1
*serue me such another tricke, neuer come in my sight | more.   1955
TRIE = 1*1
Duk. You shall trie but one fall.   365
Cel. O, a good wish vpon you: you will trie in time   482
TRIP = 2
Clo. Trip *Audry*, trip *Audry*, I attend, | I attend. *Exeunt*   2405
TRIPT = *1
Cel. It is yong *Orlando*, that tript vp the Wrastlers | heeles, and your
heart, both in an instant.   1406
TRO = 1
Cel. Tro you, who hath done this? | *Ros*. Is it a man?   1375
TROD = *1
*purgation, I haue trod a measure, I haue flattred a Lady,   2621
TRODDEN = *1
*in holiday foolerie, if we walke not in the trodden paths   473

TROILOUS = *1
*a loue cause: *Troilous* had his braines dash'd out with a   2009
TROT = 1
Orl. I prethee, who doth he trot withal?   1502
TROTH = *6
Cel. By my troth thou saiest true: For, since the little   253
Iaq. By my troth, I was seeking for a Foole, when I | found you.   1477
Ros. By my troth, and in good earnest, and so God   2094
*my troth, we that haue good wits, haue much to answer   2352
Clo. By my troth well met: come, sit, sit, and a song.   2539
Clo. By my troth yes: I count it but time lost to heare   2569
TROTS = *2
*who Time trots withal, who Time gallops withal,   1500
Ros. Marry he trots hard with a yong maid, between   1503
TROUBLE = *1
Du Sen. Welcome, fall too: I wil not trouble you,   1152
TROUBLED = *2
*Well sir, get you in. I will not long be troubled with   76
Cel. I warrant you, with pure loue, & troubled brain,   2150
TROWELL = 1
Cel. Well said, that was laid on with a trowell.   271
TRUE = 10*13
Adam. Is old dogge my reward: most true, I haue   82
Cel. 'Tis true, for those that she makes faire, she scarce   206
Cel. By my troth thou saiest true: For, since the little   253
High commendation, true applause, and loue;   431
Though in thy youth thou wast as true a louer   808
*teares, weare these for my sake: wee that are true Lo-|uers,   835
Du Sen. True is it, that we haue seene better dayes,   1097
Cor. Sir, I am a true Labourer, I earne that I eate: get   1270
Ros. Nay, but the diuell take mocking: speake sadde | brow, and true
maid.   1408
Ros. Then there is no true Louer in the Forrest, else   1493
Aud. I do not know what Poetical is: is it honest in | deed and word: is
it a true thing?   1628
Ros. Not true in loue? | *Cel*. Yes, when he is in, but I thinke he is not
in.   1735
Betweene the pale complexion of true Loue,   1761
*true louer hence, and not a word; for here comes more | company.
Exit. Sil.   2222
Ros. O, I know where you are: nay, tis true: there   2438
*cut, he would answer I spake not true: this is call'd the   2653
Phe. If sight & shape be true, why then my loue adieu   2695
If truth holds true contents.   2704
That were with him exil'd. This to be true, | I do engage my life.   2741
you to a loue, that your true faith doth merit: 2765
As we do trust, they'l end in true delights. *Exit*   2775
*Lord the Prologue. If it be true, that good wine needs   2778
*no bush, 'tis true, that a good play needes no Epilogue.   2779
TRUELY = 2*2
*none is like to haue; and truely when he dies, thou shalt   187
Clow. Truely Shepheard, in respect of it selfe, it is a   1213
Clo. Truely the tree yeelds bad fruite.   1314
Cor. If you will see a pageant truely plaid   1760
TRUEST = *1
Clo. No trulie: for the truest poetrie is the most fai-|ning,   1630

TRULIE = *1
*Clo. No trulie: for the truest poetrie is the most fai-|ning,   1630
TRULY = 3*8
Most truly limn'd, and liuing in your face,   1172
Be truly welcome hither: I am the Duke   1173
Was't euer in Court, Shepheard? | Cor. No truly.   1231
*Clo. Truly thou art damn'd, like an ill roasted Egge, | all on one side.   1235
*for no passion truly any thing; as boyes and women are   1592
*in a little roome: truly, I would the Gods hadde | made thee poeticall.   1626
*Clow. I do truly: for thou swear'st to me thou art ho-|nest: 1635
*Clo. No truly, vnlesse thou wert hard fauour'd: for   1639
*Clo. Truly, and to cast away honestie vppon a foule   1645
*Ol. Truly she must be giuen, or the marriage is not | lawfull.   1678
*Clo. Truly yong Gentlemen, though there was no   2565
TRUST = 3
(As I doe trust I am not) then deere Vncle,   510
Let is suffice thee that I trust thee not.   516
As we do trust, they'l end in true delights. Exit   2775
TRUTH = 4*2
*to take thy father for mine; so wouldst thou, if the truth   181
To the last gaspe with truth and loyaltie,   774
Cel. Nay certainly there is no truth in him. | Ros. Doe you thinke so?   1730
*Du Se. If there be truth in sight, you are my daughter.   2693
Orl. If there be truth in sight, you are my Rosalind.   2694
If truth holds true contents.   2704
TRY = 2*2
*in disguis'd against mee to try a fall: to morrow sir I   125
*I come but in as others do, to try with him the strength | of my youth.   334
Ros. I would try if I could cry hem, and haue him.   478
such offenders, and let time try: adieu. Exit.   2106
TUFFT = 1
'Tis at the tufft of Oliues, here hard by: 1847
TUNE = 2*1
*Cel. I would sing my song without a burthen, thou | bring'st me out of tune.   1441
*Iaq. Sing it: 'tis no matter how it bee in tune, so it | make noyse enough.   2134
2.Pa. I faith, y'faith, and both in a tune like two | gipsies on a horse.   2544
TURKE = 1
Like Turke to Christian: womens gentle braine   2182
TURND = 2*1
*haue liu'd manie a faire yeere though Hero had turn'd   2012
And turn'd into the extremity of loue.   2172
Read. Art thou god, to Shepherd turn'd?   2189
TURNE = 5*2
*turne monster: therefore my sweet Rose, my deare Rose, | be merry.   191
And turne his merrie Note,   893
If it do come to passe, that any man turne Asse: 937
Within this tweluemonth, or turne thou no more   1187
Do this expediently, and turne him going. Exeunt   1198
Oli. Twice did he turne his backe, and purpos'd so: 2279
*Ros. Why then to morrow, I cannot serue your turne | for Rosalind?   2457
TURNING = 1*1
*in dispight of a fall: but turning these iests out of seruice,   483
Turning againe toward childish trebble pipes,   1141
TURPH = 1
Who you saw sitting by me on the Turph,   1756

245

TUTORD = 1
And hath bin tutor'd in the rudiments   2607
TWAS = 3*1
*Iaq. You haue a nimble wit; I thinke 'twas made of   1468
Then that mixt in his cheeke: 'twas iust the difference   1896
That her old gloues were on, but twas her hands: 2175
Oli. 'Twas I: but 'tis not I: I doe not shame   2288
TWELUEMONTH = 1*1
Within this tweluemonth, or turne thou no more   1187
*and to betray a shee-Lambe of a tweluemonth   1278
TWENTIE = 3
So neere our publike Court as twentie miles, | Thou diest for it.   503
Orl. And wilt thou haue me? | Ros. I, and twentie such.   2027
Will. Fiue and twentie Sir. | Clo. A ripe age: Is thy name William?   2360
TWENTY = *1
*were there twenty brothers betwixt vs: I haue as much   51
TWICE = 1
Oli. Twice did he turne his backe, and purpos'd so: 2279
TWILL = 2*2
Oli. Call him in: 'twill be a good way: and to mor-|row the wrastling is.   94
And after one houre more, 'twill be eleuen,   998
*'twill out at the key-hole: stop that, 'twill flie with the | smoake out at
the chimney.   2072
TWIXT = 1
Some of violated vowes, | twixt the soules of friend, and friend: 1331
TWO = 9*11
*of her Vncle, then his owne daughter, and neuer two La-|dies loued as
they doe.   112
Which of the two was daughter of the Duke,   437
*Ros. Then there were two Cosens laid vp, when the   466
Enter Duke Senior: Amyens, and two or three Lords | like Forresters.   605
*of a peascod instead of her, from whom I tooke two   833
*of two dog-Apes. And when a man thankes me hartily,   914
Opprest with two weake euils, age, and hunger,   1109
*wee two, will raile against our Mistris the world, and all | our miserie.   1470
*Orl. For these two houres Rosalinde, I wil leaue thee.   2084
*Ros. Alas, deere loue, I cannot lacke thee two houres.   2085
*Orl. I must attend the Duke at dinner, by two a clock | I will be with
thee againe.   2086
*me: 'tis but one cast away, and so come death: two o' | clocke is your
howre.   2091
Ros. How say you now, is it not past two a clock? | And heere much
Orlando.   2148
When from the first to last betwixt vs two,   2293
*was neuer any thing so sodaine, but the sight of two   2439
Heere come two of the banish'd Dukes Pages.   2536
Enter two Pages.   2537
2.Pa. I faith, y'faith, and both in a tune like two | gipsies on a horse.   2544
2.Bro. Let me haue audience for a word or two: 2727
*Is but for two moneths victuall'd: So to your pleasures,   2769
TYDINGS = 1
out of thy mouth, that I may drinke thy tydings.   1398
TYRANT = 3
From tyrant Duke, vnto a tyrant Brother.   456
Ros. She Phebes me: marke how the tyrant writes.   2188
TYRANTS = 2
Are meere vsurpers, tyrants, and whats worse   669

TYRANTS *cont.*
Should be called tyrants, butchers, murtherers.   1785
VACATION = *1
Ros. With Lawiers in the vacation: for they sleepe   1520
VALIANT = 1*2
And wherefore are you gentle, strong, and valiant?   709
*reproofe valiant. If againe, it was not well cut, he wold   2654
*the Reproofe valiant: the fift, the Counterchecke quar- | relsome: 2668
VALUE = 1
I was too yong that time to value her,   532
VDDERS = 1
A Lyonnesse, with vdders all drawne drie,   2265
VEHEMENCE = *1
Ros. Nay, I pre'thee now, with most petitionary ve- | hemence, tell me
who it is.   1385
VEINE = 1
Orl. You touch'd my veine at first, the thorny point   1070
VELUET = 1
Left and abandoned of his veluet friend;   658
VENEMOUS = 1
Which like the toad, ougly and venemous,   619
VENERABLE = *1
Du Sen. Welcome: set downe your venerable bur- | then, and let him
feede.   1147
VENGEANCE = 1
That could do no vengeance to me.   2197
VENISON = 1
Du Sen. Come, shall we goe and kill vs venison?   627
VENTS = 1
With obseruation, the which he vents | In mangled formes. O that I
were a foole,   1014
VENTURD = 1
Ere he should thus haue ventur'd.   402
VENUS = *1
Ros. No, that same wicked Bastard of *Venus*, that was   2117
VERGE = 1
Stood on th'extremest verge of the swift brooke, | Augmenting it with
teares.   649
VERIE = 3*10
Her verie silence, and her patience, | Speake to the people, and they
pittie her.   539
Till that the wearie verie meanes do ebbe.   1047
*naught. In respect that it is solitary, I like it verie well: 1215
*verie vncleanly fluxe of a Cat. Mend the instance Shep- | heard.   1265
*This is the verie false gallop of Verses, why doe you in- | fect your selfe
with them?   1311
Orl. Verie wel, what would you?   1489
*Sir, you are verie well met: goddild you for your last   1682
*companie, I am verie glad to see you, euen a toy in hand   1683
*would you say to me now, and I were your verie, verie | *Rosalind?*   1983
*to kisse: verie good Orators when they are out,   1988
*before marriage; they are in the verie wrath of   2448
*of verie strange beasts, which in all tongues, are call'd | Fooles.   2614
VERILY = 1
A freestone coloured hand: I verily did thinke   2174
VERITY = *1
*but for his verity in loue, I doe thinke him as   1133

247

VERSE = 4*1

Iaq. Ile giue you a verse to this note,	933
Orl. Hang there my verse, in witnesse of my loue,	1201
*themselues without the verse, and therefore stood lame- |ly in the verse.	1367
Iaq. Nay then God buy you, and you talke in blanke | verse.	1946

VERSES = 1*7

*This is the verie false gallop of Verses, why doe you in- |fect your selfe with them?	1311
Cel. Didst thou heare these verses?	1361
*of them had in them more feete then the Verses would | beare.	1363
Cel. That's no matter: the feet might beare y verses.	1365
Orl. I pray you marre no moe of my verses with rea- |ding them ill-fauouredly.	1456
*in good sooth, are you he that hangs the verses on the	1574
Clo. When a mans verses cannot be vnderstood, nor	1623
Cel. O that's a braue man, hee writes braue verses,	1747

VERTUE = 5*1

Shall see thy vertue witnest euery where.	1208
*for you'l be rotten ere you bee halfe ripe, and that's | the right vertue of the Medler.	1317
Orl. 'Tis a fault I will not change, for your best ver- |tue: I am wearie of you.	1475
Orl. Vertue is no horne-maker: and my *Rosalind* is | vertuous.	1976
the onely peace-maker: much vertue in if.	2676
your patience, and your vertue, well deserues it.	2764

VERTUES = 2

But that the people praise her for her vertues,	448
No more doe yours: your vertues gentle Master	715

VERTUOUS = 2*1

*And thou wilt show more bright, & seem more vertuous	542
Why are you vertuous? Why do people loue you?	708
Orl. Vertue is no horne-maker: and my *Rosalind* is | vertuous.	1976

VERY = 17*5

Oli. Know you where you are sir? | *Orl*. O sir, very well: heere in your Orchard.	43
*makes honest, & those that she makes honest, she makes | very illfauouredly.	207
our very petty-coates will catch them.	474
Cor. Else are they very wretched.	852
I will your very faithfull Feeder be,	886
Sayes, very wisely, it is ten a clocke:	995
Hee, that a Foole doth very wisely hit,	1027
Doth very foolishly, although he smart	1028
*but in respect that it is priuate, it is a very vild life. Now	1216
*no wit by Nature, nor Art, may complaine of good | breeding, or comes of a very dull kindred.	1228
Ros. His very haire | Is of the dissembling colour.	1716
the very yce of chastity is in them.	1727
'Tis pretty sure, and very probable,	1782
Sil. Not very well, but I haue met him oft,	1880
It is a pretty youth, not very prettie,	1887
He is not very tall, yet for his yeeres hee's tall:	1892
Ile write to him a very tanting Letter,	1908
Cle. So, so, is good, very good, very excellent good:	2368
*great matter in the dittie, yet y note was very vntunable	2566
Du Se. I like him very well.	2630

VERY *cont*.

    *Du Se. By my faith, he is very swift, and sententious   2639

VESSELL = *1

    *the weaker vessell, as doublet and hose ought to show it   789

VGLY *see* ougly

VICAR = *1

    *Oliuer Mar-text, the Vicar of the next village, who hath   1652

VICTORY = *1

    *horns vpon his head, for a branch of victory; haue you   2131

VICTUALLD = *1

    *Is but for two moneths victuall'd: So to your pleasures,   2769

VIDELICET = *1

    *was not anie man died in his owne person (*videlicet*) in   2008

VILD = *1

    *but in respect that it is priuate, it is a very vild life. Now   1216

VILE = *1

    *Clow. A most wicked Sir *Oliuer*, *Awdrie*, a most vile   2345

VILLAGE = *2

    *Oliuer Mar-text, the Vicar of the next village, who hath   1652

    *Towne is more worthier then a village, so is the fore-|head   1667

VILLAINE = 1*3

    Oli. Wilt thou lay hands on me villaine?   56

    *Orl. I am no villaine: I am the yongest sonne of Sir   57

    *Rowland de Boys, he was my father, and he is thrice a vil-|laine   58

    *Duke. More villaine thou. Well push him out of dores   1195

VILLAINES = 1*1

    *that saies such a father begot villaines: wert thou   59

    It cannot be, some villaines of my Court | Are of consent and sufferance

    in this.   682

VILLANOUS = *2

    *emulator of euery mans good parts, a secret & villanous   141

    *teares I speake it) there is not one so young, and so vil-|lanous   150

VIOLATED = 1

    Some of violated vowes, | *twixt the soules of friend*, *and friend:*   1331

VIRGIN = *1

    *and blood breakes: a poore virgin sir, an il-fauor'd thing   2634

VMBER = 1

    And with a kinde of vmber smirch my face,   576

VNBANDED = *1

    *hose should be vngarter'd, your bonnet vnbanded, your   1563

VNBASHFULL = 1

    Nor did not with vnbashfull forehead woe,   754

VNBORNE = 1

    Neuer so much as in a thought vnborne,   511

VNBUTTOND = *1

    *sleeue vnbutton'd, your shoo vnti'de, and euerie thing   1564

VNCKLE = 1*1

    *religious Vnckle of mine taught me to speake, who was   1532

    Of many desperate studies, by his vnckle,   2608

VNCKLES = *1

    *Ros. There is none of my Vnckles markes vpon you: 1554

VNCLAIMD = 1

    Vnclaim'd of any man. But who come here?   1061

VNCLE = 4*3

    *of her Vncle, then his owne daughter, and neuer two La-|dies loued as

    they doe.   112

    *waight that I loue thee; if my Vncle thy banished father   178

VNCLE *cont*.

*had banished thy Vncle the Duke my Father, so thou	179
And here detain'd by her vsurping Vncle	442
Ros. Me Vncle. | *Duk*. You Cosen,	500
(As I doe trust I am not) then deere Vncle,	510
Ros. Why, whether shall we goe? | *Cel*. To seeke my Vncle in the	
Forrest of *Arden*.	570

VNCLEANE = 1
slut, were to put good meate into an vncleane dish.	1646

VNCLEANLIE = *1
*you kisse your hands; that courtesie would be vncleanlie | if Courtiers	
were shepheards.	1247

VNCLEANLY = *1
*verie vncleanly fluxe of a Cat. Mend the instance Shep-|heard.	1265

VNCOUTH = 1
If this vncouth Forrest yeeld any thing sauage,	956

VNDER = 6*7
*deerely hir'd: but I (his brother) gaine nothing vnder	16
Vnder an oake, whose anticke roote peepes out	638
The thriftie hire I saued vnder your Father,	743
Song. | *Vnder the greene wood tree*,	890
*the Duke wil drinke vnder this tree; he hath bin all this | day to looke	
you.	919
Vnder the shade of melancholly boughes,	1088
vnder a tree like a drop'd Acorne.	1429
Ros. I wil speake to him like a sawcie Lacky, and vn-|der	1487
*wel met. Will you dispatch vs heere vnder this tree, or	1674
*married vnder a bush like a begger? Get you to church,	1690
*Vnder an old Oake, whose bows were moss'd with age	2255
Into a bush, vnder which bushes shade	2264
*Du Se. He vses his folly like a stalking-horse, and vn-|der	2679

VNDERSTAND = 2*1
*with a matter: I am giuen sir secretly to vnderstand, that	123
And let me all your fortunes vnderstand. *Exeunt*.	1178
Ros. I am: what must we vnderstand by this?	2244

VNDERSTANDING = *2
*a mans good wit seconded with the forward childe, vn-|derstanding:	1624
*thou perishest: or to thy better vnderstanding, dyest; or	2393

VNDERSTOOD = *1
Clo. When a mans verses cannot be vnderstood, nor	1623

VNDER-HAND = *1
*vnder-hand meanes laboured to disswade him from it;	138

VNDONE = *1
*enemie, I haue vndone three Tailors, I haue had foure	2623

VNEXPRESSIUE = 1
The faire, the chaste, and vnexpressiue shee. *Exit*	1210

VNFAITHFULL = *1
*may bee chosen out of the grosse band of the vnfaith-|full:	2100

VNFORTUNATE = 1
Rosalind, I am that he, that vnfortunate he.	1577

VNGARTERD = *1
*hose should be vngarter'd, your bonnet vnbanded, your	1563

VNGENTLE = 1
To seeme despightfull and vngentle to you:	2487

VNGENTLENESSE = *1
Phe. Youth, you haue done me much vngentlenesse,	2484

VNHANDSOME = *1
*but it is no more vnhandsome, then to see the 2777
VNHAPPIE = 2
Why, what's the matter? | Ad. O vnhappie youth, ... 719
Du Sen. Thou seest, we are not all alone vnhappie: 1114
VNIUERSALL = 1
This wide and vniuersall Theater 1115
VNKEPT = *1
*more properly) staies me heere at home vnkept: for call 11
VNKINDE = 1
Thou art not so vnkinde, as mans ingratitude 1157
VNKNOWNE = *1
*it cannot bee sounded: my affection hath an vnknowne | bottome, like
the Bay of Portugall. 2113
VNLESSE = *4
*of, and would you yet were merrier: vnlesse you 173
*Clo. No truly, vnlesse thou wert hard fauour'd: for 1639
*shall neuer take her without her answer, vnlesse you take 2080
*neuer haue her, vnlesse thou intreat for her: if you bee a .. 2221
VNLINKD = 1
Seeing Orlando, it vnlink'd it selfe, ... 2262
VNMUZZLE = 1
Ros. I marry, now vnmuzzle your wisedome. 237
VNNATURALL = 2
And he did render him the most vnnaturall | That liu'd amongst men. 2273
Oli. And well he might so doe, | For well I know he was vnnaturall. 2275
VNPEOPLED = 1
Cel. Why should this Desert bee, | for it is vnpeopled? Noe: ... 1323
VNQUESTIONABLE = *1
*and sunken, which you haue not: an vnquestionable spi-|rit, .. 1559
VNREGARDED = 1
And vnregarded age in corners throwne, ... 746
VNSEASONABLY = 1
vnseasonably. He was furnish'd like a Hunter. 1439
VNTIDE = *1
*sleeue vnbutton'd, your shoo vnti'de, and euerie thing 1564
VNTO = 7*1
*Ros. With bils on their neckes: Be it knowne vnto | all men by these
presents. 286
I should haue giuen him teares vnto entreaties, ... 401
From tyrant Duke, vnto a tyrant Brother. 456
vnto the sweet Birds throte: 894
Heigh ho, sing heigh ho, vnto the greene holly, ... 1160
Committing me vnto my brothers loue, ... 2298
Who led me instantly vnto his Caue, ... 2299
Died in this bloud, vnto the Shepheard youth, ... 2309
VNTREASURD = 1
They found the bed vntreasur'd of their Mistris. 687
VNTUNABLE = *1
*great matter in the dittie, yet y note was very vntunable 2566
VNWILLINGLY = 1
Vnwillingly to schoole. And then the Louer, ... 1126
VNWORTHY = 1*2
*God made, a poore vnworthy brother of yours with | idlenesse. 36
The cost of Princes on vnworthy shoulders? 1050
*and the most vnworthy of her you call Rosalinde, that 2099

VOICE = 3*1
And in my voice most welcome shall you be.	872
Amy. My voice is ragged, I know I cannot please | you.	903
For his shrunke shanke, and his bigge manly voice,	1140
*or spitting, or saying we are hoarse, which are the onely | prologues to a bad voice.	2542

VOICES = 1
| *such a foolish song. God buy you, and God mend your \| voices. Come *Audrie. Exeunt*. | 2570 |

VOLUNTARY = *1
| *Lords haue put themselues into voluntary exile with | 103 |

VOWES = 2
| *Some of violated vowes, \| twixt the soules of friend, and friend:* | 1331 |
| For I am falser then vowes made in wine: | 1845 |

VOYAGE = 2
| After a voyage: He hath strange places cram'd | 1013 |
| And you to wrangling, for thy louing voyage | 2768 |

VP = 8*5
Orlan. Goe a-part *Adam*, and thou shalt heare how | he will shake me vp.	30
*onely in the world I fil vp a place, which may bee better | supplied, when I haue made it emptie.	354
Are all throwne downe, and that which here stands vp	416
Ros. Then there were two Cosens laid vp, when the	466
To fright the Annimals, and to kill them vp	670
And hauing that do choake their seruice vp,	765
Cel. It is yong *Orlando*, that tript vp the Wrastlers | heeles, and your heart, both in an instant.	1406
Clo. Come apace good *Audrey*, I wil fetch vp your	1615
Did make offence, his eye did heale it vp:	1891
And by him seale vp thy minde,	2207
Briefe, I recouer'd him, bound vp his wound,	2304
Iaq. And how was that tane vp?	2625
*knew when seuen Iustices could not take vp a Quarrell,	2672

VPON = 25*18
Orlando. | *As I remember *Adam*, it was vpon this fashion	3
Oli. Is it euen so, begin you to grow vpon me? I will	85
*Musicke in his sides? Is there yet another doates vpon	304
Orl. What passion hangs these waights vpo(n) my toong?	424
Grounded vpon no other argument,	447
*vpon curs, throw some of them at me; come lame mee | with reasons.	464
Cel. They are but burs, Cosen, throwne vpon thee	472
Cel. O, a good wish vpon you: you will trie in time	482
Which I haue past vpon her, she is banish'd.	545
If you out-stay the time, vpon mine honor,	549
And doe not seeke to take your change vpon you,	566
A gallant curtelax vpon my thigh,	582
Which when it bites and blowes vpon my body	614
Vpon the brooke that brawles along this wood,	639
Vpon that poore and broken bankrupt there?	665
2.*Lord*. We did my Lord, weeping and commenting | Vpon the sobbing Deere.	673
Weele light vpon some setled low content.	772
As euer sigh'd vpon a midnight pillow:	809
*broke my sword vpon a stone, and bid him take that for	829
Ros. Ioue, Ioue, this Shepherds passion, | Is much vpon my fashion.	841
Go with me, if you like vpon report,	884

VPON *cont*.

And take vpon command, what helpe we haue	1102
And let my officers of such a nature | Make an extent vpon his house and Lands:	1196
But vpon the fairest bowes, | *or at euerie sentence end*;	1333
*thy name should be hang'd and carued vpon these trees?	1370
skirts of the Forrest, like fringe vpon a petticoat.	1525
*barkes; hangs Oades vpon Hauthornes, and Elegies on	1547
*some good counsel, for he seemes to haue the Quotidian | of Loue vpon him.	1550
Ros. There is none of my Vnckles markes vpon you:	1554
*him, and this way wil I take vpon mee to wash your Li-|uer	1599
Falls not the axe vpon the humbled neck,	1775
Some scarre of it: Leane vpon a rush	1793
Her with bitter words: why looke you so vpon me?	1842
A scattred smile, and that Ile liue vpon.	1878
*the wiser, the waywarder: make the doores vpon a wo-|mans	2070
*horns vpon his head, for a branch of victory; haue you	2131
*and play false straines vpon thee? not to be en-|dur'd.	2217
There stript himselfe, and heere vpon his arme	2300
And cride in fainting vpon *Rosalinde*.	2303
*was old Sir *Rowlands* will I estate vpon you, and heere | liue and die a Shepherd.	2419
Looke vpon him, loue him: he worships you.	2489
Clo. 'Faith we met, and found the quarrel was vpon | the seuenth cause.	2626
Clo. Vpon a lye, seuen times remoued: (beare your	2644

VPPON = *1

Clo. Truly, and to cast away honestie vppon a foule	1645

VRGD = 1*1

I cannot speake to her, yet she vrg'd conference.	425
Ros. Patience once more, whiles our co(m)pact is vrg'd:	2580

VS *see also* let's *l*.*51 *200 *215 *259 276 *309 320 404 *418 *484 565 572 601 627 846 857 879 1080 1154 *1260 *1358 *1618 1654 1656 *1674 1765 1767 *1989 *2034 2036 2043 2293 2333 2747 2750 = 22*13

VSE = 2*2

*contriuer against mee his naturall brother: therefore vse	142
To burne the lodging where you vse to lye,	727
Which she did vse, as she was writing of it,	2158
*Yet to good wine they do vse good bushes: and good	2780

VSES = 1*1

Sweet are the vses of aduersitie	618
Du Se. He vses his folly like a stalking-horse, and vn-|der	2679

VSURPE = 1

And in that kinde sweares you doe more vsurpe	634

VSURPERS = 1

Are meere vsurpers, tyrants, and whats worse	669

VSURPING = 1

And here detain'd by her vsurping Vncle	442

VULGAR = *1

*you Clowne, abandon: which is in the vulgar, leaue the	2389

W = *2

*of madnes, w was to forsweare the ful stream of y world,	1597
Orl. What's that? | *Ros*. Why hornes: w such as you are faine to be be-|holding	1972

WAGES = 2

And ere we haue thy youthfull wages spent,	771

WAGES *cont*.
  Cel. And we will mend thy wages: 880
WAGGES = 1
  Thus we may see (quoth he) how the world wagges: 996
WAIES = 2*2
  haue mockt me before: but come your waies.   370
  But come thy waies, weele goe along together,   770
  Ros. I, goe your waies, goe your waies: I knew what   2088
WAIGHT = *1
  *waight that I loue thee; if my Vncle thy banished father   178
WAIGHTS = *1
  Orl. What passion hangs these waights vpo(n) my toong?   424
WAINSCOT = *1
  *Wainscot, then one of you wil proue a shrunke pannell, 1693
WALKE = *1
  *in holiday foolerie, if we walke not in the trodden paths 473
WALLD = *1
  *Is the single man therefore blessed? No, as a wall'd   1666
WANDER = 2
  therefore he giues them good leaue to wander.   105
  *the whetstone of the wits. How now Witte, whether | wander you? 224
WANT = 1
  *then no skill, by so much is a horne more precious | then to want. 1670
WANTING = 1
  That to your wanting may be ministred.   1103
WANTS = *1
  *the worse at ease he is: and that hee that wants money, 1223
WARBLE = 1
  Come, warble, come. | *Song*. *Altogether heere*.   925
WARE = 1*1
  Ros. Thou speak'st wiser then thou art ware of.   838
  Clo. Nay, I shall nere be ware of mine owne wit, till   839
WARNE = *1
  *they will spit, and for louers, lacking (God warne vs) 1989
WARPE = 3
  Though thou the waters warpe, thy sting is not so sharpe, 1166
  and like greene timber, warpe, warpe.   1694
WARRANT = 1*4
  Cha. No, I warrant your Grace you shall not entreat   366
  *you Loue beleeue it, which I warrant she is apter to do, 1571
  Aud. Your features, Lord warrant vs: what features? 1618
  him oth' shoulder, but Ile warrant him heart hole.   1963
  Cel. I warrant you, with pure loue, & troubled brain, 2150
WARST = 1
  War'st thou with a womans heart?   2194
WAS *see also* 'twas = 36*44, *2
  Ros. You haue heard him sweare downright he was. 1737
  Cel. Was, is not is: besides, the oath of Louer is no 1738
WASH = *2
  *him, and this way wil I take vpon mee to wash your Li-|uer 1599
  *(good youth) he went but forth to wash him in the Hel-|lespont, 2014
WASPISH = 1
  By the sterne brow, and waspish action   2157
WAST *l*.808 *1238 2141 = 2*1, 3*1
  Was't euer in Court, Shepheard? | *Cor*. No truly.   1231
  Ros. Was't you he rescu'd?   2286
  Cel. Was't you that did so oft contriue to kill him? 2287

WAST *cont*.
Will. *William*, sir. | *Clo*. A faire name. Was't borne i'th Forrest heere?   2362
WASTE = 2
  I like this place, and willingly could | Waste my time in it.   881
  And we will nothing waste till you returne.   1112
WASTEFUL = *1
  *leane and wasteful Learning; the other knowing no bur-|then   1512
WATCH = 1
  Lay cowching head on ground, with catlike watch   2266
WATERS = 1
  Though thou the waters warpe, thy sting is not so sharpe,   1166
WAY = 5*4
  Oli. Call him in: 'twill be a good way: and to mor-|row the wrastling is.   94
  Deuise the fittest time, and safest way   600
  Cor. That is the way to make her scorne you still.   804
  And little wreakes to finde the way to heauen | By doing deeds of
hospitalitie.   866
  The why is plaine, as way to Parish Church: 1026
  *him, and this way wil I take vpon mee to wash your Li-|uer   1599
  *the way, you shal tell me, where in the Forrest you liue: 1608
  *Well, goe your way to her; (for I see Loue hath   2218
  *to begge will not become mee. My way is to coniure   2785
WAYES = *1
  *will kill thee a hundred and fifty wayes, therefore trem-|ble and
depart.   2398
WAYWARDER = *1
  *the wiser, the waywarder: make the doores vpon a wo-|mans   2070
WE = 48*17
WEAKE = 1
  Opprest with two weake euils, age, and hunger,   1109
WEAKER = 1*1
  Or Charles, or something weaker masters thee.   428
  *the weaker vessell, as doublet and hose ought to show it   789
WEAKNESSE = 1
  The meanes of weaknesse and debilitie,   755
WEALTH = 2
  And get our Iewels and our wealth together,   599
  Leauing his wealth and ease,   938
WEARE = 5*3
  Ros. Gentleman, | Weare this for me: one out of suites with fortune   410
  *teares, weare these for my sake: wee that are true Lo-|uers,   835
  A worthy foole: Motley's the onely weare.   1007
  *that I weare; owe no man hate, enuie no mans happi-|nesse: 1271
  *lispe, and weare strange suites; disable all the benefits   1949
  His Leather skin, and hornes to weare: 2138
  Take thou no scorne to weare the horne,   2140
  thee weare thy heart in a scarfe. | *Orl*. It is my arme.   2430
WEARES = 1
  Weares yet a precious Iewell in his head: 620
WEARIE = 3*1
  Clo. I care not for my spirits, if my legges were not | wearie.   785
  Till that the wearie verie meanes do ebbe.   1047
  Orl. 'Tis a fault I will not change, for your best ver-|tue: I am wearie of
you.   1475
  Ros. I will wearie you then no longer with idle tal-|king.   2460
WEARIED = *1
  *Loue haue you wearied your parishioners withall, and   1354

WEARING = 1
Wearing thy hearer in thy Mistris praise, | Thou hast not lou'd.   820
WEARY = 1
Who after me, hath many a weary steppe   1107
WEATHER = 2
But Winter and rough Weather.   897
As the Winter to fowle Weather.   2710
WEAZEL = 1
As a Weazel suckes egges: More, I pre'thee more.   902
WED = 2*1
*are Aprill when they woe, December when they wed: 2056
Or else refusing me to wed this shepheard: 2598
Nor ne're wed woman, if you be not shee.   2698
WEDDING = 4
gone I say, I wil not to wedding with thee.   1705
Let your Wedding be to morrow: thither will I   2423
Song. | Wedding is great Iunos crowne,   2715
Thou offer'st fairely to thy brothers wedding: 2744
WEDLOCK = 1
High wedlock then be honored: 2719
WEDLOCKE = 2
Pigeons bill, so wedlocke would be nibling.   1688
Whiles a Wedlocke Hymne we sing,   2711
WEE *l.*203 *835 *1470 *1658 *1745 *2660 = *6
WEED = 1
Prouided that you weed your better iudgements   1019
WEEKE = 1
But at fourescore, it is too late a weeke,   778
WEEL = *1
Du Se. Proceed, proceed: wee'l begin these rights,   2774
WEELE = 3
Weele haue a swashing and a marshall outside,   585
But come thy waies, weele goe along together,   770
Weele light vpon some setled low content.   772
WEELL = 1
Cel. Wee'll lead you thither.   2316
WEEPE = 3*3
*blush, and weepe, and thou must looke pale and | wonder.   153
*him: now weepe for him, then spit at him; that I draue   1595
Ros. Neuer talke to me, I wil weepe.   1710
Ros. But haue I not cause to weepe?   1713
Cel. As good cause as one would desire, | Therefore weepe.   1714
*I will weepe for nothing, like *Diana* in the Foun- |taine,   2062
WEEPING = 3*1
take his part with weeping. | *Ros*. Alas.   294
First, for his weeping into the needlesse streame;   654
2.*Lord*. We did my Lord, weeping and commenting | Vpon the sobbing
Deere.   673
*cods, and giuing her them againe, said with weeping   834
WEL = 6*7
Amy. Wel, Ile end the song. Sirs, couer the while,   918
Wel said, thou look'st cheerely,   964
Ros. It may wel be cal'd Ioues tree, when it droppes | forth fruite.   1430
Orl. Verie wel, what would you?   1489
detect the lazie foot of time, as wel as a clocke.   1495
*as wel a darke house, and a whip, as madmen do: 1581
Aud. Well, the Gods giue vs ioy.   1656

WEL *cont*.
*wel met. Will you dispatch vs heere vnder this tree, or   1674
*me wel: and not being wel married, it wil be a good   1697
*woman, Ile meet: so fare you wel: I haue left you com-|mands.   2525
1.*Pa*. Wel met honest Gentleman.   2538
That heere were well begun, and wel begot: 2748
WELCOM = *1
Du Sen. Sit downe and feed, & welcom to our table   1082
WELCOME = 5*4
And in my voice most welcome shall you be.   872
Du Sen. Welcome: set downe your venerable bur-|then, and let him
feede.   1147
Du Sen. Welcome, fall too: I wil not trouble you,   1152
Be truly welcome hither: I am the Duke   1173
Thou art right welcome, as thy masters is: 1176
Iaq. Good my Lord, bid him welcome: This is the   2617
Du Se. O my deere Neece, welcome thou art to me,   2722
Euen daughter welcome, in no lesse degree.   2723
Du Se. Welcome yong man: 2743
WELL *see also* fareyouwel = 29*32
*on his blessing to breed mee well: and   7
Oli. Know you where you are sir? | *Orl*. O sir, very well: heere in your
Orchard.   43
*Well sir, get you in. I will not long be troubled with   76
*some broken limbe, shall acquit him well: your brother   127
*from his intendment, or brooke such disgrace well as he   132
Ros. Well, I will forget the condition of my estate, | to reioyce in
yours.   184
Cel. Well said, that was laid on with a trowell.   271
Cel. Well, the beginning that is dead and buried.   281
Ros. Fare you well: praie heauen I be deceiu'd in you.   359
Orl. Yes I beseech your Grace, I am not yet well | breath'd.   378
But fare thee well, thou art a gallant youth,   391
Sticks me at heart: Sir, you haue well deseru'd,   406
Shall we goe Coze? | *Cel*. I: fare you well faire Gentleman.   413
Sir, you haue wrastled well, and ouerthrowne | More then your enemies.   420
Cel. Will you goe Coze? | *Ros*. Haue with you: fare you well. *Exit*.   422
Will sodainly breake forth: Sir, fare you well,   451
Orl. I rest much bounden to you: fare you well.   454
Cel. Why should I not? doth he not deserue well?   493
Orl. Oh good old man, how well in thee appeares   760
Then to die well, and not my Masters debter. *Exeunt*.   780
Ros. Well, this is the Forrest of *Arden*.   797
Iaq. Well then, if euer I thanke any man, Ile thanke   912
His youthfull hose well sau'd, a world too wide,   1139
Duke. More villaine thou. Well push him out of dores   1195
*naught. In respect that it is solitary, I like it verie well: 1215
*in respect it is in the fields, it pleaseth mee well: but in   1217
*life (looke you) it fits my humor well: but as there is no   1219
Ros. Though it be pittie to see such a sight, it well | becomes the
ground.   1436
*well: for there he fel in loue. I haue heard him read ma-|ny   1534
Aud. Well, I am not faire, and therefore I pray the | Gods make me
honest.   1643
Clo. Well, praised be the Gods, for thy foulnesse; slut-|tishnesse   1649
*of them. Well, that is the dowrie of his wife, 'tis none   1663
*Sir, you are verie well met: goddild you for your last   1682

WELL *cont.*

Cel. Well: and what of him?	1759
But since that thou canst talke of loue so well,	1868
Sil. Not very well, but I haue met him oft,	1880
'Tis but a peeuish boy, yet he talkes well,	1884
But what care I for words? yet words do well	1885
His leg is but so so, and yet 'tis well:	1893
Ros. Well, in her person, I say I will not haue you.	2004
Ros. Well, Time is the olde Iustice that examines all	2105
*Conquerour, and it would doe well to set the Deares	2130
Why writes she so to me? well Shepheard, well,	2167
*Well, goe your way to her; (for I see Loue hath	2218
Oli. And well he might so doe, | For well I know he was vnnaturall.	2275
*Ah, sirra, a body would thinke this was well counterfei-|ted,	2321
*I pray you tell your brother how well I counterfei-|ted: heigh-ho.	2322
Oli. Well then, take a good heart, and counterfeit to | be a man.	2328
Clo. Why, thou saist well. I do now remember a say-|ing:	2372
Clo. By my troth well met: come, sit, sit, and a song.	2539
Du Se. I like him very well.	2630
*said his beard was not cut well, hee was in the minde it	2647
*word againe, it was not well cut, he wold send me word	2649
*If againe, it was not well cut, he disabled my iudgment:	2651
*this is called, the reply churlish. If againe it was not well	2652
*reproofe valiant. If againe, it was not well cut, he wold	2654
Iaq. And how oft did you say his beard was not well | cut?	2657
That heere were well begun, and wel begot:	2748
your patience, and your vertue, well deserues it.	2764

WELL-DESERUED = 1

you to a long, and well-deserued bed:	2767

WENT = 2*2

And wheresoere we went, like *Iunos* Swans,	536
Still we went coupled and inseperable.	537
*he? How look'd he? Wherein went he? What makes hee	1415
*(good youth) he went but forth to wash him in the Hel-|lespont,	2014

WERE *l.**51 *173 *182 227 *231 *233 *241 *356 *372 394 *466 579 *785 810 862 1015 *1169 1170 1182 1248 *1366 *1540 1557 1646 *1657 *1695 1862 1865 1904 *1983 *1986 *1987 *1996 2165 2175 *2255 2315 *2377 2585 *2592 *2673 2732 2741 2748 *2791 = 21*25

WERT *l.**59 *144 *1636 *1639 *2103 = *5

WEST = *1

Cel. West of this place, down in the neighbor bottom	2228

WESTERNE = 1

Ros. From the east to westerne Inde, | no iewel is like Rosalinde,	1286

WET = *1

*the propertie of raine is to wet, and fire to burne: That	1225

WHAT *l.*32 34 *41 54 *75 *120 *188 194 199 253 266 *267 *296 383 419 *424 434 565 569 572 584 588 591 594 617 651 705 707 717 *735 738 871 *873 908 930 *982 984 *1036 1037 1048 1053 1057 1066 1078 1086 1094 1102 1192 *1353 *1372 *1400 *1413 *1414 *1415 1462 1489 1490 *1491 1557 *1618 *1628 *1631 *1659 *1681 *1691 *1743 *1745 1759 1810 1814 1856 1885 1903 *1982 1998 *2010 2024 2029 *2034 2078 *2088 *2109 2137 2201 *2216 2244 2246 2253 2254 2289 2456 *2473 *2490 *2522 2772 *2782 = 62*37

WHATERE *see* ere

WHATS = 6*1

Oli. Good Mounsier *Charles*: what's the new newes | at the new Court?	98
Boon-iour Monsieur le Beu, what's the newes?	263

WHATS *cont.*
What's that to me, my Father was no Traitor, 524
Are meere vsurpers, tyrants, and whats worse 669
Why, what's the matter? | *Ad.* O vnhappie youth, 719
Amy. What's that Ducdame? 943
Orl. What's that? | **Ros.* Why hornes: w such as you are faine to be
be- | holding 1972
WHEELE = *1
*from her wheele, that her gifts may henceforth bee | bestowed equally. 201
WHEN *l.**75 *187 *190 *213 *217 355 *466 *520 521 543 588 614 717 745
762 *798 *828 *914 1001 1049 1052 *1414 *1417 *1430 *1443 *1460
*1477 *1623 1736 *1745 1805 1833 1886 *1986 *1988 2042 *2056 *2057
*2058 *2063 *2064 2249 2267 2293 *2312 *2375 *2376 2436 *2471 2551
*2584 *2672 *2673 2684 2796 = 23*33
WHENCE = 1
from whence you haue studied your questions. 1467
WHERE *l.*43 114 229 *279 *361 695 727 764 857 974 1091 1208 *1416
1523 *1527 1606 *1608 1859 *1953 2226 2246 *2438 2736 = 16*7
WHEREFORE = 3
'Tis iust the fashion; wherefore doe you looke 664
And wherefore are you gentle, strong, and valiant? 709
You foolish Shepheard, wherefore do you follow her 1822
WHEREIN = 3*3
*thoughts, wherein I confesse me much guiltie to denie 347
*wherein if I bee foil'd, there is but one sham'd that was 350
There then, how then, what then, let me see wherein 1057
Presents more wofull Pageants then the Sceane | Wherein we play in. 1116
*he? How look'd he? Wherein went he? What makes hee 1415
Trees, wherein *Rosalind* is so admired? 1575
WHEREON = 1
Tell me whereon the likelihoods depends? 518
WHERESOERE = 2
And wheresoere we went, like *Iunos* Swans, 536
Finde out thy brother wheresoere he is, 1185
WHERE-EUER *see* euer
WHETHER = 6*3
*the whetstone of the wits. How now Witte, whether | wander you? 224
Cel. O my poore *Rosaline*, whether wilt thou goe? 552
Whether to goe, and what to beare with vs, 565
Ros. Why, whether shall we goe? | *Cel.* To seeke my Vncle in the
Forrest of *Arden.* 570
**Ad.* Why whether *Adam* would'st thou haue me go? 733
Ad. No matter whether, so you come not here. 734
**Clo.* You haue said: but whether wisely or no, let the | Forrest iudge. 1319
**Orl.* A man that had a wife with such a wit, he might | say, wit
whether wil't? 2074
Whether that thy youth and kinde 2208
WHETSTONE = *2
*our whetstone: for alwaies the dulnesse of the foole, is 223
*the whetstone of the wits. How now Witte, whether | wander you? 224
WHICH *see also* w *l.**17 *24 *35 *135 168 *259 *275 *289 *354 416 437
545 561 614 619 640 657 744 1012 1014 1096 1207 1374 1482 *1555
*1558 *1559 *1560 *1571 *1573 *1588 1796 1869 *1926 *1927 *1928
*1929 *1930 *1934 2127 2158 2264 2283 2302 2387 *2389 *2390 *2391
*2447 *2478 *2542 *2614 2732 = 25*32
WHILE = 4*2
**Oliuer.* Marry sir be better employed, and be naught | a while. 38

WHILE cont.
*Amy. Wel, Ile end the song. Sirs, couer the while, 918
For my sake be comfortable, hold death a while 959
Orl. Then but forbeare your food a little while: 1104
*haue you bin all this while? you a louer? and you 1954
Which all this while had bled: and now he fainted, 2302
WHILES = 4*1
Whiles (like a Doe) I go to finde my Fawne, 1105
Whiles the eye of man did wooe me, 2196
Whiles you chid me, I did loue, 2203
*Ros. Patience once more, whiles our co(m)pact is vrg'd: 2580
Whiles a Wedlocke Hymne we sing, 2711
WHINING = 1
Then, the whining Schoole-boy with his Satchell 1124
WHIP = *1
*as wel a darke house, and a whip, as madmen do: 1581
WHIPPERS = *1
*that the Lunacie is so ordinarie, that the whippers are in 1583
WHIPT = *1
*speake no more of him, you'l be whipt for taxation one | of these
daies. 249
WHISPERD = 1
As you haue whisper'd faithfully you were, 1170
WHISTLES = 1
And whistles in his sound. Last Scene of all, 1142
WHIT = *1
*Cor. Not a whit Touchstone, those that are good ma-|ners 1243
WHITE = *1
*Orl. I sweare to thee youth, by the white hand of 1576
WHITHER see whether
WHO l.*165 *221 246 *375 *802 850 892 927 988 1044 1051 1061 1107
1375 1379 1383 1387 *1393 *1499 *1500 1501 1502 1507 1515 1519
*1532 *1652 1752 1756 1784 *1808 1854 *1994 2153 2260 2283 2297
2299 *2348 = 27*13
WHOLE see also hole = 1
hath generally tax'd their whole sex withal. 1537
WHOLESOME = *1
*is not the grease of a Mutton, as wholesome as the sweat 1253
WHOM l.45 *688 *833 1023 1473 2609 = 4*2
WHOS = 1
Orl. Who's there? | Ad. What my yong Master, oh my gentle master, 704
WHOSE = 4*2
*him, whose lands and reuenues enrich the new Duke, 104
To keepe his daughter companie, whose loues 443
Vnder an oake, whose anticke roote peepes out 638
Whose heart th'accustom'd sight of death makes hard 1774
*Vnder an old Oake, whose bows were moss'd with age 2255
Whose heart within his bosome is. 2690
WHY l.*161 298 *460 493 534 570 707 708 710 719 *733 *954 *982 1044
1060 1064 *1238 *1250 *1252 *1311 1323 *1403 *1496 *1582 *1728 1788
*1808 1814 1842 1858 1865 1906 1924 1925 *1953 *1973 *2032 2043
2167 2180 2181 2193 2246 2311 *2372 *2457 2510 2511 2512 *2513
*2695 = 32*23, 2
They most must laugh: And why sir must they so? 1025
The why is plaine, as way to Parish Church: 1026
WICKED = *3
*then thy manners must be wicked, and wickednes is sin, 1240

WICKED cont.
*Ros. No, that same wicked Bastard of Venus, that was   2117
*Clow. A most wicked Sir Oliuer, Awdrie, a most vile   2345
WICKEDNES = *1
*then thy manners must be wicked, and wickednes is sin,   1240
WIDE = 4
Cel. Heele goe along ore the wide world with me,   597
This wide and vniuersall Theater   1115
His youthfull hose well sau'd, a world too wide,   1139
With all Graces wide enlarg'd, | nature presently distill'd   1341
WIFE = 4*3
*of them. Well, that is the dowrie of his wife, 'tis none   1663
excuse for me heereafter, to leaue my wife.   1698
fortune, and preuents the slander of his wife.   1975
*Cel. Goe too: wil you Orlando, haue to wife this Ro-|salind? | Orl. I
will.   2039
*Ros. Then you must say, I take thee Rosalind for | wife.   2044
Orl. I take thee Rosalind for wife.   2046
*Orl. A man that had a wife with such a wit, he might | say, wit
whether wil't?   2074
WIL l.*277 *321 *344 908 910 *916 *919 957 960 962 966 *1152 *1257
*1472 *1487 *1544 *1599 1609 *1615 *1651 1677 1685 *1689 *1692
*1693 *1697 1705 1710 *2039 *2063 *2084 *2519 *2522 2582 *2584
2724 = 13*23
WILDE = 1
And to the skirts of this wilde Wood he came;   2735
WILD-GOOSE = 1
Why then my taxing like a wild-goose flies   1060
WILL see also heele, hee'll, Ile, shee'll, they'l, 'twill, wee'l, weele, wee'll,
you'l l.*26 31 *66 *70 *73 *76 *79 *85 114 *136 *146 *159 *184 *189
*190 *193 *259 269 *313 *323 422 451 474 *482 553 572 584 591 601
724 729 739 740 764 773 846 871 880 886 *899 942 1033 1035 1076 1110
1112 *1281 1301 1302 1309 *1316 *1403 *1469 *1470 1475 *1605 1612
*1674 1760 1764 1776 1846 1848 1870 1913 *1952 *1960 *1989 2004
*2022 *2023 2024 2036 2038 2042 *2058 *2062 *2064 2066 2067 *2071
2083 2087 *2097 2185 *2220 2245 *2312 2317 2334 2337 *2395 *2396
*2397 *2398 2412 *2419 2423 *2447 *2449 *2451 *2460 *2480 2482
*2517 *2520 2533 2587 2591 *2636 *2665 2761 *2785 *2795 = 61*56,
6*4
*bequeathed me by will, but poore a thousand   5
*father charg'd you in his will to giue me good educati-|on: 67
*you: you shall haue some part of your will, I pray you | leaue me.   77
*shall runne into, in that it is a thing of his owne search, | and
altogether against my will.   133
*Orl. Readie Sir, but his will hath in it a more modest | working.   363
A stubborne will to please,   939
Will I Rosalinda write, | teaching all that reade, to know   1335
Phe. For no ill will I beare you.   1843
Were man as rare as Phenix: 'od's my will,   2165
Will the faithfull offer take   2209
WILL = 11
WILLIAM see also Will. = 5
Enter William.   2350
Aud. God ye good eu'n William.   2355
Will. Fiue and twentie Sir. | Clo. A ripe age: Is thy name William?   2360
Will. William, sir. | Clo. A faire name. Was't borne i'th Forrest heere?   2362
Aud. Do good William. | Will. God rest you merry sir. Exit   2400

WILLING = 1*1
*neuer gracious: if kil'd, but one dead that is willing to   351
Ros. You say, you'l marrie me, if I be willing.   2586
WILLINGLY = 1
I like this place, and willingly could | Waste my time in it.   881
WILT *l*.56 *75 *542 552 553 *1268 1909 2027 2075 *2216 = 6*4
WINDE = 5*1
And churlish chiding of the winters winde,   613
Withall, as large a Charter as the winde,   1022
Song. | *Blow, blow, thou winter winde*,   1155
Hir worth being mounted on the winde, | *through all the world beares*
Rosalinde.   1288
Oliuer leaue me not behind thee: But winde away, bee   1704
Like foggy South, puffing with winde and raine,   1823
WINE = 1*3
*Wine comes out of a narrow-mouth'd bottle: either too   1396
For I am falser then vowes made in wine: 1845
*Lord the Prologue. If it be true, that good wine needs   2778
*Yet to good wine they do vse good bushes: and good   2780
WINGD = 1
Orl. So do all thoughts, they are wing'd.   2051
WINTER = 4
Therefore my age is as a lustie winter,   756
But Winter and rough Weather.   897
Song. | *Blow, blow, thou winter winde*,   1155
As the Winter to fowle Weather: 2710
WINTERS = 1*1
And churlish chiding of the winters winde,   613
*Nun of winters sisterhood kisses not more religiouslie,   1726
WINTRED = 1
Wintred garments must be linde, | *so must slender Rosalinde:*   1303
WIPD = 2
If euer from your eye-lids wip'd a teare,   1093
And sat at good mens feasts, and wip'd our eies   1099
WISE = 4*4
*I will no longer endure it, though yet I know no wise | remedy how to
auoid it.   26
*wise men haue makes a great shew; Heere comes Mon-|sieur the *Beu*.   255
That I am wise. I must haue liberty   1021
Full of wise sawes, and moderne instances,   1135
*of a good peece of flesh indeed: learne of the wise   1263
Ros. By my life, she will doe as I doe. | *Orl*. O but she is wise.   2067
Art thou wise? | *Will*. I sir, I haue a prettie wit.   2370
*The Foole doth thinke he is wise, but the wiseman   2373
WISEDOME = 1
Ros. I marry, now vnmuzzle your wisedome.   237
WISELY = 2*2
Clo. The more pittie that fooles may not speak wise-|ly, what
Wisemen do foolishly.   251
Sayes, very wisely, it is ten a clocke: 995
Hee, that a Foole doth very wisely hit,   1027
Clo. You haue said: but whether wisely or no, let the | Forrest iudge.   1319
WISEMAN = *1
*The Foole doth thinke he is wise, but the wiseman   2373
WISEMEN = 1
Clo. The more pittie that fooles may not speak wise-|ly, what
Wisemen do foolishly.   251

WISER = 1*2
*Clo. Thus men may grow wiser euery day. It is the	299
Ros. Thou speak'st wiser then thou art ware of.	838
*the wiser, the waywarder: make the doores vpon a wo-|mans	2070

WISE-MANS = 1
The Wise-mans folly is anathomiz'd	1030

WISH = 1*2
*Cel. O, a good wish vpon you: you will trie in time	482
And wish for her sake more then for mine owne,	861
*Aud. Do you wish then that the Gods had made me | Poeticall?	1633

WISHES = 2*1
*faire eies, and gentle wishes go with mee to my triall;	349
happie, in hauing what he wishes for.	2456
All made of passion, and all made of wishes,	2502

WIT = 9*10
*hath giuen vs wit to flout at Fortune, hath not Fortune	215
*wit that fooles haue was silenced, the little foolerie that	254
Ros. As wit and fortune will. | Clo. Or as the destinies decrees.	269
*Clo. Nay, I shall nere be ware of mine owne wit, till	839
*no wit by Nature, nor Art, may complaine of good | breeding, or	
comes of a very dull kindred.	1228
Cor. You haue too Courtly a wit, for me, Ile rest.	1267
*Iaq. You haue a nimble wit; I thinke 'twas made of	1468
*a mans good wit seconded with the forward childe, vn-|derstanding:	1624
or I should thinke my honestie ranker then my wit.	1997
*Ros. Or else shee could not haue the wit to doe this:	2069
*wit, and it will out at the casement: shut that, and	2071
*Orl. A man that had a wife with such a wit, he might | say, wit	
whether wil't?	2074
met your wiues wit going to your neighbours bed.	2077
Orl. And what wit could wit haue, to excuse that?	2078
Art thou wise? | Will. I sir, I haue a prettie wit.	2370
*(to wit) I kill thee, make thee away, translate thy life in-|to	2394
the presentation of that he shoots his wit.	2680

WITH = 110*85

WITHAL = 6*2
*who Time trots withal, who Time gallops withal,	1500
Orl. I prethee, who doth he trot withal?	1502
Orl. Who ambles Time withal?	1507
*of heauie tedious penurie. These Time ambles | withal.	1513
Orl. Who doth he gallop withal?	1515
Orl. Who staies it stil withal?	1519
hath generally tax'd their whole sex withal.	1537

WITHALL = 2*4
*to acquaint you withall, that either you might stay him	131
*Cel. Marry I prethee doe, to make sport withall: but	195
Withall, as large a Charter as the winde,	1022
*Loue haue you wearied your parishioners withall, and	1354
*with diuers persons: Ile tel you who Time ambles with-|all,	1499
and who he stands stil withall.	1501

WITHIN = 8*2
*is within mee, begins to mutinie against this seruitude.	25
Within these ten daies if that thou beest found	502
Come not within these doores: within this roofe	721
And you within it: if he faile of that	728
Within this tweluemonth, or turne thou no more	1187
*Orl. My faire Rosalind, I come within an houre of my | promise.	1957

WITHIN *cont.*

But at this howre, the house doth keepe it selfe, | There's none within.	2231
Within an houre, and pacing through the Forrest,	2251
Whose heart within his bosome is.	2690

WITHOUT = 3 *9

*wrastle for my credit, and hee that escapes me without	126
*one should be lam'd with reasons, and the other mad | without any.	467
*meanes, and content, is without three good frends. That	1224
*themselues without the verse, and therefore stood lame-|ly in the verse.	1367
Cel. But didst thou heare without wondering, how	1369
Cel. I would sing my song without a burthen, thou | bring'st me out of tune.	1441
Then without Candle may goe darke to bed:	1812
Ros. Say a day, without the euer: no, no *Orlando*, men	2055
*shall neuer take her without her answer, vnlesse you take	2080
*her without her tongue: o that woman that cannot	2081
*to set her before your eyes to morrow, humane as she is, | and without any danger.	2475
1.Pa. Shal we clap into't roundly, without hauking,	2541

WITH-HELD = 1

To one his lands with-held, and to the other	2745

WITNESSE = 2

And as mine eye doth his effigies witnesse,	1171
Orl. Hang there my verse, in witnesse of my loue,	1201

WITNEST = 1

Shall see thy vertue witnest euery where.	1208

WITS = *3

*but Natures, who perceiueth our naturall wits too dull	221
*the whetstone of the wits. How now Witte, whether | wander you?	224
*my troth, we that haue good wits, haue much to answer	2352

WITTE = 1 *1

*fortune makes natures naturall, the cutter off of natures | witte.	218
*the whetstone of the wits. How now Witte, whether | wander you?	224

WIUES = 1 *3

*with goldsmiths wiues, & cond the(m) out of rings	1465
*to your wiues for: but he comes armed in his	1974
*when they are wiues: I will bee more iealous of	2058
met your wiues wit going to your neighbours bed.	2077

WOE = 4 *2

Leaue me alone to woe him; Let's away	598
Nor did not with vnbashfull forehead woe,	754
That your poore friends must woe your companie,	983
*to woe me. At which time would I, being but a moonish	1588
and come euerie day to my Coat, and woe me.	1604
*are Aprill when they woe, December when they wed:	2056

WOFULL = 2

Presents more wofull Pageants then the Sceane | Wherein we play in.	1116
Sighing like Furnace, with a wofull ballad	1127

WOING = *1

*pouertie of her, the small acquaintance, my sodaine wo-|ing,	2414

WOLD *l.**1494 *2649 *2654 = *3

WOLUES = *1

*of Irish Wolues against the Moone: I will helpe you	2517

WOMAN = 11 *14

*mightily misplaced, and the bountifull blinde woman | doth most mistake in her gifts to women.	204

WOMAN *cont*.

*apparell, and to cry like a woman: but I must comfort	788
What woman in the Citie do I name,	1048
When that I say the City woman beares	1049
Ros. Do you not know I am a woman, when I thinke, | I must speake:	
sweet, say on.	1443
*Lectors against it, and I thanke God, I am not a Wo-|man	1535
Ol. Is there none heere to giue the woman?	1676
Then she a woman. 'Tis such fooles as you	1825
*then you make a woman: besides, he brings his destinie | with him.	1970
*her without her tongue: o that woman that cannot	2081
Can a woman raile thus?	2191
*wilt thou loue such a woman? what to make thee an in-|strument,	2216
Of femall fauour, and bestowes himselfe | Like a ripe sister: the woman	
low	2236
Ros. So I doe: but yfaith, I should haue beene a wo-|man by right.	2330
Will. Which he sir? | *Clo*. He sir, that must marrie this woman:	
Therefore	2387
*which in the common, is woman: which toge-|ther,	2391
Orl. And I for *Rosalind*. | *Ros*. And I for no woman.	2494
Orl. And I for *Rosalind*. | *Ros*. And I for no woman.	2499
Orl. And so am I for *Rosalind*. | *Ros*. And so am I for no woman.	2508
*me altogether: I wil marrie you, if euer I marrie Wo-|man,	2519
*woman, Ile meet: so fare you wel: I haue left you com-|mands.	2525
*no dishonest desire, to desire to be a woman of y world?	2535
Nor ne're wed woman, if you be not shee.	2698
Or haue a Woman to your Lord.	2708
*and the women, the play may please. If I were a Wo-|man,	2791

WOMANS = 2*2

Lye there what hidden womans feare there will,	584
*girle goes before the Priest, and certainely a Womans | thought runs	
before her actions.	2049
*the wiser, the waywarder: make the doores vpon a wo-|mans	2070
War 'st thou with a womans heart?	2194

WOMEN = 4*6

*mightily misplaced, and the bountifull blinde woman | doth most	
mistake in her gifts to women.	204
Ia. All the world's a stage, | And all the men and women, meerely	
Players;	1118
that he laid to the charge of women?	1539
*which women stil giue the lie to their consciences. But	1573
*for no passion truly any thing; as boyes and women are	1592
There be some women *Siluius*, had they markt him	1898
*you, and Ile begin with the Women. I charge you (O	2786
*women) for the loue you beare to men, to like as much	2787
*for the loue you beare to women (as I perceiue by your	2789
*and the women, the play may please. If I were a Wo-|man,	2791

WOMENS = 2

*and suppers, and sleeping hours excepted: it is the right | Butter-	
womens ranke to Market.	1295
Like Turke to Christian: womens gentle braine	2182

WONDER = 2*1

*blush, and weepe, and thou must looke pale and | wonder.	153
Ros. I was seuen of the nine daies out of the wonder,	1371
That reason, wonder may diminish	2713

WONDERFUL = *1
*wonderfull, and yet againe wonderful, and after that out | of all
hooping.   1388
WONDERFULL = *4
*Cel. O wonderfull, wonderfull, and most wonderfull   1387
*wonderfull, and yet againe wonderful, and after that out | of all
hooping.   1388
WONDERING = *1
*Cel. But didst thou heare without wondering, how   1369
WONDERS = 1
Orl. I, and greater wonders then that.   2437
WONNE = *1
*thought no lesse: that flattering tongue of yours wonne   2090
WONT = 1
Your Grace was wont to laugh is also missing,   689
WOO = *1
*And louing woo? and wooing, she should graunt? And | will you
perseuer to enioy her?   2411
WOOD = 4*1
Vpon the brooke that brawles along this wood,   639
Song. | Vnder the greene wood tree,   890
*but the wood, no assembly but horne-beasts. But what   1659
sight, I had as liefe be woo'd of a Snaile.   1966
And to the skirts of this wilde Wood he came;   2735
WOODS = 1
Then that of painted pompe? Are not these woods   609
WOOE see also woe = 2*2
I had rather here you chide, then this man wooe.   1838
*Ros. Come, wooe me, wooe mee: for now I am in a   1981
Whiles the eye of man did wooe me,   2196
WOOING = *2
*chopt hands had milk'd; and I remember the wooing   832
*And louing woo? and wooing, she should graunt? And | will you
perseuer to enioy her?   2411
WORD = 8*8
*he would not haue spoke such a word. Ex. Orl. Ad.   84
Not a word? | Ros. Not one to throw at a dog.   461
And in the greatnesse of my word you die. | Exit Duke, &c.   550
*parted he with thee? And when shalt thou see him a- | gaine? Answer
me in one word.   1417
*'tis a Word too great for any mouth of this Ages size, to   1420
*Aud. I do not know what Poetical is: is it honest in | deed and word: is
it a true thing?   1628
*stronger then the word of a Tapster, they are both the   1739
*true louer hence, and not a word; for here comes more | company.
Exit. Sil.   2222
*Keepe you your word, O Duke, to giue your daughter,   2595
Keepe you your word Phebe, that you'l marrie me,   2597
Keepe your word Siluius, that you'l marrie her   2599
*cut of a certaine Courtiers beard: he sent me word, if I   2646
*word againe, it was not well cut, he wold send me word   2649
Phe. I wil not eate my word, now thou art mine,   2724
2.Bro. Let me haue audience for a word or two: 2727
WORDS = 6*2
*Cel. No, thy words are too precious to be cast away   463
If their purgation did consist in words,   514
*speakes braue words, sweares braue oathes, and breakes   1748

266

WORDS cont.
Her with bitter words: why looke you so vpon me?   1842
But what care I for words? yet words do well   1885
Orl. Pray thee marrie vs. | Cel. I cannot say the words.   2036
Such Ethiop words, blacker in their effect   2184
WORE = 1*1
*Cel. And a chaine that you once wore about his neck: 1377
Thy fathers father wore it,   2142
WORK = *1
*Cel. Peraduenture this is not Fortunes work neither,   220
WORKE = 2
Of Natures sale-worke? 'ods my little life,   1816
Would they worke in milde aspect?   2202
WORKING = 2
*Orl. Readie Sir, but his will hath in it a more modest | working.   363
how full of briers is this working day world.   471
WORLD = 18*10
carelesly as they did in the golden world.   119
*so much in the heart of the world, and especially of my   164
*Fortune reignes in gifts of the world, not in the | lineaments of Nature.   210
*lament me: the world no iniurie, for in it I haue nothing: 353
*onely in the world I fil vp a place, which may bee better | supplied,
when I haue made it emptie.   354
The world esteem'd thy father honourable,   387
And all the world was of my Fathers minde,   399
Hereafter in a better world then this,   452
how full of briers is this working day world.   471
Cel. Heele goe along ore the wide world with me,   597
Oh what a world is this, when what is comely | Enuenoms him that
beares it?   717
The constant seruice of the antique world,   761
A motley Foole (a miserable world:)   986
Thus we may see (quoth he) how the world wagges: 996
Cleanse the foule bodie of th'infected world,   1034
Would'st thou disgorge into the generall world.   1043
His youthfull hose well sau'd, a world too wide,   1139
Hir worth being mounted on the winde, | through all the world beares
Rosalinde.   1288
*wee two, will raile against our Mistris the world, and all | our miserie.   1470
*Orl. I wil chide no breather in the world but my selfe   1472
*of madnes, w was to forsweare the ful stream of y world,   1597
That makes the world full of ill-fauourd children: 1826
And be not proud, though all the world could see,   1850
*Ros. No faith, die by Attorney: the poore world is   2006
*your head, and shew the world what the bird hath done | to her owne
neast.   2109
in the world: here comes the man you meane.   2349
*no dishonest desire, to desire to be a woman of y world?   2535
Both from his enterprize, and from the world: 2738
WORLDLINGS = 1
As worldlings doe, giuing thy sum of more   656
WORLDS = 1
Ia. All the world's a stage, | And all the men and women, meerely
Players;   1118
WORMES = *2
*Clo. Most shallow man: Thou wormes meate in re-|spect   1262
*from time to time, and wormes haue eaten them, but not | for loue.   2019

WORME-EATEN = 1
concaue as a couered goblet, or a Worme-eaten nut.   1734
WORSE = 2*3
*Ros. Ile haue no worse a name then *Ioues* owne Page,   589
Are meere vsurpers, tyrants, and whats worse   669
*the worse at ease he is: and that hee that wants money,   1223
*Iaq. O knowledge ill inhabited, worse then Ioue in | a thatch'd house.   1621
*fellowes, and betray themselues to euery mo- | derne censure, worse
then drunkards.   1922
WORSHIP = 4
Enter Dennis. | Den. Calls your worship?   88
Cha. Good morrow to your worship.   97
so God keepe your worship. Exit.   158
That can entame my spirits to your worship: 1821
WORSHIPS = 1
Looke vpon him, loue him: he worships you.   2489
WORST = 1
Iaq. The worst fault you haue, is to be in loue.   1474
WORTH = 5
Worth seizure, do we seize into our hands,   1190
Hir worth being mounted on the winde, | through all the world beares
Rosalinde.   1288
Is his head worth a hat? Or his chin worth a beard?   1401
Men of great worth resorted to this forrest,   2731
WORTHIE = *1
*Iaq. O worthie Foole: One that hath bin a Courtier   1009
WORTHIER = *1
*Towne is more worthier then a village, so is the fore- | head   1667
WORTHY = 1
A worthy foole: Motley's the onely weare.   1007
WOULD *l.*60 *84 *110 *128 *173 *203 274 *323 *340 *356 *372 *386
392 394 396 419 478 596 624 710 *826 979 1037 1078 *1247 *1260 1338
1351 *1363 *1394 *1441 1489 *1549 *1569 *1588 *1593 1602 *1603
*1626 1638 1655 1688 1714 *1728 1779 1780 1859 1864 1899 *1983 1985
*2002 *2011 *2020 *2052 *2089 *2130 2161 2202 2315 *2321 *2375
*2518 2559 *2583 2585 *2653 2772 *2792 = 32*38
WOULDST *l.*181 *733 *735 *1036 1043 = 1*4
WOUND = 3
And if mine eyes can wound, now let them kill thee: 1787
Now shew the wound mine eye hath made in thee,   1791
Briefe, I recouer'd him, bound vp his wound,   2304
WOUNDED = 1*2
*Cel. There lay hee stretch'd along like a Wounded | knight.   1434
*Ros. I thought thy heart had beene wounded with | the clawes of a
Lion.   2432
Orl. Wounded it is, but with the eyes of a Lady.   2434
WOUNDS = 1
Then shall you know the wounds inuisible | That Loues keene arrows
make.   1802
WRANGLING = 1
And you to wrangling, for thy louing voyage   2768
WRAPS = *1
*which by often rumination, wraps me in a most humo- | rous sadnesse.   1934
WRASTLE = 2*3
*Oli. What, you wrastle to morrow before the new | Duke.   120
*wrastle for my credit, and hee that escapes me without   126
*goe alone againe, Ile neuer wrastle for prize more: and   157

WRASTLE *cont*.
*Cel. I would I were inuisible, to catch the strong fel-|low by the legge.
Wrastle. 372
Cel. Come, come, wrastle with thy affections. 479
WRASTLED = 2*1
*Le Beu. The eldest of the three, wrastled with *Charles* 288
Sir, you haue wrastled well, and ouerthrowne | More then your enemies. 420
*in mans apparrell? Looks he as freshly, as he did the day | he
Wrastled? 1424
WRASTLER = 2*4
*Oli. Was not *Charles* the Dukes Wrastler heere to | speake with me? 90
*misprised: but it shall not be so long, this wrastler shall 166
*the Dukes Wrastler, which *Charles* in a moment threw 289
*Ros. Young man, haue you challeng'd *Charles* the | Wrastler? 331
*Ros. O they take the part of a better wrastler then | my selfe. 480
The parts and graces of the Wrastler 693
WRASTLERS = *1
*Cel. It is yong *Orlando*, that tript vp the Wrastlers | heeles, and your
heart, both in an instant. 1406
WRASTLING = 6*2
Oli. Call him in: 'twill be a good way: and to mor-|row the wrastling is. 94
*you of good wrastling, which you haue lost the sight of. 275
Ros. Yet tell vs the manner of the Wrastling. 276
rib-breaking? Shall we see this wrastling Cosin? 305
*place appointed for the wrastling, and they are ready to | performe it. 307
Du. How now daughter, and Cousin: | Are you crept hither to see the
wrastling? 318
the wrastling might not go forward. 345
That here was at the Wrastling? 438
WRATH = *1
*before marriage; they are in the verie wrath of 2448
WREAKES = 1
And little wreakes to finde the way to heauen | By doing deeds of
hospitalitie. 866
WREATHD = 1
A greene and guilded snake had wreath'd it selfe, 2259
WRETCHED = 4
The wretched annimall heau'd forth such groanes 643
Cor. Else are they very wretched. 852
Ouer the wretched? what though you haue no beauty 1810
A wretched ragged man, ore-growne with haire 2257
WRIT = 1
To shew the letter that I writ to you. 2485
WRITE = 4
Will I Rosalinda write, | *teaching all that reade*, *to know* 1335
Ile write to him a very tanting Letter, 1908
Phe. Ile write it strait: 1911
Sil. No, I protest, I know not the contents, | *Phebe* did write it. 2169
WRITERS = *1
*other. For all your Writers do consent, that *ipse* is hee: 2385
WRITES = 2*1
*Cel. O that's a braue man, hee writes braue verses, 1747
Why writes she so to me? well Shepheard, well, 2167
Ros. She *Phebes* me: marke how the tyrant writes. 2188
WRITING = 2*1
Enter Celia with a writing. 1321

WRITING *cont*.

Iaq. I pray you marre no more trees with Writing | Loue-songs in their
barkes. 1454
Which she did vse, as she was writing of it, 2158
WRONG = *1
*be so: I shall do my friends no wrong, for I haue none to 352
WRONGD = 2
My tongue hath wrong'd him: if it do him right, 1058
Then he hath wrong'd himselfe: if he be free, 1059
Y = *5
Cel. That's no matter: the feet might beare y verses. 1365
*of madnes, w was to forsweare the ful stream of y world, 1597
*as a puisny Tilter, y spurs his horse but on one side, 1750
*no dishonest desire, to desire to be a woman of y world? 2535
*great matter in the dittie, yet y note was very vntunable 2566
YCE = 1
the very yce of chastity is in them. 1727
YE *l*.*1113 *1681 2355 = 1*2
YEA = 3
Yea, and of this our life, swearing that we 668
Yea prouidently caters for the Sparrow, 748
Yea brought her hether. 2688
YEARE = 1*1
that it seemes the length of seuen yeare. 1506
*yeare old conuerst with a Magitian, most profound in 2469
YEARES = *2
*your yeares: you haue seene cruell proofe of this mans 337
Clo. Ile rime you so, eight yeares together; dinners, 1294
YEELD = 1
If this vncouth Forrest yeeld any thing sauage, 956
YEELDE *see also* goddild, god'ild = 1
That cannot so much as a blossome yeelde, 768
YEELDS = 1
Clo. Truely the tree yeelds bad fruite. 1314
YEERE = *1
*haue liu'd manie a faire yeere though *Hero* had turn'd 2012
YEERES = 4*1
From seauentie yeeres, till now almost fourescore 775
At seauenteene yeeres, many their fortunes seeke 777
He is not very tall, yet for his yeeres hee's tall: 1892
*almost six thousand yeeres old, and in all this time there 2007
Such garments, and such yeeres: the boy is faire, 2235
YERE = *1
Phe. Sweet youth, I pray you chide a yere together, 1837
YEREWHILE = *1
Phe. Knowst thou the youth that spoke to mee yere- | (while? 1879
YES = 6*5
Orl. Yes I beseech your Grace, I am not yet well | breath'd. 378
1 *Lord*. O yes, into a thousand similies. 653
Ros. O yes, I heard them all, and more too, for some 1362
Iaq. Rosalinde is your loues name? *Orl*. Yes, Iust. 1458
Ros. Yes one, and in this manner. Hee was to ima- | gine 1586
Cel. Yes, I thinke he is not a picke purse, nor a horse- | stealer, 1732
Ros. Not true in loue? | *Cel*. Yes, when he is in, but I thinke he is not
in. 1735
Iaq. Yes, I haue gain'd my experience. 1940
Ros. Yes faith will I, fridaies and saterdaies, and all. 2026

YES *cont*.
no song Forrester for this purpose? | *Lord*. Yes Sir.   2132
*Clo. By my troth yes: I count it but time lost to heare   2569
YESTERDAY = 1*1
That I made yesterday in despight of my Inuention.   934
*Ros. I met the Duke yesterday, and had much que-|stion   1742
YET = 30*22
*I will no longer endure it, though yet I know no wise | remedy how to
auoid it.   26
*physicke your ranckenesse, and yet giue no thousand | crownes
neyther: holla *Dennis*.   86
*I hope I shall see an end of him; for my soule (yet   160
*I know not why) hates nothing more then he: yet hee's   161
*gentle, neuer school'd, and yet learned, full of noble   162
*of, and would you yet were merrier: vnlesse you   173
*were naught, and the Mustard was good, and yet was   233
Ros. Yet tell vs the manner of the Wrastling.   276
*your Ladiships, you may see the end, for the best is yet   278
*Musicke in his sides? Is there yet another doates vpon   304
*Cel. Alas, he is too yong: yet he looks successefully   317
*Orl. Yes I beseech your Grace, I am not yet well | breath'd.   378
I cannot speake to her, yet she vrg'd conference.   425
Yet such is now the Dukes condition,   432
But yet indeede the taller is his daughter,   440
*him, for my father hated his father deerely; yet I hate | not *Orlando*.   490
Ros. Yet your mistrust cannot make me a Traitor;   517
Weares yet a precious Iewell in his head: 620
And yet it irkes me the poore dapled fooles   628
Your brother, no, no brother, yet the sonne   723
(Yet not the son, I will not call him son)   724
This I must do, or know not what to do: | Yet this I will not do, do how
I can,   738
Though I looke old, yet I am strong and lustie;   751
Yet fortune cannot recompence me better   779
*beare you: yet I should beare no crosse if I did beare   795
And Ile be with thee quickly: yet thou liest   965
In good set termes, and yet a motley foole.   990
Iaq. Why I haue eate none yet.   1064
Of smooth ciuility: yet am I in-land bred,   1072
As yet to question you about your fortunes: 1153
*though not with bagge and baggage, yet with | scrip and scrippage.
Exit.   1359
*wonderfull, and yet againe wonderful, and after that out | of all
hooping.   1388
Orl. And so had I: but yet for fashion sake   1450
loue too: yet I professe curing it by counsel.   1584
*Goates, *Audrey*: and how *Audrey* am I the man yet?   1616
*Cel. Do I prethee, but yet haue the grace to consider,   1711
And yet it is not, that I beare thee loue,   1867
'Tis but a peeuish boy, yet he talkes well,   1884
But what care I for words? yet words do well   1885
But sure hee's proud, and yet his pride becomes him;   1888
He is not very tall, yet for his yeeres hee's tall: 1892
His leg is but so so, and yet 'tis well: 1893
I loue him not, nor hate him not: and yet   1901
*Ros. Not out of your apparrell, and yet out of your | suite: 1999
*Grecian club, yet he did what hee could to die before,   2010

YET *cont*.
Sil. So please you, for I neuer heard it yet: 2186
Yet heard too much of *Phebes* crueltie.   2187
and yet it is not, it is but so, so: 2369
*his Art, and yet not damnable. If you do loue *Rosalinde*   2470
*great matter in the dittie, yet y note was very vntunable   2566
at any thing, and yet a foole.   2678
*Yet to good wine they do vse good bushes: and good   2780
YFAITH = 1*1
Ros. So I doe: but yfaith, I should haue beene a wo-|man by right.   2330
2.*Pa*. I faith, y'faith, and both in a tune like two | gipsies on a horse.   2544
YIELD *see* yeelde
YOND = 1
Cel. I pray you, one of you question yon'd man,   845
YONDER = 2*2
Adam. Yonder comes my Master, your brother.   29
*third: yonder they lie, the poore old man their Father,   292
Cel. Yonder sure they are comming. Let vs now stay | and see it.   309
Ros. Is yonder the man? | *Le Beu*. Euen he, Madam.   315
YONG = 11*14
Orl. Come, come elder brother, you are too yong in | (this.   55
*like the old *Robin Hood* of *England*: they say many yong   117
*yong fellow of France, full of ambition, an enuious   140
Le Beu. Three proper yong men, of excellent growth | and presence.   284
Cel. Alas, he is too yong: yet he looks successefully   317
Cel. Yong Gentleman, your spirits are too bold for   336
Ros. Do yong Sir, your reputation shall not therefore   343
Char. Come, where is this yong gallant, that is so   361
Ros. Now Hercules, be thy speede yong man.   371
Ros. Oh excellent yong man.   374
Duk. Beare him awaie: | What is thy name yong man?   382
Had I before knowne this yong man his sonne,   400
I was too yong that time to value her,   532
Orl. Who's there? | *Ad*. What my yong Master, oh my gentle master,   704
here, a yong man and an old in solemne talke.   803
Here's a yong maid with trauaile much oppressed, | And faints for
succour.   858
Cor. That yong Swaine that you saw heere but ere-|while,   874
And sayes, if Ladies be but yong, and faire,   1010
Cor. Heere comes yong Mr *Ganimed*, my new Mistris-|ses Brother.   1283
Cel. It is yong *Orlando*, that tript vp the Wrastlers | heeles, and your
heart, both in an instant.   1406
Ros. Marry he trots hard with a yong maid, between   1503
*our yong plants with caruing *Rosalinde* on their   1546
Oli. When last the yong *Orlando* parted from you,   2249
Clo. Truly yong Gentlemen, though there was no   2565
Du Se. Welcome yong man: 2743
YONGER = 1*3
*olde newes: that is, the old Duke is banished by his yon-|ger   101
*your yonger brother *Orlando* hath a disposition to come   124
Ile doe the seruice of a yonger man   758
*in beard, is a yonger brothers reuennew) then your   1562
YONGEST = 2*2
Orl. I am no villaine: I am the yongest sonne of Sir   57
Orl. *Orlando* my Liege, the yongest sonne of Sir *Ro-|land de Boys*.   384
His yongest sonne, and would not change that calling | To be adopted
heire to *Fredricke*.   396

YONGEST cont.
*you should fall into so strong a liking with old Sir | Roulands yongest
sonne?   485
YOU = 263*256
YOUL = 5*2
*speake no more of him, you'l be whipt for taxation one | of these
daies.   249
*for you'l be rotten ere you bee halfe ripe, and that's | the right vertue
of the Medler.   1317
Ros. You say, you'l marrie me, if I be willing.   2586
You'l giue your selfe to this most faithfull Shepheard.   2589
Ros. You say that you'l haue Phebe if she will.   2591
Keepe you your word Phebe, that you'l marrie me,   2597
Keepe your word Siluius, that you'l marrie her   2599
YOUNG = 1*3
*is but young and tender, and for your loue I would bee   128
*teares I speake it) there is not one so young, and so vil- | lanous   150
*Cel. Which he will put on vs, as Pigeons feed their | young.   259
*Ros. Young man, haue you challeng'd Charles the | Wrastler?   331
YOUR l.29 *40 44 *52 *63 *77 *83 *86 89 97 *124 *127 *128 158 *226
*235 237 *238 239 247 *278 *336 *337 *338 *339 *341 *343 *346 *348
360 *366 370 *378 407 409 421 469 498 505 512 517 *520 521 528 531
*548 566 567 595 624 635 689 692 712 715 722 723 726 743 750 759 796
851 853 886 887 911 917 983 1019 1079 1093 1103 1104 *1113 *1147
1153 1172 1174 1177 1178 1193 1237 *1247 *1252 *1257 *1276 1313
*1354 1399 1407 *1448 1451 1458 1467 1475 *1485 *1529 1553 *1561
*1562 *1563 *1564 *1566 *1567 *1578 *1599 *1615 *1618 1675 *1682
*1689 1722 1742 *1808 1819 1820 1821 1830 1832 *1839 1861 *1937
*1942 *1950 *1974 1978 *1983 *1996 *1999 2001 *2023 *2034 2047 2077
*2088 2092 *2096 *2097 *2101 *2107 *2108 *2109 2168 2199 2204 *2218
2230 *2322 *2325 2380 *2385 *2417 2423 *2435 2436 *2441 *2457 *2466
*2471 *2475 *2479 *2480 *2570 2581 2589 *2595 2597 2599 2605 *2637
*2644 *2675 2708 2712 2757 2763 2764 2765 2766 *2769 2773
*2789 = 108*96
YOURS = 5*2
*God made, a poore vnworthy brother of yours with | idlenesse.   36
*Ros. Well, I will forget the condition of my estate, | to reioyce in
yours.   184
No more doe yours: your vertues gentle Master   715
*thought no lesse: that flattering tongue of yours wonne   2090
You yours Orlando, to receiue his daughter: 2596
Ros. To you I giue my selfe, for I am yours.   2691
To you I giue my selfe, for I am yours.   2692
YOURSELFE see selfe
YOURSELUES see selues
YOUTH = 16*13
*Duke. Come on, since the youth will not be intreated   313
*youth, I would faine disswade him, but he will not   323
*I come but in as others do, to try with him the strength | of my youth.   334
But fare thee well, thou art a gallant youth,   391
That youth is surely in their companie.   696
Why, what's the matter? | Ad. O vnhappie youth,   719
For in my youth I neuer did apply | Hot, and rebellious liquors in my
bloud,   752
Though in thy youth thou wast as true a louer   808
Orl. Where dwel you prettie youth?   1523
*in his youth an inland man, one that knew Courtship too   1533

YOUTH *cont*.
Orl. Faire youth, I would I could make thee beleeue | (I Loue.   1569
Orl. I sweare to thee youth, by the white hand of   1576
*youth, greeue, be effeminate, changeable, longing, and   1589
Orl. I would not be cured, youth.   1602
Wil you go? | *Orl*. With all my heart, good youth.   1609
youth mounts, and folly guides: who comes heere?   1752
Phe. Sweet youth, I pray you chide a yere together,   1837
Phe. Knowst thou the youth that spoke to mee yere- |(while?   1879
It is a pretty youth, not very prettie,   1887
Iaq. I prethee, pretty youth, let me better acquainted | with thee.   1917
*(good youth) he went but forth to wash him in the Hel- |lespont,   2014
Sil. My errand is to you, faire youth,   2154
Whether that thy youth and kinde   2208
And to that youth hee calls his *Rosalind*,   2242
Died in this bloud, vnto the Shepheard youth,   2309
Oli. Be of good cheere youth: you a man?   2318
Mar-text. But *Awdrie*, there is a youth heere in the | Forrest layes
claime to you.   2346
Phe. Youth, you haue done me much vngentlenesse,   2484
Phe. Good shepheard, tell this youth what 'tis to loue   2490
YOUTHFULL = 2
And ere we haue thy youthfull wages spent,   771
His youthfull hose well sau'd, a world too wide,   1139
& *l*.*141 *207 *542 *735 889 950 972 *1082 1180 1211 *1273 1310 *1413
1445 *1465 1614 1709 *1839 *2063 *2150 2408 2482 2554 2558 2562
2579 *2695 = 15*12
&C *l*.551 932 1168 2556 2560 2564 = 6
1LO = 1
1LOR = 1
1LORD = 4
1PA = 1*2
2BRO = 2
2LOR = *1
2LORD = 1
2PA = 2

274